D1109610

Almost Innocent

JANE FEATHER

R A N D O M   H O U S E
LARGE PRINT

Almost Innocent

Prologue

CARCASSONNE, 1360

THE WOMAN WAS smiling, and it was the smile that never failed to set the serpents of lust crawling in his belly, the heat of urgent desire suffusing his skin. It did so even tonight.

The man returned the smile, reaching to touch the rich dark hair falling to her knees, glowing bright against the virgin white of her linen shift. A virgin white belied by the swell of her belly.

"It seems nothing can dim your beauty, Isolde."

The woman took the compliment as her due. She began to play with the dripping wax from the tallow candle on the table in front of her, rolling the little puddles into soft balls. Her nails were long.

The man felt the stirring in his loins. How many times had those nails raked his back in the throes of passion, those little white teeth nipped his shoulder during the violent heat of their sharing?

He turned aside, walking to the narrow slitted window set into the turret wall of the fortress monastery of Carcassonne. He could see nothing but the black strip of night sky and a single steady star. The silence in the bastion room was profound, its quality somehow undiminished by the crackle of a splitting log in the hearth, the scrape of her chair on the stone-flagged floor, the whisper of wine flowing from pitcher to cup. At the last sound, he felt his shoulders stiffen. He kept his back to the room until she spoke. And it was a minute or two before she did so.

"Come drink with me, John. You are in a strange mood this night. It is the last time we will be together for many months." Her voice was sweet and cajoling, and bile rose in his gorge.

"Aye, and this meeting was the devil's own work to arrange," he said, turning back to the room. Two pewter goblets of wine stood on the table. Her hand curved possessively around the one at her place. The man's full, passionate mouth smiled, but his blue eyes were hooded, concealing their expression. The candlelight caught his golden head as he bent to kiss her mouth, curving beneath his caressing lips. How easy it was to do that.

"I have a present for you," he said, straightening slowly.

Her gray eyes glittered as they always did at such a prospect. "What is it?"

"A christening present for our child," he replied. "I must leave tonight for the fighting in Burgundy, and you will be delivered and churched long before I may see you again."

"Where is it?" She rose from the table, tall and graceful despite her swollen belly. Vibrant, she was, with her glowing dark hair and her glittering gray eyes, and her rich red lips now parted eagerly. Her lover's generosity was always princely.

He gestured to the leather pouch on the settle beside the fire. "Why do you not see for yourself?"

She moved with measured step. She bent over the pouch. Soundlessly, he switched the positions of the pewter cups on the table.

"Why, 'tis beautiful!" She held up a golden two-handled cup studded with emeralds and rubies.

"Look within," he said softly.

Slowly, she drew out a strand of sapphires, each one the size of a robin's egg. "Ah, John, but you never fail." She regarded him with that same smile. Was there a hint of regret in her eyes? If there was, it was gone almost before it was visible.

"Let us drink," he said. "A toast to the babe." He lifted his own goblet. She took the one at her chair and raised it to her lips.

"To love, John."

"To love," he said, and drank.

She watched him drink before she drained her own cup, then she came into his arms, so warm, so loving . . . so treacherous. But yet the passion stirred even as he felt on his own body the child in her womb kicking against her belly, pressed so close to his own.

"Why do you wear chainmail?" she asked suddenly, running a hand beneath his surcote. " 'Tis hardly the garb for a lover's tryst."

"The roads are dangerous," he said, tracing the curve of her jaw with his finger. "Brigandage in these parts is beyond control." He drew her back into his embrace, tasting the wine on her lips.

Then came the sound he had been expecting. The piercing note of a bugle, his own herald, sounding the call to arms from the great court. His own men would have been ready for the attack, however it was launched, although those who attacked would know nothing of the spy whose dying words, wrenched by torment, had alerted their intended victims.

The woman in his arms pulled away. "What is that?"

Running feet, stumbling feet sounded from the stone passage beyond the heavy oak door. The door flew open.

"Lady, we are betrayed." A friar, in the corded habit of the Franciscan, stood clutching his chest where the hilt of a dagger stood out. Strangely, there was no blood. Then he fell into the doorway, and the lifeblood began to flow from the wound.

"What is this?" The woman clutched her throat, staring at her lover in the horror of realization. "What have you done?"

"What you would have done to me," he told her in a voice as flat as a summer sea.

He whirled suddenly, withdrawing the dagger from his belt. Then it was lodged deep in the chest of a man-at-arms whose springing leap across the dead friar was stopped in mid-air. He fell, the wicked, two-pronged knife in his own hand clattering to the flags.

The woman gave a sudden, choking gasp, her hand plucking desperately at her throat, her eyes widening in horror. "What have you done to me?"

"What you would have done to me," he repeated.

Her eyes flew to the goblets on the table, and terror stood out clear on her face. Suddenly, she doubled over. "Help me! In the name of pity, help me!"

He eased her to the floor, unable to feel pity for the woman who was suffering the torments she had prepared for him. Only she knew whether the poison in the goblet was mercifully quick or whether she had from her twisted soul planned a tortured death for him. Her eyes glazed rapidly, her body convulsed rhythmically, but all awareness seemed to have left her. He knelt beside her and swiftly murmured the words of absolution as papal decree permitted. For all her sins, and they were grievous and many, for all the blood she had upon her hands, he could not abandon her to hell's damnation. As he whispered over her, he became aware of something else, some other convulsive movements of her body. The child was fighting its way into the world.

For a moment he knelt, irresolute. The child was his, but it had grown in such a womb and was nothing to him. If he left, it would die beside its mother. It would probably die anyway; what chance did an eight-month child have? But there was something about the elemental struggle, the blind need of that life to emerge, that refused to allow him to turn aside.

He pushed up the woman's linen shift and helped the infant into the world as her mother died. To his amazement, the child immediately drew breath on a gulping cry. She was small, as was to be expected of an eight-month babe, but her limbs were whole, and she offered him an unblinking stare even as the thin wails shook the tiny body.

There had been enough death in this chamber. He took a small knife from his belt, cut the cord, and knotted it. Then he wrapped the child in his fur-lined mantle and left the place of birth and death.

One

IT WAS DARK in the wattle and daub hut—dark and cold. An ice-tipped wind, gusting down the hole in the roof that served as a chimney, sent smoke billowing into the dank air from the sullen fire. Despite the cold, fleas hopped in the moldering rushes laid on the earth-packed floor, and the child slapped absently at her leg, her interest centered on the scummy surface of the liquid in a shallow earthen dish set on the floor.

"What can you read therein, mad Jennet?" she whispered in awe, peering fruitlessly for the magic message that her companion never failed to see.

Mad Jennet shook her head and cackled with more irony than humor. "Mad they call me, but I've more wits than the lot o' them and don't you forget it, little maid."

"No, I will not," Magdalen said, anxious not to cause offense at such a pivotal moment. "What can you read?"

The crone began to intone in an expressionless voice, "Water and a land of wide spaces."

It was very disappointing. "Will I go to this

land?" the child asked, eager to draw some relevance from the image.

"Who's to say." Mad Jennet creaked to her feet and brought a leather flask to her lips, drinking deeply of its contents. "Who's to say." She wiped her mouth with the back of a filthy, gnarled hand.

Magdalen knew from experience that once mad Jennet started drinking from the flask, there would be no more revelations. Disconsolately, she got to her feet, brushing at her orange holland smock where she knew, although she could not see in the gloom, any number of nasty things would have collected. "You said you would prepare me a spell, so that I could make something happen."

"And what would you like to happen, little maid?" The old woman reached up to a shelf set into the wall and brought down a box.

"Anything," Magdalen said. "Anything at all."

Mad Jennet peered at her in the dim light. "One day, you'll have no such hankering. The day will come when you'll pray for all to stay the same. Bad though 'tis, you'll wish it to stay for fear of the worse that is coming."

Magdalen shivered. You could never be certain with mad Jennet when her pronouncements were based on prescience or when they were just idly made.

"Give me your hand."

Obediently, the child extended her hand, palm up, and watched as the dame sorted through the box, selected, and placed items in her palm. There were bits of hair, tiny bones, a snake's eye, a cat's tooth, and a light dusting of some ashy substance. Magdalen stared, fascinated and awed at this clear proof of the dame's power to cast spells.

"Put them beneath your pillow for three nights," Jennet instructed, "and be sure you have only broth for supper. The spell will not work if your belly's overfull."

Magdalen thought of putting such a collection beneath the pillow of the bed she shared with her aunt, and her heart quailed slightly, even as laughter tickled at the back of her throat. She swallowed the laughter, thinking her companion might find it disrespectful in the face of such an awesome gift, thanked the dame, and slipped cautiously from the hut. Unfortunately, she was not cautious enough.

The Lord Bellair stood upon the battlements of Bellair Castle, staring toward the dark huddlement of the forest of Radnor. It was from those massed and secret depths that a raid would come, and the presence of sentinels in all four belltowers of the fortress gave evidence of the castle's watchfulness. It was the task of the Lords

Marcher, of whom Lord Bellair was one, to protect the border from encroachment from the Welsh lowlands. The lords held their fiefs, strung along the border, in the king's name, and none was more sensible of the importance of his duty and the honor attendant upon it than the Lord Bellair.

This gloomy, blustery February day, however, this Lord Marcher was expecting visitors to come in peace on a matter of business that exercised him considerably. Rooks wheeled and cawed over the crenellated fortress, built for defense not comfort with its four massive towers at each corner. The vast donjon rose in the center of the enclosed space, towering over the working buildings of the compound, throwing its great shadow over the maze of cloisters and inner courtyards.

A sudden burst of raucous laughter rose above the cawing of the rooks and the background sounds of the fortress at work, the hammer on anvil from the forge, the rattle of harness, the tramp of marching feet from the garrison court. The man on the battlements swung round to look down into the courtyard below. Two pages were engaged in a game of chase, threading their way through the groups of men-at-arms, who jeered or called encouragement, depending on their mood. One of the boys held aloft a velvet cap of the Bellair livery as he dodged the grasping hands of his capless pursuer. Two yellow mastiffs plunged noisily and eagerly into the fray.

Satisfied that it was but exuberant play, more the responsibility of the master of pages than his, Lord Bellair was about to turn back to his examination of the horizon when he caught a glimpse of vivid orange hugging the wall of the outer ward.

His lips thinned in anger. There was only one possible reason she could have had for being there. Mad Jennet's hut was situated at the furthest extremity of the outer court. For fear of her powers, no one dared banish her from the castle, but she was kept in isolation, visited only by the desperate in their own need or the greatly compassionate in her need.

The Lord Bellair, his fur-trimmed surcote swaying, strode rapidly down the stone steps, reaching the inner courtyard just as the child emerged through the central archway.

"Where have you been?" he demanded, although he knew the answer well enough.

"With mad Jennet, sir," Magdalen answered. Lying would benefit her nothing.

Lord Bellair regarded the child with his usual

mixture of unease and bewilderment. It was unnatural for an eleven-year-old to find irresistible a filthy crone with her mutterings and incantations. Why was she not as afeard of the witch as he was convinced any other child of her age and upbringing would be? He took in the unspeakable dirt on her smock, the ribbon come loose from the long brown plait, and saw that she held something clenched in her fist.

"What is that in your hand?"

Magdalen examined the cobbles at her feet while she tried to decide whether she could keep her secret. But she knew she could not. Slowly, she uncurled her hand, revealing the unsavory little pile on her palm. "It's a spell."

Lord Bellair recoiled. What sort of a child was she that she would dabble in witchcraft in this fashion? Was she so tainted by her birth? He had struggled for eleven years to overcome that taint, and he would try one last time. He wanted to take the disgusting, fearsome assortment from her and hurl it to the ground. But he dared not. If there was indeed magic contained within the grouping, he dared not disturb it. The spell must be returned intact whence it came.

Taking the child's free hand, he strode with her back into the outer ward and over to mad Jennet's hut. He pushed through the skin hanging over the doorway and held his breath against the noxious stench. Mad Jennet cackled from the shadows at her visitor.

"Well, well, my lord. Are you come to visit the mad crone? What can I do for you? Is it a willing wench you'd wish for . . . or the power to enjoy one? That's long lost to you, I'll be bound." Her laughter rustled like sere leaves, mocking.

They were not words for a child's ears, and the Lord Bellair's anger rose with his discomfiture. He shoved the girl forward. "Return those revolting things!"

Magdalen stepped further into the hut and laid the spell carefully upon the ground. "My thanks, dame, but I may not accept it."

Old Jennet offered no response, and Lord Bellair and the child left without further speech.

They went in silence across the outer ward and into the court. Magdalen was resigned to the coming punishment. Her feet took little skipping steps to keep up with the impatient, angry stride of her father as he marched with her to the donjon and through an arched doorway into the great hall of the castle. An ancient hound, sprawled before the massive fireplace, raised his grizzled head at the arrival, but the servitors and wenches bustling around the vast room, laying fresh rushes interlaced with lavender, barely glanced at their lord and the child as they went up the stone staircase leading from the hall. They went down a long passage and into the women's wing of the castle.

In the bedchamber Magdalen shared with her aunt, Lord Bellair whipped her. Nothing was said by either of them until it was over. The child made no sound, although tears crowded her eyes. He replaced the switch on the shelf beside the hearth and turned back to the room, the frown still deep on his brow. She stood with her back to him, her shoulders rigid, her head averted lest he see the trembling lip and tear-sheened eyes.

He shook his head in weary incomprehension, appreciating despite himself the pride that kept her from showing him that he had hurt her, yet wishing she would offer just a hint of contrition. Just a hint, and he could make some move toward her, but she stood there, fierce in her refusal to offer him the slightest help.

Such a fierce, indomitable, *unnatural* child she was. Even as he chided himself yet again for using such a term as "unnatural" in reference to an eleven-year-old child, he knew that it expressed what he felt about her. Was she touched by destiny, or tainted by the past? One of the two. He caught himself wondering what her horoscope would foretell, then dismissed the thought abruptly. With God's grace, the child's future would be no concern of his. And it was a future to begin this day.

He walked to the door, and when he spoke his voice was without anger. "I am expecting visitors this day. You will be presented to them in the great hall. Wait here until your aunt comes to you." The door closed behind him, and the key turned in the lock.

Magdalen's tears now flowed freely. They flowed for the smarting of the switch, but more for her own perverse nature that would not permit her to behave properly, that set imps of wickedness coursing through her veins so that she wanted to dance and sing and must always be moving, could not be still with her tambour frame or lute, could not restrain her exuberance and the joy of her soul, could not feel that she belonged in this drear, damp, border land of cold stone and heavy forests. And yet she had known no other; had known no caretakers but her father and her aunt, who, she knew in her heart, did the best they could with her, although she seemed constantly to disappoint them. She could not accuse them of injustice. So why did she seethe so with resentment sometimes, with the certainty that she didn't belong, the certainty that she had never belonged, that these people were only passersby in her life? She flung herself facedown on the poster bed, but she was not made for tears and never wept for long. The tears dried rapidly as speculation about the coming visitors took her mind off her soreness.

Leaving Magdalen, Lord Bellair went in search of his sister. He found her in her square parlor, warmed by a blazing log fire, lit by thick wax candles in wall sconces. Skins covered the stone-flagged floor, and a branched candelabrum threw golden light on the long table set beneath the narrow windows, where the February gloom offered meager illumination.

The Lady Elinor, seated at the table, looked up from her embroidery as her brother entered. "Good morrow, brother." Her smile faded as she took in his expression. "Is aught amiss with the preparations for the visitors?"

"Not to my knowledge." He went to the fire, stretching his hands to the blaze. "I could wish you would have Magdalen in better care, Elinor. She has been yet again with mad Jennet."

Lady Elinor touched a hand to the crisp folds of her wimple. "She is like quicksilver, Robert. It is beyond human ability to keep up with her at all times. Did you punish her?"

"Of course." He sighed heavily. "But how long do you think the lesson will last?"

"Until the smart dies," Elinor said, laying down her silks and needle. "But your wardship will soon be over." She looked shrewdly at him in the candlelight.

"I would not be found wanting in my conduct of that charge," he said. "It is a responsibility we have borne for eleven years, yet I misdoubt our success. She is such a strange child—"

"Your charge was simply to keep her safe and well through her growing, beyond the attention of those whose interest might be malign," his sister interrupted. "You have carried out that duty with care beyond criticism. She is strong and healthy and has no knowledge of who and what she is, as you were instructed."

Bellair nodded, stroking his graying beard. His sister spoke the truth, but he could not help feeling that he had been somehow remiss. With no experience of children, he had tried to do his duty by the little girl, neglecting neither kindness nor just correction, but the expected results of such careful and impartial rearing had escaped him. Magdalen was no ordinary child. He could only believe that her upbringing had failed to have an enduring effect upon the inherent characteristics imparted to her in the womb. What would those to whom she was going find in her?

A trumpet sounded shrill and demanding from beyond the great gates of the castle. Lord

Bellair hastened to the window as the call was answered by the herald within. The drawbridge was lowered over the moat, the great gates swung open, and a troop of archers and cross-bowmen trotted into the *place d'armes*. Behind them rode six knights banneret on plumed and braided palfreys, gold-embossed surcotes over their armor. At their head rode a knight in a blue and silver jupon, a squire at his side bearing a standard on which a dragon device was displayed against a field of azure and argent. Squires and pages and a troop of swordsmen brought up the rear. Such an army to collect one small girl from a border fortress. But, then, the roads were besieged with brigands, and the girl had a destiny to fulfill.

"They are come," he said, striding to the door. "I must meet them in the inner court. Do you prepare Magdalen for presentation within the hour."

Lady Elinor hastened to her bedchamber, instructing a serving maid to bring hot water immediately. She unlocked the door and went in. Magdalen, her ills forgotten, was kneeling on the windowsill, gazing down at the busyness in the courtyard below. Pages and grooms ran to take bridles and place mounting blocks. The arriving master herald still sat his horse, his trumpet with its pennant of azure and argent dipped in recognition of their hosts. Her father was greeting his knightly visitors, who dismounted and stood exchanging courtesies under the gray sky while Lord Bellair's pages proffered stirrup cups of wine. They disappeared through the door to the great hall below Magdalen's window, their own squires and pages in attendance. The armed troop were dispersed to the barracks in the garrison court, horses led off to the stables and the pasture beyond the postern gate.

"Who are they, my lady aunt?" Magdalen scrambled from the sill as the woman entered with a restrained rustle of her billowing velvet skirts.

"Visitors from London," Elinor replied. "Show me your hands." She shook her head over their grimy, broken-nailed condition. "You must wash your face and hands well and replait your hair. Let us see what gown will be most suitable." She opened the clothes press.

"From the king?" Magdalen asked, gingerly dipping a cloth in the basin of hot water and dabbing at her face.

"For heaven's sake, child, you cannot expect to get rid of the dirt in such dainty fashion!" Instead of answering the question, Elinor took the cloth impatiently and scrubbed the child's face. "Now take off that old smock and put this on."

The gown she held out was of heavy ceremonial velvet. Magdalen's nose wrinkled in disgust. She detested the material, finding it weighty and cumbersome and itchily hot. But she said nothing, merely unfastened the simple girdle of her orange smock and pulled it over her head.

Elinor softened her tone. "See how pretty you will look. Crimson suits you well, and you may wear the silver brocade cap."

"Are the visitors come from the king?" Magdalen ventured again, standing still as the bodice of the gown was laced and its girdle of braided crimson and silver silk fastened at her waist.

"That is your father's business," her aunt told her a little sharply. "He will tell you what he deems it meet that you should know."

Magdalen's lips pursed at this, but since it was entirely true and always had been, she saw little point in inviting further reproof by pursuing that line of questioning. "Will my father order a grand feast for them?"

"Yes, indeed, and I must go to the kitchens and see that all is well," Elinor said, suddenly distracted. "Come now, we will go to the great hall and you may make your reverence. Then you may sit quietly in my parlor until you are sent for again."

The latter aspect of this plan failed to appeal to the Lady Magdalen, but, mindful of the morning's lesson, she kept her objections to herself and endured her aunt's intent examination with downcast eyes.

"There, you will do." Elinor pronounced herself satisfied after one final adjustment to the close-fitting cap of silver brocade. "Let us make haste."

Magdalen followed her aunt down the passage to the stone stairs leading to the hall. Lord Bellair and his visitors stood around the great fireplace, pewter goblets in hand. The knights' attendants were clustered beyond the circle of warmth, watchful lest they miss a summons.

"Ah, sirs, may I present my sister, the Lady Elinor, and my daughter, Magdalen." Lord Bellair had been watching for them and immediately stepped forward as the two came down the stairs.

Magdalen dutifully made her reverence to the seven knights, all of whom wore the red rose of Lancaster emblazoned on their surcotes; but the girl had eyes for only one of the visitors, a man younger, it seemed, than the others, for all that they were presented as his vassals. He was a giant of a man, above six feet tall, and broad. He was clean shaven, and his hair hung in thick red-gold waves to the sable collar of his blue and silver surcote. Bright blue eyes beneath heavy brows examined the child with more than cursory interest. Forgetting decorum, Magdalen returned the scrutiny from her own clear gray eyes and privately decided that he was a most handsome lord.

Guy de Gervais, for so the lord was named, suddenly laughed and chucked her beneath the chin. "She is well made, my Lord Bellair, straight as a sapling, and I dare swear the soul within is as straight, if one may judge by her eyes." His voice was surprisingly soft, coming from such a massive frame.

Lord Bellair inclined his head in acknowledgment. "I believe it to be so, my lord. But Father Clement will not always agree."

Magdalen flushed slightly at this reference to her *bête noir,* the castle chaplain whose care for the souls of all within was on occasion overly zealous. Since he supervised the girl's studies, she had suffered on more than one occasion from his enthusiasm.

Lord de Gervais smiled reassuringly. "Are you in mischief on occasion, little maid?"

Magdalen dropped her eyes in embarrassment, aware that this apparently well-meaning examination had made her the center of attention in the great hall.

He laughed again. "I will not expect an answer." He turned from her, taking Lord Bellair's arm and moving out of earshot of the group.

There was no laughter now in his voice. "Does the child know aught of my mission?"

Bellair shook his head, and the frown was back on his brow. "I thought it best not to trouble her with it. She has a vivid imagination and a certain liveliness that is not always well placed. If she took against the idea—" He shrugged. "I saw little point in being obliged to deal prematurely with any difficulties."

"Quite so." De Gervais stroked his chin, turning to look again at the child, who still stood rather awkwardly beside her aunt. "She knows nothing . . . suspects nothing?"

Bellair shook his head again. "She believes me to be her father."

"And her mother?"

"Magdalen knows only that she died in childbed. For one so innately inquisitive, she has shown little curiosity about the subject."

"It has been a troublesome charge?" The blue eyes gleamed suddenly with a shaft of comprehension.

"Not a light one," his companion said after a moment's consideration. "We have done what we can, but there is a strangeness about her that I will not deny to you. I have been unable to eradicate it. Father Clement would have it that we have been too lenient and must tear out the evil, root and branch, from the soul." He pulled distressfully at his beard. "But I am not convinced there is evil in her." He fell into a troubled silence, as if he would say more but hesitated to do so.

"Then what do you suspect?" de Gervais prompted gently.

Bellair shrugged. "Her birth was accursed. She must bear the mark."

Guy de Gervais frowned. It was not impossible, and if there was a taint, while it would not change the plans made for her, it would be as well for those concerned to be forearmed against its manifestations. "I would talk privately with her, if you have no objections," he said. "I would like to gain some impression of her character. We do not wish to tarry here overlong, and since the matter must be brought to conclusion, it is best done so without delay."

"The betrothal?"

"By proxy this evening, if it can be so arranged."

"After vespers," Lord Bellair agreed. "You will inform her yourself?"

"Unless you wish to." He smiled courteously.

"I lay no claims to the task. She will listen as well to you as to me."

De Gervais made no comment to this, and they went back to the group by the fire.

"Magdalen, Lord de Gervais wishes to talk

privately with you," Lord Bellair said, kicking at a slipping log in the hearth. "Keep your tongue moderate and heed him well."

Magdalen looked in startlement at the knight in question. What business could such a splendid figure possibly have with her?

He bowed ceremoniously, although there was more than a glimmer of amusement in his eyes. "Will you honor me with your company on a short walk, Lady Magdalen?"

Flustered, Magdalen curtsied. "Indeed, sir, if you wish it." She placed her hand tentatively on the proffered arm, and he immediately covered it with his own hand. In this stately fashion, they left the great hall, going out into the raw morning.

"Shall we walk in the pleasaunce?" he asked. "It will be sheltered from the wind."

"If you wish it," the figure at his side repeated with a dull docility that did not ring true.

He looked down at her. "But do you wish it, *damoiselle?*"

She turned her face up to meet his eyes. "In truth, sir, I would prefer to walk upon the battlements. It is usually forbidden, but with your escort . . ." She left the sentence unfinished, but her face was alive with eagerness.

"If you are not fearful of the wind," he said agreeably, directing his step toward the stone stairs to the battlements, "then indeed we will do so."

They climbed up, and the wind was certainly rough and needle-sharp, but Magdalen seemed unaware of the cold in her heavy velvet dress and wool underdress. She ran to the parapet, leaning over to look toward the dark forest, visible in the winter gloom only as a lowering shape stretching to the horizon.

"There has not been a raid for nigh on three months," she said, and de Gervais was certain he could detect a hint of regret in her voice.

"You sound wistful," he observed, strolling to a stone bench carved into the parapet.

She responded with the semblance of a grin. "At least it is exciting when it happens."

This was not going to be as awkward as he had feared, de Gervais reflected, if it was excitement she craved. Sitting down, he patted the bench beside him in invitation.

Magdalen regarded the hard stone with disfavor. "I was whipped this past hour."

"Ah." Comprehending, he stood up again and resumed his slow pacing. "For what offense?"

Magdalen hesitated. Would this lord be as repulsed by her actions as her father and aunt were? She found that she did not want to disgust him, yet some perverse prod compelled her to test him. "Visiting with mad Jennet," she said boldly. "And getting a spell from her."

"A spell to do what?" He sounded neither surprised nor disgusted, interested rather.

"To make something exciting happen," she replied. There was silence for a minute, and, encouraged, she continued with sudden low fierceness, "How can one be happy when there is nothing to do except study the Psalter with Father Clement, who will never be pleased and always makes bad report of me to my father, or sit with my aunt and sew seams? There is no one to play with, no one to talk with. Sometimes my father says I may accompany him hunting or hawking, but then I offend in some way and I am not permitted to go." There was an aching loneliness in her voice. "I like to dance and to sing and to play. I wish to ride and shoot with a bow and arrow and hunt with a hawk, but there is no one to do these things with except the pages, and that is not permitted. It is so cold and dark and drear in this place, and I do not seem to belong to it," she finished on a note of despairing bewilderment.

When provision had been made for the rearing of this child, no one had given thought to the loneliness she would experience in the wild border land, her only companions a confirmed

spinster and a childless widower in his middle
years. The concern had simply been for secrecy
and the safety of anonymity. She must be given
the care necessary to ensure her growth to responsible womanhood, if God willed such
growth, but happiness was not adjudged a necessary or even desirable condition of childhood.
Guy de Gervais tapped his gloved hands together in front of his mouth, thinking.

He was frowning deeply, staring at the little
girl who had fallen silent and looked anxious, as
if she had revealed something forbidden. Wisps
of brown hair strayed from the cap onto a broad
brow; the gray eyes, lashed long and dark, were
set wide beneath well-defined eyebrows. Her
cheekbones were high, the chin pointed with a
deep cleft giving her face a perfect heart shape.
Her mouth was her father's, too wide for tradi-
tional beauty in a maid, but de Gervais had not
yet seen her smile. Her nose was small and well
shaped, her ears lying flat against her head. De
Gervais had once seen a portrait of her
mother—a portrait kept in the utmost secrecy in
the duke's inner chamber. The similarity was
striking, but Isolde de Beauregard had set a land
aflame with her beauty and her venom. It was
hard to imagine this fierce yet exuberant little
girl ever developing the devious skills and
knowledge of beauty's power to—

"I did not mean to speak immoderately, sir."
The anxious words broke into his reverie. "You
will not tell my father that I did so?"

He shook his head, smiling. "Nay, I would
not dream of it. Besides, I asked you a question,
and you answered in truth. There is no fault in
that."

She sighed with relief and turned back to the
parapet. "What is it you wished to talk to me
about, sir?"

"How would you like to journey to London
with me?" He saw little point in prevaricating.

She spun round to stare at him in astonishment. "For what purpose, sir?"

"Why, to be wed."

"To *you?*"

"Nay, not to me." He laughed at the absurd-
ity. "To my nephew who is in my wardship."

Magdalen continued to stare at him. It was
not as if the idea of marriage was a novel one.
She knew that by twelve years of age she would
be considered marriageable, just as she knew
that her father would choose her bridegroom
for what benefits of alliance, power, land, or
money would accrue therefrom. Marriage was
the woof and warp of diplomacy, an incident in
the system of barter and allegiance among families and nations, and it did not occur to her to
question the decision that had been made for

her. The Lords Marcher were powerful barons, vassals of the king and of no other, so she could expect the match made for her to be an important one. But there was something abrupt and overhasty about its presentation. Why must it bring seven knights to her father's castle? Why was he not telling her of his decision, but leaving the matter to this lord? Oh, she liked the lord and felt a trust for him, but something did not sit aright, and Magdalen was quick to nose out matters that did not sit aright.

"Well, what say you?" De Gervais leaned against the parapet, watching her carefully.

"Why is your nephew not with you? Is it that he is ill favored, crookbacked, walleyed?"

De Gervais laughed. "Nay, not so. You will find him well favored enough. But this is a long journey and takes a good week on each side. He has duties and training to attend to. I am here in his stead and will stand proxy for the betrothal, which will take place before you leave this house. Now, what say you?"

"How is he called?"

De Gervais stroked his chin. He was clearly going to receive no answer until she had asked her own questions and been satisfied, for all that her answer could only be of one kind.

"Edmund de Bresse. His sire, my half brother, was the Sieur Jean de Bresse, a liege lord of

Picardy; his mother the daughter of the Duke de Guise."

"But how is he in your wardship?"

"He and his mother were taken hostage some four years past, after the death in battle of my brother. The lady died soon after, and the child was placed in my care."

Magdalen chewed her bottom lip. There were interesting puzzles there. Why was this lord a vassal of the English king, when his half brother's family was clearly for France? And why was her father desirous of forming an alliance with one of the great seigneural families of France? He took no active part in this war that had been dragging on between the two lands these last thirty years, being far too busy defending the Welsh border for his king. But she knew nothing of politics. The reasons for the choice could not concern her, and she returned to questions that were of much more moment.

"How many summers has he?"

"Fourteen."

"Of what character is he?"

"One you may find sympathetic. He is not fond of his lessons and has been often whipped for their neglect." He smiled at her. "He is more at ease with his companions in sport, tilting, archery, hawking, hunting. But he is not averse to dancing, or to music."

"He is a squire?"

"Aye, in my household, and will receive his spurs in a twelvemonth."

"But if the war continues, will he then fight for England or for France?" She was frowning in puzzlement, the problem of such divided loyalties striking her as insurmountable.

"Such weighty issues are not for the minds of maids," Guy de Gervais said, deciding it was time to put an end to the catechism which began to grow uncomfortably pointful. "Come now, how do you answer *my* question? If you can still remember it after such an inquisition as you have subjected me to."

She looked stricken at the note of sharpness, as if her trust in him had in somewise been misplaced. "If my questions were impertinent, my lord, I ask your pardon." Her voice was stiff to disguise her hurt.

"They were not, just overly numerous," he replied. "But they were fair questions. Now, must I ask you again for your answer."

"Am I to go alone?"

Lord de Gervais sighed. "The Lady Elinor and your own maids will accompany you, and Lady Elinor will remain until it is seen that you are well established in the care of my lady wife."

He would have a wife, of course, although

Magdalen strangely found herself rather wishing he had not. "And . . . and my father?" she continued. "But of course he cannot leave the king's defense." She answered her own question. "He will remain here."

"Lord Bellair will remain here," he replied, quietly deliberate in his choice of words. The child's father would be present at her wedding.

"When must we leave?"

"Is that my answer?"

Magdalen looked out from the battlements, over the bleak, frowning country. She heard the tediously familiar sounds of fortress life rising from the courts beneath. Her father must come to London sometimes to do homage to his liege lord, the king. And she was tired unto death of this dreary place . . . and a maid must be wed, after all. What would it be like to see London? To live there? She had never left her home before. Her prospective husband sounded pleasant enough . . . and a maid must be wed, after all.

She turned a pair of sparkling eyes upon him and a radiant smile, the first he had seen. "I will be ready to go with you, my lord, whenever you wish."

He laughed. The smile was delightfully infectious. "Then let us rejoin the company. The betrothal will take place this evening after vespers."

A thought struck her as she followed him back down to the court. "Edmund de Bresse, sir—what does he know of me?"

"Why, that you are comely, wellborn, well dowered," he responded easily. "He needs to know no more."

"But how could you know I was comely if you had not seen me? I might be most dreadfully pocked, or crooked of limb, or squint-eyed, or—"

"But you are none of these things," he rejoined. "And I was told so by the Lord Bellair in a letter some months past. These matters are not decided in haste."

"It is strange it was never mentioned to me before," she mused, prancing down the stairs at his side. "And I consider it most unjust that I should be whipped on the day of my betrothal. Had I known you were to come, I would have had no need to visit mad Jennet for a spell to make something happen."

Lord de Gervais fortunately found the logic impeccable. He managed to murmur a soothing agreement of the injustice while avoiding any discussion of the reasons why she had not been forewarned of the plans made for her.

All was bustle in the great hall when they returned as preparations were made for the feast in honor of the visitors. Lady Elinor left her supervision of the setting of the high table when she saw them and hurried down the hall.

"Magdalen, you must go and sit quietly in my parlor. You are to dine in the hall this day, but until you are summoned I would have you keep well out of trouble. My lord, I will have you conducted to the guest chambers. My brother will await you in the south turret when you have refreshed yourself."

"Oh, but I will conduct my lord to his chamber," Magdalen said eagerly, slipping her hand into the enormous one beside her. "I will fetch rosemary from the pleasaunce to lay upon his pillow."

Lady Elinor blinked in some startlement and Guy de Gervais laughed. "I'faith, my lady, I would be honored if you would permit her to do so. Such tender consideration for a guest can only be commended."

"Indeed, sir, I believe you are right," Lady Elinor said. "But 'tis somewhat unusual. However, one must not stifle good intention. Go then, niece, but afterward you must go directly to my parlor."

BELLAIR CASTLE MIGHT be designed for defense, not domesticity, but Lord de Gervais could find no fault with the accommodations prepared for him. The sheets to the bed were of finest linen, daintily stitched by the lady of the house and her women. The hangings were thick and draught-proof. Soft skins lay upon the floor, and a fire roared in the chimney. His page was already awaiting him with lavender-scented water and fresh garments.

De Gervais watched with amusement as his small companion proceeded to take inventory of the chamber, for all the world like an accomplished chatelaine. "It lacks but the rosemary," she declared. "I will fetch it directly." She ran off, and the page came forward instantly to help him divest himself of the great swordbelt, the surcote, and the chainmail beneath.

He was in the process of removing the padded leather gambeson beneath the mailshirt when the door opened again without ceremony and the child reappeared, sprigs of rosemary in her hand. These she laid with some care to artistry upon his pillow and turned to smile at him.

"There, that is well done, do you not think?"

De Gervais handed the heavy tunic to his page and stretched mightily in his soft linen shirt with the fine drawn openwork set by his wife at neck and wristbands. "It is well done indeed, *damoiselle,* and I thank you for your kindness." The response was in the nature of a dismissal, and he was somewhat disconcerted when she perched on a high stool beside the fire, still bathing him in that radiant smile.

"I will sit and talk with you while you dress. Then I can show you to the south turret to my father's room."

"And how will you explain your truancy when your aunt goes to the parlor and finds you absent?" He took the linen cloth his page had soaked in the warm, scented water and laid it over his face, taking pleasure in the luxurious caress easing into his travel-worn skin.

"It is customary for the daughter of the house to assist a knightly guest with his armor," she said innocently, swinging her legs.

"I do not think such sophistry either should or would save you from the consequences of further disobedience," he observed, putting his arms into the full sleeves of a particolored tunic of green and gold cloth.

"But if you asked me to remain—"

"But I have not." He fastened the large gold buttons of the knee-length tunic. "Hand me my belt, Edgar." The heavy, emerald-studded belt with its gold buckle was fastened at his hip.

The page was grinning in open amusement, and disconsolately Magdalen slipped from the stool. "When I am wed," she announced, "I shall go where I please."

"When you are wed," Guy de Gervais pronounced with great deliberation, since it seemed to be time to straighten matters out, "you will be lodged beneath my roof until you are both old enough to set up your own establishment. You will not find the discipline in my household any easier than it is here . . . as Edgar will tell you."

The page's grin widened. "Indeed not, my lord. And the Lady Gwendoline can be most severe on occasion."

Magdalen looked suspiciously between them, trying to decide if they were teasing her. Then she heard her name called from the passage outside. Her hand flew to her mouth. "Oh, 'tis my lady aunt. I will hide in the clothes press."

"Indeed you will not." The lord had joined his page in laughter now. He strode to the door, flinging it wide. "Do you look for Magdalen, my lady? She had just returned with the rosemary, and I begged her to bear me company for a few minutes more." He beckoned her forward.

Magdalen fell in love with the Lord de Gervais at that moment. She stepped up beside him. "I was just going to the parlor, madam. But who is to escort my lord to the south turret?"

"Why, Giles, to be sure," Lady Elinor said, indicating the Lord Bellair's page, who stood waiting outside the guest chamber. "Hurry along now, child. You must not weary our guests with your chatter."

Lord de Gervais smilingly watched the small figure trail off toward the circular stairs leading down to the family quarters on the second floor of the donjon. If Edmund could be persuaded to devote some part of his widely scattered attentions to his bride, they might deal in companionship extremely well. At all events, he was not concerned about this strangeness Lord Bellair sensed in her. The Lord Marcher was not accustomed to children, but Guy de Gervais was. Although his own marriage was childless, he had in his wardship, besides his nephew, two cousins and his young half brothers and sisters, the progeny of his mother's third and final marriage. He believed he could detect in Isolde de Beauregard's daughter no more than a nature ill-suited to restraint—and that, it was to be assumed, she had inherited from her dam, if not from her sire. It was, after all, a defining characteristic of the Plantagenets.

Ten minutes later, attired in his green and gold tunic over emerald-green hose, his marten-trimmed surcote and similarly lined velvet mantle, he followed the lad Giles to a round chamber in the south turret. It was a businesslike room, furnished simply with an oak table and several chairs, the floor bare except for one skin before the hearth. Candles provided bright illumination over the stack of parchments lying on the table. It was Lord Bellair's administrative office, and his secretary sat hunched over the papers on the table, his quill pen scratching busily.

"How did your discussion with Magdalen fare?" Bellair set a chair for his guest and instructed Giles to pour wine.

De Gervais waited until the page had been dismissed before replying. "Without difficulty. She was curious about many things, but in no wise reluctant."

"I trust her curiosity was tempered with courtesy," said Lord Bellair dryly.

De Gervais smiled. "You need have no fears on that score. Master Secretary is gathering together the necessary documents, I see."

"The original document, placing the babe in my charge until such time as the duke would claim her, is here. Master Cullum is drawing up the necessary release of that charge, naming you as my successor in the matter. It will be witnessed under seal."

De Gervais nodded. He could well understand Lord Bellair's desire to have no loose ends. His responsibility must be officially declared completed. With such parentage and the destiny planned for her, Magdalen could well be the focus of some future plot, and a sensible man would want no past ties hanging loose to incriminate him.

"When is the wedding to take place?"

De Gervais pulled his chin. "Within six months. There is the matter of legitimacy to be dealt with first, but the duke is working closely with Rome. There are bargains to be struck." He shrugged as if to say there always are. One could always buy what one needed from the papal court with some kind of currency if one was powerful enough, particularly in these days of the papal schism when competition between the papal courts at Avignon and Rome obscured all spiritual considerations. John of Gaunt would not be remotely interested in spiritual considerations, only in what his power and currency would buy him from one amenable pope—he only needed one, after all.

"You will wish to discuss with Lady Elinor certain matters, I daresay," Robert Bellair said directly. "She will know what stage the child has reached in her maturing." Receiving a nod of agreement, he called for Giles and sent him for Lady Elinor.

The lady had been expecting the summons and addressed the subject with the same directness as her brother. "There are as yet few indications of womanhood, Lord de Gervais. She is, I believe, somewhat behind in her developing. I have known other girls at eleven who could be bedded within a short time after their twelfth birthdays, but I believe that in Magdalen's case it will be more than a twelvemonth before her terms come. Her body is still unformed."

"There will be no hurry for consummation," the lord said. "Once the alliance is formalized, the rest may take its time. The duke is besides concerned that her breeding ability be not over-taxed, as so often happens if maids are bedded too young. But I am glad to have your opinion, my lady. You will remain with her for a few months at Hampton, I trust, and will be able to pass on your knowledge of the child to my wife, the Lady Gwendoline."

"I will be happy to be of what service I can to your lady. But my brother will have need of me before the spring forays, and I would return by Easter."

Lord de Gervais recognized that the brother and sister felt their duty to be done, and he understood this. For eleven years they had fulfilled a responsibility, knowing always that the duty would end within twelve years. They had affection for the girl, but the affection would have been tempered with the knowledge of the impermanence of the relationship—a knowledge that the child had not had to aid her through her confused sense that in essence she did not belong in this place with these people. But then childhood was a time of confusion, was it not? If it were not, then grown men would be ill prepared to deal with their world.

"Indeed, madame, whatever time you feel able to spare will be most welcome."

Lady Elinor curtsied in acknowledgment. "When will you wish to go in to dinner, brother?"

"Whenever we are summoned," Robert said heartily. "I believe my Lord de Gervais and I are concluded with our business. There is but the betrothal. Father Clement will officiate, and it should take place in the chapel after vespers. Magdalen understands that Lord de Gervais will stand proxy for his nephew?"

"I have explained it to her," de Gervais said. "Would you permit her to sit beside me at dinner, Lord Bellair? I would further our acquaintance. It may make matters run more smoothly."

Robert Bellair offered a small smile, tapping the document now handed to him by his secretary. "By the words here written, Lord de Gervais, you make what disposition you see fit for the person of one Magdalen, daughter of his grace, the Duke of Lancaster, and Isolde de Beauregard."

"But I would not have her aware of that," the other said sharply. "She must believe, until his grace decrees otherwise, that you still hold a father's authority over her."

"We will proceed in that fashion," the Lord Marcher acceded. "Let us repair to the hall."

THAT EVENING, MAGDALEN stood beside Lord de Gervais before the altar in the castle chapel, feeling both important and excited. "What am I to do?" she asked, blinking her eyes, which stung from the censer smoke.

"I will put a ring upon your finger and plight you my troth in Edmund's name, then you are to say, 'I, Magdalen, plight thee, Guy, proxy for Edmund de Bresse, my troth, as God is my witness.' Then you will give me a ring."

Lord Bellair was standing beside her and now handed her a plain gold band, advising in accustomed fashion, "Do not drop it."

"Of course I will not, sir," she responded, injured.

It was as simple as she had been told. Questions were asked; Lord de Gervais and Lord Bellair answered them all. Guy de Gervais slipped a thin gold ring on her middle finger, and she spoke as she had been bidden, giving her own ring to de Gervais, who slipped it into his pocket.

At dawn the following morning, Magdalen hastened downstairs in search of Lord de

Gervais. She did not bother to examine why she wished to see him, but since he was her betrothed, even if only as proxy, she considered she had a right to his company. She was most disconcerted to be told that he and his knights had gone stag hunting with their host.

Reflecting that it showed a fine want of feeling to abandon the main player in this present drama as if her affairs were of no further concern, the child trailed disconsolately back to the women's wing, where she was pounced upon by her aunt and obliged to participate in the preparations for departure.

The hunting party returned with much revelry and elation, bugles blowing, two stags slung across poles borne in the rear by four huntsmen apiece. The great hall resounded with their feasting, with the music of pipe and lyre, but Lord Bellair had decreed that today the women should dine apart, and Magdalen ate in her aunt's company in the parlor, silently lamenting the unjust lot of women.

Nor did she have private speech with Lord de Gervais before their departure, three days later, by which time she had decided that being betrothed was a sad and sorry condition, according none of the expected advantages. But not even this disgruntlement could spoil her excitement at the sight of the cavalcade drawn up in the *place d'armes* at dawn on the day of departure. A small troop of Lord Bellair's men were to accompany them to the border of Bellair territory, as a matter of courtesy. The knights' own force, refreshed after the generous hospitality they had been accorded, sat alert and ready, and the train of pack mules loaded with the baggage stood in resigned patience.

Magdalen looked in vain for her own horse. Lord de Gervais was standing talking to her father when she hurried over. "I beg pardon for interrupting, sir, but where is my mount? I cannot see Malapert anywhere."

"You are to ride with me, Magdalen," de Gervais informed her. "Your aunt and her women will ride pillion with the grooms."

"But I would ride by myself," Magdalen blurted without thought for discourtesy. "I will not be carried like a baby."

Lord Bellair's reaction to this insolence was entirely predictable. De Gervais interrupted the threats of summary punishment with a raised hand. "Nay, we will excuse the impertinence. If the child wishes to ride, then she may do so until she is fatigued."

"I will not become fatigued," Magdalen declared stoutly, emboldened by this championship.

"I will give you four hours at the outside," he

challenged, laughing. "Go and tell a groom to have your mount readied."

In her pleasure and relief, Magdalen failed to remark the subtle shift in authority revealed by that exchange. In any other circumstances, she would have been mightily puzzled that her father would have permitted the intercession of a stranger in such an instance. The intercession itself would ordinarily have been an unthinkable act. But Lord de Gervais was rapidly assuming godlike qualities in the child's vivid imagination, and whatever he did was becoming invested with a magic that set his actions outside the normal run of things.

Then came the flurry and excitement of departure. Lord Bellair promised that he would be in London within the year, and she threw her arms around his neck and hugged him with a fierceness that surprised him. She made a decorous farewell to the pages and then spoiled the effect with a broad grin and a mischievous wink. The servitors who had known her through her growing were there to call their good wishes, and she rode through the great gate and across the drawbridge, waving frantically over her shoulder at her home and wondering why she felt suddenly melancholy.

Then the bugle sounded, and the thrilling prospect of what lay ahead drove all from her mind but the need to meet the Lord de Gervais's challenge. She rode proudly upright at his side as the sun rose, and it was near midmorning before her aching back caused her shoulders to slump slightly. The third time she put her hand behind her in an unconscious gesture, rubbing the small of her back to ease the stiffness, Guy leaned down from his palfrey, caught her under the arms, and lifted her onto the saddle in front of him.

"If you exhaust yourself this day, you will be fit for nothing on the morrow."

"But was it more than four hours?" she asked urgently.

He smiled, looked up at the sun, and gave her the benefit of the doubt. "By a hair," he said.

With a sigh of satisfaction, Magdalen settled comfortably into the crook of his arm.

Two

It was May morning, a delicate cobweb of a morning dawning under a sky so pale as to be almost translucent, the faintest tinge of pink in the east offering the sun's promise.

"Up, you slugabeds. This is no morning for maids to be stewing beneath the sheets! You must bring in the May." The words were laughingly spoken and a large hand swooped, stripping back the bedcovers, creating tickling havoc with the squealing, wriggling children, nesting like baby voles beneath.

"Oh, 'tis our brother," squeaked Mary obviously. "Is it time for the Maypole, sir?" She squirmed away from her half brother, giggling as he reached for her.

"Lazybones, you will be lucky to see the Maypole at all. The bell for prime sounded some ten minutes ago," he declared, catching her and swinging her out of the bed, the rest of his sisters jumping for his knees in a futile attempt to throw him off balance. Within an instant, they were joined by their equally exuberant little brothers from the next-door chamber, and the match became somewhat uneven.

Magdalen watched the rough-and-tumble as she always did with the bedclothes pulled up tight over her nakedness. As always, part of her wished he would play with her in the same jolly, uninhibited way, but a larger part knew that she would sink with embarrassment if he did. He didn't . . . he never did. The bed she shared with his cousin, Catherine, was always inviolate. When he called a halt to the morning's game, he would greet the older two cheerfully, sometimes giving their hair a teasing tug, before leaving the bedchamber and his vociferous brood of brothers and sisters to their dressing.

"My lord, they will never be ready if you do not cease this foolishness." Lady Gwendoline, half laughing, half scolding, appeared in the open door. "Sounds of revelry are come already from beyond the gates, and it would be a sorry thing indeed if this house were the only one bereft of the May."

Her husband shook the children from him like a dog shaking his coat after the rain. "Make haste, then, or you will miss the crowning of the queen."

"I think Magdalen should be crowned May queen," little Margaret announced. "She can dance better than anyone and has such pretty hair."

"Oh, such silliness, Meg," Magdalen chided, blushing against the pillows.

Guy de Gervais smiled at her. "I am not sure it is silliness. What do you think, my lady?" He turned to his wife, the tenderness of his smile as always overlaid with anxiety. It took no experienced eye to see that the Lady Gwendoline was in poor health. Her skin was of a deathly pallor, her body thin and frail, her eyes sunken.

She stood leaning for support against the doorjamb and returned her husband's smile. There was much love between them, and it was there for all to see. "I think the poor girl has been put to the blush quite sufficiently," she said. "Do you go to your breakfast, husband, and leave the nurse to her work."

At the door, he turned as if reminded of something. "Magdalen, you and I are to journey to the city later this morning. It would be as well for you to dress with more than usual care."

He had gone before she had absorbed the statement sufficiently to respond. Her companions, however, burst into a chorus of envious speculation.

"It must be about your wedding," Catherine said, standing naked beside the bed and stretching. "But he did not say Edmund was to journey with you."

Magdalen's head was buried in the clothes press, and her reply was muffled. "I am not to be wed for months yet," she said more clearly, backing out with a gown of embroidered linen in her hands. "I do not seem to be growing quickly enough." She looked with frank envy at the other girl's budding breasts, the faint dusting of hair beneath her arms and at the base of her belly. "My Aunt Elinor said I could not expect to have my terms for a year at least."

"Then you are most fortunate," declared Catherine. "For they are a great inconvenience, are they not, madame?"

Gwendoline, who had been helping the nurse with the little ones' dressing while listening without comment to the older girls' conversation, agreed with a sigh. For her, the bleeding was more than an inconvenience; it was a near permanent condition and had been these last six months. She had tried physicians' remedies and midwives' cures. She had been cupped to the point of fainting, had lain upon her bed for weeks at a time, but nothing would stop the steady, life-draining flux. And now there was the pain, a deep inner stabbing that wrenched her vitals and took her breath away. But she had told no one of that. Guy could not bear the suffering that he knew about, and it was easier for her to endure in fortitude if she did not feel his pain and fear and anger.

"But such a lack, Magdalen, will not delay your wedding, only the time at which you and your husband can be truly man and wife," she said, wondering why no one had thought to explain this to the child before.

"Oh." Magdalen thought about this for a minute, then shrugged. It did not seem to make much difference. "Do you know why I am to go to London, my lady?" She fastened the buttons of her gown. "Is it then because of the wedding?"

"It has something to do with it," Lady Gwendoline said vaguely. "Lord de Gervais will explain all, I am certain. Let me tie your girdle. It is twisted at the back."

Why was it, Magdalen thought not for the first time, that one was so rarely afforded a straight answer to a straight question? Lady Gwendoline did know why she was to go to London, the child was sure of it. However, whatever the reason, the journey itself promised joy. Lord de Gervais's exclusive company was a rare treat, and in the months since she had been established in his household, he had lost none of his divine luster.

Finally dressed, the excited troop of children ran from their wing of the stone manor house. The house stood on a hill and was therefore not fortified with moat and drawbridge, although watchtowers stood at the corners of the outer walls. In one of the two inner courts, a group of

young men, the pages and squires of the de
Gervais household, waited for the children.
Among them was Edmund de Bresse. As his betrothed came bounding down the hall steps, her
plaits flying, he came toward her, in his hands a
bunch of marigolds that he had picked along the
riverbank before the first touch of the sun had
dried the dew. He was very conscious of the
correctness of his romantic gesture as he presented the bouquet with a flourishing bow.

Magdalen looked both pleased and surprised,
but the significance of the gift in terms of
courtly etiquette completely escaped her, and
she failed to respond to the bow with the appropriate curtsy. "Why, how pretty, Edmund.
We will put some in our hair," she said gaily, distributing the flowers among her companions.
"But we must pick more in the fields as we go
to the village, for we must all have crowns and
garlands."

Guy watched the little scene with an inner
smile. He approved Edmund's gesture as indicative of chivalric lessons well learned, but
Magdalen's response showed how ill prepared
she was to be the object of a suitor's ardor. She
had too little artifice in her nature, he reflected,
perhaps ever to become adept at the game of
flirtation. Edmund was doing his best, but his
betrothed was more inclined to jump with joy

at the prospect of a visit to the mews or a ride to hounds than she was to sentimental tunes on Edmund's lyre or soulful walks in the pleasaunce. He rather suspected that soon the lad would give up and return to his neglected companions and the sport and training at arms that had always given him the most pleasure. And Lord de Gervais would not blame him, for all that he understood Magdalen's inability to enter into the spirit of the game. When a girl was thrust directly from childhood into matrimony, there was little enough time for the development and enjoyment of romantic play.

It was inappropriate in marriage, anyway, he reflected, turning back to the house. That institution was purely instrumental, and romantic entanglements were the province of illicit relationships. But even as he thought this, he caught a glimpse of Gwendoline through the arch to the second court talking with the steward. Her frailty tore at him. They both knew she had upon her the mark of death, and there were many nights when he knelt at the altar rail in the chapel praying for the strength to bear her loss.

Ten years they had been married, he at sixteen, she at thirteen. During a lull in the long, drawnout conflict between England and France, he had been sent to England to the court of the Duke of Lancaster as page. John of Gaunt had taken a liking to the lad and had arranged the alliance for him with the powerful Saxon Redefordes. It was an alliance that transformed the fortunes of the younger son even as it brought him the responsibilities of an English liege lord, responsibilities which compelled his loyalty to his adopted land. Gwendoline brought him land and a dowry of majestic proportions, and with such possessions came power and an earldom. John of Gaunt's personal patronage was extended to the Redeforde family in return, and the duke bought himself a vassal who could be trusted to act for him in the most delicate matters, as well as bear arms in his service and the service of the king.

The union had been childless, but since the nurseries at Hampton had been occupied by Guy's wards, both the lord and lady had had their hands filled with the concerns of children. There were inheritances to manage, educations to order, physical health to attend to, and marriages to arrange. And throughout all this ordering, the Duke of Lancaster's thread had been sewn. The child responsibilities of his vassal were to be put to his own use, and in no more particular an instance as the wedding of de Gervais's nephew to Magdalen of Bellair.

"Guy?" Gwendoline left the steward and came through the arch to meet him, the extreme thinness of her frame accentuated by her close-fitting gown. "Have the children left?"

"Yes, with much excitement. Poor Edmund presented Magdalen with a posy which she immediately distributed to the others, causing him some considerable mortification in front of his friends." He laughed, slipping a hand beneath her arm as if in casual affection, yet they both knew that it was for support, although neither of them would acknowledge it openly.

"I wonder what the duke will make of her," mused the lady. "Let us walk in the orchard, my lord."

"I doubt he will trouble himself to make anything of her." Guy turned toward the gate of the court. "He has shown no interest in her up to now. The child is merely a useful pawn. The church has granted legitimacy, finally. Rome is willing to accept that a binding contract existed between Isolde de Beauregard and the Duke of Lancaster before his first marriage, a contract subsequently dissolved, but nevertheless all children of the union are deemed legitimate."

"But Magdalen must have been conceived when the duke was married," Gwendoline objected as they walked through the wicket gate leading to the orchard.

"Nevertheless, Rome has decreed that she is legitimate," her husband told her, reaching up to pluck a sprig of apple blossom. "Rome has been well paid to do so." He placed the blossom behind her ear, where her hair curled beneath the white linen coif. "There, now you are queen of the May, sweet lady." Bending, he touched his lips to hers, and she leaned into him.

"I know how hard it must be for you, husband," she whispered against the supple, weather-worn skin of his cheek. "I ache to lie with you again, and I am filled with such guilt that I cannot be a wife to you."

"Hush! What folly is this?" He sounded genuinely angry, and she shrank from this most unusual manifestation. "You may not speak so, Gwendoline. You are all the wife I wish for, and I will not hear you say otherwise."

"Nevertheless . . ." She steeled herself to say what she had long lacked the courage to say. "I would wish that you ease yourself in the way that men must. You must take a mistress—"

"Be silent!" he interrupted her, horrified by her words, yet also horrified by the deep inner response he had to them. He was a young, virile man, accustomed to working his body hard and easing it with the same vigor, and the long months of chastity had tried him sorely, although he had done all he could to hide this from his suffering wife.

"If you will not take a leman," she persisted, her voice low, anguished with her own humiliation, "then you must visit the harlots in the stews."

"I have said I will not hear you talk in this wise," he said harshly, "and you would do well to cease this instant." But even as he spoke so harshly, he took her in his arms, gentling her, wiping the tears from her cheeks with a smudging thumb. "Hush now, sweetheart, hush now. 'Tis no great matter for me. 'Tis nothing beside your sufferings."

"My sufferings are not so very great." She gave him a watery smile. "I could endure them easily enough if it were not for the pain they cause you. But I pray daily with Father Benedict, and there is a woman in the village come from Shrewsbury who has most marvelous powers, Elfrida tells me. I will take counsel of her on the morrow."

Guy could place no faith in prayer or the miraculous powers of an itinerant dame, but he would not say so. Instead, he smiled and kissed his wife again. "Then you will soon be well. Let us go back to the house. The children will be returning, and I must take that misbegotten little rogue to her sire." He spoke with a great softness, and his lady smiled with a tinge of sorrow. He was a man who loved children . . . a man who should have children of his own. But she would never bear him any.

MAGDALEN HAD HAD A morning of unalloyed joy. May Day in the border fortress had tended to pass with little ceremony. There had been Maypoles in the surrounding villages, but there had been no one to take the child to participate in the revelry. Erin, her maidservant who had come with her from Bellair, had told her what went on in the village of her own childhood, and this morning's experiences exactly matched those oft-told tales to which Magdalen had listened with aching envy. Barefoot, garlanded with primroses, bluebells, marigolds, and cowslip, they had danced around the Maypole, been chased across the dew-wet fields by the boys and youths of both village and manor while a troop of itinerant minstrels had played and sung the ancient, cheerfully ribald songs of virginity about to be lost.

The manor children were now returning home, laughing and singing, their arms filled with May branches of apple and cherry blossom to fill the great hall of the manor. Magdalen cast Edmund covert glances from beneath her lashes. He had made a great point of catching her in the chase and an even greater play of kissing her soundly. She was not at all sure whether the experience had been pleasant, but Edmund was looking very pleased with himself, and everyone had laughed and cheered him on heartily. Her linen gown, carefully chosen for the journey to the city, was grass-stained and rumpled now, her hair escaped from its braids, the ribbons on her plaits hanging loose. But they were all in similar state, and there was no fear in the de Gervais household that such disarray would bring censure.

It had taken her no more than a day or two to realize that Edgar and Lord de Gervais had indeed been teasing her about the strictness of discipline in the manor at Hampton. It was a place of light and laughter, although there was routine, lessons to learn, and tasks to perform; but always plenty of time for music and play and mirth. The only serious offense for anyone in the household was to cause the Lady Gwendoline the least distress, and since she was a lady much beloved by all, it was an offense rarely if ever committed, and never intentionally.

Lord de Gervais, with a party of liveried retainers, all of whom, like their lord, wore at their shoulders the red rose of Lancaster, was waiting for them in the inner court. His caparisoned palfrey was held by a squire, who had been obliged to forgo the merriment in the village since it was his task this day to serve the lord. Magdalen's small mare stood patiently in the hands of a groom.

The child came running over to him. "Are we to go immediately, my lord? I fear I am sadly untidy."

"I fear you are, too," he agreed affably. "You had best find one of your maids and make haste to change your dress. Do not keep me waiting above a quarter hour." He gestured with his whip to the sundial in the center of the court where the new-risen sun threw its shadow. Magdalen scampered off, narrowly missing a head-on collision with Lady Gwendoline, coming out of the hall.

"You will not return this day?" Gwendoline walked over to her husband, smiling ruefully at the precipitate Magdalen.

He shook his head. "We will sup at the Savoy, and it will be too late to bring the child home afterward."

"The roads at night are ill for traveling anyway," his wife said.

"We are well protected, sweetheart," he said, but there was a frown between his brows as he ran his eyes over the armed retainers. "I trust there will be no danger."

"Do you fear danger for the child?"

"At some point, it will be inevitable. But I

cannot think it will come this soon. Her identity cannot yet be known for certain beyond the duke's confidants, although there are bound to be whispers, both busy and malevolent. But that is another reason why we will travel only under the sun."

He glanced with a hint of impatience at the sundial again. The quarter hour he had allotted Magdalen was all but over. However, she reappeared even as he thought this, fresh and pretty in a clean gown of blue damask, full-skirted with a white collar, her plaits looped at the side of her head beneath a *chaperon* of dark blue silk.

"I am not late, am I?" she asked anxiously, hurrying across to them.

"Not unpardonably. I am accustomed to waiting for maids and ladies while they beautify themselves."

She blushed prettily as he said this. Laughing, he lifted her astride Malapert, and she arranged her full skirts decorously around her. "What is our business in London, my lord?"

"All in good time." He turned from her to bid farewell to his wife. "Try to rest, sweetheart. You had little enough sleep last night."

Gwendoline had thought she had succeeded in keeping her sleeplessness from her husband, gritting her teeth on the gnawing pain, clenching her muscles so that her restlessness would not disturb him. But she should have known that he would be aware of it. "I am going to take counsel with the dame from Shrewsbury in the morning," she said again, almost like an incantation, lifting her face for his kiss. His gaze lingered over her upturned face as if he would read some hope therein, then he bent to kiss her with ineffable tenderness.

Magdalen grew impatient with this whispered congress and the extended salutation. For some reason, it made her uncomfortable and a little cross. She shifted on her mount. The mare skittered on the cobbles as her rider's heels accidentally nudged her flanks. Guy looked round sharply at the sudden clatter, catching the mare's bridle above the bit.

"It's not like you to be clumsy, Magdalen," he said, frowning. "Sit still now, until we are ready to depart."

Magdalen flushed deeply at what was, however gentle, an undeniable rebuke. A lump grew in her throat and she swallowed hard, wondering why she should mind a mere word of censure from Guy de Gervais so much more than the most severe strictures at Bellair Castle.

They were off at last, however, and she sat silent, nursing her resentment, as the cavalcade rode down the hill from the manor and onto the road to London. The river wound between grassy banks alongside the uneven roadway, where the winter's mud was dried into razor-edged ridges. The hedge-rows were massed with hawthorn, periwinkles, and buttercups opened beneath the warmth of the late spring sun. Guy was too preoccupied with thoughts of his wife's illness and the words they had had in the orchard to notice the nature of his companion's silence, and her sense of injury increased as the silence stretched. He had not even told her why they were making this journey. He had been too busy with the Lady Gwendoline to spare her so much as a word. And she was wearing her prettiest dress. She had no mirror, but Catherine, when her opinion had been solicited, had said the *chaperon* also was most elegant and made her look quite womanly. So why would he take not the slightest notice of her?

The road was crowded, but all gave way to the cavalcade in its blue and silver livery, the red rose of Lancaster emblazoned for all to see and recognize. The knight at its head was clearly a baron of considerable substance and power, and the small figure riding at his side caused interested speculation in the villages where the de Gervais livery was known.

After a while, Magdalen found she could no longer nurse her grievance. It kept slipping out of her mind when some sight caught her interest. First there was a dancing bear being led on a long string by a raggedy man flourishing a long-tailed whip, then a peddler with his pack spilling goods, scarves, and packets of needles and bundles of ribbon. A grinder had set up beside the road, and women from the nearby villages were bringing their knives for sharpening, while a troupe of jongleurs offered entertainment as they waited.

Magdalen wished she had a silver penny to throw to the jongleurs. She wished they could stop for a few minutes and watch. She wished she could sample the wares of a pastry cook, calling his pies from a stall set up in the market square of the little town of Kingston. But they pressed on through the narrow streets, the herald blowing his horn to clear the way for them when they met an obstruction in the form of an oxen-pulled ploughshare or a haycart or a straggle of barefoot pilgrims.

A heavy sigh escaped her as they clattered over a small bridge across the river, and she craned over her shoulder to catch a last glimpse of the entrancing bustle they were leaving behind.

"I'faith, but that's a sigh to move the devil himself!" Guy looked down at her in surprise, shaken out of his self-absorption. "Whatever is the matter?"

"Nothing, sir."

"That was a most grievous sigh for nothing." He took in her forlorn expression and frowned. "Come, tell me what is distressing you."

"I do not like to be scolded, and you will not tell me why we are journeying, and there is so much to see but we are going so fast I have not time to look."

"That is a catalogue of woe, indeed," he said solemnly. "But who has scolded you?" He had completely forgotten his flash of sharpness in the manor court.

Magdalen set her lips and would not say, realizing suddenly that it seemed rather silly.

"Well," he said, when it became clear she was not going to answer his question, "let me see what I can do to put right the other wrongs. We are going to London so that you may be presented to the Duke of Lancaster, my overlord. He has an interest in Edmund's affairs as well as my own and has given order that you be brought to him."

Magdalen's eyes widened. "He is a son of the king, is he not?"

"And one of the most powerful men in the realm," Guy said without exaggeration, reflecting that with John of Gaunt's faction controlling the Parliament at Westminster, he had undisputed control over the affairs of the land.

"Perhaps I shall see the king," Magdalen said in hushed tones. "Do you think I might, my lord?"

"Not today, although we will sup at the Savoy Palace and lie there overnight."

The child was silent at this information. She knew enough to realize that in such a case, she would be separated from de Gervais, given into the charge of strangers. It was an alarming prospect.

"As to the sights you do not have time to enjoy," he continued cheerfully, "today we are in somewhat of a hurry, but tomorrow we will proceed at a more leisurely pace, and you may look your fill."

"May I have a silver penny, too?" The thought diverted her attention from the upcoming visit.

"I think I could spare such a sum." He laughed. "What gewgaw have you set your heart upon?"

"None in particular."

"But one must have money to burn, is that it?"

She laughed up at him and nodded. "Edmund kissed me this day. Do you think he should?"

"That rather depends upon whether you think he should," he responded. "Did you find it agreeable?"

Her nose wrinkled. "I am not certain. My

lady says I am to be wed even if I do not yet have my terms. Is it truly so?"

"Yes, but you will remain with the others in the children's wing until you are old enough to be a proper wife to your husband."

"Catherine has her terms already, but she is not yet betrothed. She says she would wish for the religious life, but I think that would be very drear, do you not, my lord?"

"Not everyone thinks the same way," he pointed out. "But how long has Catherine had this yearning for the cloister? I did not know of it."

"She had a vision two months past, when she was walking in the pleasaunce," Magdalen informed him. "It was of an angel and a beggarwoman. The angel was very beautiful, in shining robes with a large halo, and he told Catherine she must devote her life to the poor . . . That was the beggarwoman, you understand. And when Catherine woke up—for she said it was as if she had been asleep although she was still standing up—she had been transfigured."

"I see." Religious hysteria in girls of Catherine's age was hardly unusual, Guy reflected, but he had best talk with his young cousin. He had begun tentative discussion of a betrothal with the son of Roger de Mauroir, but if she really wished for the religious life, then he would not stand in her way. The abbess of Cranborne Priory was his kinswoman and would be delighted to receive a well-dowered cousin as novitiate. And the young de Mauroir could be saved for Alice, who was nearly nine and could soon be betrothed.

Magdalen's merry prattle continued until they reached the gate of the city. There she fell abruptly silent in mid-sentence, her mouth slightly agape as she stared upward at the peculiar frieze over the gate. It took her a minute to realize that they were heads, disembodied heads, fleshless, although some still had straggling locks wisping in the breeze. She had never seen such a sight, never before having spent time in a city.

Her awed silence continued as they rode through the narrow streets. She did not think she had ever seen so many people gathered in one place. And what a people they were. They walked with an air of belonging to no man, the air of those who inhabit the kingdom of heaven and know it. Burghers and master craftsmen in rich mantles bedecked with jeweled chains jostled with leather-aproned apprentices and sober-gowned merchants. The noise was incessant, a cacophony of shrieks and bellows, of blows and laughter. Street vendors called out their wares, and children darted between the hooves of cart horses pulling heavy drays. In a square they came upon a man in the stocks. That was not an unfamiliar sight, but it was always an amusing one. Someone had slung a dead, decomposing cat around the prisoner's neck, and the crowd roared at his predicament as he tried to turn his head away from the stench and crawling vermin. Magdalen laughed with the rest until suddenly she caught the villein's eye. Her amusement vanished at the sheer misery revealed in that desperate gaze. An F was branded on his left cheek, the mark of the fugitive serf, and she wondered who or what he had run from. Then they left the square behind, and she forgot the branded villein.

Her mare tittuped delicately on the crown of the causeway which sloped steeply on both sides to the filth-clogged kennels. An old woman, bent double beneath a bundle of kindling, was pushed from the relative cleanliness of the crown by a stalwart youth with a basket of fish and was forced to continue her journey splashing through the stinking mud at the side of the road. A strident warning came from above a second before a pot of night soil was emptied from a gable window, cascading into the kennels, splashing all in its path.

Lord de Gervais muttered an oath as the foul contents splattered the palfrey's saddlecloth. City ordinance forbade the emptying of chamber pots from upper windows, but he took no action against the offender. None could take action against the citizens of London. They were a law unto themselves; militia, magistrates, and mob, they accepted the dictates of no lord, not even the king.

It was with relief that they rode out of the city on the road to Westminster, some two miles distant. The roofs of the abbey and the great hall were visible as they reached the magnificent white stone mansion of the Savoy Palace, the seat of the Duke of Lancaster, commanding the road between London and Westminster. The Lancastrian flag flew from the central donjon, and, to Magdalen's fanciful eyes, the palace's four white towers gleamed like the towers at heaven's gate in Father Benedict's illustrated book.

The de Gervais herald blew his note of identification. "Here is come the Lord de Gervais, vassal of the House of Lancaster, on business with his overlord."

The great gates to the outer court were flung open, and they rode through into the bustle within. They were received with swift and ceremonious courtesy by the duke's servitors. Magdalen was helped from her mare and stood waiting while Guy dismounted and spoke with the duke's chamberlain. It was clear she was the subject under discussion, judging by the chamberlain's swift sideways glance, then Guy beckoned her forward.

"Come, you will be taken to the women's wing, where you may ease yourself after the journey." Seeing her unhappy expression, he took her hand. "There is nothing to alarm you."

"But you are going to leave me."

"I must for a while. You will be sent for soon enough."

There was nothing to do but obey. She was conducted across the quadrangle and into the vast mansion by a waiting page who offered her not a word of greeting, maintaining a haughty silence as if she were beneath his notice. He ushered her down bewilderingly long and twisting corridors, up a flight of stairs, finally showing her into a long gallery. Soft sunlight sparking off water filtered through the diamond panes of the narrow windows overlooking the river. The air rustled with the light tones of women, the swish of their richly colored gowns, the merry plucking lilt of a lute. They sat around on low stools, on the cushioned seats carved beneath the windows, coiffed heads bent over tambour frames, whispering gently among themselves, lost in the absorption of their private world.

The page left her at the door, and she stood awkwardly, unacknowledged. She was in need of the privy and most desperately thirsty, but she

had no idea how to relieve either of those conditions. Which of these women was the lady of
the house? She must surely make her reverence
to her grace, but how could she do so if she
could not identify her? Angry tears of resentment at Guy de Gervais for abandoning her in
this predicament pricked behind her eyes.

Hesitantly, she stepped further into the gallery.
The women were all most magnificently
gowned, she noticed, but her attention was
drawn to a knot of women by the far window.
A lady was plucking a lute and singing softly to
the group. Magdalen summoned her courage
and walked as boldly as she dared toward them.

"I pray you, good mesdames, where is the lady
of this house that I may make my reverence?"

"Good heavens, child, where did you spring
from?" A young woman in a dark red cotehardie beneath a sideless surcote laughed, not
unkindly.

"I was told to wait here until I am summoned," Magdalen said. "I am come with Lord
de Gervais."

There was a sudden silence. Then an older
woman, one who sat in the center of the group,
said with an accent that Magdalen found strange
yet not unpleasant, "Come here, child. I am
Constanza, Duchess of Lancaster."

Magdalen stepped over to her. The lady was

large and swarthy, with dark eyes lost in rolls of flesh, her hair hidden beneath a jeweled cap over a netted caul. Her gown was so smothered with gems that it was hard to see the material beneath. Magdalen made her reverence and waited while she was inspected with considerable care.

"How are you called?"

"Magdalen, my lady. I am daughter of the Lord Bellair, Lord Marcher of Bellair Castle."

A little ripple ran around the room, but the duchess shook her head, frowning at her women, and they fell silent.

"You are a long way from the border lands, Magdalen of Bellair."

"Yes, my lady. I am betrothed to Edmund de Bresse, ward of my Lord de Gervais." Magdalen answered the questions in the formal manner she had been taught to adopt in the company of adults, her eyes lowered, her hands clasped in front of her. It was only in the de Gervais household that such formal deference between child and adult was not insisted upon, nor even particularly encouraged.

"And you are come with Lord de Gervais." The lady of the house touched her chin, where, to Magdalen's fascination, sprouted some astonishingly long black hairs. "For what purpose?"

"To be presented to his grace of Lancaster, my

lady, because he takes an interest in my lord's ward." Magdalen had spotted a crystal jug and goblets upon a table against the wall and looked longingly at it, even as she squeezed her thighs tightly together beneath her gown in an effort to contain her other pressing need.

Constanza followed her eyes. "Are you thirsty, child?"

"Yes, my lady, dreadfully, but I also have need of the privy," Magdalen blurted in a rush, lest the moment pass her by.

"You may ease yourself beyond the garderobe." The duchess gestured toward a curtained doorway in the corner of the gallery and Magdalen, without further ceremony, hastened to avail herself of the offered relief in the latrine set into the wall and opening over a deep drainage ditch below.

When she emerged, she was told to pour herself mead from the pitcher and come and sit on the stool beside the duchess. The gentle activities in the long gallery resumed, no one appearing to pay any further attention to the new arrival, although Magdalen was puzzlingly aware of looks and whispers directed at her from the four corners of the gallery.

Meanwhile, Lord de Gervais had been escorted to the duke's presence chamber. The antechamber was thronged with those hoping for audience with Lancaster, petitioners, courtiers, merchants. Lord de Gervais was left among them for a very few minutes before the chamberlain emerged from the presence chamber and bade him enter.

His overlord was seated in a carved oak chair, slightly elevated on the dais at the far end of the room. He wore a loose gown with dagged sleeves over a particolored tunic of red and gold. His golden hair was fading to gray now, but the power in his frame was as evident in his middle years as it had been in the stripling, and the blue eyes were as sharp and bright.

De Gervais crossed the carpeted floor, knelt to take and kiss his lord's hand.

"You are well come, Guy," the duke said with jocular familiarity, raising him up. "Let us leave this crowd. I would have private speech with you." With the impatient arrogance that always marked his step, he moved to a door in the paneled wall. The courtiers and attendants in the room fell back as the door closed behind the duke and his vassal.

"Well, it is done. The papal decree arrived three days past." The duke went to the table in the windowless inner chamber that had an almost womblike quality to its seclusion. The walls were hung with heavy tapestries, the floor covered with a thick carpet, the furniture all

dark and carved. The only light came from the
wax candles which burned at all hours. There
were two ways into the room, through the
presence chamber and by a stairway from the
duke's bedchamber above, the door cunningly
concealed in the paneling. Both doors were
guarded at all times, because in this room were
contained all Lancaster's secrets, and many of
those secrets were too dark to see the light
of day.

He handed Guy the parchment with the papal
seal and began to pace the chamber, the quiet
satisfaction in his voice the only indication of his
inner triumph. "With the marriage of my
daughter to the hostage, Edmund de Bresse, we
will secure the service of the de Guise and the
de Bresse. Such an alliance cannot help but win
us Picardy and Anjou."

Guy nodded, examining the parchment. With
the death of Edmund's father, the de Bresse fiefdom in Picardy had been put in the control of a
regent appointed by the king of France until
such time as the heir grew to adulthood and his
ransom had been paid, when he could take up
his inheritance. A regent was necessary because
an empty nest of that richness was an open invitation to any cuckoo with even the slightest pre-
tensions to the estate. However, had the child
heir been in the hands of the French, there

would have been no danger of a change in political allegiance within the fief. But Edmund was a hostage in England, under the influence of the English not the French king. His fealty to England could be secured by marriage to a Lancastrian, and forgiveness of his ransom. When he took possession of his vast inheritance, then he would bring to the English cause the loyal service of the de Bresse of his paternal line and the de Guise of his maternal. Two such allegiances would be of enormous benefit to the English king in his hotly disputed claim for the French throne, and Edmund de Bresse would breed Plantagenet heirs to his great fiefdom.

The boy would have to fight to regain his heritage, though, Guy thought. Charles of France would not hand it over to a vassal of King Edward's without a murmur. But the lad's claim to the fief was unshakable. There would have to be a campaign, one in which young Edmund would earn his spurs. And he would have the mighty power of Lancaster at his back, because Lancaster would be claiming for his acknowledged daughter's husband. It was a clever piece of deceptive diplomacy that could only misfire if aught should occur to prevent or destroy the marriage. The permanent removal from the scene of John of Gaunt's daughter would be the most effective means of achieving such a breakdown. And such a removal might seem to the de Beauregards an adequate vengeance for their defeat at Carcassonne at the hands of Lancaster eleven years previously. They might well choose to be Charles's agent in such a matter, and it was a business to which that devious, unprincipled clan was well suited.

"What is she like?"

The abrupt question, asked with an underlying fierceness that seemed to have no justification, interrupted the gloomy turn of de Gervais's thoughts. He considered Magdalen.

"Lively, impatient of restraint. Strong of character, yet with a softness that craves and responds to affection. She learns quickly if she is so minded, but she is more interested in the pursuit of pleasure than of learning. However, that is not unusual."

"Of what complexion is she?"

"Fair, gray eyes, dark brown hair. Small frame, as yet unripened, but she bids fair to beauty."

Guy de Gervais knew that Lancaster wanted to ask: Is she like her mother? But he could not ask that question. Guy would not know how to answer it.

"I will see her for myself," John of Gaunt said, as if he had heard his companion's thoughts. He went to the door concealed in the paneling and gave low-voiced instructions to the guard who stood without.

When Magdalen received the expected summons, she sighed with some relief. She curtsied to the duchess, thanking her for her hospitality, and followed the guard, eager to be with de Gervais again. The passageways were thronged with servitors, men-at-arms, pages and squires in every kind of livery, accompanying the courtiers and hangers-on at the court of the Duke of Lancaster. None gave the child hurrying after a sentry more than a cursory glance. She was not taken to the antechamber, however, but up a wide, winding stone staircase and into a bedchamber hung with red and gold brocade, the Lancastrian rose embroidered on the tester and the curtains, set into the carpet and the upholstery. Privately, Magdalen thought the design overused.

"This way." The sentry pressed a panel, and a door swung open leading to a narrow stair, seemingly within the wall. Her companion plucked a torch from the sconce beside the door and held it high to light their path.

Mightily puzzled, the child followed him down the stair. At the foot stood a narrow doorway set into the stonework. The sentry banged on the door with the heavy stave he carried at his belt. A call answered the knock, and the sentry opened the door, gesturing to his companion that she should enter.

Magdalen stepped into a dim, warm heaviness. The door closed behind her. Lord de Gervais and another man were standing by a long table, goblets in hand. The other man moved to place his goblet on the table, and the candle on the wall above cast the gigantic shadow of his hand. The child's scalp crept and her skin prickled in the smothering atmosphere. Someone walking over her grave . . . Why would Lord de Gervais say nothing to her? Why was he standing there, so immobile?

"Come over here." The other man spoke, moving into the more vigorous light of two torches above the fireplace, where burned a fire, despite the warmth of the May morning outside this secret burrow.

Hesitantly, Magdalen crossed to him. She glanced in appeal at de Gervais, but his face was unsmiling. He had no part to play in this scene, but he was filled with a nameless apprehension.

The duke took his daughter's face between both hands and tilted it to the light. She felt the fire hot through her damask gown; his hands, hard with the calluses of a swordsman, on her jaw; the edge of the massive ruby in his signet ring touching cold against her cheek. She had no choice but to look up at the expressionless face staring into her rather than at her with such frightening, unwavering intensity.

"God's blood!" He flung her face suddenly from him and swung away to the table, lifting his goblet and draining it to the dregs. "God's blood! I never thought to see those eyes again."

Magdalen knew that something was dreadfully awry. She began to shake, although she knew not why. De Gervais came over swiftly. "Wait outside," he said softly, hustling her to the paneled door.

"But how have I offended?" she whimpered. "I do not know what I have done wrong."

"You have done nothing wrong," he assured her, pushing her through the door. "Wait abovestairs with the sentry." He turned back to the room, his face grave as he dared to speak. "That was ill done, my lord. She is but a child."

"She is Isolde's child!" the duke said with a hiss. "The child of a faithless, murdering whore. May her black soul be damned! Think you that one will be any different? Whores breed whores." A laugh of scorn and disgust cracked in the humid air.

"You cannot visit the mother's sins upon her. She never knew her mother," Guy said urgently. "It is not the church's teaching."

"You know how that child was born." The

duke refilled his goblet, and pain twisted, ugly and harsh, upon his face. "I pulled her forth from her dam's body as the whore convulsed in her death throes, convulsed with the poison she had intended for me! And you say such a birth was in innocence!"

"If you felt thus, my lord, why did you take the babe in charge? She was but an unacknowledged bastard."

Lancaster shook his head. "I had acknowledged the coming child as my own, with documents witnessed in proof." His voice was low with self-disgust now. "I loved the whore, would you believe? I intended to provide for the child." His voice took on a distant, pensive quality. "Besides, there was too much death in the room already." He seemed to look inward, to see again that dim chamber in the fortress monastery at Carcassonne, the slaughtered monk at the door, the young squire with the dagger through his heart. He could smell again the reek of death, the blood of birthing. He could hear again the shrillness of agony on the lips of the woman he had once loved more than life itself. The woman he had killed, turning her own weapon upon her.

"I saw her mother in those eyes," he said bluntly, offering the explanation without apology for his harsh rejection of the child as he came back to his surroundings again. "What features does she have of mine, de Gervais?"

"Your mouth, my lord," de Gervais said promptly, sensing that some crisis had passed. "And some of your arrogance, I believe."

The duke's lip curled in slight amused acknowledgment. "She may have her dam's eyes, but there's the mark of the Plantagenet upon her." He refilled his goblet and drank deeply. "The proclamation of legitimacy will go out across the land, and she will be wed at Westminster. We will throw down the gauntlet to France with much trumpeting. And after the marriage, her husband will go into Picardy and lay claim to his fief."

"And what of Magdalen? She will be in some danger once her paternity is proclaimed."

"You will keep her safe until she is wed. Then she may return to Bellair until this business is ended. The Lord Marcher will ensure her safety behind the walls of his castle."

Guy de Gervais felt a pang for the child so soon to be abandoned once more in the wilderness of the border lands, her role played for the moment. But he knew she would be safer there than anywhere, and he had no reasonable alternative to offer. He himself would take up arms with Edmund, and since her father would not shelter her, there would be none here to protect her.

"Will you not say some words of softness to her, my liege?" he asked. "She is afraid she has offended but does not understand why."

Lancaster shook his head. "No, I do not wish to see her again this day. But you may assure her that she has not offended. Explain matters to her as you see fit."

A loyal vassal must perform many services for his liege lord, de Gervais reflected caustically. This last task that Lancaster had laid upon his shoulders he would dearly like to forgo.

FROM THAT DAY, Magdalen entered a world of terrifying confusion. Her reception at Lancaster's hands had shattered some deep-seated confidence in herself. Yet she was told that this man was her sire. She did not believe that she was the duke's daughter, whatever she was told by de Gervais and the Lady Gwendoline. Such a thing was not possible, so she would not even permit her mind to examine it. But the person she had believed herself to be, they said did not exist. She had lost one, could not accept the other, and thrashed in a torment of hideous loss and bewilderment. The constant surveillance under which she now found herself turned a stable, generally happy child into a violent rebel, alternating be-

tween frenzied storms and equally impassioned
sulks. It was as if the escort who had been as-
signed to protect her became the symbol of this
appalling thing that had happened to her. She
would talk to no one, refused to go to her lessons, refused to play with the others. All her
mental and physical energies were devoted to
evading her guard, and she succeeded often
enough to drive Lord de Gervais to distraction.

He told himself that her behavior was not surprising, that she was frightened and uncertain,
thrust so suddenly upon center stage in this devious play of Lancaster's composing. She was
taken to court, was visited by all and sundry,
whispered about, exclaimed over, and she sat
sullen and unmoving throughout, planning her
next move in her battle with her escort. She
climbed through windows, down apple trees,
hid with the hawks in the mews, put spur to her
horse and set her to jump the river, catching her
guards completely by surprise.

Gwendoline grew weaker by the day, and
Guy watched in wretchedness as she faded before his eyes. But throughout, she struggled
with Magdalen, giving her all the loving understanding and kindness that she had within her,
praying that acceptance would come to the
child soon and this dreadful destructive storm of
uncomprehending rage would die.

One evening, Guy found his wife weeping quietly in despairing frustration at Magdalen's latest intransigence, and his patience deserted him. He beat the child and sent her supperless to bed. The effect was devastating. Magdalen wept all night with such violence that she became febrile, locked in some wracking tussle with her grief and perplexity. The apothecary cupped her, they purged her until she could barely struggle from the bed, but still the harsh sobs tore through the fragile frame. Finally, summoned by his distraught wife, Guy came into the chamber, leaning over to push the soaked strands of hair from her brow. Her eyelids were so swollen as to be almost closed, and his heart turned over with remorse and pity.

"There now," he said softly, aware of his inadequacy in the face of this monumental unhappiness. "Hush now, pippin. Hush now." He lifted her from the bed and sat with her on his knee. Gradually, words began to emerge through the sobs, gasping, disjointed words of apology.

"We must pardon each other," he said when he could finally make sense of what she was saying. "I lost patience, but I cannot suffer it when my lady is unhappy, and you had made her so."

Her sobs began to die down as he held her, and the words began to flow as the tears had done. All her fear, her bewilderment, her anger came forth, and Lady Gwendoline sat beside her husband, holding the hot damp hand in hers. "He does not like me," Magdalen said with a final gulp. "If he is my sire, why did he look at me with such hatred? Why did he send me to Bellair to make me think that Lord Bellair was my father? Where is my mother?"

"Your mother is dead," Gwendoline said, "as we have explained to you." Gritting her teeth, she told the tale that all knew to be a blatant falsehood. "She was but briefly wed to his grace of Lancaster and died in giving birth to you."

"Your identity had to be kept secret for reasons of policy," Guy said. "As now, for reasons of your safety, you must remain under guard at all times. I have explained that."

The child in his arms was very still, the violence of her earlier weeping evident now only in an occasional gulping sob as her body found its ease. Finally, she lifted her head from his chest. Her voice was scratchy after the tempest of weeping, but it was calm. "If it must be, then it must be."

The Lord and Lady de Gervais looked at each other in silent relief. It was over.

TWO WEEKS BEFORE the Lady Magdalen of Lancaster married Edmund de Bresse at Westminster, Gwendoline died. She died in her husband's arms, and he could only be thankful for the merciful oblivion that brought an end to sufferings that had become unendurable. His own grief was a canker, spreading from his soul to infect all around him, darkening his vision so that he saw the sun as a dim cold circle in a murky sky, dulling his senses so that the richness of new-mown hay, the freshness of lavender, the tang of cinnamon were as savorless as chaff upon the tongue.

Everyone grieved for a lady so beloved, but all were thankful that her torment was concluded, and in no breast lurked the fear that the Lady Gwendoline's soul was destined for anywhere but heaven.

Magdalen's sorrow was twofold. She grieved for the Lady Gwendoline, but she could not endure Guy's grief. She did not know how to comfort him, yet she was unable to stand aside. The wedding would take place as decreed, because how could such a state and politic event be postponed for the death of a peripheral figure? But she ignored all the preparations. Her betrothed was far too busy training for the grand campaign that would win him his spurs and the power of his fiefdom to concern himself with anything outside the basic facts of the marriage that must be solemnized before he could depart for France. All his previous efforts at courting

Magdalen had fallen upon stony ground, so he returned his attention to the other and most important function of the knight—war.

Magdalen spent her time following de Gervais. She was always to be found at his side at the long refectory table, picking the choicest morsels for him from the serving platters, filling his cup. She crept into his privy chamber, sitting in a corner, quiet but watchful as he attended to his affairs or simply sat, staring into the wasteland of memory. When he went forth on business, she was waiting for his return, watching critically as his page cared for his needs.

Guy was but vaguely aware of her until the evening before her wedding, when he went into the pleasaunce, a place painful to him because in every shadow he saw Gwendoline, picking lavender, dabbling a finger in the birdbath, bending to pluck a weed from the unsullied beds. The place was painful to him, yet he could not keep away from it and would pace for long hours along the walks.

On this evening, he found Magdalen sitting beneath an espaliered apricot tree, and he remembered with guilty remorse that she was to be wed on the morrow and he had had no speech with her in days, it seemed.

He sat beside her, but before he could say anything she whispered with a strange, fierce passion, "If I do not have my terms, then I cannot be bedded with Edmund before he leaves for France, and the marriage could be annulled and then we could be wed, you and I."

Shaken from his absorption, Guy stared at her in shock. "What folly is this, Magdalen. You are distempered."

"Nay, sir," she returned stoutly. "I love you and I have always loved only you, and I will always love only you. When the Lady Gwendoline was your lady wife, then of course it could not be. But now——"

He stood up abruptly. "We will forget this ever took place, Magdalen. You are still but a child and in the midst of much excitement and confusion. The day after tomorrow you will return to Bellair Castle, and you must pray for your husband's safe return and successful enterprise."

"I will pray for yours," she said, the gray eyes glittering with a determination that chilled him with its strength. She was indeed the child of Isolde de Beauregard and John, Duke of Lancaster.

Three

LADY MAGDALEN DE BRESSE had come to the conclusion that tourneys were simply occasions where bouts of murderous sound and fury alternated with irksome heraldic ceremonies. As a child, she had longed passionately for the opportunity to watch a joust. Maybe it was simply that the years that now separated her from her childhood had invested her with a certain cynicism, but she could not, however hard she tried, see why these men would wish to enclose themselves in pounds of plate armor on a steaming August afternoon in order to ride at each other, their war cries rending the air, and belabor each other with lance or the flat of a sword until one of them fell off his horse to lie helpless like some monstrous chrysalis in an iron cocoon.

She kept such heresy to herself, however. In the crowded tiers surrounding the lists, excitement and pleasurable fear were nearly palpable. In the midsummer heat, such emotions brought damp foreheads and clammy hands, not helped by the richness of dress, the fur-trimming of surcotes. But neither man nor woman would let comfort dictate when wealth and status were adjudged by dress. Magdalen herself was sweltering, feeling sweat trickle beneath her arms and collect between her breasts, and she surreptitiously eased the heavy damask of her gown away from her skin so that it should not become stained.

The lady on her right had been whispering prayers to the saints for the safety of her lord throughout the morning's combats, whether the knight in question was engaged in a joust or no, and at every clash of steel, little moans of mingled excitement and terror broke from her lips, interrupting the incantations. The dust was so thick it was impossible to see exactly what was going on during the jousts and melees, for all that Magdalen was seated on the front bench of the Lancastrian loge. The king was absent this afternoon, so the adjoining loge was empty, the tournament falling under the command and patronage of Lancaster. The banner of the Plantagenets, displaying the lily of France and the leopard of England, flew over the scarlet canopied booth. The duke was seated in the center of the velvet-covered platform at the front of the loge, his carved chair all hung about with scarlet draperies embossed with the red rose. He was in morose mood, misliking the role of spectator on such occasions, and his wife, the Duchess Constanza, sat beside him in nervous silence, knowing better than to intrude upon his grimness.

The marshals entered the stockade, followed by the heralds and their pursuivants. Magdalen sat forward expectantly. The event which required her presence was about to be announced. The dust from the preceding melee had settled somewhat, aided by the buckets of water sprinkled over the surface of the arena. Trumpets blared as the heralds announced a private joust between the Sieur Edmund de Bresse and the Sieur Gilles de Lambert.

The two knights on massive destriers entered from opposite ends of the lists, but instead of waiting for the marshals' ritual call to arms, they both rode forward to the Lancastrian loge. There they raised their visors and spoke as one.

"My lord duke, we request to do battle *a l'outrance.*"

From the gallery tiers people craned forward, demanding to know what was being said. The peasants and servitors who had scrambled up to the barriers the better to view the sport began a low-voiced grumble at this delay.

Magdalen, well aware of the unorthodox nature of such a request, felt her husband's eyes upon her. He wore her favor, a scarf of silver gauze twisted around his helmet, and he held her gaze for a long, burning moment. Puzzled, she glanced sideways at John of Gaunt. His displeasure was apparent.

"The rules of this tourney state that all combat will be *a plaisance.* Is this some private quarrel you bring to a trial of skill undertaken beneath the banner of friendship?"

"We make request, my lord duke," Edmund said simply.

"Young hothead!" The voice was that of Guy de Gervais. He appeared suddenly at John of Gaunt's elbow, his jupon of blue and silver over his armor, but he was unhelmeted and wore only the two-pronged dagger at his belt. He had taken part in the morning's combat but would not enter the lists again until the final melee.

A low-voiced conversation took place between the duke and de Gervais. Magdalen strained to catch some word of what was said without obviously turning her head. Surprised and not a little embarrassed by this disconcerting turn of events, she avoided returning Edmund's look, keeping her eyes fixed on the waving pennants of the knights' tents beyond the stockade, occupying her mind with trying to identify them, remembering lessons in heraldry from her months in the de Gervais household.

The two young knights sat their destriers, rigid with honor and purpose as they awaited judgment on their request to fight in earnest.

The lords and ladies of the duke's household sitting around Magdalen made no attempt to hide their curiosity, and their whispers and glances were directed more often than not at the young wife. Newly established at the king's court under the aegis of the House of Lancaster after her husband's return from France, she was an object of fascination and not a little envy for many. Her husband was young and noble, had distinguished himself in the campaign in Picardy, and was now in possession of his wealthy fiefdom. They were a couple upon whom the world smiled, it must be believed. So what lay behind this disruptive request of the Sieur de Bresse?

John of Gaunt listened to de Gervais, then he turned his head and his eyes rested on his daughter. A bleak shaft pierced the brilliant blue of his gaze. He said something to de Gervais, then took the emerald-studded hanap held by the squire at his elbow and tossed back the contents. Leaning forward, his hands resting on the arms of the chair, he spoke.

"The rules of this tourney state that all deeds of arms will be *a plaisance*. You will abide by those rules of combat."

There was nothing further to be said. The knights dropped their visors and returned to their own ends of the lists. But this combat had acquired unusual interest for the spectators, even for the majority who had no idea what issue had been raised before the duke. Something unusual had taken place.

"In the name of God and St. George, come forth to do battle!"

Guy de Gervais stood beside his liege lord watching as the marshals gave the call and the two bore down upon each other in a crash of steel. The length of stirrup and the high ridge of saddle ensured that they were all but standing on the backs of the mighty horses, all the better to control and empower the thrust of their lances. They met. The lances, correctly foiled as the rules of *a plaisance* combat decreed, clashed and splintered evenly. They separated, received new lances from their squires, and settled for the second course. Lance slid off shield, wood splintered, the dry earth flew up in great clods beneath powerful hooves as the destriers, carried by their own momentum, pounded past each other. Guy frowned. It was an ill-run course, and the crowd were making clear their disappointment. It was ill-run because these two were battling for something other than the thrill of the tournament, and it added misjudged ferocity to something that should rather have the elegance of a deed of arms, perfect in technique.

His gaze drifted to the intent figure of

Edmund de Bresse's wife. She was staring at the scene with a fixity that seemed to indicate she was aware of some underlying cause to this display of clumsy ferocity. In the years since her wedding, she had grown upward like a watered sapling and now displayed a tall figure, slender but well-shaped. Her gown of rose damask was cut low at the neck, revealing the soft cleft of her breasts; her neck rose long and sinuous; her rich brown hair was confined beneath silver cauls and a pearl-encrusted headband. Her beringed fingers played restlessly with the ruby buckle of her girdle, underscoring her perturbation. But she could not know the cause of her husband's suddenly erupted quarrel with the Sieur Gilles de Lambert. If it was as her father and Guy de Gervais suspected, it would do her little good to know it.

Magdalen felt Guy's eyes upon her. She was always vibrantly aware of him whenever he was in her ken. She turned her head to look at him and smiled in both appeal and invitation.

It was her father's mouth, full and passionate, Guy thought, not for the first time, as he debated whether to answer the appeal and move to sit beside her. She wanted to know what was going on, and he could hardly blame her, but he would have to fabricate both for her ears and for those around, and he was not sure he had the mental agility to do so at the moment. He shook his head, and disappointment crossed her face, followed rapidly by annoyance. He should have expected such a response, he supposed. The willfulness of the child had now hardened into Plantagenet arrogance and determination, and they were certainly more difficult characteristics to withstand.

She rose and turned her back on the joust, making her way past the rows of knees crammed tightly along the bench. Surprise and disapproval rustled at her passing. It was hardly seemly for a wife to refuse to watch her husband in the lists, particularly when he wore her colors.

"What's this?" demanded the duke when she reached his chair. "You turn your back on your husband in combat, madame?"

She curtsied low. "I wished to talk with Lord de Gervais, my lord duke. I believe he has some knowledge of why my lord would wish to change the rules of combat."

"I suggest you ask your husband, madame," the duke rasped. "He will tell you if he considers it meet."

The crowd roared behind her, and she turned slowly. The Sieur de Lambert had been unhorsed and lay heaving in the dust in his effort to right himself. His squires came running to offer assistance. It should have signaled the end of the trial, but Edmund dismounted, drawing his sword when his opponent had struggled to his feet.

"God's nails," muttered the duke. "He must needs pursue this. I've a mind to call a halt and banish de Bresse from my court for a month."

The other combatant had now drawn his own sword, and the two stood facing each other amid the roaring crowd, a crowd now acknowledging the antipathy between these two and eager to see what was to come of it.

"Let them have it out, my lord." Guy offered the low-voiced suggestion at the duke's ear so Magdalen could hear only a word here and there. "It will not do to seem to make more of it than the unruly impulse of a pair of hotheads. Punish Edmund for it afterward on the grounds that such choler is dangerous on the field and he does himself no service by it."

"Lady, I suggest you return to your place," the duke said testily to Magdalen, who still stood in frowning puzzlement. "You serve no useful purpose standing there, and you interrupt my view."

"Your pardon, sir." The man whom, in her soul, Magdalen still refused to acknowledge as her father had never a kind word for her, and she had learned to expect no more than a measure of courtesy. It did not trouble her since she disliked him at least as much as he disliked her, and she had given up wondering about the cause of his antipathy. Now, thwarted, she looked at Guy, but he studiously avoided catching her eye so she was obliged to return unsatisfied to her seat.

The two in the arena fought with all the vigor of youth and the skill garnered in the years of boyhood training. They used only the flat of the sword, but the blows crashed through the lists as the weapons came down on helmet and hauberk with a viciousness that was obvious to all.

Magdalen watched Edmund as he forced his opponent inexorably toward the side of the lists. The Sieur de Lambert would be *hors de combat* if he touched the stockade, and such an outcome began to seem inevitable. Edmund had perhaps the edge of strength and he was using both hands on his sword, his incomprehensible fury somehow enabling him to receive and ignore the blows that fell upon him so that they did not deter his attack in the least. He pressed closer to his opponent, his sword thwacking across his shoulder, and then the Sieur de Lambert stumbled over a stone and went to the wall.

The crowd bellowed as, with hands upraised

in submission, de Lambert acknowledged his defeat.

Only then did Magdalen realize how tensely she had been holding herself. The palm of one hand was imprinted with the rings of the other, so tightly had she been clenching them, and her shoulders ached. She sat back as the ceremonies of the marshals and heralds commenced. Edmund raised his visor and came on foot to the duke's loge to receive what should have been his lord's congratulation on a bout well fought.

Instead, his reverence was accorded a frozen silence. The hectic flush on his cheeks faded to a dull pallor. His eyes still retained some of the fury that had driven him during the joust, and now that simmering glow flared again at this public humiliation.

Guy de Gervais saw the danger at the same moment Magdalen did. The young man was still so locked in his own world of private frenzy, the battering he had taken surely still pounding in his blood, that he had forgotten in whose presence he stood.

"My lord . . . my lord." Magdalen's voice rose clear and sweet, breaking the dreadful, anticipatory hush. Edmund dragged his livid gaze from the duke and turned toward his wife.

She stood up, plucking a rose from a vase at her side. "You have worn my colors well, my lord." Smiling, she leaned over the balcony and tossed him the flower. "I claim a gift in exchange."

Edmund caught the flower without conscious thought as her words penetrated his fog, and he realized with a shock how close he had come to disaster. "Indeed, my lady, what would you have of me?" He bowed his head in acknowledgment.

"Why, a kiss, sir," she returned. Delighted laughter rose around them at this elegant courtly play that bid fair to banish any unfavorable impressions of the joust.

Edmund stepped up to the loge. "Why, lady, it is a gift gladly given." Reaching up as she leaned over, he put his hands on her arms and then, to the surprise of all, lifted her bodily over the rail to the ground beside him. He kissed her on the mouth with a lusty vigor that brought applause from the spectators and a blush to Magdalen's cheek.

"Fie, my lord," she said. "How am I to return to my place?"

Guy de Gervais, smiling, leaned over the rail. "Lift the lady to me, Edmund, and I will take her."

The exchange was effected without difficulty, and as he set her on her feet, Guy said in soft approval, "That was prettily done, Magdalen." Her eyes glowed at the praise from the only person whose opinion mattered to her in the least.

"Does it not deserve a kiss, also, my lord?" The whispered question seemed to speak itself.

The smile vanished. "Indeed, it does, my lady," he responded without expression, lifting her hand to his lips in a formal salute. He turned from her, excused himself to the duke, and left the loge.

He made his way to the tents beyond the lists, intending to have a serious word with his erst-while ward, but Magdalen's whispered question, the soft glow of her eyes, would not be banished from his mind. He had not forgotten the pas-sionate declaration of the child before she be-came a woman, but he had believed himself untroubled by it. It had been simply the inten-sity of a grieving, overexcited child. Now, un-ease stirred. The demand she had just made had not been of the order of a small girl begging for a sweetmeat or a silver penny. There had been undeniable sensuality in her voice and eyes. Her body was no longer a child's body, her speech and conduct no longer that of a child, and he knew because he had been there exactly when Edmund had made a woman of the child.

Magdalen returned to her place, a fixed smile hiding her discomfiture. Fortunately, only she was aware of that discomfiture and the reasons for it. What had passed between herself and the Lord de Gervais would draw no remark from other eyes. But she was deeply mortified. Yet she knew she had no right to be. She was the truly bedded, wedded wife of the Sieur Edmund de Bresse . . .

THEY HAD ARRIVED at Bellair Castle the previous January, a messenger sent on ahead to warn of their coming. Magdalen had stood on the battlements, huddled into her fur-lined, hooded mantle, watching for them. The long and wearisome years of seclusion stretched behind her, years when the existence of the Duke of Lancaster's daughter, wife of Edmund de Bresse, seemed to have been forgotten by all. When Edmund and de Gervais had prevailed in Picardy and Edmund was in possession of his castle, the duke had sent a formal note of congratulation to his daughter, informing her of her husband's safety and prowess in the field. The message had not mentioned Guy de Gervais, and she had received no word of him in all those years until the day before, when the heralding messenger had told her that Lord de Gervais accompanied her husband on this journey to the border lands, when Edmund de Bresse in victory was come to claim his wife.

Standing on the battlements, she had stared

out across the plain until spots began to dance in front of her eyes. The sentinels in the watchtowers would see them coming before she did, and the subsequent bell ringing would reach her wherever she might be in the castle. But she still stood, exposed to the bitter snow-tipped wind, straining her eyes into the distance.

The bell clanging its alert from the eastern tower came the instant before she herself could make out the slight shifting on the horizon. In the courtyard below, the call to ride out was heard, and the sounds drifted upward of men running, booted feet ringing, iron-shod hooves clattering, harness jingling. She turned to lean over the parapet, looking down on the scene. Lord Bellair was about to mount his palfrey. He was dressed with his usual lack of adornment, a heavy plain wool surcote over his tunic, but he rode forth to greet his guests with an escort that could only do them honor.

Magdalen left the battlements and on impulse crossed the inner court and went through the arch to the outer ward. Mad Jennet's hovel was still standing against the far wall, its outer structure sadly in need of patching, the reed-thatched roof showing gaps. But smoke curled from the central chimney hole, and the flicker of a tallow candle showed in the unshuttered window.

She had no time to pay this visit, yet some

powerful need that she could not put into words
was driving her. She pushed aside the skin at the
doorway and stepped within. These days, when
she visited the old woman, it was always to
bring her something from the stillroom to ease
her aching limbs, or a basket from the kitchen to
fill her empty belly. Occasionally since her return to Bellair, she had prevailed upon the castle servants to clean out the filthy rushes and lay
fresh, but the stench still caused her to put a
hand across her mouth and nose.

"Jennet?" She could make out nothing for a
moment in the dimness, then saw the huddle on
the straw pallet in the corner. "Are you ailing,
Jennet?"

A knotted, twisted hand emerged from the
filthy scrap of blanket. "Fetch the friar to me,
child. I'm minded to lay down this mortal coil."
The old voice creaked like unoiled leather. "I'd
be shriven before I die."

Magdalen peered at the wizened face. She had
no idea how old mad Jennet could be. The
woman herself probably didn't know. But she'd
been occupying this corner of the outer ward
for as long as Magdalen could remember, and
she'd never looked any younger.

"My husband comes within the hour," she
heard herself say. "And another with him. Will

you read the water for me, Jennet, one last time?"

"Give me your hand." The command was surprisingly crisp, issuing from a toothless mouth set in a near skeletal head, the scalp gleaming white beneath lank wisps of dirty gray hair, the cheeks fallen in, eyes sunk so deep in their sockets they were almost invisible.

Hesitantly, Magdalen held out her hand. The twisted claw grasped it, turned it palm up. "Raise the candle; my eyes fail." Magdalen lifted the reeking tallow candle from the floor by the pallet and held it up. There was silence in the frigid gloom. Then Jennet fell back on the pallet. "Love," she said. "There is love, much of it, the love of men; there is love and blood in your hand, daughter of Isolde."

"How could you know that was my mother's name?" Magdalen felt a fear greater than she had ever experienced. She knew nothing of her mother beyond the bare bones of circumstance she had been given.

"Send the friar to me. I would have absolution."

Magdalen stood irresolute, unable to believe that Jennet would not expand on her cryptic statement. But then she heard the piercing call of the bugle, announcing the approach of her future, and she knew that her time of hiding in the shadows was drawing to a close. "I will tell Father Clement."

She slipped outside and hurried into the donjon.

"Oh, there you are!" Elinor came down the staircase into the hall, her cheeks pinkened by her morning's exertions. "I have been looking everywhere for you." She tucked a straying gray lock back beneath her linen coif. "I had thought you were to give order for fresh rushes to be laid in the hall, but when I came in a minute ago it was not done and now there is no time before they arrive."

"Your pardon, madame." Magdalen looked at the floor at her feet. "It slipped my mind. But indeed they are quite fresh, still. They have been down but a week."

"Maybe so, maybe so," Elinor muttered. "But I would not be lacking in due courtesy to our guests. Have you made all seemly in your husband's chamber? I have ordered matters in the Lord de Gervais's apartment, and the dorter for his knights and attendants, but I think it is for you to look to your husband's comfort."

"Yes, madame, and I have done so," Magdalen said, tossing back her hood, revealing the rich dark coils of hair confined with a delicate silver filigree fillet. "There is a good fire and water heating. The sheets and hangings are new washed, the floor swept."

"And are you yourself clothed to do him honor?" Elinor peered shortsightedly. She was very flustered. She had had little or nothing to do with weddings and beddings in her reclusive spinsterhood, but she wished to conduct matters correctly. Since the bride and groom had been separated immediately after the wedding feast, Elinor saw this coming reunion as a simple extension of the wedding, but whether it should be conducted on those lines or not she did not know. They were, after all, a married couple of some years' standing.

Magdalen loosed her mantle, exposing her gown of turquoise silk and the cream brocade surcote, trimmed with the royal ermine to which her paternity entitled her. "Will this do, madame?"

"Oh, yes, it is most suitable." Elinor looked relieved. It did appear as if Magdalen were able to take charge of this situation herself, so perhaps Elinor could let matters go their own way. "I must repair to the kitchens. There was some difficulty with the roasting of the swans. One of the scullions neglected to oil the spit. Do you be ready to greet your husband in the court."

Magdalen smiled as the lady whom she no longer called aunt hastened into the kitchen, muttering anxiously. It was strange how these two, who had governed her early life with such absolute authority, had now become quite ordinary souls, with their faults and foibles, their kindnesses and virtues. Magdalen called one of the servitors to her and sent him with Jennet's summons to the chaplain, then moved restlessly to the door of the great hall. The wind was gusting, lifting the rushes at the doorway and sending smoke belching from the hearth. The dogs, crowded near the fire for warmth, blinked against the smoke and moved backward. If the wind did not veer before late afternoon, the feasting in the hall would be a mite uncomfortable, but that was an ordinary enough hazard.

She stood on the steps of the hall, waiting, both eager and apprehensive.

The bugle call at the drawbridge set her pulses beating fiercely for all that she had been expecting it from minute to minute. She could see through the far arch into the *place d'armes* as the sizable combined force appeared in files of three from the drawbridge. The Lancastrian standard flew beside the dragon of Gervais and the falcon of Bresse. At the head rode the Lord Bellair and his two guests.

Magdalen walked down the steps to the court as pages came running from the hall with the stirrup cups of welcome. She stood at the bottom, her palms moist, as the cups were proffered, the contents quaffed.

Edmund de Bresse bore only superficial resemblance to the lad she remembered, the squire who had picked marigolds for her and kissed her on May Day. He was lean and hard, his face bronzed, his mouth and chin set firm in the manner of one grown accustomed to command, and he wore well the knight's spurs and belt, the great sword at his waist.

Even as she became aware of these things, her eyes sought Guy de Gervais. He looked as he always had done, except that his hair was now close-cropped. His eyes were as blue, his frame as powerful, his smile as merry, for he was laughing at something the Lord Bellair had said. The heaviness of his grief in those last days at Hampton seemed to have slipped from him.

She moved to Edmund's stirrup. "I bid you welcome, my lord, and thank God for your safe return and the success of your enterprise."

He looked down at her, his eyes raking her face as if he too would see what changes the years of his absence had wrought upon the bride he barely knew. "My thanks, lady," he said, handing his bridle to his squire, standing ready to receive it. He dismounted and took her hand, raising it to his lips.

"Forsooth, Edmund, is that any way to greet your wife!" Guy swung from his own horse and came over to them. "It's a kiss she needs." Laughing, he cupped her face and kissed her brow. "You must pardon him, pippin, but we have been long in the field and have sorely missed gentle company."

His tone was teasing yet affectionate, just as it used to be, and Magdalen felt a sharp stab of acute disappointment, followed rapidly by resentment. Could he see no change in her, that he would treat her like the little girl she had been?

She inclined her head in haughty acknowledgment and turned back to her husband. "Pray come within, my lord." She led the way up the steps and into the hall.

Guy was both hurt and puzzled. He had been about to offer some light compliment on her very clear beauty, and she had dismissed his greeting with all the cold arrogance of the Plantagenets. He had had little time or opportunity to think of her in the last years. The campaign in Picardy had been hard fought and hard won, and had been followed by an engagement in Brittany which had tried them all sorely. But he was freed from warmaking for a space and had thought to complete the business that he felt somehow lay within his purview, the final joining of his erstwhile ward to his erstwhile charge. But it rather appeared as if John of Gaunt's daughter held some grievance against him. He followed them into the hall, where Lady Elinor claimed his attention.

Edmund stood to one side with Magdalen, allowing his goblet to be filled and refilled. An awkward silence lay between them. He was angry with himself for neglecting to greet her in correct manner. Of course, he should have kissed her properly. She was his wife, not some lady to whom it was necessary to pay court. He did not need Guy de Gervais to demonstrate how he should have conducted himself. He had been in a ferment of excitement on the journey here, an immoderate excitement at the prospect of possessing his wife at long last, a possession that would be his final step into the true world of men, for one did not count whores. That agitation now mingled with a seething annoyance at all and sundry, an annoyance he was attempting to drown in Lord Bellair's wine.

Suddenly, he handed his wine cup to a hovering page and spoke to Lady Elinor, his tone sadly unceremonious as wine loosened his tongue and gave voice both to his annoyance and his passionate eagerness. "Your pardon, my lady, but I would ask leave to repair to my chamber. I am but poorly clad and would do you more honor."

"But of course," Elinor said, flustered. "I will have you shown—"

"My wife will attend me," he declared, two spots of color burning on his cheeks. "It is customary for a wife to attend her husband in such case."

Magdalen paled, then as swiftly reddened as she felt the eyes of all upon them.

Guy de Gervais turned away to the fire, bending to stroke a brindle hound thrusting its massive head against his knee. Edmund could have behaved with more delicacy, but then he was still young for all that he had conducted himself in France with the courage and strength to match any man's. It was not strange that he should now be anxious, desirous also, and therefore tactless, about the business that had brought them hither. They were best left alone to sort themselves out, so he remained stroking the hound, gazing pensively into the fire, until Magdalen with a stiff curtsy of agreement left the hall with her husband.

Edmund's squire moved to follow them, but his lord gestured with an abrupt irritability, expressive more of nervousness than annoyance, and the lad fell back at the foot of the stairs.

Magdalen preceded her husband up the stairs to the third-floor guest quarters. Lord de Gervais, as befitted his greater age and rank, was allotted the foremost guest chamber, and she passed the massive oak door at the head of the stairs, moving instead to a corner chamber at the rear of the passage.

"My lord." Opening the door, she stepped aside to allow him to enter ahead of her. "I trust you will find all is to your liking."

"Close the door," he said, his voice suddenly thick.

Magdalen did so, her heart thumping against her rib cage, and stepped over to a small table by the hearth. "May I pour you wine?"

"My thanks." He took the hanap, drank, and held the cup to her lips. "Will you not drink with me?"

For form's sake, Magdalen wet her lips with the wine. Then she turned aside to pour water from the pitcher into the bowl of beaten copper. "You will wish to wash, my lord." Her voice was low, expressionless, disguising the tumultous pulse of nervous anticipation.

He tossed his beaver hat onto the window seat and pulled off his surcote. "Help me with my mailshirt."

Inexperienced though they were in the ways of married couples, they both knew what each was to expect of the other. Magdalen knew well what her duties were in this instance. Her lord's body was hers to care for after his exertions spent in her defense, or in providing for her needs and those of his household. She helped him with the chainmail, with the quilted leather tunic, with the linen shirt, with the boots and hose. She wrung out a soft cloth in the warm water and hesitated. She should sponge his body herself, but somehow she could not. She held out the cloth. Edmund also hesitated, then he took it from her and rubbed himself down. She passed him the towel. They were tongue-tied while they performed these rituals that neither had performed before.

Magdalen was not unaccustomed to the sight of a naked man. The garrison soldiers often enough stripped under the summer sun to bathe in the river beyond the postern gate, or threw buckets of water at each other from the well in the garrison court. Her viewings of these uninhibited activities had of course been clandestine. The garrison had always been absolutely forbidden to her, but that had not prevented a bored and lonely child from creeping where she should not. At Hampton, the simpleton Jack had frequently been found skipping, naked as a shorn lamb, in the village, and no one had taken the least notice. But the intimacy of Edmund's naked body in this small, secluded chamber shocked her into silence, and she tried to avoid looking at him even as she attended him. But it was impossible not to notice the shape and texture of him, impossible to be unaware of the youthful suppleness, the firm swell of muscle in arms and thighs.

Since their marriage, Edmund had lived the life of a warrior. He had slept in ditches and hedgerows, in castles and abbeys; on one occasion, exhaustion had overtaken him in a doorway of a sacked town and he had slept deeply amid plundering troops, fired buildings, screams of the ravished and wounded. He had seen men bludgeoned and hacked to death on the battlefield; he had bludgeoned and hacked to death in his turn. He had fought hand to hand with nothing but a dagger, had known the headiness of bloodlust and the incandescent glory of victory. He had witnessed torture, gratuitous slaughter, dreadful injuries, unjust executions, and he accepted them as necessary in the business of war, a business that he now knew would be his for as long as God preserved him.

He had had many women in that time, whores for the most part . . . except for one. But he tried not to think back on that deed. He had confessed and done penance and was shriven. The memory should trouble him no more. He knew nothing of virgins and nothing of ladies, and his nakedness in the presence of this delicate, willowy, utterly silent girl both stirred and disconcerted him. Her mute attentions thrilled him, and he knew it was because she was his wife. Wives were not whores, and the submission they made to their lords was of a very different order from that made for coin or kind.

She turned from him when he had finished washing, folding the towel carefully, paying most deliberate attention to the creases, smoothing the damp material repeatedly, hesitating to replace it on the chest and thus indicate that her task was completed.

"Magdalen!"

The voice at her back was low but emphatic, the hand on her shoulder hard as he turned her to face him. She read the passionate message in his eyes, blue like those of his uncle, and she quivered like a kitten taken too soon from its dam. She was overwhelmed with terror at the potential power of such passion, at the contemplation of the force in the warrior's body, at the sense of her own frailty in the face of such superior strength. She thought of the way Guy de Gervais had looked at his lady, the softness of his speech, the tenderness of his touch and kiss. She did not know—how could she?—of the years of passion Gwendoline and her lord had shared, of the vigor of their healthful, youthful couplings, of the many times Guy de Gervais had poured forth his lust and need upon the delicate body of his wife, and she had accepted it in love and as love's gift. Magdalen knew none of these things, only the need for gentleness and her fear of an unleashed power in an unknown man.

Edmund pulled her against him, one hand circling her waist, flattening against her buttocks, his other hand pushing up her chin as his mouth came down upon hers. She could taste the wine on his plundering tongue; clamped to his body, her breasts were painfully crushed. A great lassitude swamped her with the knowledge that she neither could nor should do anything to alter the course of the next minutes. It happened to all women at some point, unless they took the veil or, like Elinor, were permitted to settle for spinsterhood as the pensioner of a male relative.

She fell back on the bed beneath the weight of his body, felt a hand under her gown, urgent, scratching her thigh in haste and need. She shifted her body to release the gown bunched beneath her, anxious now simply to be done with this, hating the roughly probing hand yet knowing absolutely that he intended her no harm, bore her no ill will, would not hurt her if he thought to avoid it.

But he did not think. It did not occur to him

to behave with Magdalen any differently than with any of the other women he had enjoyed. He knew no better.

When it was finished, he rolled away from her and fell instantly into a deep sleep induced by a week's hard riding, wine, and the body's fulfillment.

Magdalen eased her bruised body on the sheets and stared dry-eyed into the winter gloom of the chamber. The candles had not been lit, and only the fire's flicker enlivened the gray dimness. Her gown and surcote were twisted under her, the rich material scrunched into a hard ridge in the small of her back. Gingerly, she got off the bed, shaking down her clothes. There was blood on the sheet where she had been lying. At least her husband could rest easy in the incontrovertible evidence of his wife's virginity, she reflected, walking softly to the door, wincing at the soreness between her thighs.

Quietly, she unlatched the door, stepping out into the passage, closing the door behind her with an uplift of relief. But the relief was short-lived. In the peace and solitude of the passage, tears of reaction sprang to her eyes, and she leaned for a moment against the stone wall beneath a flaring torch.

Guy de Gervais mounted the stairs at the far

end of the passage. He was about to turn into his own chamber when he saw the figure, the ermine and ivory of her surcote glimmering in the torchlight. His immediate impression was of a limp and broken doll, and panic flared, turning his gut to water. He strode, half running, toward her, but she pushed away from the wall before he could reach her and began to walk slowly to the stairs.

"Magdalen." He caught her arm as she made to pass him, her head lowered as if she did not wish to see him. "Magdalen, what is it? What has happened?"

She shook her head but would not meet his eyes. "Nothing out of the ordinary, my lord. I must go to my own chamber, if you please." She pulled slightly at the arm he still held.

He maintained his hold for a second longer, trying to puzzle out her meaning. But of course it was obvious; he had just put out of his mind all thoughts of the inevitable conclusion to the couple's departure from the hall. He let her go, and as she walked away from him he saw a bright spot of blood on the back of her surcote, and he cursed Edmund de Bresse for a clumsy, selfish, insensitive lout. Then it occurred to him that Edmund knew no better, and no one, least of all Guy de Gervais, had taken the trouble to educate him in such matters. Sensitivity did not make a warrior, and one did not attempt to sensitize a youth on the brink of violent death dealing. No, husband and wife must come to their own peace on such issues, as he and Gwendoline had done. He went into his own chamber.

Magdalen reached the room she still shared with her aunt on the second floor and rang the bell for Erin. She was struggling out of her mangled clothes when the maidservant hastened in. "I wish to bathe, Erin," she said shortly.

"Yes, my lady." Erin curtsied. "Shall I help you out of your gown before I fetch water?"

"If you please." Magdalen ceased her struggles with the laces that had knotted themselves under her impatient and shaky fingers and allowed the girl to unravel them.

"Why, my lady, there's blood on your surcote," Erin exclaimed, tutting. "It is early for your terms."

"It's not that," Magdalen said wearily. "Take the gown away and see if you can sponge it clean. It's too fine a garment to be ruined after but three wearings."

Erin pursed her lips but made no comment. She was not herself averse to a tumble with a lusty groom or servitor on occasion and had no difficulty reaching the correct explanation for the stained surcote. Her lady's husband was returned victorious from the war.

Magdalen bathed before the fire, the hot water easing her bruised flesh. The bleeding had stopped, and she could find no signs of injury, so clearly she had suffered no more than the natural consequences of lost virginity. She contemplated the sense of violation that had accompanied that possession and decided that it was because for the man who possessed her there had been no sense of a person inhabiting her body. Well, Edmund de Bresse did not really know her yet, maybe when he did he would see her differently.

On that thought, she stepped out of the bath, allowed Erin to dry her, and selected a cotehardie of gold velvet with a matching gold brocade surcote edged in sable. The Duke of Lancaster's daughter had been lavishly supplied with a wedding trousseau, most of which she had had little opportunity to wear during her seclusion in the wild border lands.

Dressed, her hair caught beneath a dainty jeweled cap, she left her room and went to Edmund's chamber above. He was still asleep as she entered, but stirred when the door closed with a snap.

"My lord, it's past time you rose and dressed for the feast." She approached the bed, her voice calm but strong.

Edmund groaned, heavy-headed now that the

euphoria of the wine had passed. He rubbed his eyes with the heel of one hand and blinked at the figure beside his bed. Then he remembered. He reached for her, intending to pull her down to him, but she jerked away.

"My lord, I am bathed and dressed for the feast. Shall I call for your squire?"

He frowned, sat up, then saw the blood, dried on the sheet beside him. He scratched his head and looked up at Magdalen, clearly at a loss for words.

"It is supposed to happen," she said matter-of-factly, "when a maid loses her virginity."

"Yes, I know that." He sounded impatient and swung himself from the bed. "Come, I would have another fall, sweeting."

She drew away from him. "You hurt me. I must heal first."

He looked dismayed. "Hurt you? But none has ever complained of that before."

"Maybe they were not virgin," she said in the same matter-of-fact tone. "I will summon your squire."

"I would wish you to sleep with me in this chamber," he said, hesitantly now in the face of her calm assurance. "You do not appear to have your belongings in here."

"As my lord wishes," she replied, gliding to

the door. "I will return when you are dressed, and we will descend to the hall together."

That night, and every subsequent one, she had slept beside her husband in a marital bed . . .

MAGDALEN MOVED RESTLESSLY on the velvet bench under the August sun, still puzzling over what could have caused her husband's extraordinary performance in the joust. Since last January at Bellair, his passion for his wife had become a powerful obsession. Far from moderating under the generally dampening effects of familiarity and unhindered opportunity for satisfaction, his ardor raged unchecked. Magdalen found this passion neither flattering nor unpleasant. He was her husband, as good as any and better than most, judging by what she saw around her. While it was true to say his nightly lovemaking afforded her little enjoyment, he certainly took pains not to hurt her anymore. But however ardent and eager he might be in the bedchamber, in matters of chivalry and knightly duty he was always clear-headed, ruthless, but rarely out of temper.

Her gaze drifted around the arena where preparations were being made for the final melee of the tournament. All the knights who had participated over the last two days would

take part in this bout, divided into two opposing teams. She had been hoping all day that Guy
de Gervais would ask to wear her colors, and
she had a silk handkerchief in her sleeve, in anticipation of such a moment. But after the last
awkwardness, she was disappointingly certain he
would not make the courtly request.

In Edmund's tent, Lord de Gervais surveyed
the young man thoughtfully. "Why would you
behave in such rash manner?"

Edmund's lips set. "It was a matter of honor,
sir." His squire was rubbing a strong-smelling oil
into his sword arm, bruised through the heavy
armor plate by a blow from his opponent's
sword. He flexed the muscles, anxious there
should be no reduced mobility for the coming
melee.

"Explain!" Guy's exasperation crackled. It was
an exasperation based on his own concern.
Gilles de Lambert was related by marriage to the
de Beauregard clan, as Guy had just informed
John of Gaunt. Had he attempted to force a
quarrel on the husband of John of Gaunt's
daughter?

Edmund looked sullen, resenting this interro-
gation yet knowing that he was not entitled to.
The Duke of Lancaster was his overlord, and
Guy de Gervais was the duke's representative.

He sent his squire away with an uncharacteristically unmannerly oath.

"The Sieur de Lambert informed me that through my wife the de Bresse name was tainted with bastardy," he said stiffly. "By such accusation, he sullies both my honor and my wife's."

Guy nodded. It was as they had suspected, then. The long shadow of the de Beauregards had fallen, finally. "How did you answer him?" he asked quietly.

Edmund flushed with remembered anger. "I gave him the lie. The issue can now be settled only in combat."

It was so; and such combat must inevitably end in the death or maiming of one of the combatants. De Gervais frowned, considering. Edmund had appeared to have the edge in both strength and skill that afternoon, but not by much. It would be a close run combat if it were permitted to take place, and whichever way the sword fell, the repercussions would reopen wounds that would bleed across England and France.

At that point a page in the Lancastrian livery pushed through the tent opening. "Sieur de Bresse," he said, bowing.

"What is it?" Edmund frowned his displeasure at being so unceremoniously interrupted.

"I bring a message from his grace of Lancaster," the page said.

Guy rather thought he knew what the message was going to contain, and that it would infuriate Edmund, but he also knew it to be a sound move on the duke's part.

"His grace forbids the participation of the Sieur Edmund de Bresse in the melee," the page intoned. "He also forbids his attendance in the great hall of the Savoy for three days."

Edmund whitened. The page, his message imparted, beat a hasty retreat. "I will not accept it!" Edmund raged.

"Do not be any more foolish than you need," Guy advised. "It is a light enough punishment for your unruly behavior. Accept it with a good grace." He left the tent and its fulminating occupant.

Edmund bellowed for his squire. "Help me out of this!" he demanded, indicating his hauberk.

"But . . . but the melee, my lord," stammered the astonished squire. "It is to start within the quarter hour."

"Not for me!" snapped de Bresse, still white with this fresh humiliation. How was he to explain his absence in the melee to Magdalen, who would be watching and waiting for her knight, expecting to take pride in his prowess? But she would know soon enough . . . Everyone would know of his punishment, and she would be shamed also.

His cheeks burned with anger and mortification as he was slowly released from the great plates of iron that had encased his body. "Fetch my palfrey," he ordered curtly, belting his surcote at the hip over the leather tunic. If he could not take part in the jousting, then he would leave the tournament altogether.

"Shall I accompany you, my lord?" the squire asked, holding the bridle as de Bresse swung astride his riding horse.

"No, I go alone." He touched spur to the stallion, and the horse pounded away from the field, the sounds of clashing steel and the roar of the crowd coming from the lists adding spur to his own desire to leave the scene of his present shame.

Two men in brown leather jerkins, daggers at their belts, heavy staves in their hands, moved away from the massive trunk of a copper beech behind the de Bresse tent. Their horses, already saddled, were tethered a few yards away. It was a matter of a moment before they were mounted and cantering off on the heels of Edmund de Bresse.

Edmund veered away from the riverbank and toward the forest. He was in no mood to con-

sider the dangers attendant upon solitary riding
through a forest crawling with outlaws, fugitive
serfs, petty thieves, and not-so-petty murderers
with whom the land was riddled. He heard
branches snapping behind him as he rode along
a broad path in the dappling light thrown by the
sun through the umbrella of leaves over his
head, but the first prickle of unease did not disturb him until he had ventured away from the
well-trodden path and into the green dampness
of the inner wood.

The prickle of unease prepared him, however.
He turned, drawing his sword, as the first of the
two men jumped his horse out of the trees to
the right of Edmund's path. His assailant's dagger
swept down in a wicked curve, slashing
Edmund's shoulder, penetrating the leather
gambeson, and he cursed his stupidity for not
wearing his mailshirt. But the sword was in his
hand, and he parried the next blow with sufficient force to unhorse the man. Then the other
one came at him out of the trees, dagger poised,
and he was locked in silent, vicious combat. The
palfrey went down beneath him, screaming with
a severed tendon, and he jumped clear just in
time. On foot, he was hard pressed, embattled
by the two men, one of whom remained
mounted and wielded his stave from his superior
position with bone-shattering, deadly accuracy.

His head reeled from a massive blow, blood trickled into his eyes and poured from a gash in his sword arm. His breath came achingly from his chest, and he felt the cold, deadly certainty of imminent defeat. Backed up against a tree trunk, he parried blow after blow from the heavy staves, until agony rent his shoulder and the black cloud took him.

IN THE LISTS, Magdalen looked in vain for her husband's black and gold jupon embroidered with the falcon of de Bresse. She recognized de Gervais's blue and silver, and immediately her husband's puzzling absence took second place to her interest in the other's prowess. Despite her professed scorn for the entire exercise, she was inordinately pleased and proud when Guy was one of the few remaining knights still mounted on the field at the end of the melee.

She leaned over the edge of the loge, applauding with the rest, trying to catch his eye. He rode over to make his reverence to the duke, and she hastily plucked another rose from the bouquet, intending to toss it to him. In her haste, she pricked her finger, the thorn driving beneath her nail. With a little whimper, she sucked her finger, and by the time she had recovered, the moment was past. He had received his lord's congratulations and those of the ladies in the box, most of whom had showered him with their own flowery favors. Magdalen, seeing his attention now diverted to one of the duchess's ladies, disconsolately dropped her rose to the floor of the booth.

She observed from beneath her lashes the elegant play between Guy de Gervais and the Lady Maude Wyseford. The latter was not much older than Magdalen herself and had been recently widowed. She was a matrimonial prize in the gift of the Duchess Constanza, and Magdalen regarded her this afternoon with great disfavor.

Guy saw the pout and ascribed it to her husband's unexplained absence. There was little pleasure for a lady in watching a joust when her own knight was not participating. It was not for him to tell her of the duke's decree, at least not in public. Indeed, rightfully, it was her husband's prerogative, unless John of Gaunt chose to enlighten her. Dismissing the issue as being none of his business, he rode out of the lists, back to his own tent to divest himself of the burden of armor.

Magdalen waited for her husband to escort her back to the Savoy Palace. The tournament had taken place in the lists at Westminster and the crowd was dispersing quickly, anxious to be off the roads before sundown. The duchess, on being informed that Magdalen's husband had told her to await his escort, left with the duke and those of her ladies who had not been claimed by their knights.

Magdalen waited for a very long time. The two pages in attendance tried not to fidget as the shadows lengthened and the men at work within the stockade completed their tasks. At last, she sent a page to seek out her husband in his tent while she remained in the loge in seething resentment, too angry and generally disgruntled to reflect that such lack of chivalry where she was concerned was most unlike Edmund.

The page found the Sieur de Bresse's tent deserted. All around was bustle as the tents were struck and the pennants furled, but the knightly combatants had all dispersed. He stood in a quandary. His orders to attend the lady until Sieur de Bresse came for her had been most explicit, and his lord had a short way with disobedience, but at the same time he had a duty to the lady, who must be conveyed home with all speed before the sun finally sank beneath the horizon. It was with a surge of relief that he saw Lord de Gervais emerging from his own tent, a jeweled goblet in his hand. This lord held the duke's authority over Edmund de Bresse and would know how to advise.

De Gervais listened to the boy's anxious tale, then nodded and sent him back to Lady Magdalen, instructing him to wait with her until he came to the loge. He drank off the wine in the hanap, tossed the cup to his own page, and strode off to the duke's loge. He guessed that Edmund had ridden off under such a burden of hurt pride and sense of injustice that he had completely forgotten about his arrangement with Magdalen. It was a perhaps understandable omission in the circumstances, but it was inexcusable nevertheless, reflecting poorly on de Gervais's training of his nephew.

De Gervais found Magdalen in exceeding ill humor. She turned her anger upon him as if he were in some way responsible for her husband's humiliating neglect.

He waited patiently until the tirade subsided for want of further fuel, then stated calmly, "If you have said your piece, madame, I suggest we take the road. It grows dark, and I have no men-at-arms."

"Where is Edmund?" she said, deflated by his tone. "I do not understand why he would do this."

Guy told her of Lancaster's prohibition as they left the loge. "He was deeply distressed," he said. "I would imagine he took his distress elsewhere and forgot all else."

"He will not forget again," Magdalen said grimly as de Gervais lifted her onto her horse. "And if he is forbidden to sup in the great hall, I am not. I shall do so, and he may take his supper where he can."

"That is hardly wifely," Guy chided, but without much conviction. Edmund certainly deserved some censure.

"Why did he wish to fight the Sieur de Lambert *a l'outrance?*" she asked suddenly as they took the road, her two pages and Guy's squire their only attendants.

Guy shrugged. "A private squabble that had no place in a public tourney. They should both have known better."

"But de Lambert was permitted to joust in the melee." Her anger had died, and she began to find herself allied with her husband in his sense of injustice.

"So he was," her companion agreed. "But if you dare to question his grace's decisions in such an instance, I do not." To what extent had he stilled her curiosity? It was to be hoped that Edmund would offer her something other than the truth if she questioned him. The technical nature of her legitimacy was known to them both by now, but she would be deeply distressed if she thought her husband could believe himself dishonored by it.

The attack came when they reached a stretch of road winding between thickets of bramble and laurel. The scent of bay hung in the evening air, mingling with the rich loamy smell of the luxuriant undergrowth.

There were six of them in the jerkin, hose, and boots of the peasant, but they were armed with the staves and knives of the outlaw robber. On foot, they set upon the horses with their knives, aiming for artery and tendon. Guy and his squire were armed with sword and knife, but the pages had only their daggers with which to fend off the murderous assault, leaning down to slash wildly as their assailants ran at the horses, dodging hither and thither, evading all attempts to ride them down. Guy, wielding his sword with deadly calm, noticed on the periphery of his awareness that they seemed less interested in the human prey than in the destruction of the horses. He supposed it made some kind of sense. Unhorsed, Guy's party would be four against six. But none of the attacking rabble would be a match for his great sword, or even his squire's, and the pages had months of discipline and combat training behind them. Such a disorganized attack was self-destructive madness. One of the horses went down, the page leaping clear, his knife flashing. A heavy stave swung at the lad's wrist. Bone crunched, and the boy screamed. The next instant, his assailant crumpled, his head cleaved in two by de Gervais's great sword.

Magdalen sat her trembling horse, desperately trying to think of some way of helping. She carried only her little jeweled hip knife and could not imagine it doing the least good, except in close quarters. So far, the robbers had ignored both her and her horse, and then with shocking suddenness one of the brigands ran toward her and sprang up behind her with an agile, twisting leap. He kicked the mare's flank viciously, lashing the horse with a thorny bramble, and the animal bolted down the road, leaving the bloody turmoil behind them.

It was Magdalen they had been after! That was why they had been interested in unhorsing Guy's party, who without mounts could not hope to pursue. Their assailants must have been well paid to venture such an assault against superior fighting power when death for some of them was inevitable.

Guy realized all this with a bolt of self-directed fury. He should have been ready for something. The de Beauregards had already shown their hand; they would not delay in following up. He set his horse in pursuit, but one of their attackers had firm hold of the bridle now and was slashing upward. The horse kicked, reared, screamed in fear and pain, all but unseating his rider, who was forced to waste precious minutes eliminating the stabbing brigand at his bridle.

Magdalen was initially so stunned by what had happened that she sat like stone on the saddle, feeling the hot, sweaty weight of the man behind her, holding her against him as he reached to wrest the reins from her hands. Her mount was a lot more powerful than little Malapert had been and seemed to be eating up the ground beneath them. She realized the truth with sudden terror. She was being abducted by this villein, and no one seemed to be coming after her.

Terror and desperation galvanized her. She drove her elbows backward into the man's ribs and heard with grim satisfaction his grunt of pain as the breath whistled through his lips and his hold loosened. She did it again, immediately, aiming lower for his belly, then, hardly knowing what she was doing, she kicked her feet free of the stirrups and tumbled sideways off the plunging horse, catching at an overhanging branch. The horse careened down the path, its rider now hauling back on the reins. At any minute, he would halt the mare's bolt and would turn back for his quarry. She dropped to the ground, preparing to run into the undergrowth, when Guy de Gervais hurtled toward her. His horse was bleeding profusely from a gashed neck, foam flecked around the bit, and the whites of his eyes rolled wildly. Guy charged straight past her, intent on the destruction of her would-be abductor, who was now off balance, struggling to turn the frantic mare.

The man had no time for his prayers. He would have been aware only of blue eyes, pin-pricks of death, and a massive form rising in the saddle above him, the hilt of the great sword clasped between both hands. The sword took off his head.

Magdalen was still standing by the roadside, staring at the carnage around her. To her shocked gaze, there seemed to be dead men and horses everywhere. It took her a minute to realize that all members of their party were still standing, and that one of the fallen horses was struggling to its feet. The page whose wrist had been shattered was leaning against a tree, barely conscious.

Guy rode back, sheathing his bloody sword. He dismounted when he reached Magdalen, his expression grave as he took in her deathly pallor and the gray eyes blank with shock. "You've a mind as nimble as your body, pippin," he said, taking her hands. "But it's finished now."

With a gasping sob, she flung herself against his chest. For a minute, he resisted, feeling her soft and warm against him, pliant and graceful. He could smell her skin, the slight tang of fresh sweat, the rich scent of her hair. But she was quivering like a frightened kitten, and he could not deny her the comfort he had offered her as a child. He enfolded her in his arms, and her sob became a sigh of contentment. His body stirred at her closeness.

Abruptly, he put her from him. "Come, there is no time for this, Magdalen. You have done well, and you are unharmed, but we must hurry to the Savoy. Dick has urgent need of the physician." Turning from her, he led his palfrey back to the little troop waiting with the two relatively unharmed horses.

Magdalen watched as he spoke gently to the injured Dick, bound his arm in a handkerchief, and helped him onto the back of the squire's horse. The squire mounted behind; the other page mounted his own horse again. She supposed she should be helpful and reclaim her own mare, still standing, head hanging uneasily, along the road. But the headless corpse of her abductor lay close by, and she found she was feeling rather sick.

Guy, fortunately, seemed to understand her reluctance, because he fetched the animal himself. "Do you feel able to ride, Magdalen?" His voice was as calm and gentle as if the last blood-sodden half hour had never happened.

Magdalen considered. If she said she did not, then he would take her up before him. But somehow she knew that he did not wish to do that, and it was her fault that he did not wish to. She offered him a shaky smile.

"Yes, I am quite able to ride, my lord."

It was such a pathetically gallant little smile that for a moment he was tempted to ignore the dictates of caution and scoop her up as he had been used to do so naturally in the old days. But those days were long gone, and Magdalen de Bresse was now the embodiment of dangerous temptation. He didn't know how or when it had happened, only that it had.

"You have a true Plantagenet's courage, Magdalen of Lancaster," he declared with calm approval, and lifted her onto her palfrey.

Magdalen did not find his approval an adequate substitute for the comfort of the physical proximity she craved, but she accepted it as she must.

Four

MAGDALEN SAT AT the high table in the great vaulted hall of the Savoy Palace, looking in vain for Guy. He had escorted her to her apartments when they had completed their limping journey earlier and left her with her women and the advice that she take a little wine as restorative. It had been sensible and concerned advice, but she had felt dismissed, her part in the afternoon's drama discounted. There had been no message from Edmund, either, and his squire, with some anxiety, had told her that his lord had ridden off alone when the final melee had begun.

She had sent one of her pages to the duchess with the request that she be excused attendance at the banquet in the great hall that evening. The request had been denied, not by the duchess but by John of Gaunt, who insisted upon her presence at the high table. She could only assume that the duke wished to emphasize Edmund's punishment by making his absence all the more noticeable with his wife's solitary presence.

It had done little to improve her humor. She had said nothing about the attack on the road and wondered if she should have pleaded that as an excuse for her absence. Surely the duke would have been more considerate of her well-being, if he knew of her ordeal. She assumed she was to have been abducted for ransom, a common enough crime since the companies of brigands and mercenaries had begun their reign of terror both in France and England—a direct consequence of the war that taught armed men to live by plunder in war, and in periods of truce threw them upon the land, unemployed and unpaid.

His grace, however, was well aware of the incident. Guy had wasted no time in telling him of it, and of his suspicions that it was part and parcel of Edmund's trouble at the tournament. There had been no time before the start of the banquet for extended discussion, and Lancaster now sat in his carved chair, deep in thought, his eyes occasionally flickering sideways to the still figure of his daughter. The chair at her left was empty, and she was making no attempt to converse with anyone else at the table. Despite her stillness and the unmistakable expression of an annoyed Plantagenet on her face, she seemed to exude her mother's vibrancy. There was a sensuality about face and form, a quivering about her that made a man think of lusty tumbling, of limbs white and naked, twined in passion. But there was something else, too, something Isolde had not had, and John of Gaunt could not fail to recognize and acknowledge it. There was a straightness to her, an honesty that against his will tugged at him.

Magdalen played with a morsel of goose patty, pushing it around her bowl with her trencher of white bread. She responded monosyllabically to attempts to draw her into conversation and was soon left to her own reflections. She knew she was not generally liked by the duchess's ladies. An isolated childhood, broken only by the few months in the de Gervais household, had left her with a certain shyness, a reluctance for intimacy, an inability to engage in the gossip, frequently malicious, that passed for conversation among the women at court. She also knew that her anomalous position as the clearly disliked, suddenly revealed daughter of the duke left people unsure how to treat her. They did not treat her with the reverence accorded Lancaster's other children, the ladies Elizabeth and Philippa, and his heir, young Henry Bolingbroke, but neither dared they offer her the least discourtesy. Nevertheless, her history was a matter for fascinated speculation.

What Magdalen had failed to notice was that the ladies were also aware of the effect she had on the men of the court. One would have to be

blind to fail to see the eyes that followed her, to
fail to notice how there was always someone at
her elbow, eager to help her mount, to pick up
a glove, to proffer a new-picked bloom for her
hair. Such attentions did not make the ladies any
more drawn to her, although the recipient
seemed blithely unaware of them. But then, no
one else knew that for the Lady Magdalen only
one man existed, and that man was not her
husband.

Magdalen took another sip of her wine, letting
her gaze roam over the hall below. Chamber-
lains were directing new arrivals to tables appropriate to their rank, and the guests threaded
their way between scurrying varlets carrying
laden trays of roast meats, boar, venison, swan,
all thickly smothered in slightly sweet sauces
that disguised any detectable taint, inevitable in
the midsummer heat. Jugs of mead and wine,
shipped in quantities from the English fief of
Aquitaine, were passed down the tables, and
voices were rising commensurately, drowning
the minstrels in the gallery above.

A herald's alerting note came from the great
double doors. "My Lord Guy de Gervais, Earl
of Redeforde, enters here," the marshal cried,
and Guy strode unhurriedly into the hall, followed by a squire and a page. He looked magnificent, his powerful body clad in a tunic of

black and gold, the dragon of Gervais embroidered on his shoulder, a massive gold belt at his hip, golden spurs at his heels. Heads turned at his entrance, and servitors scuttled out of his path. He smiled and greeted acquaintances as he came up to the dais, where he knelt briefly before his lord, offering a word of apology for his tardiness. The duke merely smiled at his favorite and bade him get to his supper.

Guy came immediately to the vacant chair beside Magdalen. "Since I stood proxy for your husband at his betrothal, I trust it will not come amiss if I take his place now, my lady," he said.

It was a simple pleasantry, designed to lessen her discomfiture at the obvious emptiness of her husband's seat, but he felt the charge jolt through her as he sat down beside her. He could feel the heat of her body, smell the scent of her skin, and as her head turned toward him, he read again the message in her eyes, clear and determined, saw the eager promise in her parted lips, felt within himself the deep sensual throb of her body. His skin felt as if the blade of a knife had been passed, sharp-edged, across it, lifting the hairs in an assurance of danger and excitement.

But he was accustomed to danger. "You are recovered from your ordeal, I trust, madame," he said neutrally, turning to wash his hands in the bowl held at his elbow by his page.

"I suffered no hurt," she said. "I was afraid you had perhaps discovered some injury yourself when you were absent from the table."

He gestured to his page to fill his goblet. "Nay, madame, not I. But I remained with poor Dick while the apothecary set the bone. The lad had an uncomfortable time of it."

"Why, what has happened, Lord de Gervais?" Lady Maude asked, and everyone within earshot craned to hear the story.

"We were attacked by brigands," Guy said with a chuckle that sounded perfectly natural as he helped himself to meat from the platter held by his squire. "It would seem they had it in mind to carry off the Lady Magdalen for ransom."

There was much clamoring for the story, and he told it succinctly but with the narrative skills acquired during training in his youth. Magdalen contributed nothing, since no contribution was asked of her. But as she sat in her silence, the certainty came to her that something was being withheld here. Her eyes drifted over the hall again. She had told Edmund's squire to bring her word as soon as his lord returned, but so far Carl's blunt, square face had not appeared.

"Your appetite is sadly lacking this even," Guy observed as Magdalen waved away a basket of boiled raisins and a platter of almond sweetmeats. He knew of old that she had a sweet tooth, and he had often teased the child Magdalen over her passion for nutmeg custards and marchpane.

"I do not know where Edmund is," she said, speaking her thought with customary directness. "I feel that something has happened, and we must send out men to search for him."

"Nonsense," he said, nibbling on a honeyed almond. Yet this concern for her husband relieved him somewhat, enabling him to put aside that disturbing moment earlier—that moment, and the others that had occurred on this troublesome day. "He is sulking, somewhere." Probably in the city stews, he thought but did not say. It would be the natural recourse for any young man in similar circumstances—one he would have taken himself before Gwendoline had given him a distaste for such coarse dishes.

He glanced at Lady Maude. The duchess had intimated that if he wished for the prize it was his for the asking. The lady had good Flemish blood mixed with the Saxon, and had given birth to a full-term child in her previous marriage, so it was to be assumed she would bear him children. She was well dowered, and the duchess had promised to augment the dowry with an annual pension of five hundred pounds.

But there was something about the florid complexion, the certain dullness in the flat green eyes, the broadening of the hips, the looseness to the flesh beginning to bulge at upper arm and around her midriff, from which he recoiled. His eyes drifted sidways to his neighbor. The comparison did not bear making.

"I do not believe he is sulking," Magdalen declared, her mouth taking a stubborn turn. Abruptly, she pushed back her chair just as the duke and his lady rose from the table to retire to their own apartments.

As the entire company got to their feet in reverence, Magdalen went quickly along the table, her words hasty, their urgency unmistakable. "My lord . . . my lord duke, may I have speech with you?"

The duke paused, and his eyes sought those of Guy de Gervais, who had taken a step in her wake. Everyone at the table listened unashamedly.

"What is it, Magdalen?" Lancaster said. He used her name rarely, although it was the one he had bestowed upon her himself.

"It is about my husband." Her eyes, Isolde's eyes yet not Isolde's eyes, burned their appeal. "I believe some ill has befallen him."

John of Gaunt's frown was fierce enough to

send the devil scurrying. "Your husband has been banished from this table for three days, madame. That is all the ill that has befallen him."

She shook her head. "I am aware of that, my lord. But I believe there is something else." Her hands moved in an inarticulate gesture, the candlelight sparking off the ruby and emerald rings she wore. She seemed as unaware of the immediate audience at high table as of the distant one below, where a silence had fallen, servitors paused in their duties, all eyes directed toward whatever drama was taking place among the highborn.

"Come with me," he said shortly. "Guy, would you bear us company?" He strode from the dais and through the hall, his wife beside him, the assembled company remaining on their feet until they had passed. Magdalen was suddenly aware of the stir she had caused, and her cheeks flew bright flags of color as she walked behind him. She wanted to look at Guy, who was at her shoulder, but she dared not direct her eyes anywhere but ahead.

In the court, the duke bade his wife a brusque good-night and left her with her ladies-in-waiting, turning himself toward the stair that led to his own bedchamber and the privy room in the wall beneath. Magdalen and Guy followed.

"Well?" In the womblike seclusion of his

privy chamber, the duke turned to his daughter. "You have something of considerable moment to impart, I assume. There can be no other excuse for such a public disturbance."

"Something untoward has happened to my husband," Magdalen said simply.

The duke signaled to the accompanying page to pour wine, then dismissed him. "What flight of fancy is this? Are you gifted with second sight, madam?" He drank, raising his goblet in salutation to Guy, who drank also.

Magdalen had not been offered wine. "It is necessary to send a party in search of Edmund," she said, quietly determined. "I know that some ill has befallen him."

"Your husband is licking his wounds in some congenial haven," the duke declared harshly. "I have no time for this."

"No!" Her voice shocked her with its sharpness. "No, my lord duke, he is not. Something has happened, and I insist you send men in search."

There was a moment of silence. John of Gaunt looked as surprised as he felt, then a gleam appeared in his eye as he examined the intent, vigorously assertive figure in front of him. "Take heed, daughter," he said, for the first time acknowledging her to her face. "You may have the Plantagenet temper, but remember well that I have it, too, and have been used to exercising it."

Magdalen said nothing, but she did not drop her gaze.

"Why do you believe this, Magdalen?" Guy spoke, recognizing the appropriate moment for his own intervention.

"Because he would not knowingly cause me anxiety," she said. "I am with child."

The two men exchanged a look that Magdalen could not fully interpret. "You are certain of this?" her father asked slowly.

"Yes," she replied. "I have missed my terms."

"There have been no other signs?"

"Some nausea when I rise."

"Your husband knows of this?"

"Yes, my lord, and is most pleased with the news. He would not risk causing me unnecessary anxiety at this time."

The duke pulled at his neat, forked beard. "There is little point attempting a search in the dark. We will set off at first light."

"A sizable force with torches might yet achieve something," Guy said. "If the lady is right in her supposition, then we should not delay."

The duke turned abruptly to Magdalen. "Get you to bed, lady, and have a care for yourself and the child you carry. You may leave this matter in my hands."

Magdalen curtsied to both men and left the chamber by the conventional route, via Lancaster's presence chamber.

"You see the hand of the de Beauregards in this?" Lancaster refilled his goblet, his eyes hard.

"It seems not unlikely. The removal of both husband and wife would ensure that the de Bresse fealty reverts to France. Had de Lambert prevailed in combat *a l'outrance,* Edmund would not have lived. Had de Lambert failed, then there was a secondary plan."

"And the attack on Magdalen was another arm," the duke mused. "If they used mercenaries in that attack, it is to be assumed they would have done so in an assault on de Bresse. The de Beauregard name would not therefore be involved, but Charles of France would know whom to reward, and . . ." He paused, staring bleakly into the ruby contents of his goblet.

"And any personal satisfaction they might gain from revenge upon the man who turned the tables on them would be for private gratification," Guy said.

"Aye." His voice was harsh. "They are a treacherous tribe, yet they will not understand the treachery that foils their own. They planned my death by poison, the ambush and massacre of my men, and their treachery was defeated by their own weapons. To me that is fitting, but to the de Beauregards my actions stand alone, unconnected to theirs." He placed his goblet on the table. "And they will never forget that I took the child, a child they would claim for their own, and used her against France, and therefore against them. Therein lies the crux, Guy."

"I will have the sergeant-at-arms organize a search party," Guy said. "The sooner we discover if there has indeed been foul play, the better able we will be to plan our next move."

MAGDALEN HEARD THE commotion in the court an hour after the bell for compline had rung and the night silence had settled over the palace. Her chamber windows stood open to catch any breeze that might relieve the muggy air, and the sound of jingling harness, shouted orders, clattering hooves, and running feet shattered the quiet of the outer ward. She leaped from bed and ran to lean out of the window. The court was brilliantly lit by torches held aloft by mounted men-at-arms in Lancastrian livery. This was no ordinary search party. It had more the appearance of a sizable force setting forth for a skirmish. Guy de Gervais was at the head, mounted not on a palfrey but on a massive black charger. He wore a steel helmet and chainmail and carried his shield.

Magdalen leaned her elbows on the broad windowsill, propping her chin in her palms. A cold finger of apprehension touched her spine. Why must he take part in this enterprise? The party could surely be as well led by someone else. Venturing forth into the countryside at night was not to be undertaken lightly. She was afraid for Edmund, of what they would find, but she feared in her soul for Guy de Gervais.

It was a long night, spent in tossing and turning amid tumbled sheets that twisted around her as if they had a life of their own. The bell from the east tower rang at midnight for matins, then at three o'clock for lauds before she finally fell asleep, just before prime, when the palace rose under the first streaks of the dawn of what promised to be another steaming day.

"My lady . . . my lady . . ."

Erin's urgent voice, a rousing hand on her shoulder, brought Magdalen out of sleep with a groan of reluctance. "Leave me, Erin. I am not ready to wake," she mumbled, diving deeper into the pillow.

"It is my lord duke, my lady," Erin said with the same urgency. "He is without and wishes speech with you. He and my Lord de Gervais."

Memory brought her wide awake. "He is

back?" She meant Guy, but Erin assumed naturally that she was referring to her husband.

A shadow crossed the woman's face. The entire palace knew by now of the nighttime errand and its outcome. She answered evasively, because it was not her place to anticipate the men waiting outside. "I do not believe so, my lady. Shall I bid his grace entrance?"

"Yes, do so." Magdalen struggled up on the pillows, blinking as Erin drew aside the hangings and the early light of day offered gray illumination. "But first, bring my hairbrush." It had been a long time since Guy had come into her bedchamber of a morning, and for some reason, despite the urgent nature of this occasion, her vanity would not permit him to see her in sleep-tossed untidiness.

Erin looked faintly disapproving. Surely, Lady Magdalen ought to be too anxious to hear news of her husband to fidget about such conceits. However, she brushed the rich sable hair until it glowed in the dimness, then went to the door, where the impatient John of Gaunt stood with Lord de Gervais.

The two men entered the bedchamber. Magdalen knew immediately what they were going to say and bit her lip. "He is killed?"

"We found his horse," Guy said gently, coming to the foot of the bed. "Dead. There was evidence of a struggle, blood upon the ground . . ." He fell silent.

"But you did not find Edmund?" She frowned, leaning forward suddenly so that her hair fell over her white shoulders and the deep cleft of her breasts showed above the sheet. "If you did not find his body, how can you be sure he is dead?"

"It is a reasonable assumption," John of Gaunt said.

"But not a fact," she persisted.

"No, not a fact," Guy agreed, thinking he understood that she was having difficulty accepting such grim news and so was looking for some way of denying it. His voice was gently firm. "But there can be no hope, pippin. We went deep into the forest, following the trail where the bracken was trampled."

"But if it was outlaws, they would surely have stripped the body and left it," she persisted.

"That may be," Lancaster spoke briskly. "But we must assume your husband is dead, although for the nonce we will simply let it be known that he has disappeared, so there will be no need for you to go into mourning. You now have a duty to his lands and possessions in Picardy. They must be secured for his heir."

Magdalen touched her flat belly beneath the sheet and said nothing.

"It is only met if that child be born in his father's house, so you will journey to France without delay. Lord de Gervais will act as escort and counselor."

"You fear that when the knowledge of my husband's disappearance is widespread, Charles of France will attempt to retake the de Bresse fiefdom?"

Lancaster looked a little surprised at this insight. "Yes, madame, that is exactly what I fear, and that fiefdom must be held for England. It is for you to play your part now."

"I will of course do so," she said slowly. "But have I not been playing it all along, my lord duke?"

"What mean you?"

"You would hardly say I have had my destiny in my own hands," she said boldly.

"That is not women's lot," he replied, but he thought of her mother, who, until the last when he had taken it from her, had had her own hand on her own bridle.

Her eyes sought Guy de Gervais, and the hunger was in them again. He tried to draw back from it, wondering why she would never attempt to dissemble. But he was vibrantly aware of her naked body beneath the sheet, the slope of her shoulder, the swell of her breasts, and for an instant her intensity held him bound.

He understood now that for Magdalen nothing about her husband could affect the declaration she had made to him all those years ago, and was continually reaffirming whether her husband were there or not. It was a thing quite apart from anything she might feel for Edmund de Bresse, and she would never deny it. The power of it was reaching out to him, drawing him ever closer to its center where he was sure, although he knew not how, swirled danger and passion as yet untouched.

Was this how John of Gaunt had been drawn to Isolde de Beauregard? Isolde had drawn many into that center, but none as powerful as Lancaster; and Guy de Gervais knew of the many youths lovesick for her daughter, and the many men whose lusting eyes hungrily followed her. Just as he knew that she had held her husband in thrall from the moment he had first bedded her. He wondered if she truly understood this force that had been her mother's strongest weapon. He wondered if he understood it. He wondered if he could resist it.

John of Gaunt intercepted the look, and for a moment the present dimmed, the past surging forward. He felt the power between these two because he had felt its like, and he knew the danger in which they stood. He drew a harsh breath. It was no concern of his if Guy de

Gervais made whore of a whore's daughter . . .
yet she was his daughter, too . . .

But only insofar as he could use the blood relationship for his own ends, he reminded himself with the same harshness. He had never
before been in danger of losing that perspective,
and the present moment of weakness angered
him. He turned on his heel from the bed,
breaking the spell that for a minute had held
them all.

"Make your preparations for departure, lady.
You will travel in the style consonant with your
rank, your women accompanying you. Lord de
Gervais will have a force of fifty lances and two
hundred men-at-arms."

Fifty lances . . . one knight or squire and two
attendants for each lance—one hundred and
fifty men. It was an enormous force for simple
escort duty. Magdalen wondered why they
would be expecting trouble on the journey. A
truce existed between France and England at the
moment, an uneasy and spasmodic one, certainly, but it was always thus. She could only assume they felt the need for such protection
against the companies of disbanded knights and
men-at-arms terrorizing the countryside.

The door closed behind her visitors, and she
lay thinking of Edmund. Why was she so certain
he was not dead? He must be in some trouble,

but he lived. She thought of mad Jennet's words: love and blood in her hand. There was love and blood here, she knew, just as she knew Edmund de Bresse had not departed from her life. She would not yet grieve for him, but she would do her duty by him and his child that she carried. She would take her rightful place as chatelaine of the castle of Bresse, in a land of open spaces across the sea.

She remembered Jennet's reading of the water that long-ago day, when she had been whipped for consorting with the witch and Guy de Gervais had ridden into her life . . . had ridden into it and would not soon ride out of it.

The love she bore him was a force not to be denied. For so long it had been an essential, defining part of her self, comforting in its absolute certainty, growing at its own pace. It would come to fruition in its own good time; she knew that as assuredly as she knew that Edmund was not dead. What would come of such a tangle, she neither knew nor cared to know. Such future concerns seemed to have little relevance beside the fact of love and its driving force.

Five

THEY SET SAIL from Portsmouth harbor two weeks later in three ships, all of which had been requisitioned together with masters and crews by John of Gaunt from their merchant owners, who had no choice but to yield them up to the prince for as long as they were required. It was standard practice and caused no comment, the merchants keeping their resentment to themselves.

Magdalen was excited. She stood at the rail of the *Elizabeth* as the three ships took the morning tide, square-rigged sails set fair for Calais. From the forecastle, *Elizabeth*'s master called instructions to the hands in a vocabulary that meant nothing to the eagerly listening girl, but all three ships fanned out over the calm waters of the Solent, running before the wind, sails bellying under the fresh breeze. The escorting force, horses and grooms, were quartered on the accompanying ships; Magdalen and her women, Lord de Gervais and his own personal retinue, and twenty vassal knights sailed on the *Elizabeth,* the de Gervais dragon fluttering at the masthead beside the Lancastrian rose.

Guy came to stand at the rail beside her, infected by her excitement and her pleasure in the wheeling gulls, the salt tang of spray, the easy lift of the hull across the calm, bluegreen waters of the Solent. Her attitude toward Edmund's disappearance puzzled him. She had said with quiet assurance that she did not believe him dead and therefore would not grieve, but she would do what she perceived as her duty in his absence. Guy had not known how to respond. Eventually, he had decided that accepting her certainty could do no harm. She would come to her own realization of the truth when she was ready.

Since the day of the tournament, however, he was generally at some pains to keep a distance between them. Had he been able to behave with her in the old ways, the easy avuncular attitude he had found so natural with the child, it would have been simple enough. But he could not. Magdalen de Bresse was no child, and he was all too vibrantly aware of her womanhood and the disconcerting clarity of her gray-eyed gaze, so often turned upon him with an undaunted purpose.

This early morning, the crispness of the sea air, such a welcome change from the humid airlessness of summer in London, seemed to blow aside the cobwebs of confusion, to sweep through the chambers of his mind where lurked desires that he dared not acknowledge. He laid a hand on her shoulder, and she turned her face up to smile at him.

"Is it not wonderful, my lord? To be able to breathe again!"

It was so exactly his own sentiment that he laughed in agreement. "See, there is the Isle of Wight." He pointed to the long shape, its out-line blurred by a sea fret, crouching against the horizon. "We will pass the Needle Rocks by this afternoon. There has been many a wreck upon them."

"But we need have no such fear," Magdalen said, unable to disguise the anxiety in her voice. Much as she was enjoying the fresh air and the unusual motion, she held the firm belief that God had not intended people to travel upon the water. "The weather is set fair, is it not?"

Guy looked up at the sky, where a haze smudged the sun so that it showed as a diffused light against the thin cloud. "Perfectly fair," he assured her. "But in any case, we will be well past the Needle Rocks before dusk, and there is little to fear on the open water."

Magdalen accepted this news trustfully and drew him to a sheltered spot on the deck in the lee of the cabin housing, where cushions had been set beneath a striped canopy for the passengers to enjoy the sea air, and a minstrel was strumming his lute in plaintive melody.

There was little to do but enjoy the warmth, the gentle motion, and the enforced idleness. Dinner at midmorning was a lavish meal with venison pasties, preserved goose, fresh white bread, and a compote of mushrooms, new picked that morning in the fields outside Portsmouth. They should not be at sea for more than three days, so should suffer no more hardship than the staling of the white bread, Magdalen reflected contentedly, sipping hypocras from the pewter tankard, closing her eyes to the sun so that its warmth fingered her lids and created a soft rosy glow beneath. The lute player continued his soft plucking, and she drifted pleasantly into sleep.

When she awoke, there was a chill to the breeze, and Lord de Gervais was no longer beside her. Shivering, she sat up. "Erin, fetch me my mantle; 'tis cold of a sudden."

Erin went to the cramped cabin where Magdalen and her two women were accommodated. Iron-bound chests containing the clothes, china, glass, and domestic linens that were part of Magdalen's dowry were stacked against the sides. There were two straw pallets on the floor for the maids, another for Magdalen set on a wooden shelf carved into the bulkhead beneath the tiny porthole.

She found the fur-lined mantle and brought it on deck. Lord de Gervais had reappeared and was standing at the deck rail, a frown between his brows as he felt the more accentuated lift and drop of the hull across foam-tipped waves. The sky had taken on a salmon tinge.

"Something feels awry." Magdalen stepped up beside him, huddling into her cloak. "What is it?"

"Nothing," he said with an easiness he did not feel. "See, we are passing the Needle Rocks."

Magdalen looked to her left, seeing the wickedly jagged points rising from a surging sea at the furthest edge of the Isle of Wight. She shivered slightly and without thought sliped her hand into the pocket of her mantle, her fingers closing over the beads of her rosary, her lips moving in silent prayer. There was a boiling to the sea at the base of the rocks that made her think of hell and the damnation that awaited the unshriven.

They passed the rocks and the natural shelter provided by the island. The open sea had a different quality. It was gray, not blue-green, and the swell was more pronounced. Magdalen thought of venison pasty and wished she had not.

"I think perhaps I will go to my cabin."

Guy merely nodded as if he barely heard her, and indeed he was hardly aware of her departure. Something did feel awry. He went to the forecastle, where the master and the helmsman stood, eyes fixed upon the great square sail that tugged with the wind, stretched taut as a drumskin. The helmsman's hands on the wheel were white-knuckled with effort as he fought an increasing power.

"What is it?" Guy asked.

The master shook his head. "A squall's coming, my lord. 'Tis the only explanation. I've known it like this before, and it's always the worst when it creeps up on you. There was no sign of this one an hour ago, and still it's little more than a stirring in the air."

"Why do we not turn back?" Guy could feel the sailor's apprehension and looked over his shoulder to the still reassuringly close bulk of the Isle of Wight.

"Tide and wind's against us, my lord. We'd never round the Needle Rocks. We've no choice but to sail as far into open water as we can, then reef and sit it out, hoping we'll not be blown onto rocks." The master turned abruptly and bellowed over his shoulder to batten down the hatches. "You'd best get below, my lord."

Guy stood for a while longer at the rail,

watching as their sister ships went through the same maneuvers as *Elizabeth*. The wind was increasing and there was a wet, bitter edge to it. The waves slapped against the hull now, the spray no longer a gentle refreshing mist but an icy sheet. The sky had darkened to an almost night-dark, although it was but five in the afternoon.

"My lord, you'd best get below!" The master's shout was lost in a sudden scream of wind. The sea ahead boiled, rose in a swirling cone, and hurtled toward the tossing craft that seemed to Guy to be now made of matchwood. A gray-green trough opened up before the hull, and *Elizabeth* dived nose first into the flat wall of water.

Water slammed on the deck with a solid, bruising impact that knocked Guy from his feet. He grabbed the deck rail and hung on with every last ounce of strength until the ship lifted her nose out of the trough and the sea ran from her decks. But the next wall of water was racing toward them, and he hurled himself at the companionway hatch, recognizing that he could be of no use on deck and was in imminent danger of being swept away. Through the raging of the wind and the roaring of the water, he could hear the horses on the ships nearby, their hooves thudding against the wooden partitions of their stalls, their shrill neighing snatched away by the tempest.

Below, there was a merciful cessation of the battering tumult of wind and sea. But there was utter darkness, no possibility of candlelight in the ship's bucking, twisting, heaving fight with the ocean. He could hear cries from all around, cries for mercy as sailors and passengers called upon the saints and prayed for deliverance. He stumbled into his own cabin and flung himself onto his pallet, aware that only by lying prone would he escape injury. Miraculously, he was not sick, although he could hear, through the thin bulkheads, the acute wretchedness of his fellow travelers. The dreadful moans of his squire and page, stretched retching upon the floor of the cabin, filled his ears like souls in torment. After an hour, when there was no surcease and the cries around had become weaker with exhaustion and more despairing, he crawled off his pallet, stepped over his still vomiting attendants, and made his unsteady way to Magdalen's cabin.

His eyes had become accustomed to the darkness by now, and he was aware of the bodies twisted upon the floor, their cries for mercy and deliverance mere broken groans. Magdalen was lying upon her pallet, and she made no sound.

He stumbled over to her, fear a vise around his gut. The vessel heaved and he fell to his knees, grasping the edge of the shelf on which Magdalen lay. He saw then that she was clutching a chamber pot as if it were a lifeline, but her eyes were flat and open.

He touched her face. Her skin was clammy, but she responded to his touch. "I am bleeding," she said in barely a whisper, then with a wrenching moan rolled over the pot in her arms, the slight body convulsing as she retched with no possibility of relief.

For a moment, he did not understand what she had said, then he saw the darkness puddled beneath her before she fell back on the pallet again. The image of Gwendoline rose in dread memory. He turned desperately toward the two women on the floor, but one look was enough to convince him of the hopelessness of expecting help from that direction. They were both prostrate, beyond helping themselves, let alone their lady.

"I am bleeding," Magdalen said again. "It will not stop."

He staggered across to the stack of chests, opening them feverishly, searching for something that would soak up the flow. He found the sheets and towels in the third chest and came back to the pallet. He lifted her gently, feeling the wet stickiness against his hand as he pushed her skirts aside and spread a double sheet beneath her. He wrapped a towel around her body, drawing it up tightly between her legs in the desperate hope that it would staunch the bleeding.

"Is it the child?" she whispered, accepting his attentions with the helplessness of a newborn infant.

"I believe so," he said softly. "Try to lie as still as you can." He lifted her head, holding the pot for her when she moaned again in desperation, but she had nothing left inside her and fell back in the torment of unrelief, while the violent pitching and rolling continued unabated.

Her stomach cramped violently, and sweat stood out on her forehead. "I am going to die."

"You are not going to die!" He spoke fiercely out of his own fear. "I am going to fetch you something that may ease you."

"Do not leave me!" Her hand sought his, terror in her voice at the thought of being left alone again in the dreadful darkness, with the flooding blood, the cramping of her stomach that was inextricably bound with the dreadful retching, yet had a different cause. "Do not leave me," she entreated again.

"Only for a minute," he promised, and resolutely put her hand on the cover and struggled to his feet.

He was gone no more than five minutes, but

when he returned she was weeping soundlessly with pain and terror at her body's betrayal.

"Drink some of this." He unscrewed the top of a leather flask and put it to her lips. She turned her head from the powerful, stinging aroma, but he was insistent and finally she opened her mouth. The fiery liquid burned her throat and settled in her stomach, making a hole of fire, it seemed.

"More," he said. She swallowed again, and imperceptibly some ease came to her tortured body. The cramping became less painful the more she swallowed, and a great lassitude swamped her. Even the violent pitching of the ship ceased to matter as her body gave up the struggle.

Throughout the night, he remained beside her, changing the soiled sheets and towels repeatedly, dosing her with the aqua vite whenever her body seemed to be about to wake up to pain and nausea again. He had no idea whether the powerful spirit would have a deleterious effect in the long run, but beside the need to ease her present torment, such considerations were irrelevant. She slept fitfully, and he agonized over the bleeding that seemed not to abate throughout the long hours of darkness.

At dawn, the storm finally blew itself out. The ship, heavily reefed, came head to wind, and they could all draw breath after the night's beating. Ruthlessly, he roused Erin and Margery from their own exhausted unconsciousness. They staggered up on their pallets, whey-faced, and looked in horror at their lady, who seemed barely conscious, the blood-soaked linen piled around her.

"Water, my lord," Erin managed to croak. "We shall need hot water."

"You shall have it." He left the cabin and went on deck, gulping the clear, cold air with relief after the fetid stench below. The master was distracted, assessing the night's damage, which seemed amazingly to be confined to two broken spars. He had little time for his passengers' woes, but agreed to the lighting of a brazier in the cook's cubby beneath the forecastle. Guy instructed his deathly pale page to see to the heating and supplying of water to Lady Magdalen's women. Then he went to a sheltered corner of the deck and breathed deeply, trying to still his panic.

An hour later, he was aware of a soft voice at his shoulder. He turned to see Erin, still white and trembly from her own ordeal. "Well?" The one word came out more harshly than he had intended, but he was afraid.

"My lady has lost the child, my lord," Erin said.

"I assumed as much. But how is the Lady Magdalen?"

"The bleeding has slowed, my lord, and I believe she will recover. But she is much weakened."

Relief cast a golden glow over the gray morning, tipped with rose the greasy, lethargic swell of the sea. The loss of the child was a grave setback for Lancaster's plans, but at that moment Guy de Gervais gave not a damn for those plans.

"I will come below and see how she is."

In the cabin, he found Magdalen in a linen shift, lying on clean sheets, her face and lips still colorless but her breathing even. She opened her eyes as he stood above her, his body casting a shadow from the faint light at the porthole.

"My lord?"

"Aye." He took her hand. "You will be well soon enough, pippin. It is no great matter."

Her fingers tightened feebly around his. Throughout the dreadful reaches of the night, an intimacy had been forged between them that changed their relationship in ways she did not yet understand. "But I think my lord duke will consider it to be a great matter," she whispered through her aching throat, scraped raw with the violence of her sickness. "The child was to have made firm the Plantagenet claim to the de Bresse lands."

"You will make firm that claim," he said.

"You are the rightful heir to your husband's lands, and you are a Plantagenet."

"Yes, I suppose that is so." Her eyes closed. She had not had long enough to become accustomed to the idea of the coming child to feel more than minor disappointment at its loss. Such losses, after all, were a commonplace occurrence. "I seem to be very sleepy, my lord."

"Then sleep." He bent and brushed her brow with his lips. Her skin was cool, the earlier clamminess gone, and for a moment he was almost light-headed with relief. He was not going to lose her as he had lost Gwendoline. The comparison was formed before he could prevent it, and when he examined it, he knew it to be the truth in all its implications.

THE LITTLE FLEET limped into Calais harbor in the early afternoon of the sixth day. Guy sent his squire ashore to see about accommodations and then conferred with his companions over the storm damage to men and horses. They had lost five horses, all of which had contrived to break legs in their wild, terrified trampling and pounding and had had to be put down. Two grooms had suffered injuries in their efforts to restrain the animals, but apart from the debilitating weakness engendered by ten hours of racking seasickness, Guy had reason to feel they had been let off lightly.

The squire returned with the information that the nearest abbey large enough to offer their entire party accommodation was at St. Omer, some twenty miles inland.

Guy frowned. They could not make twenty miles before dark. Magdalen was fully recovered; the miscarriage had occurred too early in the pregnancy for any extended ill effects, and youth and general good health had their usual advantages. But she had not left her cabin since that storm-tossed night, and he did not want to tire her with a journey of any distance, bumping over ill-paved roads in a horse-drawn wagon.

"Take the Lady Magdalen's women and go to the largest inn in the town," he instructed. "Arrange a privy chamber for the lady. Her women can see to its preparation with their own linens and hangings. Any kind of accommodation will do for myself."

The men would have to fend for themselves. They could seek quarters with willing townspeople, or unwilling as the case may be, or make camp on the beaches or in the surrounding countryside until the morning.

He went below, finding Magdalen sitting fully dressed on her pallet. She was brushing her hair, but she put the brush aside, a brilliant smile lighting her face when he entered the cabin.

"Are we to leave this ship now? I do not think I will ever again sail on the sea."

"I fear you may have to," he said, returning her smile, as unquestioning as she of the new bond they shared. "Unless you intend never returning to England. Come, I am going to carry you on deck." He lifted her against his chest, and her arms went naturally around his neck, her head resting on his shoulder.

"I'm certain I could walk, but this is much more pleasant."

There was a coquettish note to her voice, and her eyes sparkled up at him. His body stirred in response, but he said severely, "Magdalen, I am not interested in hearing such observations."

"But I think you are," she said softly, and that clear determination chased the coquette from her eyes, bringing to him a shiver of premonition, a heady intoxicating rush of blood. Before he could say anything further, she moved upward in his arms, her hands gripping his scalp with a fervent urgency as she brought her mouth to his in a heated conjunction that drove all else from his mind but the warm moistness of her mouth, the curve of her body beneath his hands, the press of her breasts against his chest.

Her mouth tasted of honey, her skin smelled sweet as new-drawn milk, her body in his arms lay soft and tender as an infant's, yet with all the pulsing ardency of aroused womanhood.

For too long he yielded to the moment she had orchestrated, the union she had compelled . . . yielded because she was drawing him ever closer to that center where swirled danger and passion beyond previous knowing. This was a kiss in which a man drowned, he in her, she in him, a kiss bearing no relation to past kisses, which were as milk and water to the fire and ice of this joining of mouths.

But reality at last forced its way between them. He dropped her on the pallet as if she were a burning brand. "God's blood, Magdalen, what devil drives you?" He ran his hand through his hair, touched his still tingling lips. "You are not a free woman. Would you embrace adultery? 'Tis a mortal sin."

"I love you," she said simply. "I do not see it as sinful. I said long ago, after the Lady Gwendoline died, that I should never have married Edmund, but you would not listen."

"Stop this!" His voice shook with the fear of his own unleashed desires. "It is dangerous madness that you talk. Your wits are addled."

Stubbornly, she shook her head. "They are not. I do not know what is to be done about

Edmund, but perhaps I will be able to make him understand."

Guy stared at her, for the moment convinced she had indeed lapsed into some madness, perhaps brought on by her ordeal. "Your husband is dead," he said finally.

She shook her head. "If you believe that, then I do not understand why you would talk of mortal sin; but he is not dead. I know it."

Guy turned on his heel and left the cabin, slamming the door behind him. His anger was directed as much at himself as at Magdalen. She had acted on an impulse that he should have been able to forestall, or at least cut short. But he had been lost, with neither will nor power to alter the course of those moments, and he knew without a shadow of doubt that he must keep away from her if he was to avoid a repetition.

Magdalen was carried up to the deck by a stalwart young squire and placed in a litter, her women walking beside her. She caught a glimpse of Guy giving orders to the sergeant-at-arms, but he did not glance in her direction. At the Coq d'Or, she was put to bed in a chamber overlooking the market square. The sheets on the straw mattress on the square box bed were her own, as were the hangings, and the floor had been energetically swept by Margery herself when the lackadaisical efforts of the inn's kitchen wench had failed to satisfy. These amenities were small compensation for the noise, however.

The chamber was directly over the inn's main room, and shouting, laughter, the occasional burst of song drifted up through the cracks in the ill-fitting floorboards. From the square outside came incessant street noises, the rattle of iron wheels over the cobbles, the shouts of street vendors, the brawling of drunken sailors. The smell of fish was pervasive. The inn stood in the shadow of the church, and over all, the bells rang for the day's offices, until Magdalen's head was fit to burst and she knew even the bumpy road would be better than this.

She sent Erin to ask Lord de Gervais to visit her chamber, but the girl returned with the message that my lord was too busy to come to her. He would hear any message through her maid.

Magdalen chewed her fingernail in frustration. "Ask my lord, then, how long he intends that we should remain in this place, for my head is splitting."

Guy was no happier with his own accommodations, a cramped and dirty loft where black beetles scurried into the corners and the reek of fish oil came from the great barrels set against the wall. However, he had no intention of con-

tinuing their journey until the morning, and
Magdalen's petulant message did nothing for his
temper. He advised Erin, somewhat sharply, to
tell her lady to put cloth in her ears if the noise
troubled her.

Magdalen received this advice with a hiss of
annoyance and announced her intention of getting up. "Oh, my lady, that were foolish," Erin
protested. "You're still weak as a new-dropped
lamb."

"Nonsense. I am perfectly strong and will be
more so if I cease this melancholy lying about.
Help me with my gown, for I go to find my
lord. If he will not come to me, then I must
needs go to him."

She was somewhat disconcerted, however, to
discover how shaky her legs were when she
stood upon them properly for the first time. She
clung to the door frame for a minute, then resolutely stepped into the unsavory passageway. A
rickety wooden stairway led to the inn's main
room, and she walked carefully down it, lifting
her skirt from the piles of dust and other more
unsavory debris in the corners. Her pointed-toe
slippers stuck occasionally on the step and had to
be pulled free of whatever grim substance held
them.

The room below was crowded and reeked of
sweat and stale beer, overlaying the fish. She felt

a moment's dizziness, then pushed forward through the throng, heading for the door to the square. Erin had said Lord de Gervais had been about to go out with his page, so presumably if she waited for him outside in the fresh air and sunshine, she would catch him on his return.

She sat down with some relief on the ale bench against the inn wall and closed her eyes for a minute.

"My lady, you will forgive the impertinence, but this is no place for you."

The unfamiliar voice brought her eyes open, and she found herself looking at a man of middle years, booted and spurred as a knight. Her first thought was that she must have seen him somewhere before, because there was something about him that she recognized, although she could not pinpoint it. It was something about the eyes, perhaps; gray like her own. His face was thin and pointed, the nose large and dominating, his mouth barely there at all. She did not care for his looks in the least. Her second thought, more fanciful, was that, although he was bowing and smiling in the most unexceptionable fashion, there was a shadow over him, a strangely menacing shadow.

"Sir?" Her brows lifted haughtily, with pure Plantagenet arrogance.

"Sieur Charles d'Auriac, my Lady de Bresse."
He bowed again, taking her hand and bringing
it to his lips. "Forgive my intrusion on your
peace, but indeed the public street is no place for
a lady. If you will accept my escort, there is a little garden a few paces from here where you may
enjoy the sun without annoyance."

"I had received no annoyance until now, sir,"
she said, her rudeness arising as much out of un-
easiness as out of irritation at his presumption.

His eyes darkened, and that shadow of menace
became almost palpable. Magdalen was suddenly
afraid. But she had no need to be, surely. The
inn door was at her back, its noisy safety within
easy reach.

"I can assure you I wish only to be of service,"
he said, laying a hand lightly on her arm. "Pray
permit me to show you the garden. You will
find no one there but monks. It belongs to the
presbytery, but they will be happy to offer you
their seclusion."

Why, when everything he said was so reasonable, when there was nothing about his attire or
demeanor to give the lie to his claim of knightly
status, why then was she so certain he meant her
no good? Her eyes flickered sideways along the
street as she felt the hand on her arm tighten just
a little. Lord de Gervais and his page turned

onto the square from the far corner just as she was about to wrench her arm free and plunge back into the inn without further ado.

"My Lord de Gervais!" she called loudly. Charles d'Auriac glanced over his shoulder, then he released her arm and strode off without a word.

Guy hurried over to her. "What are you doing out here?"

"I wanted to talk to you," she said. "Since you would not come to me, it seemed I must come to you."

He frowned and sent his page into the inn. "Who was with you just then?"

"A man I did not like in the least," she said. "Sieur d'Auriac, I believe he said. He knew my name without my telling him."

"That is hardly surprising. Calais is a small town, and one person's business is everyone's business." He stood frowning down at her. "You should not be out here unaccompanied."

"That is what he said. He wished me to go with him to the presbytery garden, where he said I could enjoy the sun without fear of annoyance." She shivered slightly. "I do not know why, but he frightened me."

"In what way?" Guy felt a prickle of unease.

"I felt he might have made me go with him," she said, feeling for words.

"Abduct you?"

"It is folly, I know, but I felt it. I also felt as if I ought to know him, as if there was something familiar about him . . . almost like a memory . . ." She stopped and shrugged. "I cannot find the right words."

Guy's frown deepened. He could think of no reason why a French knight should threaten Magdalen, however obliquely, if he knew her for a lady. Had he believed her a woman of the town, taking her ease outside a tavern in open invitation to all comers, it would have been different. In such a circumstance, an element of roughly persuasive sport would have been perfectly natural. In addition, Calais was an English possession, and the lady but newly disembarked from an English ship, flying the Lancastrian colors. No Frenchman would have offered her insult or discourtesy if he knew she had come from that ship. Unless . . . But no, it was far too soon for the de Beauregards to make any kind of move on French soil.

"Go back to your chamber," he said. "It must be clear to you by now that the open street is not a suitable place for you."

"Will you not bear me company? It is sadly tedious on my own, and I really do not need to be in bed any longer. Perhaps we could walk a little way?" She smiled hopefully.

De Gervais felt the ground slippery beneath him again. "I have no desire for your company," he said brutally. "Go within. If you wish to leave this place in the morning, you will ensure that you spend the intervening hours resting."

What little color she had drained from her cheeks, and the look in her eyes was the one she had worn when he had punished her all those years ago for causing Gwendoline such distress. It reminded him now as then of a betrayed and wounded fawn. Then she turned and without a further word went into the inn.

The bell for vespers rang from the church, but the noise from below did not lessen. Erin brought supper to the chamber, a dish of lampreys and an eel pie. "Why have they no meat?" Magdalen demanded palely from her pillow. "The stench of fish is trapped in my nostrils, and I cannot suffer the thought of its taste upon my tongue."

"But 'tis a good pie, my lady," Margery piped, looking up from her own platter. "And you will not regain your strength if you do not eat."

Magdalen turned her head into her pillow and closed her eyes.

An hour later, the sounds of music and loud laughter came up from the square. "Oh, there are jongleurs, my lady," Erin exclaimed, leaning out the window. "And mummers."

"Oh, yes, and see, there is a group of those mad dancers," chimed in Margery, hanging so far out that Erin seized hold of her apron at the back. "I have seen them in Lincoln. They dance like that because they are possessed. Do come and see, my lady."

Magdalen sighed wearily. She could summon no enthusiasm for the demonic dancers. Her head still ached, but it was not that that led to her present joylessness. "Why do you not go down, then, if you wish to join the crowd?"

"Oh, we could not leave you, my lady," Erin demurred, although her eyes shone. "Why do you not come too?"

Magdalen shook her head. "Nay, I do not feel like it, but do you both go. I have no further need of you this night."

After only a token protest, Erin and Margery donned their hooded capes and ran down to the square where the shrieks and hilarity grew more wanton by the moment. It sounded to Magdalen's jaundiced ear as if the revelry were growing out of hand. She pulled the sheet over her head and buried her face in the pillow.

She must have drifted off to sleep because when she next opened her eyes, the chamber was in darkness, although the noise from the square continued and the light from the flambeaux illuminating the gaiety flickered in the

window. She did not know what had wakened
her, but whatever it was had set her heart ham-
mering against her ribs and dried her mouth.
Then she saw the shadow against the window, a
huge fluttering batlike shape, and she knew that
some sixth sense of danger had pulled her from
sleep. She opened her mouth to scream as the
figure seemed to swoop upon her, arm upraised,
something curved and glittering in its hand.

She threw herself sideways as the glittering
thing came down upon her, and the knife ripped
into the pillow. The scream would not leave her
throat but stuck there, heavy and useless. She had
hurled herself to the floor when the cowled figure freed his weapon and came at her again.
Then the scream came loose, but it was lost in the
noise from the square below. She grabbed the
sheet off the bed and flung it toward her assailant.
It twisted around his knife hand, and a foul oath
came from him. She screamed again, running
naked toward the door. Her fingers were slippery with the sweat of terror, and she fumbled
with the latch. The huge shadow grew on the
door above her, and she knew he was at her back.
She ducked desperately beneath the upraised
hand just as the door flew open.

What happened next was a blur. She cowered
against the wall as Guy de Gervais and the man
struggled with silent fury. Then Guy was sud-

denly left holding a brown monk's habit, and the figure in britches and shirt threw itself at the open window. With an agile twist of his body, he swung himself onto the gable overhang and disappeared across the roof.

"Why did he wish to kill me?" she gasped on a sobbing breath, flinging herself against Guy, shaking from head to toe with terror. He held her, enfolding her nakedness in his arms, whispering softly into her hair until the trembling had ceased. "I did not think anyone could hear me scream," she managed to say. "There is so much noise outside."

"I was passing the door," he said, adding soberly, "I would not have heard you else." Her trembling began again, and he was abruptly, vibrantly conscious of her nakedness, of the silken curve of her buttocks beneath his hands, the rise and fall of her breasts against his chest. He let his hands fall from her, but with a little moan of protest, she burrowed closer.

"Hold me. I am so cold and afeared."

There didn't seem to be much else he could do. He wrapped her in his arms again, letting his hands rest where they would. "Where are your women, pippin?" He frowned over her head at the empty chamber.

"I gave them leave to join the sport in the square," she said, cuddling closer, feeling warmth from his body lap her skin, and feeling something else as well . . . Where his hands touched her, her skin seemed to come alive, and a deep tingling sensation was in her belly.

"That was foolish of you in such a place as this. They should not both have left you." The statement did not, however, sound as angered as he intended. He became aware of her nipples peaking hard against his shirt and the stirring of his own body in response. With supreme effort, he stepped away from her and picked up the fallen sheet. "Put this around you, then you will not be cold."

She took the sheet with a reluctance that was unmistakable. "I'd prefer it if you would hold me."

He looked at her helplessly, powerless to make any impact on her determination to plunge them both into a swirling morass of danger and dishonor. "You would commit mortal sin," he said, yet hearing his own lack of conviction. There was no point denying his own desires any longer, to himself or to her. He was no longer even sure whether it was worth attempting to manage those desires. But until John of Gaunt declared her officially widowed, adultery was the name of the game she would play. True, it was a game played lightly by all and sundry, but it did not sit easy with him.

"I love you," she said as she had so often before. "And I believe you love me."

He did, of course, and had known it without
acknowledging it for some time. But it did not
alter facts. Without replying, he went to the
window and looked down at the riotous scene
in the square. It had deteriorated to a melee of
debauchery, wine spilling into the gutters, con-
joined bodies heaving in the shadows, and some
indeed not even bothering to seek that concealment. A woman's shrieks came from an alley,
but it was impossible to judge whether they
were shrieks of fear or pleasure. Magdalen's lusty
wenches had presumably been up to no good,
he reflected. It was to be hoped neither of them
acquired a swollen belly as a result.

Magdalen came to stand beside him, swathed
now in the sheet. She laid a hand on his arm,
looking up into his face as if she would read
some affirmation there, but when she spoke it
was no longer of illicit passion. "Why would
someone try to kill me?"

"Such a night of revelry and debauchery
breeds robbers, assassins, brigands," he said, having no intention of telling her the truth at this
stage—that tonight's attack was no coincidence.
She seemed to find nothing to question in the
explanation, and he turned to pick up the
monk's habit from the floor, examining it with a

frown. It was an ordinary garment with no identifying marks, offering no clue to its owner—or wearer if the two were distinct, as seemed likely.

"I am going to post a sentry at your door," he said. "I daresay it will be long before your women decide to return."

"Don't leave me alone," she said, fear again in her voice. "He might come back while you are gone."

Guy stood irresolute. It occurred to him that his entire force was likely the worse for wear by now, and the sounds of feet stumbling drunkenly along the passage outside the chamber did not bode well for the courtesy and consideration of the inn's other occupants. "Very well, I will stay with you until your women return. But get into bed."

She looked at him for a minute, considering, as if weighing the situation, then turned to the bed, slowly shook off the sheet, and as deliberately brought one knee up onto the mattress. He inhaled sharply, aware that her movements were purposely provocative, were constituting some kind of an invitation, although their present surroundings did not lend themselves to the issuing or acceptance of such an invitation.

"Behave yourself," he said roughly, coming over to the bed. "Get in." He slapped her rounded behind in emphatic punctuation and she jumped, hastily putting herself between the covers.

"Spoilsport," she accused.

"I have told you that that is a sport I will not play," he declared.

"Yes, you will." She closed her eyes, drawing the sheet up to her neck. "I bid you good night, my lord."

He stood looking down at her for a moment, unable to prevent the slight smile curving his mouth. He was lost, it seemed, but lost or no, he had to ensure her safety. He sat on the window seat as the noise from below finally died away and the bodies in the square either went slinking off into the surrounding alleys or remained where they were in sterterous sleep. Had the Sieur d' Auriac anything to do with tonight's attack? Who was d' Auriac? He would have to set some inquiries in motion. He would put the matter in the hands of Olivier, a swarthy native of Provence with the physique and agility of a monkey, who was as adept at ferreting out information as he was at slipping in and out of places where he had no business. He was probably the most valued and valuable member of de Gervais's retinue.

MARGERY AND ERIN reappeared at midnight, disheveled, flushed, and slurred of speech. At the sight of Lord de Gervais sitting on the window seat, fear and guilt flared in their suffused eyes.

"My lady said we could go, my lord," Erin whimpered.

"Did she also say you could return in this condition?" he demanded in a caustic whisper. "While you've been tumbling and debauching in the streets, your lady has been in grave danger. You are fortunate I do not have you beaten for your negligence and dissolute behavior." He strode to the door. "We leave at dawn. Make sure you and your lady are ready to travel at first light."

It became very clear at dawn, however, that rounding up his household and widely scattered men-at-arms was a near impossibility after the night's excesses. Those who could be found were generally incapacitated, and it appeared that the only two members of the sizable party not suffering the ill effects of debauchery were himself and Magdalen. Even his page moved his head with the greatest care and showed a reluctance to move speedily on his errands. Guy resigned himself to another day and night in their insalubrious lodgings in Calais, but it was three days later before they were able to leave. Two of his men were accused of theft by an outraged citizen of the town, and the subsequent inquiry and peace making took a full two days. Guy fretted but knew he could not afford to ignore such complaints of the French townsfolk, who were already all too inclined to resent their involuntary subservience to the English crown.

Magdalen's objections to their continued residence in the noisy, ill-smelling tavern were lessened when Guy gave her permission to go about the town with an armed escort of two squires and pages. It would have seemed an overly large escort but for the previous night's attack, and Magdalen accepted the protection with cheerful gratitude. Her strength returned rapidly as she wandered the busy port, enjoying the foreign sights and sounds and smells under a warm September sun.

At last, however, they resumed their journey, Magdalen and her women installed in a covered wagon whose heavily cushioned bench offered little protection as the vehicle lurched and jolted over the uneven roadway. The accompanying force in glittering mail presented a fearsome aspect as they marched, the herald sounding his trumpet at each potential obstacle in their path, the attached pennants of Lancaster and de Gervais lifting in exclamation as he raised the horn for each blast. The impression was that of a fighting force, one not to be tangled with, and the local inhabitants, accustomed to such companies roaming the land, set upon plunder and spoiling, trembled until they had passed in peace.

They sighted the roof of the abbey at St. Omer as the bells were ringing for vespers, but when they reached the gate-house in the enclosure walls, Guy immediately sensed something amiss. They would have been seen approaching from some distance away, and he would have expected the hospitaller to be waiting to greet them and show them to the guest hall. But the stone gate was resolutely closed, and the inset grille offered only a blind eye to the travelers. He told his page to pull the bell beside the gate, and they all listened as the echoing peals flew repeatedly within with a strange hollowness, as if those who inhabited this place were absent.

Finally, there came a sound of dragging footsteps, as if each step entailed more effort than could be easily borne. The grille slid open, and a tired, lined face looked out at them, pale eyes haunted with sorrow beneath the white wimple and black cowl.

"I can offer you little succor, friends," the porteress said, making no attempt to open the gate.

"Why, how is this?" Guy demanded. "We ask

a traveler's rest of the good sisters of this abbey. There are women in our party—"

"And there is plague within these walls," the sister said simply.

Guy took an involuntary step backward, a swift prayer to St. Catherine, his patron saint, rising unbidden to his lips. Since the catastrophic pandemic of forty years ago, the plague remained a recurrent scourge, and none was untouched by it. It struck down rich and poor, lord and peasant, God's servants as often as the damned.

"May God have mercy upon you, Sister, and all within your house," he said. The grille closed, and he turned back to his assembled company. His page regarded him with wide, frightened eyes.

"My lord, are we touched?"

Guy shook his head. "Nay, lad. We have not stepped within the gates."

"What is it, my lord? Why are we denied entrance?" Magdalen clambered with relief from the wagon and walked somewhat stiffly toward him.

"The sisters have the plague," he told her. "We will seek shelter in the town for this night."

But when they reached St. Omer some ten minutes later, they found the gates closed to them, the watchmen within both fearful and threatening—fearful because of the size and warlike appearance of the group, and threatening because they had no other recourse. "There is plague abroad in the land," they told Guy. "We admit no traveler within these walls."

They showed sense, Guy reflected. Isolation was the only way for a community to protect itself, but it left him stranded in the countryside. Of course, he could attempt to force entrance, and with the men at his command he would probably succeed, but he was not at war with the citizens of St. Omer and had no wish to spend the night among hostile people.

Magdalen, who was now heartily sick of the wagon and extremely hungry besides, stepped down purposefully. "If you have tents, sir, why can we not make camp like the soldiers?" She gestured to the plain around them. "There is a pretty river, and firewood aplenty."

"We may do so," he said, "but 'tis hardly fit accommodation for the Lady de Bresse."

"The Lady de Bresse thinks it is," she said stoutly. "I can think of nothing pleasanter. It is such a lovely evening."

It was a lovely evening, the air as soft as wine and rich with the fragrances of sweet basil and sage thick upon the riverbank. The cooks would have little difficulty preparing supper on the braziers they carried in the baggage train, the men would sleep beneath the stars easily enough, and they carried sufficient tents for those who would need them.

"I have always wished to," Magdalen said, judiciously adding more weight to her side of the scale.

Guy laughed because he could not help himself, she had such a look of eager mischief about her. Then he saw the deep sensual glow in her eyes belying the mischief, saw that full, passionate mouth opened slightly in her own laughter, the little white teeth clipping her bottom lip, and desire stronger than he had ever known washed through him, leaving him breathless.

"By the Holy Rood, Magdalen," he whispered, "what bewitchment do you work? You are indeed your mother's daughter."

"What of my mother?" The gray eyes widened in surprise. "What do you know of my mother?"

"That she held men in thrall," he said, his gaze suddenly distanced. "That she drove men to distraction with the power of her beauty and the—" But here he stopped, brought suddenly back to awareness of what he was saying and to whom he spoke. *And the power of her treachery*, he would have said, but he could not say such a thing to this sweet-scented innocent, whose knowledge and understanding of her own powers was but still undeveloped.

No one had ever spoken to Magdalen of her mother beyond the mere mention of her name, and now a new vista opened as she saw Guy's expression, heard his words, heard even more the sudden cessation of his words.

"I do not understand," she said hesitantly. "Is it good that I should be like my mother?"

Guy's eyes focused again. "We all belong to our parentage," he said briskly. "It is only meet that we should do so. You have John of Gaunt's mouth, his arrogance and his determination, and you have some things of your mother."

With that, he turned from her and went to take counsel with his vassal knights as to the wisdom of making camp outside the walls of a hostile town.

Magdalen wandered down to the river, imbued with a strange seeping excitement, as if something was at last to come to fruition. Whatever it was that she shared with her mother, it was something that set Guy de Gervais aquiver, something that cut through his determined withdrawal like a dagger through wax.

Tents were pitched on the rise above the riverbank, and the air soon filled with the rich aromas of roasting venison haunch and sides of beef that formed part of their provisions from England. A long trestle table was set up outside the grouping of tents, and the company sat down on plank benches to supper as the evening star appeared in the sky. The meal was conducted with all the ceremony of high table at the de Gervais manor at Hampton, the knights served by their pages, servitors bearing laden platters of meat from the braziers to the table, minstrels playing as torches were lit, chasing the dusk away from the bright, hospitable scene.

Magdalen picked up the great dipper and ladled meat juice lavishly onto her bread trencher. She was so hungry she forgot for the moment the obligation to eat daintily and swallowed the bread almost whole before reaching with her little jeweled hip knife to hack at the roast of beef in front of her.

"I do not remember when I was last so hungry," she confided to Guy, feeling guiltily for her handkerchief on which to wipe her greasy fingers. "I expect it was because we have had no dinner."

"Fasting tends to have such an effect," he observed gravely, drinking deep of the wine cup as his neighbor passed it to him. "But I am glad to see you quite restored to health."

"Yes, and on the morrow I intend to ride," she informed him in no uncertain terms. "The jolting in the wagon is insupportable. Besides, 'tis an unhandsome, scurvy means of journeying."

Guy laughed. "I would not care for it myself. But if you intend to ride, you should perhaps seek your rest soon."

"Do you think there are wolves?" Magdalen said suddenly, aware of the dark plain lurking just outside their magic circle.

"Probably. But they'll not venture within the fires, and there'll be watchmen posted throughout the night."

Magdalen shivered. "I'd rather face a monk with a knife than wolves."

He looked at her sharply. "You've no need to fear either, pippin."

"But do you not think it a strange coincidence that twice someone should have attempted to harm me? That time with the brigands at Westminster, and then yesterday?"

"These are lawless times," he said casually. "At Westminster, we were journeying late in the day, without proper escort. It was inviting trouble. That night . . ." He shrugged. "The whole town was in an uproar, and robbers thrive on chaos."

She nodded, playing with a crumb of bread. "But there is Edmund, also."

"Edmund was alone in the forest, where it is known outlaws are supreme."

"Yes, I suppose that is true." She put a hand up to stifle a yawn.

"Come, I will take you to your tent where your women await you." He stood up. "The tent is too small for all three of you, but they may sleep just outside."

Magdalen frowned. "You do not fear they might be molested?" She looked around at the busy scene, where men-at-arms sat by the braziers, cleaning armor, eating supper, passing flagons of ale and mead. It seemed orderly enough, but what would happen when the lights went out?

"I doubt they will receive unwelcome attentions," he said dryly, remembering the previous evening's unlicensed sport.

Magdalen chuckled and deliberately slipped her hand into his. He stiffened for a second and made to withdraw his own hand, then he yielded the issue. It seemed such a natural gesture. But the quality of the gesture changed in the most disturbing fashion. Her little finger began tracing tiny circles against his palm. It was the most secretive, sensual movement, hinting at moist and humid places, at soft openings and knowing caresses. He looked down at her sharply and saw that her face was upturned toward his, reading in his expression the effect of her wicked game. He felt himself slipping again, pulled inexorably to that center from where she sat drawing in her line. Where had she learned such things? They were the opposite of innocence. But why should he assume innocence? She had made it very clear what she wanted of him and that she knew he wanted the same of her. Such clarity and singlemindedness of purpose were not components of innocence. Perhaps she had never been innocent. Women were, after all, put upon the earth to lead men into temptation, and, as John of Gaunt had said, Magdalen had entered the world in a moment accursed, a moment of evil. She brought double jeopardy with her.

But even as he thought these things in a harsh attempt to hold himself from the brink of that jeopardy, she chuckled again, low, sensuous, mischievous, and he knew he was already lost, that he was only playing for time. Nevertheless, he left her abruptly at her tent, with no more than a word of good-night.

It was a very small tent, with room only for a single straw pallet. It was too cold to sleep naked as she was accustomed to doing, so Magdalen crawled beneath the fur coverlet in her shift and lay listening as the camp grew gradually silent. A wild dog bayed, and the melancholy sound was picked up by others. Magdalen's skin prickled. There was something about the call, something wild, elemental, urgent, that lodged deep inside her, bringing forth some answering response that needed little enough now to emerge. Slowly a surging took over her body, a deep-rooted, passionate urgency that heated her skin despite the freshness of the night.

She knew what she wanted, and she knew the time had come, although no words of explanation or of planning formed in her head.

Drawing the fur closely about her, she crept to the tent opening. A sentry was dozing at his post, and she could hear Erin and Margery's snores from the ground beside the tent.

Wraithlike, she slipped out, standing upright, the dark fur and her dark hair blending into the gloom. Fires flickered dimly ahead. A few torches held by watchmen offered points of light further afield, demarcating the camp circle. Horses shuffled and whickered, tethered to stakes within the fires' protection. Otherwise, there was no disturbance of the sleeping camp.

The dragon of Gervais fluttered over his tent in the night breeze. She flitted soundlessly, dark-shrouded, across the ground, feeling the coarse grass against her bare feet dampening with the night dew. There was no one to see her pass except for a half-wakeful page who had indulged himself on green apples from an orchard they had passed and was now suffering the ill effects.

But he believed the figure to be some imaginary shade produced by his griping, disordered belly and simply whispered a prayer to St. Christopher as the dim ghost slipped by.

Guy was not asleep. A lantern burned dimly in the tent. His head was full of dreams, his body alive with longings. He had believed himself essentially a continent man. He had been faithful to Gwendoline except for the occasional heated skirmish during campaigns, when spilled blood and mortal danger threw up lust's demands like some boil on the skin and they had to be lanced quickly and cleanly, lest they fester and pollute the mind and body. Since his wife's death, he had had only encounters of like kind, and only when his need was imperative. Since Gwendoline, he had never wanted a particular woman.

Until now. His desire for the girl was fleshly desire, the powerful, throbbing obsession of the body, but there was more. Had it been only the former, he would have sought release elsewhere, calmed the heated flesh, and forced his mind to other things. But there was something about Isolde's daughter, some aura of danger and passion and promise that held him fast in gossamer coils. And there was something about the quicksilver nature of her, the arrogance and determination, the ready laughter, the singleminded

loyalty to person or purpose, that filled him with
deep delight.

He caught the scent of her, that special scent
reminiscent of new-drawn milk and honey,
even before he was aware of the shadow slipping
into his tent. And a profound knowledge of
inevitability drove all self-denying protest from
him.

Dropping her fur shroud, she slipped beneath
the cover beside him. "I was afeared to sleep
alone, with the dogs and the wolves and the
monks with knives."

"Why did you not call your women?" He
pushed up the shift, freeing it from beneath her.

"I called, but none came." Naked, she
stretched beside him.

"Madame, I believe you lie."

"Yes," she agreed, kissing the line of his jaw,
touching the tip of her tongue into the corner
of his mouth. "But what else is one to do in
such an instance?"

He drew her against him, fitting her body to
his. There was warmth where her skin touched
his, and cool places where they were apart. He
moved aside the cover, baring her shoulder to
the lantern light. The creamy slope glimmered,
leading his eye down to the delicate blue-veined
swell of her breasts. He touched the line of her
body from below her ear to her hip, feeling the

tender curves, the deep indentations. His palm cupped the flare of her hip, flattened against her thigh, drew her leg across his own thighs, opening her body.

Magdalen shuddered as she unfolded to the fervid, deeply intimate caress. Her lips sought the shadowy hollow of his shoulder, her tongue dipping, savoring the salt-sweetness of his skin, her thighs slithering against the muscled hardness of his. She felt him rise against her belly and moved her hand to clasp the nudging shaft, stroking as she reached down further, exploring the heated furrows of his body as she was explored.

The glowing, impassioned, whispering lovemaking had its own integrity, separate from all past experiences and creating its own future promise. When he was within her, she felt herself encompassed within his flesh, with nothing to define the shape of her body on the pallet as distinct from the one loving her; and when, after an eternity of dissolution, he withdrew from her, she felt a great sense of loss and tears started in her eyes, her arms tightening around him as if she could bind him to her.

He understood the tears and held her secure in his embrace as he rolled onto the pallet beside her. She wept silently into his shoulder, her warm body locked against him, and he felt the great vulnerability of her frailty where before he had been only aware of the immense power of her passion that had matched his and inflamed them both.

She fell asleep with the tears still wet on her lashes, his shoulder damp beneath her cheek. And he lay listening to the joyous, passionate descant of a nightingale, a harmony that seemed to acknowledge no limits to love, no insurmountable obstacles to joy.

Six

"THERE IS LITTLE more I can do for him, Father Abbot." The monk rose wearily from his knees by the pallet in the small, stone-walled, stone-floored chamber off the main infirmary. "This night will see the end, if the end is to be."

The abbot stood looking down at the broken body on the pallet. His hand rested lightly on the crucifix on his chest in an unconscious gesture, as if seeking strength, purpose, true decision from the contact. "He is anointed and absolved. He will meet his death in grace." Bending over the body, he touched the cross to the livid lips. "Go in peace, my son, if depart this life you must." The breath was a mere whisper, a sigh of life, from between those lips in a face as cold and gray as putty.

The tending monk took a cup of warmed wine, aromatic with herbs, and held it to the man's mouth. The liquid dribbled unswallowed. Brother Armand wiped the lifeless mouth, passed a cool, lavender-soaked cloth over the broad forehead where a great purple swelling throbbed at the temple.

"Send for me if he should stir. It is hard for a

man to die unnamed and among strangers." The abbot left the room, and Brother Armand sat on the stool beside the bed to keep the night's vigil. It was near impossible to believe that a man could live after such hurts, and if he should die, it would be impossible to know which of his dreadful injuries had caused his death. The gash on his head was deep enough to have fractured the skull. One alone of the many stab wounds and sword cuts would have been sufficient to drain the lifeblood from him. Yet, somehow, the faint stirring of breath continued, although the cleansed, bandaged, splinted body beneath the covers remained motionless.

Dawn broke, and the man still lived. Brother Armand touched his mouth again with the cup of wine, and this time there was the faintest movement in his throat, an effort to swallow. The eyelids flickered, the faintest tremor, and the apothecary waited for the first recognition of pain. It would be a remote recognition to begin with, but it would indicate that life still pulsed deep within the shattered frame. The mouth quivered, the nostrils flared almost imperceptibly, but it was enough to tell the watching apothecary of the return of sensation. A tension passed across the hollowed, shadowed, deathly pallor of the man's face, the tension of alarm as the pain now bit deep.

Brother Armand moved to the brazier in the corner of the room and began to prepare the draught of poppy juice that would keep the sufferer this side of sanity during the long agony of healing.

"MY LORD . . . MY LORD . . ."

Guy de Gervais paused, looking around. The whispered summons was repeated, but there was no sign of the whisperer. The long outer corridor of the castle of Bresse stretched emptily ahead of him, the arras rustling against the cold stone walls where slitted windows looked out over the moat and the flat plains of Picardy. The whisper came again. He was in no doubt as to the identity of the whisperer, but where in the name of St. Catherine was she? He continued down the corridor, and the whisper seemed to keep pace with him. At the end of the corridor stood a door onto a circular chamber set into a bastion of the castle. The door was slightly ajar. There was no whispering now, only the silence of the deserted corridor and the faint call of a bugle from the garrison court. It was midafternoon, and it seemed the castle dozed under an unseasonably warm October sun.

Guy de Gervais stepped into the turret room. The door closed behind him instantly, the heavy bar falling across with a decisive thud.

"There, my lord, I have lured you into my web!" Laughing, Magdalen stood with her back against the door. "It is a clever trick, is it not? I discovered it many years ago at Bellair Castle. You must whisper from behind the arras, and the sound carries straight down the passage as if through a hollow tube. I did it once to a scullion, and he ran screaming like a soul in torment, convinced that a spirit was after him." She chuckled. "But you did not think it was a spirit, did you, my lord?"

"No," he agreed affably, "I didn't think it was a spirit." He perched on the deep stone windowsill, his eyes narrowed with amusement. "I realized it was a naughty girl up to mischief."

"Not so," Magdalen denied with a touch of indignation. Guy on occasion seemed to take what she considered a perverse delight in resurrecting old memories. Her fingers worked busily with the hooks of her gown.

"Magdalen, there is no time for this," Guy said, still amused but resignedly aware of something else stirring beneath his amusement.

"Yes, there is," Magdalen asserted in customary fashion. She unfastened the jeweled belt caught under her breasts. "And if there is not, one must make the time. Don't you agree?" The belt dropped to the floor with a muted clatter, and she slipped the opened gown off her shoulders. Soft silken folds fell to her ankles. She wore now only her white lawn undergown that she discarded with the same swift efficiency.

During this disrobing, Guy had not moved from his perch on the windowsill, enjoying his spiraling arousal, feeling the sun warm on the back of his neck, inhaling the scent of Magdalen in the small room, the warm womanly scent of her clothes, her skin, her hair, feasting on the creamy curves of her body. She was a woman to drive a man to the fervid white heat of distraction, and having long recognized his inability to withstand that power, he let it build within him, slow and inexorable.

"If we do not have time for this, I consider it wasteful of you to sit and do nothing." Magdalen crossed the small space to the window. Frowning with concentration, her sharp little teeth closed on her bottom lip, she attacked the great buckle of his belt. His dagger hung in the sheath at his hip and she handled it carefully, her head bent so that the sun drew forth the rich dark depths of her coiled hair.

"I wish you would lower your head," she said. "I cannot remove your collar otherwise. You are too tall for me."

Obligingly, he bent his head so she could lift off the heavy gold-linked collar of rank and office. She unfastened the buttons of his tunic, pushing it off his shoulders. He wore only his shirt beneath, there being no need on a quiet afternoon within the citadel walls for the leather gambeson or chain-mail. Her fingers were deft as they unfastened the lacing of his hose from the eyelet holes in the hem of his shirt. Then the shirt came off to join its fellows on the floor.

Still with the same frown of concentration, Magdalen brushed a finger over his chest, lingering on the narrow white line of an old wound running down his belly. She looked up at him as he still perched immobile, and she smiled a soft, secretive smile before touching his nipples with the tip of her tongue, moist darting touches that shortened his breath and brought the flush of arousal to his skin. Her fingers moved to the unfastened waistband of his hose.

"Boots first, pippin," he said, managing to sound lazily nonchalant.

She nipped his shoulder in swift punishment before dropping to her knees to wrestle with his booted feet that he obligingly held out for her, bracing himself with his hands on the sill at his back as she pulled.

"Stand up," she demanded, returning to his hose. "You are being most vexatious, my lord."

"I had thought I was being entirely accommodating," he protested, standing up as she pushed the hose off his hips. "Does it not look as if I am prepared to accommodate you, madame?" He grinned wickedly at her, pushing the garment off his feet.

Magdalen examined his body with her head consideringly on one side. "I would say so, my lord," she pronounced, then said plaintively, "but when are you going to do something about it? I have done everything so far."

"It's a plan of your making," he informed her. "It seems only right you should be responsible for its conduct." He gestured around the small, round room. It was furnished with a rough plank table and two stools, a wolfskin before the empty hearth. Nothing else. Not, he reflected, that it needed aught else in his present state of excitement. He could imagine a variety of satisfactory ways of managing with what they had, but a devilish impulse led him to see what Magdalen would make of their sparse props.

Her eyes followed his gesture, seeing for the first time the paucity of their surroundings. "The floor?" she suggested tentatively.

He shook his head. "Too hard, pippin."

"The wolfskin?" she tried, but even more tentatively.

"Fleas."

Magdalen was for a moment nonplussed, then deliberately she moved against him, her hands sliding around his body, her flat palms moving in heated circles over his back and buttocks, her lower body pressing against his, her breath warmly whispering over his chest as she nipped and nuzzled with the sureness of one on familiar ground, certain of her ability to produce the desired, expected response.

He held his hands away from her for a moment of aching anticipation, teasing her still with his refusal to take the initiative. He had himself well in hand, knowing that the surrender would be all the more climactic for this present playful denial. Suddenly unsure, Magdalen drew away from him, puzzled. Then she saw his expression, and the hesitation faded from her eyes.

Laughing, he caught her around the waist and swung her onto the windowsill. "Let me show you how loving is to be contrived in such unfavorable surroundings, my impetuous pippin." Taking her face between his hands, he held her head still, bringing his mouth to hers. Her lips parted to welcome the hot thrust of his tongue, her legs curling around his waist, offering her opened body to the thrust of his. She wriggled on the cold, scratchy stone sill, fitting herself to him so that she could move with his rhythm. His hands left her face to support her hips, holding her against him as the passion coiled tight and deep within them both, and when the spring could be wound no tighter, it sprang apart in a sunburst of delight. He held her still against him while their bodies melted together under the sunburst, tension replaced with exquisite languour.

"There should always be time for that," Magdalen murmured when she could speak again. "I think we should make this room ours. I don't think anyone else uses it, and it is such a deserted part of the castle."

He laughed and withdrew from her, lifting her off the sill. "If we are to make a habit of this, then, we should contrive a blanket, or some such. I'm afraid you will become sore and scratched from repeated use of the windowsill." He kissed her swiftly. "But in truth, love, you waylaid me at a most inconvenient time. My men have come in from the countryside with their reports and I must hear them, and then visit the garrison. There is talk of brigands abroad, and the outer fortification is in need of repair."

"Can we not go hawking by the river this evening?" Magdalen slipped her undergown over her head.

"Have you no tasks of your own this afternoon?" Guy fastened his belt, raising an eyebrow at her. Magdalen was well versed in the duties and responsibilities of a chatelaine, her lord's primary assistant in the management of his

vast household, a management Guy was under-
taking for the absent Sieur de Bresse. He had
noticed, however, that there were some tasks
she undertook with more enthusiasm than
others.

In confirmation of this reflection, she sighed
heavily. "Yes, I have, and 'tis one I mislike. The
pantler says that three loaves of bread are missing, and he will have it that one of the serving
maids is responsible. If I cannot solve the mys-
tery, then the matter must go to the seneschal,
who will probably refer it to you in the hall after supper, and a little matter will become a
great one."

Guy nodded. He was the final arbiter on all issues, both domestic and military, affecting the
castle, its inhabitants and the surrounding villages dependent upon it. It was for him to settle
quarrels, dispense justice, bestow rewards and
favors, but he much preferred to leave the minor, day-to-day issues to his household officers.
"Why do you mislike the task?"

"Because I do not believe it is one of the serving maids." She picked up the jeweled belt from
the floor where it lay winking in the sunlight. "I
believe the baker from the town has an arrangement with the guardian of the bread. He supplies less than he is paid for and they share the
profit. But they have both served the household

for so long that no one will believe them dishonest."

"If that is so, then I do not think the matter to be a little one," he said. "I will relieve you of the duty if you wish it."

"I do wish it," she said with a rueful smile. "But I think I must confront the baker and the guardian myself."

Guy laughed, advising, "Do so, but in the company of the seneschal. He will appreciate being involved and his presence will augment your authority . . . and when you have concluded who is responsible, you may leave the administration of justice to me." He tilted her chin and kissed the corner of her mouth. "If I can finish with my reports, we will go hawking before vespers."

He left her then, retracing his steps toward the inner chambers of the castle, where the family apartments were situated over the great hall. In the lord's private study adjoining the big conjugal bedchamber at the heart of the family residence, he found his secretary waiting for him, together with Olivier, whom Guy had left in Calais with the task of discovering what he could of Charles d'Auriac.

Olivier's shrewd black eyes darted hither and thither while he made his report, noticing everything in the instinctive and invaluable way he had. Nothing, however innocuous, escaped him, and he observed his surroundings in the same way whether they were familiar, as now, or quite new to him.

The spy's investigations had taken him to Toulouse, the home of the de Beauregards, and from there to Carcassonne, the fortress monastery that Bertrand de Beauregard held in stewardship for the king of France. Charles d'Auriac's mother had been sister to Isolde de Beauregard. Charles d'Auriac was therefore first cousin to Magdalen de Bresse. Three weeks as scullion in the kitchens of the de Beauregard castles had taught Olivier a great deal. Guy de Gervais listened in growing perturbation.

Olivier told of an urgent summons to the men of the clan, called from their own fiefs to attend their father. He told of the whispers of a failed attempt on the life of Isolde's daughter in Calais, whispers heard behind arras and through oak doors, whispers easily heard by a man who knew where and how to listen. He told of the man, Charles d'Auriac, who had the air of one with a burning purpose, and of Bertrand de Beauregard, uncle of Charles d'Auriac, the patriarch whose own purpose seemed not to mesh with that of the nephew. There had been words spoken in heat, the nephew silenced by the authority of the elder, but Olivier had been unable to discover the nature of the disagreement, except that it had something to do with what had happened at Calais. He knew only that the gathering of the clan, the sons of Bertrand, was to settle the matter.

Anxious to bring this information to his lord, he had left the province of Roussillon before the grand conference and made all speed into Picardy. His dusty clothing and the lines of fatigue, etched sharp around his mouth, were ample evidence of his haste.

"You have done well," Guy said, opening the strongbox on the iron-bound cedar chest. He drew forth a heavy pouch and tossed it to the man, who caught it deftly. Guy smiled, despite his concern over the spy's information. "A good and faithful servant, Olivier. Go to your rest now."

The man went off with his soft, swift tread, and Guy stood frowning, gazing out of the window toward the south, from whence the threat would come . . .

MAGDALEN, MEANWHILE, DECIDED to postpone the vexatious issue of missing loaves of bread and was walking in the orchard. It was hot and sultry, and wasps buzzed busily in and out of the windfalls littering the long grass. The orchard stood close to the outside fortifications of the castle and was surrounded by its own high wall, affording a seclusion hard to come by in the teeming life of a castle that resembled a sizable town in constitution and in its many and varied functions.

She was filled with the wonderful languour of bodily fulfillment, her mind at peace as it gently probed and explored the tangle of love in which she found herself. She knew her husband was not dead. It was a knowledge she no longer reiterated to Guy because it distressed him and cast a cloud over the joy they took in and of each other.

She had not told him either of her growing certainty that she was again with child. The latter fact was a source of secret happiness, one she would keep to herself for a while longer. Only Erin and Margery knew of the lost pregnancy on the ship, and they would keep still tongues in their heads. This child, Guy's child, would take the place of the lost one for the rest of the world, any awkwardness in timing easily glossed over behind these walls and at such a distance from England. John of Gaunt's grandchild would stand heir to the de Bresse fiefdom, and Guy de Gervais's child would bind him absolutely to the child's mother. The residual honor-born doubts Magdalen sensed in Guy beneath the force of the love that held them would lose all strength, becoming mere whimpers with no power to rise up and damage their love.

She knew instinctively it was for her to manage the tangle, that Guy at the moment was moving in the magic world of bewitchment, that he was entranced by her and willing to drift, enthralled; but that once circumstances changed, intruded on the magic world, as they were bound to, then so too would his bewitchment wane. Unless she could find a way to salve his conscience, smooth out his doubts, underpin bewitchment with more solid, tangible ties, she would lose this love that was as it had been since childhood, more than life itself to her. There was love and blood in her hand, mad Jennet had said. Much love: the love of men. If such was her destiny, then she had but begun upon it.

Curiously, these reflections did not disturb her contented languour as she strolled beneath the gnarled fruit trees, gnawing around the maggot holes in a windfallen pear. The daughter of John of Gaunt and Isolde de Beauregard did not doubt her ability to make happen what she wished to happen, what she knew had to happen if her life and that of Guy de Gervais were not to be rendered dross.

THERE WERE FIVE men in the tapestry-hung, windowless inner chamber. There was no fire in the chimney, but torches threw out both light and heat from their wall sconces. One of the men threw off the short cloak he wore over a particolored tunic and reached for the pitcher of mead in the center of the table. He poured the dark, honeyed spirit into a pewter tankard and drank deeply.

"Charles has not convinced me that we gain more by her abduction than by her death."

He was older than the others, his hair and beard grizzled, but his eyes were as gray and the family resemblance as pronounced.

"She is Isolde's daughter," Charles d'Auriac said quietly.

"We know that," said one of the others, Marc, with a snap of impatience.

"I meant, cousin, that she is truly Isolde's daughter," Charles clarified as quietly as before.

There was a short silence in the warm, airless room. "You imply that she could perhaps be . . ." The speaker paused, choosing his words. "She could be used as her mother was?"

"Isolde was never used, Marc," the older man corrected sharply. "She did only what she wished, and in most cases the seductions were entirely of her own making."

"But with Lancaster . . . ?"

"With Lancaster she met treachery." Bertrand de Beauregard, brother of Isolde, spoke the plain truth as he saw it. "We would be revenged upon him for that and do the king's work at the same time. I say she must die."

Charles d'Auriac looked for words. In the face of the elder's pronouncement, rules of submission and courtesy demanded that he yield his own point. He had done so once, agreed to put the matter to arbitration, but he could not yield without one further attempt to bring them to his own viewpoint. Ever since he had seen her, sitting outside the inn at Calais, her image had filled his waking thoughts and disturbed his nights. He had arranged the murder attempt, and if it had succeeded he probably would not have thought again of that mouth, those eyes, the unconscious grace and arrogance of the slim body, the haughty voice, some rare and subtle quality emanating from her that filled a man's head with images of white and tumbling limbs and the hot breath of lust. But she had survived the monkish assault, and now he could not endure the thought of that body laid to waste, that sensual promise crumbled to dust when so much could be made of it and so many could benefit from it.

"My lord," he began. "Consider Isolde resurrected in the shape of her daughter. Her husband is dead. She must know that, for all that it does not suit her father's purpose to have it openly acknowledged at present. Once she is removed from Lancaster's sphere, she will cease to be the glue holding the de Bresse fealty to England. I can think of few more satisfactory revenges against Lancaster than turning his own daughter upon him, remaking her in the shape of the woman he murdered."

"So you would persist in this." Bertrand sat back, stroking his beard. A glimmer lurked in the back of his eyes that encouraged Charles. "And having abducted her, then what would you do with her?"

"Why, wed her, my lord," Charles declared boldly. "Bind her doubly to her mother's family, and then employ her for our own purposes. I believe she has the power, if she is taught to acknowledge it and to use it, to do all and more that her mother did."

"It would seem the girl has captured *you,* Charles." Bertrand smiled slightly. "Do you argue this course because you would bed her yourself?"

"Not just for that," his nephew said. "Although I'll admit I've a powerful lust for her. But that is secondary to what we could do with her once she is under our control."

"There is a certain pleasure, I'll admit, in contemplating such a subtle revenge on Lancaster. To reclaim our own and turn her into the weapon that would foil him."

"Maybe she could be turned into the weapon that destroys him." Gerard de Beauregard spoke for the first time.

"Aye, to assume the task her mother failed to perform." The glimmer in his father's eye flared into a spark. "How, I do not know at this point, since she cannot use with her father the methods by which her mother caught the prince. Lancaster has few scruples, but I do not think he will succumb to incest."

They all laughed, and the atmosphere in the room lightened, legs stretching beneath the table, hands reaching for the pitcher of mead. Charles d'Auriac knew his battle was won.

"If the lady should prove recalcitrant . . ." mused Gerard. "How do we compel her cooperation?"

"There are ways and means." Bertrand shrugged. "I see no difficulty there."

"Or anywhere," Charles said. "I would journey into Picardy immediately, to welcome our kinswoman to France. In the truce existing between our two countries, it would be an entirely appropriate move."

"Indeed." Bertrand rose from the table. His legs cramped rapidly these days. The blood didn't flow as it had, and an old wound in his thigh flared when he sat still for extended periods. He paced the room, one hand caressing the curiously shaped hilt of the dagger in his belt. It was the neck of a sea serpent, a bloodred ruby for the single eye. "And how do you propose dealing with Lord de Gervais? The girl is under his protection, and he is not a man to be easily circumvented, I believe."

"He knows no ill of me," Charles said. "He may have suspicions, but he cannot turn away a visiting kinsman on a mission of courtesy in a time of truce. I will do what I can to lull his suspicions and will gain the confidence of the lady. The abduction will wait until he is away from the castle." His eyes lost their focus for a minute. "There are many things that could call him away . . . a brigand attack on the towns falling under de Bresse suzerainty would not be unusual, or a summons from his own overlord, perhaps, or an invitation from a neighboring fief. That is the least of our difficulties, I believe."

"Then we will leave the matter in your hands, Charles." Bertrand went to the door. "Draw on the support of your cousins as you see the need. And bring Magdalen of Lancaster to the fortress at Carcassonne as expeditiously as you may. This family has waited overlong for its revenge."

The door closed on the patriarch, and the four younger men relaxed visibly. "He will not rest easy in his grave if the wrong done the de Beauregards by Lancaster is not redressed," Marc said. "But you are drawn to the woman, cousin. Is it bedsport she promises?" A laugh ran around the table, but it was not one in which their cousin participated.

"Something more than that," he said, considering his words. "Something that promises a man fleshly dissolution. Unless I much mistake, she has *le diable au corps,* and I would sample it, my friends."

"Dangerous sport," muttered Philippe de Beauregard. "It was said her mother had that mark of the devil upon her, and those who fell into temptation burned with the taint as if it were acid."

"Her mother was a dangerous woman." Charles d'Auriac rose from the table. "Dangerous because she bore no man's yoke. I intend that Magdalen of Lancaster shall bear my yoke and that of her maternal family. We will harness the power and the devil's mark to our own mills." He went to the door. "We will talk again when I return from Picardy. I will know more then how to proceed in this affair."

Seven

MAGDALEN WAS BORED. She nibbled on an almond cake and wished her neighbor at the high table would divert some of his attention to her. Guy de Gervais was playing host to a large party of traveling knights who had sought lodging beneath his roof, and the feast prepared for them had been going on for an eternity, it seemed. Her head ached a little from the wine and the heat of bodies and the clamor of voices from the crowded hall. Immediately below the dais on which she sat in the center of the table beside the man who stood proxy for the lord of the castle, the lesser knights of this household and of the traveling party were gathered, squires and pages beyond them until at the rear of the hall were the jostling noisy groups of the humbler members of the household.

There were no highborn women among the travelers, so Magdalen's was the only female presence on the dais. This relieved her of the burden of entertaining but consequently left her with little amusement. She could barely hear the minstrels from the gallery, so loud was the noise from the hall, and the conversation around her

was all of the expedition that united their guests.
They were on their way to Italy in support of
the Duke of Anjou's claim to the throne of
Naples. The level of excitement was growing as
the level of wine in the pitchers sank. War was
the only work understood by knights, and in the
absence of the fighting between England and
France, some other righteous cause had to employ their swords and lances. Guy was being encouraged to join them, and it was fairly clear to
Magdalen that his present occupation as protector and counselor for a lone and rather youthful
chatelaine was considered a poor substitute and
an unconvincing excuse.

Her armless chair was so close to Guy's that
the tiniest movement would bring her thigh
against his. The realization brought the devil's
gleam to her eyes. She slipped one hand beneath
the concealing folds of the heavy damask table-
cloth. Her fingers trailed over his thigh, and she
felt the hard muscles clench involuntarily.
Mischievously, she explored further, smiling innocently around the table as his body came to
life.

Guy was in something of a quandary. He
wanted to laugh as much as he wanted to luxu-
riate in the wickedly skilled caress, but neither
response struck him as appropriate in the present circumstances. He reached under the table,

firmly grasped the wandering wrist, and placed her hand in her own lap.

Magdalen sipped her wine, contemplating her next move. This little game would certainly enliven an otherwise tedious suppertime. She moved her foot in its gold embroidered velvet slipper sideways, brushing up against his leg, curling her toes against one iron-hard calf. There was no immediate response, so she increased the pressure, her toes dancing, sliding up into the hollow behind his knee. Her smile broadened as he drew a quick breath and moved his leg away. Her foot followed. She forgot about their table companions, the scurrying varlets, the attentive squires and pages behind every chair in her concentration on this delicious play.

Guy could not move his leg farther without involving his other neighbor in Magdalen's mischief, and the thought of how Sieur Roland de Courtrand would react to a little intimate footwork from his host beneath the table didn't bear thinking about if he wished to keep a straight face. He held himself very still and inquired casually of Sieur de Courtrand if he and his companions would be interested in a boar hunt on the morrow. The question fortunately elicited a flood of inebriated reminiscences of past hunts, and Guy was able surreptitiously to turn his attention to Magdalen, who was clearly demanding it. Nonchalantly, he closed what little space there was between their chairs.

He had begun to notice something different about her these days. It was indefinable, a softness, as if her edges were slightly smudged; an aura seemed to hang over her, translucent as a pearl yet imparting a glowing warmth from deep within her. She was as mischievous and as flatly assertive as ever, as joyfully sensual as she had ever been, but with this other dimension, one he sensed was more pronounced when she was alone, as if she were contemplating some secret and private source of contentment.

He moved his hand beneath the table and pinched her thigh, hard enough to make her jump. She looked up at him in startled reproach and rubbed her thigh, but he merely smiled blandly and turned back to Sieur de Courtrand.

Magdalen was reflecting on her next move when she felt something slipping beneath her. She sat frozen for a second, then, less disciplined than Guy, gave a little choke of laughter as she realized it was his hand worming its way sideways under her bottom. The long, voluminous dagged sleeve of his gown fell casually against the full silken skirts of her cotehardie, concealing his fingers' busy work. She wriggled, initially in mock protest, and then with more purpose as she realized how her movements would mesh with his. Her tongue touched her lips and she reached again for her wine cup, moving her tingling body deliberately as her excitement grew and the faces around her blurred with the slurring of voices.

Guy continued to discuss boar hunting with his neighbor even while he brought the utterly silent Magdalen to fever pitch and kept his own arousal well in check. He felt her grow rigid against his hand, her breath suspended for one climactic moment, then she relaxed on a tiny sobbing breath, and he slipped his hand out from under her.

"A lesson well learned, I trust," he said into her ear. Her face was most becomingly flushed, her eyes extremely bright, her lips moist and red, and his own wanting hit him with the force of a mace.

Magdalen pushed back her chair. "I beg you will excuse me, *mes sieurs*. I will leave you to your wine." And she fled the hall to cool her fevered blood in the evening air.

She hurried across the inner court and through the gate into the outer ward. The *place d'armes* was quiet, the garrison gone to its evening rest except for the sentries marching the battlements and the watchers in the four bell-towers. Battlements were no longer forbidden territory, and she made her way up the steep stone staircase to the broad parapet overlooking the town at the bottom of the hill and the plain and forests beyond—the land of wide spaces, perhaps, that mad Jennet had seen in the water all those years ago.

The Castle de Bresse was built on the hilltop, its massive donjon and family residence in the center, outbuildings sprawling across the enclosures up to the outer fortified wall. A deep moat encircled this wall; the only access to the castle lay across the drawbridge and through the portcullis. It was difficult to imagine an attack succeeding on such a fortification, Magdalen thought, leaning her arms on the parapet. Beyond the moat on the hillside were dotted peasant cottages with their little plots of land, and at the base of the hill the town of Bresse, itself fortified by the castle at its back and walls on three sides.

She could hear the carousing from the great hall behind her growing more intemperate. The torches of the sentries flared in a sudden gust of wind from the dark plain ahead. The cottages and town were all in darkness, safe in the knowledge that they were watched over by their liege lord, protected by his defenses.

The sky was overcast, no moon and just the north star pricking faintly through the clouds. Magdalen shivered suddenly in her silk gown.

She had left the overheated hall without a cloak, and it was already the beginning of November, the sultry summery weather of October almost a memory. She bade good night to the sentry as he passed her on his rounds and went back down to the outer ward. As she passed the granary, the sounds of scuffling reached her, and she noticed the door was ajar. She paused, curious. There was a distinctly female squeak and a giggle, followed by a deeper chuckle and more scuffling.

They were obviously enjoying themselves. Magdalen went swiftly on her way. The conduct of the castle women was her responsibility, and she should have descended upon the two play-fellows in righteous wrath, but she had no stomach for a role that ill suited her in her present position. Bastard children were absorbed easily enough in the castle community, which maintained a pragmatic acceptance of human frailty while condemning it vociferously from within the chapel walls.

The doors to the great hall stood open, and the sounds of revelry showed no sign of abating. She looked inside and saw that the scene had degenerated since her departure. The Lord de Gervais did not normally permit the unruly public conduct all too often sanctioned by others, but this evening he had obviously decided to indulge his guests and therefore his own household. He still sat at the high table, his hands clasped around his wine cup, his eye roaming over the disorderly scene below, where dancing and singing and a certain amount of purposeful chasing was taking place around the tables. His guests were for the most part occupied with wine and those women who had shown themselves willing for a little knightly sport and whatever rewards might then ensue.

Magdalen stood watching, fascinated despite herself. She did not know, as Guy did, that there were times when a certain amount of license was necessary if men were to have an outlet for energies usually exercised in battle. A species of battle was taking place in the hall, and he knew it would release the tensions developed through two months of relative inaction, much as cupping a man released the bad humors in the blood. They would all be cleansed in the morning, if somewhat the worse for wear.

He looked up abruptly, sensing Magdalen's presence before he saw her, standing wide-eyed at the far end of the hall. His hand moved in a swift, imperative gesture of dismissal. For a minute she hesitated, then with obvious reluctance turned and left. She still could not suffer his displeasure with equanimity and would do nothing to court it, frequently curbing the in-

herent impulses of a nature impatient of restraint. If Guy was aware of his power in this respect, he never took advantage of it.

She climbed the outside staircase to the second
floor of the vast residence. Her own apartments,
since she could not take up her abode in the conjugal apartments that naturally were occupied by
the proxy lord of the Castle de Bresse, were in
the women's wing of the castle. Her bedchamber
was lavishly furnished with a feather bed,
wardrobe, woven floor covering, and tapestry
wall hangings. The privy chamber adjoining
contained the commode and the curtained bath-
tub, but more important for Magdalen's purposes, a concealed door behind the tapestry
which led into one of the inner passageways that
ran within the thick stone walls. The castle was
riddled with such secret doors and narrow passageways, providing a clandestine network for
travelers who wished not to make their internal
journeys public.

Erin and Margery were waiting up for her,
dozing beside the fire. "There's much carousing,
lady," Erin said, yawning as she stood up. "It's
not like my lord to permit it."

"No," agreed Magdalen. "But he has guests,
and maybe it is appropriate hospitality for
them." She stood still as the two women undressed her, then drew a fur-trimmed velvet

robe around her. "Brush my hair well, Erin." She sat on a low stool before the fire.

"Of course, my lady." Erin smiled as she unfastened the dainty silver fillet that held the rich dark coils in place and removed the silver pins. She knew well why the Lady Magdalen wished her hair brushed to a burnished glory. The dusky mass fell almost to the floor, and she drew the brush through it with long leisurely strokes.

"The sickness has not troubled you these last days, my lady." Margery turned from the wardrobe where she was hanging the silk gown in its cedar-fragrant depths.

"No, I think it has passed." These two knew of her pregnancy, and knew whose child she bore. But they had accompanied her from Bellair Castle when she had first left it as an eleven-year-old child, and Magdalen was sure of their loyalty. "Will you bring me a cup of hypocras, Margery? Then you may go to your beds. I'll not be needing you further this night.' "

Margery curtsied and went off to the kitchens, connected to the residence and the great hall by a covered passageway. The kitchen was emptied of its usual bustling cooks and servitors, the license in the hall spreading throughout the domestic staff. The fires were neglected, burning low without the attentions of the potboys, who had taken advantage of the absence of supervision and run off about their own business. Margery prepared the hot spiced wine, kicking impatiently at a brindle puppy wandering in from the court in search of scraps. She was anxious to join the merriment herself and hastened back to her lady's chamber with the steaming pewter tankard.

Erin was as eager as Margery for the promised entertainment, and the two women needed no encouragement to leave their mistress sitting before the fire with her drink, her hair gleaming in the candlelight. And they needed no persuasion to accept that they need not look in upon her unless she called, which would most probably not be until the morning.

Magdalen slipped into a dreamy trance, sipping the hypocras, stretching her toes to the fire, wondering how long it would be before Guy decided he had satisfied the demands of courtly etiquette and could abandon his guests to their excesses for the night.

When the sounds from the hall below seemed to have muted, she lit a taper from the candle and slipped from her room by the concealed door, skimming down the long dark passageway, her taper dimly flickering but providing comforting illumination. Doors were set into the passage wall at various intervals, doors opening behind tapestries or within the garderobes to give access to the secrets of other chambers. The door opening onto the lord's chamber was not hidden from within, since the entire network of concealment had been designed for his own use by the father of Guy's half brother, Jean de Bresse, when he had constructed the castle.

Magdalen listened and could hear no sounds from within. She lifted the oiled latch gently, pushed the door open a fraction. The room was empty as she had expected. Guy's pages and squire were attending him in the hall, and he would command only one of them to light him to bed when he chose to come. She slid into the room, drawing the door closed behind her. It fitted snugly against the wall. She tossed her taper into the fire and drew the rich velvet curtains around the great feather bed. Then she slipped into the dark cave, discarded her robe, and huddled beneath the heavy covers, waiting.

She must have slept for a while, because the sound of voices from beyond the bedcurtains startled her, yet she had heard no one come into the room. She lay still, listening. Guy was talking to young Stefan as the page helped him out of his clothes and into his long robe. The conversation dealt with affairs in the great hall and contained some pithy advice for the lad on the subject of temperance. Magdalen sat up and hugged her knees.

When Stefan went to draw back the bedcurtains, Guy shook his head. "No, lad, leave them. Get you to bed now." The significance of the enclosed bed had not escaped him and as the door closed on the sleepy page, he sat down by the fire to await developments.

Magdalen's head appeared from between the curtains. "I give you good night, my lord."

"And I you, my lady," he responded courteously.

Magdalen regarded him quizzically. "Are you drunken, my lord?"

"Not in the least."

"Everyone else is," she observed.

"Sots, all of them," he agreed. "I had thought you long gone to your bed."

"As indeed I am, sir." She pushed aside the curtains and jumped lightly to the floor. "If you are intending to sit up all night, then I must join you."

He opened his arms to her and she nestled onto his lap, warm and soft and naked, her head resting on his shoulder. He ran his hands over her in a leisurely caress, then caught her chin and lowered his mouth to hers in a kiss as leisurely as the caress.

"You were very wicked this evening, Magdalen."

"Yes, wasn't I?" she agreed with a chuckle. "But not near as wicked as you, my Lord de Gervais."

He laughed against her mouth. "It was a lesson most richly deserved."

"And most richly enjoyed."

"I believe so," he concurred solemnly, shifting her slightly on his knee so that he could explore more thoroughly the luxurious curves of her body, the silken skin rippling beneath his touch. Her hair was fragrant with the scent of apple blossom from the distilled flower water her women used to wash it, and the perfume mingled headily with the honeyed hints of burgeoning arousal. She arched and purred, all sensual promise, as always instantly, supremely responsive.

"I have something to tell you," she murmured, moving her mouth to his ear, her tongue a hot, moist lance darting within. He groaned softly, his body hardening beneath the warm, seductive weight of her.

"Then tell me quickly, love, before I lose the ability to hear anything."

"I am with child." The words emerged in a whispered rush against his neck.

His hands stilled. So this was what was different about her, that indefinable quality he had noticed in the last weeks.

"Does it not please you?" She looked up at him, anxiety in her voice and eyes.

On one level it afforded him a sweeter pleasure than any he had ever known. But on another . . . He put the other from him. "Yes, my love, it pleases me." He smiled reassuringly, brushing a dark swatch of her hair from her forehead. "I should have expected it, of course, but for some reason I didn't."

"It must have happened at the very beginning," she said. "Erin believes the child will come in May or June."

He said nothing for a minute, calculating as she had done earlier that the child she had lost would have been born in March or April. With a little management, this baby could be passed off as the heir of Edmund de Bresse. The thought brought him neither pleasure nor relief.

"Are you well?" he asked.

"Wonderfully." She stretched against him, her arms sliding around his neck. "I am most wonderfully content to be carrying your child."

He allowed the soft assertion of her love to embrace him, to seep into him, to bring him a joy deep enough to overcome the sorrow he felt for all that could not be. He stroked her back, thinking of the perilous nature of childbearing, of that dreadful storm-tossed night on the ship. "You must look after yourself, pippin. There's to be no more riding to hounds, no long journeying."

"But I am perfectly well and strong, not even sick anymore." She sat up. "I cannot retire to bed for six months, Guy."

"You must take no risks after the last time," he said, sitting back, holding her hips lightly. "God knows it is a hazardous enough business at the best of times, and this is soon after you miscarried."

"I wish I had not told you if you are going to fret me with cosseting."

"Sweetheart, I will not cosset you, but I *will* forbid unnecessary exertion."

"But how are you to know what is unnecessary? What do men know of these matters?"

"Quite enough," he declared. "And what we do not know we can guess. Now, I will hear no more argument."

Magdalen chewed her thumbnail, regarding him with a frown, half vexed and half touched by this concern which she sensed was going to prove both confining and exasperating. Then she shrugged. This was hardly a good moment for argument, and there were much pleasanter ways to occupy themselves. She was about to initiate one of the ways when the night was shattered by a frenzied pealing.

"The tocsin," she said, even as Guy with a muttered oath lifted her from his knee and stood up. "They are ringing the tocsin."

"Get back to your own apartments," he commanded, striding to the door. "Immediately."

"Is it an attack?"

"Go!" The sounds of running feet came from the corridor outside.

Magdalen just had time to seize her robe from the bed and leap through the door into the private passage before the door to Guy's chamber burst open to admit his squire and pages.

"My lord . . . my lord . . . they are ringing the tocsin," Stefan gasped. "It is a brigand attack on the town."

"Cease your gabble and fetch my lord's gambeson," the squire said brusquely. "And you, Theo, bring the chainmail."

Geoffrey was a squire to gladden the most exacting heart, Guy reflected, thankful that he did not have to take his pages to task himself while his mind was whirling. Of all the damnable nights to have picked, when half the castle was in no fit state to take up arms and ride abroad. At least the men-at-arms in the garrison would be sober. They had not been given permission to join in the debauchery and knew full well the harsh penalties for disobedience in such a matter.

Magdalen flew down the passage to her own apartments, casting aside the robe and rummaging in the wardrobe for her clothes. Erin and Margery, flushed with more than excitement, came running in answer to her summons.

"It's an attack on the town, they are saying, my lady," they both gasped. "In the middle of the night!"

"Hardly Christian," Magdalen said dryly. "Help me dress. There will be much to do before this night is over . . . No, not that gown, 'tis too fine for the work we will have to do. Bring me the brown wool."

The brown wool gown was of simple cut and adorned only by the silver belt clasped at her hip. Her little jeweled dagger hung in its sheath, beside it a velvet pouch containing such useful articles as scissors, needles, and the key to the strong-box where her jewelry was kept. She took the cloak Erin handed her and hurried from her apartment by the public way, down the outside stairs and into the inner court. All was bustle and confusion as people were hauled from stupor and dissipation by the clarion call of the tocsin, still rending the night.

In the *place d'armes,* there was more order, the

scene brilliantly lit with flaming torches, the men-at-arms mounted, archers in neat ranks behind them. Magdalen noted that their guests were all there, armed and mounted on their destriers, the call to arms and the smell of battle clearly potent enough to dispel the effects of the evening. Standards snapped in the sharpening wind, and she saw Guy instantly, his jupon with the Gervais dragon over his armor, his visor for the moment up as he surveyed the scene. The standards of Gervais and Bresse flew at the head of his own knights.

She wanted to go to him, to offer him a word of encouragement, a prayer for his safety, but she knew he would not welcome such womanly weakness. She could sense, even at a distance, the warrior's excitement at the prospect of battle. It was an excitement that transcended the tenderness of the lover. His life was dedicated to this and to nothing else, and it would be so until he met his death.

He dropped his visor, the heralds blew the battle cry, and Guy de Gervais, his knights at his back, rode beneath the portcullis, the iron-shod hooves of his massive destrier ringing on the drawbridge.

Magdalen ran up the staircase to the battlements, watching the thundering force, the bugles calling their eerily magnificent call, descend upon those who dared to attack the dependents of the suzerainty of de Bresse. The drawbridge was raised when the last archer had crossed, the portcullis lowered, securing the castle from the possibility of invasion in the absence of its defenders. Smoke from the town filled the air, and she could hear screams and cries and the thud of the bombard against the town walls.

Abruptly, she turned away and went back to the outer ward. She had her own work to do, and there was little point speculating on what was happening outside the castle. The great hall still bore the evidence of the night's excesses, tables upturned, wine spilled on the rushes, dogs nosing for scraps. But the seneschal had already begun to gather the sleepy, drunken varlets together.

"We will need water, seneschal," Magdalen said, going over to him. "Hot water in abundance."

"Aye, my lady, I will have order sent to the kitchens." The seneschal looked rather pale around the gills himself, Magdalen noted, but he was doing his best to supervise the clearing of the hall to receive the returning warriors, who would need water and space to remove their armor and tend to what minor hurts they might have garnered.

Major hurts would be the province of the infirmary, and Magdalen hastened there next. She

was relieved to see that Master Elias, the apothecary, had obviously not joined in the evening's
dissolution. He greeted her briskly, indicated the
rows of pallets, the piles of bandages, the oils and
salves, the simmering cauldrons on the fires at
each end of the long room. Her supervision of
the arrangements made to receive the returning
force was unquestioned. It was the task of a
chatelaine, and she had grown up in the border
castle of a Lord Marcher with the example of
Lady Elinor of Bellair before her.

Satisfied that all was in order, she returned to
her watch upon the battlements. The screams
from the town had ceased, although a pall of
smoke still lay heavily in the graying light. Faint
sounds of steel upon steel floated in the dawn
air, but they came from the plain beyond the
town. The brigands had clearly been driven off.
Had they not expected such a sizable defensive
force? Perhaps, in the usual manner of these
wandering bands, they were satisfied with seiz-
ing what they could before being forced to
retreat.

Magdalen stood watching as dawn broke fully
and she could look down on the town and make
out that the north wall had been breached by
the bombard. If the brigands had entered the
town, there had been ample cause for screaming. Later, she would visit the town and see

what succor could be provided to the townsfolk
from the castle supplies, but for now she could
think only of Guy's return.

It was full morning, however, before she
could see the moving mass of horsemen on the
plain below, growing more identifiable as they
approached the town. They were moving in orderly fashion, stragglers, walking wounded, and
litter bearers protected by a group of men-at-
arms. The bugle called in the still morning air,
the call of victory. The standards all flew
proudly as the party ascended the hill and the
portcullis was raised and the drawbridge lowered, and they filed into the *place d'armes.*

Guy de Gervais rode at the head, his natural
advantages of height and breadth accentuated by
his erect bearing. Magdalen drew a deep,
steadying breath as she watched him ride into
the *place d' armes,* then she sped down the staircase, slowing on the bottom step to walk to his
stirrup with the stately, measured pace of the
chatelaine.

"I give thanks for your deliverance, my lord.
And thanks for your protection." The ritual
words came easily to her tongue, but they were
invested with so much more than ritual as she
looked up at him. His visor was one more
pushed back, and the bright blue eyes scanned
her face, assessing the effects of her vigil. She

took the cup handed to her by a page and held it up for him.

"My thanks, lady," he said quietly, and drank the stirrup cup before riding to the mounting block and swinging his cumbersomely clad body from the great height of his destrier.

Magdalen went into the hall, waiting to receive the knights and their attendants as they came within. The women of the castle were waiting to assist them with hot water as they stripped off armor and the clothes beneath, to proffer the cups of mulled wine to invigorate tired blood and the fragrant oils and salves to soothe bruised muscles.

Magdalen moved among them until Guy came into the hall. Then she went purposefully toward him. "I will attend my lord," she said to the page who came forward. "If you will assist him to remove his armor." It was her duty, as lady of the castle, to attend the man who had defended her, her property, and her vassals. "But first do you fetch me the oils."

"You would be better in bed," Guy said as the page departed on his errand. He discarded his helmet. "And I do not think this is work for you." He gestured to the crowded hall, where bare-chested men, their hose unlaced, were receiving the ministrations of the attendant women and pages.

"I believe it to be so," she attested quietly. "It was not a work from which the Lady Elinor turned. Why should I?"

"The Lady Elinor attended her brother," he reminded her with a weary sigh. "You would be expected to attend your husband."

"You stand in the place of my husband," she returned with the same quiet determination. "If you will not accomplish this work here in the public hall, then let us repair to your chamber and I will attend you there."

Guy looked at her, and a slight smile touched his eyes despite his weariness. Magdalen was at her most determined, again and, in truth, he could not dispute her logic. No one would question the rightness of her attentions, but they must take place here in the hall with the rest. He removed his jupon. "As you wish, my lady."

She gave him a little nod and beckoned one of the serving wenches. "Bring hot water for my lord."

As always, she took delight in the lean hard body, the breadth of chest, the swell of muscle in thigh and arm, but she gave no indication of her inordinate pleasure in performing the ritual ministrations, readying the hot, wet cloths to cleanse and moisten the skin in preparation for the oils, massaging the oils into muscle and sinew with all the strength she could muster.

"There, my lord." Slightly breathless, she stepped back from him. Tiny beads of perspiration glistened on her brow, witness to the heat in the hall and her effortful completion of her self-appointed tasks. "You are eased, I trust."

"On the contrary, lady," he murmured. "You have merely created tensions where there were none before."

"For shame, sir," she chided, her eyes sparkling for all their tiredness. "After a night of battle, I do not believe you have strength for aught but rest."

"Oh, ye of little faith," he mocked, putting on his shirt again and beginning to lace his hose. "But it's certainly time *you* sought your bed."

"My work is not done, my lord." She wiped her oily hands on a damp cloth before passing her forearm across her brow. "There is meat and drink to be served to the defenders of this castle."

"But not by you," he said. "You have kept vigil all night."

"I am not alone." She gestured around the teeming hall. "I dare swear there is not a soul in the castle who has had rest this night."

He regarded her with a slight frown. It was unlike Magdalen to offer him argument, although he knew her more then capable of it. "I would like you to go to bed," he said slowly.

"And have me renege on my duties?" she said. "I am chatelaine of this castle, sir."

"And I am lord of this castle," he declared. "And as such I excuse you from your tasks and bid you seek your bed."

Magdalen stood irresolute. She felt the need to complete her work in the hall as a personal imperative. It was not right that she should absent herself before all was properly ordered for the comfort of those who had defended her and her vassals this night. But as always, she shrank from incurring Guy's displeasure.

"I am not in the least weary," she ventured. "I would wish to finish what I started."

He looked at the tired eyes, the smudged purple shadows in the hollows beneath them. There was a translucency to her pallor that reminded him suddenly of Gwendoline, and he was touched with the old spur of fear. "You will oblige me in this," he said in a tone he had used with her but once before, and that long ago. He looked around the hall. "Erin! Margery!"

The two women left their tasks and hastened to answer the summons. "Escort your lady to her chamber and put her to bed," he directed. "Tend her well. Her condition ill fits her for a night's vigil."

"Yes, lord." The two curtsied. "I will prepare

a bowl of white bread and curds," Erin said. "Come, my lady."

Even had Magdalen wished to continue the argument, it was inconceivable that she do so in the presence of her women. Magdalen went with them without a backward glance, and Guy stood reflectively, regretting his flash of harshness. He understood why she had wished to discharge her responsibilities, and he gave her credit for it. If she had not been pregnant, he would have encouraged her, but suddenly she had become acutely vulnerable in his eyes, the focus of all his fears, the living reminder of his helplessness in the face of Gwendoline's agonized wasting. He would not lose Magdalen to the inherent perils of womanhood, not if extra vigilance and care could ensure her health and safety.

Magdalen said little as Erin and Margery put her to bed, hearing but not responding to their excited chatter and speculation as to the night's battle and present conditions in the town. The women put her silence down to fatigue, and in truth she was not sorry to sink into the feathered softness of her bed, her belly soothed with the bowl of curds and white bread sweetened with honeycomb. The sun shone through her casement onto her pillow, but when Erin went to draw the hangings around the bed, she told her to leave them open. There was something pleasant and comforting about lying in warmth and softness with the bright security of daylight and the ordinary sounds of castle life reaching her in muted busyness.

It was midafternoon when she awoke with a wonderful sense of well-being, her body warm and lethargic, her limbs heavy with relaxation. The sun still shone, and she could hear the call of the bugle from the garrison court sounding the change of sentries. Sitting up, she reached for the bell that would bring her women to her.

"Ah, you are awake, my lady." Erin bustled over to the bed bearing a tray. "I have brought you broth and a manchet of bread. You need to keep up your strength. My lord says we are to have the most particular care for you."

Magdalen remembered for the first time her grievance of the morning. She sighed. It was clearly going to be as bad if not worse than she had feared. "My lord is overly concerned," she said, taking the tray. "I would have you temper his instructions with common sense." She sipped appreciatively at the broth, rich with oxtail.

"My lady, I dare not," Erin said candidly. "He was most precise in his instructions. He bids you attend him in his study when you are risen," she added, going over to the wardrobe. "Which gown will you wear?"

Magdalen considered. "Are the knight travelers still with us?"

"Aye, my lady, but my lord has given order that he and the guests will sup alone in the great hall this even."

"Then it matters little what gown I wear," Magdalen said, a shade tartly. Lord de Gervais clearly intended that she should spend the remainder of the day and evening in restful seclusion.

Dressed in a plain gown of apple-green linen, a simple braided girdle at her waist, she took the public corridor to the lord's study.

Stefan opened the door at her knock. "I bid you good day, my lady." He bowed.

"Good day, Stefan." She smiled at the lad, who was no more than twelve. "You acquitted yourself well in the fighting last night, I understand."

Stefan blushed. It had been his first engagement, and he was still unsure whether the heart-stopping terror he had felt for one dreadful moment marked him forever as an irredeemable coward.

"You may leave us," Guy de Gervais said. He was standing by the hearth, one arm resting on the carved mantel, one foot on the andiron. He smiled at Magdalen as she stepped into the room. Stefan closed the door behind him.

"You slept well?" He beckoned her over to him.

"Yes, I thank you, my lord." She came to stand in front of him.

He took her face between his hands, examining it carefully, running a fingertip beneath her now unshadowed eyes. "You are angry with me, pippin," he said, still holding her face.

Magdalen found to her surprise that she was, if not angry, definitely annoyed. "I understand you would sup alone with your guests this even." Her tone was stiff.

He nodded. "I did not receive the impression that you enjoyed their company last night. I thought to relieve you of it today."

A tinge of color appeared on her cheekbones. "Was that the only reason?"

"What other should there be?"

"I had thought perhaps you would recommend I spend the evening in my bed," she said. "You seem to feel it is the best place for me for the next six months."

"Ah, Magdalen!" He couldn't help laughing and bent to kiss the aggrieved pout from her mouth. She responded as always without reservation, utterly direct and without artifice, her annoyance slipping from her as if it had never been.

He held her against him, feeling the warm

throbbing life of her, so precious and so fragile, even as he felt her power, the paradoxical power of the same womanhood that rendered her vulnerable. He drew back from her.

"You must indulge me, sweetheart. I was peremptory this morning and I will try not to be so again, but I will not permit you to take any risks with your health at this time."

Magdalen sighed and shook her head in resignation. She loved Guy de Gervais and would not cause him pain. If she must submit to his excessively solicitous protection to secure his peace of mind, then she supposed she would do so.

"I shall expect more of your company, my lord, if I am to be deprived of my usual pursuits. If I must sit sewing fine seams instead of going abroad, then you must find the means to entertain me."

Her mouth curved in a smile of such invitation and promise it would deprive a man of breath, and Guy de Gervais was aware again of the uneasy sense of bewitchment, of losing himself, his direction, the core of his soul in the magic she conjured. For a minute, he wanted to fight it, but it was only a minute . . . and the surrender was as sweet as he had known it would be.

Eight

Charles d'Auriac saw the commanding edifice of the Castle de Bresse long before the castle's inhabitants were aware of the approach of the party. Apart from the cooks, laundresses, chaplains, and general attendants necessary for comfortable travel, the company consisted of the Sieur d'Auriac, three knights banneret of his household, their squires and pages, and a small troop of mounted archers. Enough men to ensure their protection on the journey but not enough to appear threatening—just sufficient for a courtesy visit to a kinswoman.

He drew rein, looking across the plain to his destination. It was early afternoon, but the December sky was lowering, promising an advanced dusk. They could not travel beyond dusk, and he was trying to decide whether to hasten the pace now and knock upon his cousin's gates in the exigency of travelers about to be benighted, or whether he should seek lodging from the next hostelry and make a ceremonial arrival in the morning.

On the whole, he favored the latter course as

having more grace and consequence. But against that he must weigh his overweening desire to see his cousin again. Would she be as he remembered? Would he feel again the murky depths of a serpentine lust when he looked into those gray eyes, superficially like his own but eyes like her mother's, eyes to draw a man to perdition; that full passionate mouth, the lips that he would crush like ripe strawberries beneath his own mouth; the supple body, soft yet hinting of a writhing promise . . .

No, he would wait. The decision made itself even as his body hardened under the mental indulgence of lust. Too precipitate an arrival might give the wrong impression, and he was not prepared to put a foot wrong. Too much was at stake.

His troop received with relief the information that they were to stop for the night at the next monastery, convent, or hostelry offering adequate lodging. The journey from Toulouse to Picardy was a long one for winter travel, and they had pressed themselves to make good time along roads growing wetter and muddier as they left the soft southern climes for the gray, drizzle-ridden northern lands. The nights were cold, the days wet, the climate inhospitable for those accustomed to the silvery glimmer of olive groves, the lush green of vineyards, the distant sense of blue seas, the sandy mountain soil of Roussillon.

At dusk, they sought hospitality of the sisters at the convent at Compiegne, ten miles from their destination. Charles d' Auriac went to his chaste rest in one of the private chambers of the guest hall set aside for visitors of rank, secure in the knowledge that he and his party would arrive at the Castle de Bresse by midmorning and he would sit down to dinner in the company of his cousin, who would not this time run from him, who would not this time offer him discourtesy, who would be obliged by the rules of hospitality and kinship to offer him all due reverence and welcome.

IT WAS STILL dark when Magdalen awoke, a fact which gave her great satisfaction. Her bedfellow continued to sleep and did not stir when she slipped from the bed and ran to the casement. There was just a hint of lightening in the square of darkness but no sounds of stirring from castle and garrison as yet. The bell for prime would not ring, she calculated, for at least another half hour. Which meant that she had won and they would go hawking along the riverbank.

She lit a candle from the ashy embers of the

fire and threw more sticks upon the coals, then tiptoed back to the bed and gently shook the sleeper's shoulder. "My lord? My lord, I am awake betimes and we are to go hawking."

Guy opened one eye in the light of the candle she held above him. "Come back to bed," he said.

"No, my lord. You promised that if I awoke before prime, then we should go. And I have awakened."

Guy opened the other eye and decided reluctantly that Magdalen spoke the truth. "Come back to bed," he repeated drowsily.

Magdalen, half laughing, half impatient, stamped one bare foot in frustration. "No, for if I do, you know what will happen and then the bell for prime will ring and you will say that I was not up betimes."

"A kiss," Guy said.

Magdalen shook her head. "No, for it will lead to other things. Please get up, Guy. I do so want to go out. I have been immured in the castle for a whole week while you have been away, and you promised."

Her eyes were eloquent with urgency and appeal, her lips slightly parted in her eagerness. With a swift movement, Guy reached up, caught her around the waist, and pulled her down hard upon him.

"Caught you," he declared with some satisfaction, laughing into the indignant face above him. "Now I will have that kiss, lady. A week's deprivation works ill for me also."

"But you promised, and now you will be forsworn," she protested, trying to move her head away. He cupped her face firmly and held her still. "You will stand as a faithless perjurer, my lord!"

"Not so," he said, drawing her face down to his. "We will go when I have had my kiss."

Magdalen sighed and yielded, her body softening against his, her lips warmly pliant, her tongue lightly probing. She moved seductively beneath the caressing hands that explored, rediscovered as if he had eyes in his fingertips. But when his knee pressed upward, nudging her thighs apart, she wriggled sideways with a protesting chuckle. "I said you would not be satisfied with a kiss."

"Oh, so you would withhold your favors, would you, lady?" With a threatening growl, he lunged for her as she slid off the bed. "Come back here."

"No." She danced away from him. "I would go hawking, sir. And you must come with me if you would not be forsworn."

Guy regarded her with desirous amusement as she stood well away from the bed, her breasts rising and falling swiftly with her exertions and determination, her hair tumbling, dark and rich, down her back, falling across her shoulders to lie against the creamy whiteness of her skin, her lips rosy and eager, her eyes alight with a resolution that, strong though it was, could not completely mask the spark of arousal engendered by kiss and caress.

Purposefully, he flung aside the quilted coverlet and stood up. "If you will not come to me, then I must come to you."

"No! Oh, no, Guy! You promised!" Laughing, she backed away, dodging behind a cedar chest. Guy stalked her around the room, enjoying her frantic darting rushes to spurious safety, ruthlessly driving her into the far corner of the chamber, where she found herself backed up to the wall, the tapestry hanging prickling her bare back.

"Now," he said, standing in front of her, his arms folded across his chest. "What would you like to do?"

Magdalen put her head on one side, seeming to give the matter grave consideration. "I would go hawking, sir," she said finally, with a mischievous chuckle.

Guy scratched his head thoughtfully. "I seem not to be making myself clear. Let me ask you again: What would you like to do?"

A speculative gleam appeared in the gray eyes as she continued to regard him with her head on one side. "Go ahawking, sir?" she suggested, impishly tentative.

"God's nails! But you're an obstinate little rogue! Let me tell you, madame, that there will be no hawking, now or later, until you get your priorities straight."

"Oh." Still with that quizzical gleam in her eye, Magdalen stood on tiptoe, slipping her arms around his neck, pressing her body against his. "Like this, you mean?"

"It's certainly a step in the right direction."

Her tongue slipped from between her lips, dampening the corner of his mouth with a little darting caress. Her breasts pressed warmly against the muscular expanse of his chest, and she moved one knee, suggestively stroking against the inside of his thigh. "Like this, you mean?" she repeated in a rustling whisper against his mouth as her knee pressed upward and her foot curled around his leg.

Guy made no answer, but his hands drifted down her back, coming to rest lightly on her hips, steadying her in her one-legged stance. Her upraised knee continued its teasing pressure between his thighs as her tongue darted over his mouth. Her nipples peaked, hard and burning against his skin, and she felt the little shuddering ripple where her flesh touched his.

Slowly, she returned her foot to the floor, standing back for a second to gaze with soft satisfaction at the sight of his arousal springing with unmistakable power from the curly nest at the base of his belly. She smiled, no impish smile this, but the smile of one who knew what she was about as she moved against him again, feeling the thrust of that power against her thigh. Delicately, she kissed his nipples, teasing them into hard erection with the tip of her tongue. Her hands moved to palm the lean hips, slipping behind to the hard, muscular buttocks that rippled in immediate response. A light sweat misted her skin now as the tension built deep in her belly and her inner muscles contracted in involuntary preparation as she leaned into him, her grip on his buttocks tightening with the sudden urgency of passion.

"Hawking can wait, can it not?" Guy teased gently, globing her breasts, tracing tantalizing circles with his thumbs, circumventing the taut, wanting nipples until she thought she would die of the wanting. Her head fell back in a gesture of pure abandonment as her lower body moved with a sinuous urgency against his, seeking the fusion that had now become imperative.

"Sweet heaven, but you were made for loving, pippin," Guy whispered, his voice husky, breath rustling against the fast-beating pulse at the base of her throat. He looked down at her upturned face, the delicate complexion flushed with desire, the great gray eyes enormous, deep pools of passion, the warm red lips parted. It was the face of a mature woman who knew her own depths, who knew how to give as well as to receive, who was not afraid to express her desire, nor afraid of another's desire.

She locked her arms around his neck, rising again on tiptoe to reach against his length as his hot tongue took possession of the warm sweet cavern of her mouth and the roughness of his unshaven chin rasped deliciously against her cheek. The pressure of his lips made her own tingle, and she inhaled his special fragrance of the wind and sun embedded in his skin, mingling with the lingering scent of the lavender strewn among his shirts in the linen press. When he lifted her against him, without releasing her mouth, she curled her legs around his back and tightened her grip on his neck, clinging like a limpet as he stepped backward to the bed.

She loosened her grip as he bent to lay her down on the high feather mattress and stood looking at her, his hungry eyes taking in every line and hollow of her body, its lights and shadows thrown into relief by the steady glow of the candle she had lit earlier.

Her own gaze ran over the body towering above her, broad and strong, a smooth-muscled fighting machine that for this moment was become an instrument of delight, hers and his. Reaching out a hand, she enclosed the pulsing shaft of pleasure, feeling the warm corded throb against her palm, the wondrous pliancy that soon would enter and fill her, joining them both in transcendent bodily fusion.

"I need you," Guy whispered.

Drawing her knees up beneath her, she knelt on the bed, lowering her head to take him in her mouth, concentrating with every stretched nerve in feeling his desire and pleasure through the movements of her lips and tongue and fingers. She felt his hands on her bent head, fingers twisting convulsively in the tumbled hair at her neck, heard his breath, fast and uneven, as she moved her hands round to grasp his buttocks, her fingers digging into the hard, driving muscle as his mounting passion spread to enclose and involve her in the tight spiral that he broke abruptly, taking her by surprise as he pushed her urgently onto her back on the bed.

She looked up into a stranger's eyes, deep, dark blue oceans of self-enclosed passion, and she knew that this time she must be responsible for her own desire and fulfillment because the man was lost in the swirling intensities of his body. And she gloried in the knowledge that it was her body that had released such a tempest.

Kneeling over her, he spread her thighs wide to receive the thrust of his turgid flesh. Magdalen heard herself whimper as her body closed around him and her belly tightened, her hips arcing as he pressed deeper, reaching her very core, it seemed. With each thrust, he drove harder, further, beyond the boundaries of her self. His head was thrown back, eyes closed, hands on her shoulders, so that she bore the weight of his upper body. But she was able to bear the weight without difficulty, just as she found that she was able to take responsibility for her own pleasure, matching him thrust for thrust, her fingers biting deep into the flesh of his buttocks as she expressed her urgency the instant before the explosion wracked her body and her cry rang through the room, joined by Guy's a split second later.

It was an eternity before the weight of him crushing her breasts, the soft press of his lips against her neck, brought Magdalen back to recognition of her own identity in the world. Her arms were flung wide on either side of her body as they had fallen in the aftermath of that explosion. Her legs were still spread wide around him, her skin damply melded with his. She brought her hand to his back, running a slow caress down the lean, muscular length. Guy raised his head and kissed her mouth.

"Enchantress," he said softly. "You took me into a world I have never entered before."

"I took us both," she replied, and there was a hint of smugness in her voice that made Guy chuckle weakly.

"I know you did, love."

"And now we may go a-hawking," she declared, sitting up with a resurgence of energy. "I know it is past prime, but that is not my fault."

"I thought we just agreed that it was," he teased, running his hand over her thigh. "If it weren't for your intemperate desires and consummate skills, we'd be long gone from here."

Magdalen flung herself upon him with a squawk of outrage, and he laughingly defended himself, catching her wrists in one large hand, throwing a leg across her thighs, holding her still with his weight.

"Peace, or I shall be obliged to take reprisals and then we will never have time to go hawking."

"But I did not start it," she protested, wriggling to no good effect. "I said you were a faithless perjurer, and you are."

"Oh, unjust!" He released her and sat up. "I suggest you remove yourself before such impertinence receives its due."

"It was not impertinence, sir. I was much afraid that it was true, and I was afeared for your soul." She tossed him a wicked grin as she leaped off the bed and ran for her robe, hastily wrapping it around her.

"Off with you!" Chuckling, Guy reached for the handbell to summon his attendants. "Make haste with your dressing and be in the mews court in half an hour. I've much work to accomplish this day and little time for more sport."

Magdalen dressed swiftly, aware that Guy was indeed taking precious time out of his day to grant her the indulgence of a morning flying hawks beside the river. He had been absent a week, touring the de Bresse fiefdom, visiting the three other castles belonging to the suzerainty, arbitrating quarrels and disputed claims, dispensing justice and inspecting defenses. In his absence, matters requiring his attention at home had accumulated, and he had a tedious day's work ahead of him. She had deputed for him as far as she was able, but a chatelaine's authority was dependent upon the lord's, and there were many issues in which she could make only temporary adjudication.

She felt no guilt, however, in having insisted upon the sporting expedition. In his absence, she had been confined to the castle enclosure, as was customary when a lady was left without the protection of her lord, and she was sorely in need of a broadening of horizons. Hawking and gentle rides through the countryside were the only physical activities approved by Lord de Gervais in his anxiety for her health, and he became visibly uneasy if she took such exercise in company other than his own. In light of this fact, Magdalen felt entitled to make certain demands of her own.

A wintry sun was offering a suffused pinkening of the horizon when she presented herself in the mews court. Guy was already there, in conversation with the falconer, idly tickling the neck of his peregrine with a blade of grass. Dogs milled on the cobbles, dodging beneath the hooves of the horses, saddled and held by grooms, whose breath coiled whitely in the cold morning air.

Magdalen hurried over to the falconer. "I give you good day, Master Falconer. I trust Aleria is in placid humor." She laughed, and the falconer smiled grudgingly. Magdalen's merlin was an ill-tempered bird on occasion, challenging the falconer's training and trying his patience sorely. He would have given her up as a bad lot if it hadn't been for her owner's cheerful insistence that the hawk was entitled to her moods.

"She's not been flown for three days, my lady, so I trust she'll be anxious to conduct herself well."

Magdalen drew on the thick embroidered glove handed to her by her page. "If she misbehaves the first time, I will not fly her again. What of the gerfalcon?"

The gerfalcon was Magdalen's pride and joy. It had been an unexpected gift from her father just before she left England, a gift symbolic in many ways. The laws of falconry were immutable, certain birds allotted to certain ranks of society. Guy de Gervais flew the peregrine of earls, and while merlins were flown by noble ladies, only those of royal blood could own a gerfalcon.

The hawk had been bred in Lancaster's mews but had been untrained when he presented it to his daughter, and it would still be long before the bird could be flown by her new owner. But Magdalen kept a constant watch on her progress.

"She's stubborn, my lady," Master Falconer said with his grudging smile, but they could all hear the pride in his voice.

"But worth your pains," Guy said.

"Oh, yes, indeed, my lord. Next month, my

lady should be able to fly her on a creance. Do you care to see her?"

Magdalen was already halfway to the mews, her furtrimmed surcote swinging with her impetuous strides.

It was gloomy in the mews, and the ripe smell of bird droppings and the blood of small animals hung in the cold air. The birds sat leashed to their perches, bright eyes, wickedly curved beaks; gripping, ripping talons, all stilled; the malevolent power of the predator harnessed to the will of man.

"Do you have a name for her?" Guy stood beside Magdalen in front of the half-trained gerfalcon.

"Diana," Magdalen said promptly. "The huntress."

He nodded, smiling. "A royal name for a royal bird. Let us start out now. It is almost full day."

They rode from the castle by way of the postern gate and down to the river which circled the base of the hill, meandering through the town before wending its way to join with the Oise on the outskirts of the forest of Compiegne. The ground was frost-hard beneath the horses' hooves, and there was a bite to the air that brought a pink tinge to Magdalen's cheeks and reddened the tip of her nose. She lifted her head, tossing back the velvet hood of her *chaperon,* breathing deeply.

"Ah, it is such pleasure to be outside. When I may not leave the castle, it reminds me of being a child at Bellair."

Guy laughed. "Unfortunately, we have no witch to cast spells for you to make something happen."

Magdalen glanced sideways at him. "She once said to me that the time would come when I would pray that everything would stay the same, bad though it would be, because it would be better than what is to come." The memory sent a graveyard chill down her back, and she saw that Guy was frowning, shadowed by the words.

"It was just mad Jennet," she said, attempting to laugh it off. "I do not believe any of her spells came true."

But inadvertently she had shattered the mood of the crisp morning, the reminiscence infecting the laughing intimacy with which the day had begun. She sensed the sadness that she dreaded descend upon her companion and could find no words with which to dispel it. She knew he lived this life with her under the shadow of guilt, a guilt she did not feel, because how could such love as they bore each other be in any way associated with wrongdoing?

They flew their hawks along the riverbank

where the bullrushes gathered thickly at the edge of sluggish brown water. A flock of geese rose, screeching, necks elongated, from the rushes as the menacing shadow of the peregrine fell across them. But they were too large to be prey for the hawk and settled down again with much chattering and wing flapping.

"We will go back if you are anxious to be at your work," Magdalen said in subdued tones, all pleasure in the expedition extinguished by the heaviness that had settled over her companion.

He gave her a slightly strained smile. "I own I have much on my mind, pippin, and the morning advances. It must be all of eight of the clock."

"Yes," she agreed, turning her palfrey. "Then let us return."

Guy was looking for some way to chase away the bedeviling gloom when Magdalen abruptly kicked her mount's flanks and set off at a canter along the riverbank, her hood flying. He set his own horse to follow, coming up with her when she drew rein at a clump of trees.

"Don't be vexed," she said, reading his expression correctly. "I needed to do that."

"Did you?" He sounded unconvinced.

"Well, I would rather you were vexed than sad," she responded a mite defiantly.

"I am not sad."

"Yes, you are. You are remorseful and sad."

Guy sighed. "I wish things were other than they are. Surely you can understand that?"

She shrugged. "I suppose I can understand it, but they are as they are. I am grateful for love."

There was, as always, nothing to be said in the face of this assertion. The issues for Magdalen were as clear-cut as ever. She had asked for nothing, she had warned him long ago of the folly of her marrying Edmund, she had declared her love as an absolute, and beside that nothing else was truly important.

He wondered if it was her youth that gave her this single-minded confidence in the rightness of her beliefs and instincts, but in his heart of hearts he knew it was not that. Magdalen of Lancaster was the child of two supremely dominant personalities, and they had both left their identifying traces on their self-willed daughter.

She was looking at him now with her candid gray eyes, assessing his reaction. "Would you truly wish things were otherwise, my lord?"

Slowly, he shook his head. "Not if it would mean that I had not known the joy of you, love. I will bear the remorse for the greater joy."

She smiled, her face illuminated with pleasure, her soul touching him through her eyes. "Then we may return in peace?"

"Aye, love, in peace." Leaning sideways, he

stroked the delicate curve of her cheek and jaw with the back of his gloved hand. "I will put sadness from me."

They rode back to the castle, contented although reflective, and in the mews court parted until midmorning when they would meet in the great hall for dinner.

Magdalen had changed her gown and was discussing with the butler the wines to be served at dinner when the exchange of bugles came from the battlements.

She heard first the alerting cry of an approaching party, followed almost immediately by the heraldic demand for identification.

"It would seem we are to have guests, Master Butler," she said matter-of-factly. "I must consult with the seneschal and the chamberlain." But instead of doing so immediately, she went up to the battlements, curious to see the new arrivals for herself.

Guy left his study when he heard the heraldic exchange and hastened to the inner court, waiting for the sergeant-at-arms to tell him who was requesting hospitality. The degree of hospitality offered and his own involvement would depend on the rank of the visitors. He caught sight of Magdalen on the battlements and went up to join her.

They looked down on the party gathered at

the far side of the moat. The standard was unfamiliar to Guy. He listened as the herald blew his note and lowered the pennon on the bugle in respect for their potential hosts.

"Here comes the Sieur Charles d'Auriac, who claims kinship with the lady of the Castle de Bresse, requesting the hospitality of his kinswoman."

Guy drew breath sharply. So it was come, the threat from the south. What form would it take? There was little they could do within the castle walls. He became conscious again of Magdalen beside him, conscious of her rigidity.

"That is the man who accosted me in Calais," she said. "He would have me go with him to a presbytery garden, but I was afeared—"

"Yes," Guy said swiftly, knowing he must diffuse her unease until he had some sense of d'Auriac's purpose. "But he is in truth your kinsman. Olivier discovered that his mother was sister to your mother. And as such you must extend all hospitality."

Her face was ashen, although she did not know why she should be so afraid, except for some deep, instinctual recognition that she tried to express. "But I do not wish to. There is an evil in him."

He knew it to be true, but must deny it. Magdalen knew nothing of a de Beauregard

threat to herself or her father, or of their implication in Edmund's death, for to understand
such things she would need to know their cause,
and he could not bear to inflict upon her the
pain of such knowledge . . . to know of the
blood and murderous treachery that had attended her conception and birth. "Do not be
fanciful," he chided sharply. "You cannot turn
away your cousin." He spoke to the sentry beside him, and the man ran to the court below.

The herald blew the note of welcome and the
drawbridge was lowered, the portcullis raised.
Magdalen, still white-faced but recognizing she
had no choice, walked with Guy to the inner
court to welcome the new arrivals at the foot of
the steps to the great hall.

Charles d'Auriac rode beneath the tower into
the *place d'armes* and through the archway into
the inner ward. He saw his cousin standing motionless beside the Lord de Gervais, and a throb
of satisfaction pulsed deep in his belly. She was
as he remembered.

Why had Guy set Olivier to discover
d'Auriac's identity? And why had he said nothing to her before? The man had never been
mentioned, the incident at Calais never referred
to since that day. And why did she feel this sick
apprehension as he rode into the court? There
was nothing about his physical appearance to

promote apprehension; indeed, she experienced the same sense of familiarity she had felt before, as if she had known him in some other place and time.

He took the stirrup cup of welcome from the page who ran from the hall. Guy stepped forward.

"Sieur d'Auriac, you are most welcome to this hearth." He waited for Magdalen to offer her own greeting, but she remained silent behind him.

"My Lord de Gervais." Charles swung from his horse and extended the hand of friendship. "I claim kinship with the Lady Magdalen de Bresse."

"Your kinship is acknowledged," Guy said, clasping the hand. Magdalen still did not come forward, and the awkwardness hung, heavy with discourtesy, over the crowd gathered in the court.

"Cousin, I bring you the greetings of your mother's family." Charles d'Auriac took the initiative, stepping over to her, his hand extended.

Still she stood, ignoring the outstretched hand, her eyes fixed upon his face, realizing what was familiar. In his eyes, she saw herself. It was the family resemblance. But why did he fill her with such loathing and such terror?

"Magdalen!" Guy spoke her name in sharp re-

buke, and she came out of her trance. "You offer our guest and your kinsman discourtesy!"

"I crave pardon, sir." She spoke quietly and
held out her hand, barely brushing her cousin's
flattened palm before withdrawing it and surreptitiously wiping it against her skirts. "My
mind was elsewhere." Still she did not bid him
welcome, and it gradually dawned on them
all that she was not going to do so without
prompting.

"Come within," Guy said, gesturing to the
open door of the hall. "You and your party will
accept the hospitality of our guest house, I
trust."

"We should be glad of the courtesy," d'Auriac
said with a pointed glance at his cousin. He and
his knights followed Guy into the hall, where
the fire burned and the tables were being prepared for the main meal of the day.

Magdalen did not accompany them. She
knew she was committing an unforgivable sin
against the rules of hospitality and kinship, but
somehow she could not help herself. She went
to her own apartments and summoned Erin.

"You will go to my Lord de Gervais and you
will tell him that I find myself unwell and unable
to attend in the hall this day."

Erin hastened to the great hall where Lord de
Gervais and his guests were drinking wine be-

fore the fire, the conversation stilted, the absence of the lady of the house conspicuous.

"My lord?" Erin sidled up to him, her voice low and conspiratorial.

Guy regarded her sharply. "Well?"

"It's my lady, my lord."

"Where is she?" It was clear to Erin that the Lord de Gervais was very put out, not a usual occurrence.

"She says she is unwell, my lord, and unable to attend in the hall this day."

Guy's lips thinned. He could not imagine what game Magdalen thought she was playing, but he could not play his own and discover that of Charles d'Auriac if she continued with this distempered discourtesy. "You may tell your lady that I excuse her until dinner, but I will require her presence then at the high table."

Erin bustled off, and Charles d'Auriac, who had overheard the conversation, observed, "It would seem I have in some way offended my cousin. I would ask forgiveness for my fault, but I cannot think wherein it lies."

Guy's discomfiture increased a hundredfold. "Do not, I pray you, refine too much upon it," he said stiffly.

"Some whim which requires curbing?" gently inquired d'Auriac. "It is frequently the way with women, I have noticed."

Something in his voice set the hairs on Guy's neck prickling. Yet it was hardly an unusual sentiment. He was certain the de Beauregards would not attempt any harm to Magdalen while they were her guests and she was under his protection. Within these walls, he could ensure her safety easily enough with little more than ordinary vigilance. He had but to discover what treacherous intent lay behind this apparent social visit. And he could not do that if Magdalen persisted in behaving in this disgraceful fashion. They must both offer only smiles and courtesy, seeming to accept the visit of a kinsman at face value. But why was Magdalen behaving like this? It was not in the least in character, and a mere aversion to d'Auriac, based on that encounter in Calais, was no excuse.

Erin delivered the Lord de Gervais's message to Magdalen. "He was most displeased, my lady," she added, looking in puzzlement at Magdalen, who sat huddled on the window seat. "Should I send for Master Elias to physick you?"

Magdalen shook her head, shivering although it was not cold in the chamber. "No, but I do not wish to leave here until the knight travelers have departed the castle."

"But they say the Sieur d'Auriac is your kinsman, lady." Erin's puzzlement was now outspoken. Her lady was not behaving like herself.

Maybe it was one of the strange humors of pregnancy.

Magdalen said nothing, and Erin stood irresolute for a moment, then went again in search of the Lord de Gervais. He was escorting the visitors to the guest house where they would refresh themselves before dinner, and he frowned as he saw Erin anxiously hovering on the outskirts of the group of attendants. She was clearly burdened with some communication but unwilling to force herself upon his notice again.

He waited until he had parted with his guests, then beckoned her over. "What is it now, woman?"

"It's my lady, lord." Erin twisted her hands in her apron. "Something is amiss with her."

"She was perfectly well an hour ago," he said, frowning.

"It is not a sickness of the body, my lord." Erin's work-reddened hands tied knots in her apron as she struggled to put the strange thought into words. "It is of the soul."

"What nonsense do you talk, woman?" Guy stared at her impatiently.

"She looks most strangely, my lord, and she speaks most strangely," Erin said. "She will not have Master Elias to physick her, but perhaps she will have Father Vivian. Maybe there is a curse laid upon her, my lord."

"Don't talk such nonsense!" Guy exclaimed again. Magdalen for some extraordinary reason was behaving like a willful and insolent child. Of course there was no curse laid upon her. But he crossed the court with urgent step, ran up the outside stairs, and hastened to her chamber in the women's wing. He threw open the door without knocking and closed it smartly behind him, in the face of the breathless Erin.

"Whatever is the matter with you, Magdalen?"

She still sat huddled on the window seat and now looked up at him, her eyes wide with what he recognized as fear. "I will not see that man again," she said.

"You will not show him further discourtesy," Guy stated, as flatly as she. "This unseemly conduct must cease immediately, Magdalen."

"There is an evil in him," she said. "He means me harm, Guy, I know it."

Guy shook his head. "You can have no possible reason for such a fancy. And even if it were true, do you imagine I would permit harm to come to you?"

"Maybe not, but there is an evil in him," she repeated. "I knew it in Calais, and I knew it the minute he entered the court."

"You are talking arrant nonsense!" He forced himself to speak with the dismissive harshness he believed would bring her out of this strange, trancelike obsession that could only make matters worse. "I have no wish to lose patience with you, but if you continue with this foolishness, then I shall do so."

Magdalen lowered her eyes to her lap. His words cut through the web of nameless terror that had gripped her in the last hour, the very real prospect of Guy's anger superseding the shadow of the unknown threat.

"I cannot like him," she said, her voice once more her own.

"That is no excuse for discourtesy." He came and sat beside her on the window seat. "I do not expect this of you, pippin. Do you not trust me to protect you?"

"Yes, but you cannot always be here."

"Your cousin is simply paying a visit. I will be here all the time he is." That was most definitely the truth, but Guy was careful to imply with a casual tone that his reason for such a statement was simply to reassure Magdalen in her groundless fears. "Now, are you going to conduct yourself in proper fashion?" Catching her chin, he lifted her face to meet his steady scrutiny. "For if you do not, I must warn you that you will most certainly suffer my extreme displeasure." He softened the declaration with a smile, but Magdalen was in no doubt that he meant it.

"I will do my best to be courteous," she said. "But I can promise no more."

"That will be sufficient." He kissed the tip of her nose. "You are the chatelaine of this castle, and it ill becomes Magdalen of Lancaster to behave like a petrified child for no reasonable reason."

"Maybe not, my lord." Her candid gaze met his. "But there is evil in my cousin, and it is directed at me. You may say what you will, but it will not alter that fact."

For a moment he debated abandoning his resolution and telling her the truth, if perhaps the truth would make sense of her fears and therefore diminish them. But no, there was no cause to be found in her vague terrors to justify the infliction of the pain of that knowledge. Not while he stood between her and the de Beauregards.

"I am here," he promised quietly and stood up. "No harm will come to you while I am here."

She nodded. "I believe that."

"Then dress yourself to do honor to such guests at dinner and greet your cousin with a chatelaine's smile."

"As my lord commands." It was an attempt at her usual mischievous mock-meekness, but it lacked true conviction. However, he accepted it in the spirit it was meant, kissed her again, and left her.

Erin, who had been waiting outside, ear pressed to the keyhole, hurried in. Disappointingly, she had heard little of the conversation, but her lady greeted her cheerfully enough and showed no signs of having experienced a lord's anger.

"I will wear the crimson brocade cotehardie," Magdalen said, opening the wardrobe and examining the contents. "Over the purple underdress."

"And the gold chain, my lady?" Erin entered into the spirit of preparation with enthusiasm. Such magnificence of dress indicated the importance of the visitors.

"Yes, and the silk caul with the gold thread."

"And sapphires," Erin stated.

"And sapphires," agreed Magdalen.

Thus it was that Charles d'Auriac arrived in the antechamber of the great hall as the herald sounded the call for dinner to be greeted by his cousin, a woman who bore little superficial resemblance either to the pallid invalid outside the inn at Calais or to the equally pale, sullen girl who had so signally failed to greet him on his arrival.

The massed dark hair was caught up beneath a caul of white silk, overlaid with gold thread.

Her cotehardie of richly patterned crimson brocade fell from a low, wide neckline and followed the lines of her body to her hip, where it fell in a lavishly full skirt caught up on one side to reveal the deep purple silk of her underdress. The sleeves of the overgown ended at the elbow, showing the delicate curve of her forearm encased in the tight sleeves of the underdress. She was a vivid, vibrant vision in royal crimson and purple, a heavy necklace of sapphires around the long slim column of her throat, a chain of delicate gold filigree clasped at her hip where the cotehardie clung to the curve of her body. Gold silk slippers were on her feet, their exaggeratedly pointed toes pinned up, and her long fingers sparkled with amethyst and a ruby the size of a thumbnail.

Charles d'Auriac drew a deep breath as the throb of excitement in his belly pulsed yet more strongly. This was a woman to draw a man to hell and back. This was Isolde's daughter.

Guy sensed the other man's reaction as he would feel the vibration of a lute string. He examined Charles d'Auriac from beneath drooping lids and was chilled by what he saw. There was a predatory look in his eyes, mingling with the eagerness of a rutting stallion. He moistened his meager lips, and his large, dominating nose in the thin, pointed face seemed to quiver, as if sniffing out his prey. It occurred to Guy with unpleasant force that there was more threat here than simple vengeance.

Magdalen felt the power of d'Auriac's response to her as some kind of evil, all-pervasive miasma that brought a knot of nausea to her throat. She had to force herself to remain still, her smile fastened to her face, her hand extended. "You have found your apartments comfortable, I trust, my lord," she said in the neutral tones of a hostess asking a routine question.

"Yes, I thank you, cousin." D'Auriac took the hand and carried it to his lips. "You are most gracious." For some reason, her manners had improved immeasurably since his arrival, he reflected, glancing sideways at Guy de Gervais and wondering how seriously he took his duties as protector and counselor. "We met, I believe, at Calais, just after your arrival from England. Perhaps you do not remember?"

Magdalen shook her head. "No, I do not recall," she lied, the memory too entangled with her present unfathomable terror to be casually admitted.

Charles d'Auriac had seen the conscious flash in her eyes, the tiny telltale quiver of her lip, and he wondered why she would trouble to lie to him about such a matter. What purpose could there be to it? Unless she suspected his intent. But she would have been told nothing by her mentors. She was simply a pawn on Lancaster's board, a female child, on both counts rendered unimportant except insofar as she could be used.

"Let us go in to dinner." Guy moved forward to lead the procession into the hall, bringing an end to such speculation. "My lady."

Magdalen took her place at Guy's side with barely concealed relief, and he could feel her tension as she walked beside him up the main body of the hall, where the household stood at the long tables, to the dais at the end. Charles d'Auriac took the place on her left, as befitted an honored guest, and she steeled herself to perform the duties of hostess, selecting choice morsels for him from the dishes as they were presented.

Meals were public showcases of the household wealth and importance, and Charles d'Auriac noted that this household displayed much of both. The platters on the high table were of the heaviest silver, the wine cups bejeweled, the assortment of meats and side dishes lavish, the bread plentiful and of the softest and whitest consistency. Wax candles were lit in front of every guest and senior member of the household, while in the main body of the hall, the tables were laid with pewter, and the bread, while not white, certainly was not of the hard black variety so often served.

Magdalen de Bresse was clearly a very wealthy woman, and that wealth at present was being used in support of the English crown.

"If you care to hunt after dinner, d'Auriac, we have both boar and stag in the woods," Guy said, resigned to the fact that his overdue administrative duties would have to be postponed under the demands of hospitality.

"I'd be glad of the sport," Charles said. "We have been too long upon the road." He turned to his neighbor. "Do you hunt also, my lady?"

"I enjoy the hunt," Magdalen replied, "but I am with child, and my Lord de Gervais does not consider it an advisable activity."

With child. Charles reached for his hanap and took a considered sip. A child could not be left for Lancaster to claim. The child must share the fate of its dam. He smiled. "My felicitations, lady. Your husband must be grateful that God has so blessed your union. I understand he has remained in England for the nonce."

Magdalen inclined her head. "Since he is not here, sir, that seems a reasonable conclusion."

Charles gave no indication of his angry discomfiture at her arrogant tone. It was the arrogance of those damnable Plantagenets, a natural haughtiness they wore like a second skin. But it certainly served to disguise the truth, he reflected. She had evinced not the slightest sign of awkwardness at his question, and they both knew that Edmund de Bresse was dead, whatever the rest of the world might be told. Maybe she was more devious than he had believed.

He laughed lightly. "A foolish observation of mine, cousin."

She took a spoon and dipped into the tureen at her elbow, selecting a succulent chunk of eel from the aromatic stew of river fish. She laid this on his platter. "Not in the least foolish, sir. Entirely reasonable." She smiled at him, indicating the fish on his platter. "Do you not find this an excellent *pauchouse*?"

"Excellent," he concurred, drawn despite his anger by that smile, the small white teeth, the rose-red lips so full and passionate. Or was it that his anger gave spur to desire?

"If you do not hunt, cousin, perhaps we may walk a little in the pleasaunce, instead," he suggested. "I am sure Lord de Gervais has matters to occupy him this afternoon and can ill spare the time for entertaining guests."

Magdalen controlled her urge to look in appeal at Guy. The prospect of an afternoon in the company of her cousin filled her with as much horror as if he had suggested she spend the time in the oubliette beneath the donjon with its black spiders and slimy crawlers.

"Walking in the pleasaunce is hardly exciting sport, my lord," she said. "Would you consider it to be so, my Lord de Gervais?"

"That would rather depend upon the company," he said with a smile. "But your cousin does not know that you are required to rest with your women for some hours after dinner." He directed a bland smile at d'Auriac. "It is on the advice of the midwives. Unfortunately, the Lady Magdalen is frequently impatient of such restriction, which I daresay is why she neglected to mention it."

"And you would enforce such instructions, I gather."

"It is within my purview," Guy said, almost carelessly. "So, do you care to go out with the hounds, d'Auriac?"

Rescued, Magdalen sat back and let the hunting talk flow around her. Rescued for the moment. One could not avoid the close company of one's guests indefinitely.

Nine

CHARLES D'AURIAC WAS uncertain exactly
when he became aware of the understanding
existing between Madgalen de Bresse and Guy
de Gervais. The latter was always casually cir-
cumspect, the former generally submissive in his
company as one would expect of a young
woman with her father's representative, invested
with her lord's authority.

D'Auriac, housed in the guest quarters across
the inner court, remained in ignorance of the
clandestine network of passages in the main castle and could know nothing of the figure wisping nightly between the women's wing and the
lord's chamber. He was never party to the
laughter and the loving that took place in that
chamber, or to the violent explosions of lusting
passion that would leave the two drained of all
emotion, all strength, beached upon each other
in the velvet-hung bed, inhaling the pungent
aroma of fulfillment, sweat-slick skin melding
with sweat-slick skin.

But there were other things: a look that
would pass between them, a smiling exchange
when the lady's eyes would gleam mischievously

and the lord's would narrow with amused understanding; a touch, a brushing touch of fingertips or a white hand laid for no apparent
reason upon the lord's arm or his large hand
moving with proprietorial direction to the small
of her back, the curve of her shoulder. These
were not things that an observant man with
malevolent intent and his own fervid interest in
the lady could either miss or ignore.

Charles d'Auriac watched closely. He watched
when Lord de Gervais played his lute and the
lady sat with her tambour frame beneath the
window of a pleasant square parlor, on a rainy
day that prohibited outdoor activities. He heard
the note in Lord de Gervais's voice as he sang
softly, melodiously, the troubadour's tales of love
and chivalry, and he heard the yearning in the
voice beneath the words.

He watched the lady beneath a bright blue
December sky as she sat gazing with fixed intensity upon the jousting knights in the *place
d'armes*. There was a quality to her intensity that
transcended the pleasurably fearful interest to be
expected in the sight of Lord de Gervais in
friendly if potentially injurious combat with one
of the visiting knights. She had little to fear for
the knight who wore her favor, d'Auriac considered with dispassion. Guy de Gervais was
known as one of the most accomplished knights

in England and France, and watching the speed and daring of his horsemanship, the uncannily accurate placing of his lance, it was easy to see why. A cool head, lean body, and massive strength combined with years of chivalric training to make the man invincible in fair combat.

He watched as the lady clapped her hands in their fur gloves, her cheeks pink with more than the crisp afternoon air, her eyes alight with more than simple congratulation as her knight, triumphant, saluted her from atop his destrier.

He watched and noticed how everything concerning Magdalen de Bresse received the close attention of Guy de Gervais. What she ate, what she drank, when she walked or rode and how far, when she retired for the night, all came under his scrutiny. A hint of fatigue, or a touch of pallor to the ivory and cream complexion, brought some soft-voiced instruction, occasionally drawing from the lady a half-laughing protest, but Lord de Gervais always prevailed and the lady would excuse herself and retire to her own apartments to rest.

Such concern for his pregnant charge struck Charles d'Auriac as excessive, even taking into account the importance to the Duke of Lancaster, de Gervais's overlord, of a safe delivery and a healthy child. A healthy child of Plantagenet stock would secure the de Bresse inheritance for England despite the death of the child's father, Edmund de Bresse.

Charles d'Ariac stroked his pointed chin and thought. The Lady Magdalen showed few overt signs of her pregnancy as yet. Edmund de Bresse had been killed at the beginning of August. If she had conceived immediately before his death, she would now be five months into her account. He found himself wondering how likely that could be.

Magdalen did not become inured to her cousin as the days of his visit continued. Guy took on the responsibility of entertaining the visitors in the style to which the claims of kinship and rank entitled them. There were hunting and hawking parties, tournaments, great feasts, and evenings of music and dancing, but still she shrank from Charles d'Auriac's close company. He continued to remind her of the oubliette, to carry around him the aura of malignity; the reek of fetid, dank, and frigid air; the horror of unseen crawling things in dark and secret places.

He did his utmost to make himself agreeable. He could dance, tell stories, compose elegant songs while accompanying himself on the lute. He paid her the pretty compliments of accomplished chivalry, courted her delicately as the unattainable lady of the manor. And her fear and loathing grew by the minute.

She no longer mentioned it to Guy because he would chide her for being fanciful and untrusting. She behaved toward her cousin with superficial courtesy for the same reasons, struggling to hide her detestation under a casual archness. She indulged in a certain sharpness of tongue and wit on occasion, although she realized that that sharpness angered her cousin. He always disguised his annoyance with a smile or a laugh, but the smile never reached his eyes and the laugh carried little humor. It satisfied her to annoy him, though, and she continued to do so, always under the guise of a flirtatious wit, and always swiftly glossed over as if it had meant nothing.

But Guy would not have accused her of distempered freaks and childish mistrust, because he sensed, as Magdalen did not, the true nature of d'Auriac's feelings toward his cousin. Perhaps because Guy also was touched with her magic, he found it easy to see the effect in others. He had seen it worked upon Edmund, and now he saw another man's burning eyes following her as she moved, fixed upon her when she was still, and he read the hunger therein and understood it. What man would not be touched by the warm, vibrant promise of her? By the grace of her movements, the suppleness of her body? But it was more than that. It was something contained in Magdalen herself, something that welled from deep within her, a knowledge of her own sensuality that came out to meet a man whether she would or no.

Charles d'Auriac was not deceived by Magdalen's apparent compliance. He did not understand why she remained impervious to all his efforts to gain her confidence. Women were in general susceptible to his charm and the light courtly play at which he was skilled. He had made no move to frighten her, had kept his ardor well leashed in her company. He thought he had made it clear that he was simply playing the conventional games that made courtly life so pleasant, but he was convinced she was only polite to him because Guy de Gervais had insisted that she be so. He could feel her repugnance, the shrinking of her flesh when he stood close to her, yet it did nothing to lessen his desire for her. If anything it added spur and rowel to an already galloping steed. But it made little difference in the long run, he decided. How she felt about him was of no importance, and could not affect either the fact or the conduct of her abduction.

Guy de Gervais evaded him also. Charles could not fault the hospitality offered him, yet he knew himself to be mistrusted. On the surface, there was no cause for mistrust when a man came extending the hand of friendship. The de Beauregards had not once attempted revenge for that long ago night in the fortress at Carcassonne. It had been a secret defeat, one known only to John of Gaunt and themselves, and it was Lancaster who had chosen to throw down the gauntlet in the shape of this child of Lancaster and de Beauregard.

But as Charles had half expected, de Gervais looked beneath the surface. He must have been alerted to the possibility of a de Beauregard move against Lancaster, a move that would involve his daughter. D'Auriac was in no doubt as to the quality of his present opponent. Forewarned and perspicacious as he was, Guy de Gervais would not be lightly lured away from his charge.

But Charles d'Auriac believed that he held a knowledge regarding Magdalen and Guy de Gervais that could only play into his hand, once he realized how best to play the hand. Knowledge of mortal sin was a powerful arrow to have to one's bow.

On the twelfth day of his visit, he decided no more could be achieved at present and informed his host at the supper table that he would take his leave on the morrow.

"Do you return to Roussillon?" Guy inquired. "The winter roads are ill for traveling."

"No, I go on to Paris, to make reverence to the king," d'Auriac replied. "It is but eighty miles and the highways are in good repair around the city." He turned to Magdalen. "When you are delivered, lady, I assume you also will journey to Paris to make reverence to Charles of France."

"I imagine my husband will do so, sir," Magdalen said calmly. "If the present truce continues between our two countries."

Charles realized that he had slipped. He said, "Your mother's family owes fealty to Charles of France, my lady. I meant only that it would be right for you also, as chatelaine of Castle de Bresse, to acknowledge your double allegiance. That your husband will do so goes without saying."

"You assume my husband has a double allegiance," she said, playing with the crust of her bread. "On what basis?"

"There is now no quarrel between our two countries," Guy interposed swiftly, praying that Magdalen had not noticed Charles's revealing slip. "So talk of allegiances, single or double, is hardly relevant."

There was a warning note in his voice that ensured Magdalen's silence, although she had been enjoying the sparring. It wasn't as if her cousin didn't know the situation perfectly well. He must be aware that Edmund's ransom had been forgiven and he had been gifted with a wife of the Plantagenet line in order to buy his exclusive loyalty to England.

"How true," Charles said with a light laugh, as happy as his host to change the subject. He did not believe the lady had noticed anything amiss, but what of Guy de Gervais? "But you will enjoy a visit to Paris, my lady. It is a great city."

Magdalen meekly acquiesced and retired from the conversation, puzzled over Guy's warning. Later that night, once Guy bade Stefan and Theodore good-night and the door closed behind them, she pulled back the hangings around the bed and brought the subject up again.

"Why did you not wish me to talk of Edmund's fealty?"

Guy, in his long robe, was looking over papers on the table beneath the window. So she had not noticed her cousin's slip, the implication that he knew Edmund de Bresse was not alive to make reverence to Charles of France. Relieved, he appeared to debate her question for a minute, then turned to the bed. Magdalen was sitting up, hugging her drawn-up knees, her expression both curious and just a little disgruntled.

"Charles d'Auriac may be your cousin, but

like all the de Beauregards he is fiercely loyal to France. I saw little point in entering a possibly acrimonious discussion."

Magdalen remembered again that Guy had taken the trouble to discover the identity of the man who had accosted her at Calais, while apparently dismissing the incident as easily as she had done herself. That sense of there being something awry hit her anew. "I believe there is something else," she declared with unthinking candor.

"Are you giving me the lie?" His red-gold eyebrows met in incredulity.

"No, of course I am not," she denied hastily. "But I do not think you have told me everything."

"Perhaps I consider that you have heard all you need to hear." It was said very gently.

Magdalen flushed. "I am no child, my lord."

"No," he concurred, "you are not, and as such you should understand the unwisdom of discussing fealties with one who could as easily be enemy as friend in different circumstances."

"You do not trust him, either." The statement had an accusatory note to it, her attention abruptly switched from the previous issue to this more immediate contentious certainty.

"I never said I did. I said only that *you* should trust *me*."

"But you chided me for my fears."

"For the ill conduct your fears encouraged," he corrected.

"Why would my mother's family wish me harm?" She frowned, plucking at the quilted coverlet, her loosened hair hiding her face from him. "My mother was declared by Rome to have been wedded to my father. There was no acrimony, was there, between my father's family and my mother's?"

Should he tell her the truth? Again he asked himself the question, wondering how long the truth could be kept from her anyway. But still he felt a deep repugnance. It was for John of Gaunt to tell his daughter that story; Guy de Gervais had already shouldered too many of his prince's burdens in this regard. He would never forget the atrocious distress she had suffered when he had told her the truth of her parentage. He would not subject either of them to such a hideous experience again.

"It is simply a matter of politics," he said. "Your mother's family are for France, your father's for England. Either side would go to some lengths to gain *your* allegiance. Now that you have no husband, only you hold Bresse for England." He turned back to the papers on the table.

"I do have a husband," Magdalen whispered,

but so low he did not hear her. She was as sure of that fact as she was that Guy had still not told her everything there was to tell.

But it seemed that he was not going to, so she tossed aside the questionable issues with a shake of her head that sent her hair rippling down her back and contemplated the real reason for her presence in this bed.

"Are you intending to be at your papers all night, my lord?" The dulcet tones told him to his relief that she had laid the contentious matter to rest for the time being.

Deliberately, he did not answer immediately, instead seeming to be absorbed in his work.

Magdalen nibbled her lip thoughtfully. Then she slipped from the bed, tiptoed across the room, and with a deft wriggle interposed herself between Guy and the table, then agilely hitched herself onto the table, sitting very firmly on top of his papers.

"That will do them no good at all," Guy observed.

"I believe I am worthy of at least as much attention as some dusty parchment," Magdalen declared, the paper crackling beneath her.

His eyes narrowed speculatively. "You may have to convince me of that fact, lady. Let us discover whether it is indeed so." Lazily almost, he stretched sideways and withdrew one of the feathered quills from the holder. "Now, I am accustomed to applying quill to parchment. Since I have a most novel parchment in place of the usual, it will be interesting to see whether the results are the same . . . or," he amended, "as interesting."

Magdalen quivered, a jolt of desire deep in her belly setting her nipples burning with anticipation as she waited to see what he would do. "You have no ink upon your pen," she murmured, hearing the throb of excitement in her voice.

"So I have not." He dipped the tip of the pen in the pitcher of water standing on the table. "Now, what message would I inscribe here?" He drew the pointed tip in a delicate curlicue over one cheek, too delicate for her to feel more than the most delicious prickle. "No message, I think, but a portrait," he said softly. "Shall I inscribe the course of my living model?"

She shivered, and the papers beneath her crackled again, crisp against her bottom and thighs. Guy seemed unconcerned about the fate of his documents. He dipped the pen again and began with great concentration to trace the outline of her face, the whorls and contours of her ears. He drew around the fullness of her mouth, the pen pricking within her eagerly parted lips, before moving down the straight column of her

throat, delineating the sharpness of her collar-
bone, dipping and circling in the hollows of her
neck.

She sat still on the edge of the table, only her
skin moving in shivering ripples as he dipped
the pen again, and the thin wet line moved to
her breasts, circled the pregnancy-darkened are-
olas, lifted her nipples beneath the gentle goad.
He held the ripe heaviness of her breast in one
hand as he wrote a stanza of joy upon each, inscribed his own pleasure on the delicate, blue-
veined tautness cupped in his palm. Then, when
her breath came swift and the glow of arousal
misted her skin, he took her hands, drawing
tickling circles on the flat palms, turning them
over to trace her fingernails while her body
hung in breathless suspension during this tantalizing, utterly entrancing interlude.

The pen inscribed its message between the
deep cleft of her breasts, pricked delicately over
her ribs, wrote poetry in the soft indentation of
her navel, but it was the feathery silkiness of the
top of the quill that brushed over the small
mound of her belly, bringing a hushed moan of
delight from her as the muscles contracted, her
legs shifted, thighs parting in eager expectancy.

She wanted to lie back, to make all of herself
open and available for this blissful game. She

moved to do so, but with a hand warm and firm at her waist, he held her upright, dipping the pen point again into the water as he drew the tapering keenness finely over her thigh, moving ever closer to the dark fleece concealing the moist, heated core of her. A soft moan escaped her as the fleece parted and her opened body lifted to the punctuation marks of the pen. Now she could not master the need to fall back, to unfold herself utterly to the alternating sensations of the nerve-tingling prick of the pen tip and the brushing joy of the flickering feathers.

Only then did Guy move his hand from her waist, easing her backward, so that she lay in sprawled abandon upon the table, feeling the parchment crisp and crackling beneath her, a sensation that simply melded with the others. Her skin was alive, every nerve ending at the exquisite point where pleasure bordered pain. The quill slipped between her widespread thighs, and she no longer knew which end aroused her now to an extremity of pleasure, a swirling, heart-stopping whirlpool of bliss in which she tossed and tumbled, to come only slowly back to the awareness of the candlelight on the mantelpiece and of her body, surfeited with pleasure, incapable of movement.

Gently, very gently, as if he would not disturb

the magic of her lethargy, Guy lifted her from the table and carried her to the bed. He laid her down and covered her with the quilt.

"But you—" She whispered a beginning, but he stopped her words with his mouth.

"I took my pleasure from yours and I would not tax you further this night, love. Not after such a dissolution."

She would have protested if she could, but there was no sinew to body or brain, and the words would not come. In truth, she was not sorry to be left alone with the slow and smoky embers of her pleasure. Her eyes closed.

Guy stood looking down at her. He was smiling, but shadows lurked in his eyes. The deep shadows of knowledge, of the expectation of the pain of loss. How long would it be before John of Gaunt declared his daughter widowed? And even when he had done so, Guy de Gervais could not expect to be gifted with the prize. He had received one wife from his overlord, and the wealth and power that accompanied that union. He was owed no more, and, in truth, there was nothing he had to offer his overlord as inducement that Lancaster did not already have from his vassal.

He drew the bedcurtains to shield her from the candlelight and went back to the table, straightening the crumpled papers, inhaling the scent of her, feeling her body warmth beneath his fingers. Such sensations were not conducive to work, but he drew the candlestick closer and sat down.

MAGDALEN AWOKE FILLED with the sense that something wonderful was going to happen. She had felt like this once or twice as a child, but usually without adequate reason, she reflected without undue resentment. Now, she lay for a second before she remembered. The Sieur Charles d'Auriac was leaving today. Her spirit lifted as if the burdens of the world were gone from her. She and Guy would be alone once again.

He was sleeping heavily beside her, and she could see from the guttered candle and the still glowing fire that he had sat up long into the night. Her body still burned with the memory of what he had done for her, what he had given her before she had so selfishly fallen asleep and left him to his papers.

Propping herself on an elbow, she leaned over him, gazing at his face in the dim gray light of dawn. In sleep, the tautness of mouth and jaw was absent, giving his mouth a full, well-shaped curve that invited kisses. Red-gold hair waved thickly on his broad forehead, and she wanted to brush it aside, trace the thick line of his eyebrows, kiss the tip of his nose. But she did none of those things, unwilling to disturb his sleep, not even to repay some of the pleasure he had given to her. She would repay the debt with interest soon enough.

She lay down beside him again, but her blood was dancing, her muscles quivering with the urge to be up and doing on a day that seemed to promise only the very best of things. Silently, she slipped from the bed, drew on her robe, and left by the inner door, her heart skipping at the thought that in a few short hours she would see the last of the loathsome man she was obliged to call cousin.

In her own apartments, she leaped into the unslept-in bed for form's sake and rang the bell for her women.

"I am ravenous," she greeted them without preamble. "I would break my fast with coddled eggs and meat, and I will bathe this morning."

"Yes, my lady," Erin said placidly, well aware that the appetites of pregnant women were unpredictable and should always be indulged. "Margery will fetch food and have hot water brought up from the kitchen."

She went into the adjoining privy chamber to assemble bath necessities, and Magdalen jumped from the cold bed and followed her.

"Sprinkle lavender on the water, Erin."

"I always do, my lady," the woman said as placidly as before. "I understand the visitors are to leave this day."

"Yes, indeed!" Magdalen affirmed with an enthusiasm she realized was not entirely appropriate in front of Erin.

"There'll be some sorry to go," Erin said with a chuckle, taking soap and towels from the chest.

"Why, how should that be?"

"Young Berthe, my lady," Erin said. "The laundress in the *sieur*'s company. Fancies herself in love with my lord's servant, Olivier." She shook her head, her mouth pursed. "Can't imagine what she sees in him. Scrawny little man, he is, always creeping around and turning up when he's least expected. But they say he's smitten with the wench, too."

Magdalen's nose wrinkled. She could not imagine finding any member of her cousin's party in the least appealing. She wandered back to her bedchamber just as Margery came in with a tray. Hungrily, she took a mutton chop from the platter and began to chew on it while continuing to drift from privy chamber to bedchamber, from wardrobe to window.

"You're very restless, lady," Margery observed. "It must be the child, quickening."

"I feel nothing as yet," Magdalen mumbled

through a mouthful of mutton, patting the small swell of her belly. "Did you bring buttermilk?"

Margery handed her the cup, and she drained the contents with a satisfied gulp.

"Your bath is ready, my lady," Erin announced. "Will we wash your hair?"

"Yes, certainly." Magdalen stepped into the round wooden bath. For some reason, she felt the need to start the day fresh and clean, all traces of the last twelve days washed from her skin and hair, so that when Charles d'Auriac rode from her gates, she would be left cleansed of anything that might remind her of his touch, of that dark and slimy aura that had sullied her during his visit.

When she appeared in the great hall two hours later, however, she gave no indication of her intemperate joy, unless it was in the added sparkle in her eyes, a certain coiled expectancy in her body. Dressed in emerald velvet and an ermine-trimmed surcote, her hair hanging down her back in heavy, gleaming plaits threaded with pearls, she took d'Auriac's breath away as he became immediately aware of her suppressed excitement. For some reason, he did not associate the excitement with his impending departure—a mistake Guy de Gervais did not make.

Guy's heavy eyes were matched with a heaviness of spirit that he could not explain except in terms of a too short night. But he had spent many such nights in his life, many nights where sleep of any duration was absent, and had felt not the least ill effect. He looked at the radiant Magdalen, remembering her joy of the previous evening. She certainly had the air of a satisfied woman this morning. Maybe his own restraint and consequent lack of satisfaction lay behind his present disaffection.

"I give you good morrow, my lord." She greeted him with a smile, a hinting, glinting glow in her eyes that told him she too was remembering the artistic experiences of the previous evening. "We are to bid our guests farewell this day." She turned to Charles d'Auriac and his knights. "I wish you Godspeed, *mes sieurs,* and a safe journey."

"My thanks, my lady." Her cousin bowed slightly, his eyes hooded. "Your mother's family welcomes you as a de Beauregard, Magdalen of Lancaster."

A cold shiver lifted the downy hairs on her spine. The words seemed invested with a meaning she could not understand but knew instinctively were sinister. Yet it was a perfectly reasonable courtesy, an acknowledgment of the ties of kinship. She inclined her head, a wintry smile on her lips. "I am of de Bresse now, sir."

"Ties of diplomacy, cousin. In ties of blood, you are of de Beauregard and Lancaster."

"Magdalen." Guy spoke her name quietly. When she turned to him, her relief at his interruption transparent, he gestured to the table where a two-handled emerald-studded hanap stood beside a chased silver pitcher.

She had not forgotten this ritual but was grateful for a reminder that, however unnecessary, had spared her the need to respond to her cousin's intense declaration. She went to the table and filled the goblet with wine from the jug.

"Cousin, the cup of friendship." Her tone was neutral as she touched the rim of the chalice with her lips before offering it to her guest.

He took it, drank, and passed it around. Guy took it last, and by then Magdalen's unease had dissipated under the knowledge that her cousin's departure could not now be delayed.

They accompanied their guests to the inner court and saw them to their horses, then watched them ride into the outer ward. Magdalen on impulse gathered up her skirts and ran across the court and up the stone steps to the battlement, spurred with the need to see them well gone from her gates.

The heralds blew the exchange of civilities as

the party rode forth, standards snapping in the wind, and Magdalen began to dance on the tips of her toes. She ran back to the court, to where Guy still stood. "Oh, come into the orchard," she demanded. "I must shout my joy to the skies and may not do it here."

Shaking his head in mock censure, he followed her to the seclusion of the orchard where Magdalen instantly began her prancing dance of delight again.

"He has gone! He has really gone! Oh, I could sing such a song!" She flung her arms wide in a gesture to encompass the earth. "I need never see him again. I *will* never see him again. My heart is so light, my lord, I feel as if I have been carrying the burdens of mankind and they are suddenly lifted from me." She laughed in pure delight. "Is it not wonderful? Do you not feel wonderfully lighthearted?"

Guy wearily rubbed his temples. "Not really. In truth, you make me feel old." It was the truth, he realized, at this moment, when she was so full of life and energy and unregarding happiness, made so easily happy by the simple immediate relief of something that had been causing her discomfort. It was the way in which the young and innocent were made happy.

Magdalen stopped her prancing. She regarded

him with a frown in her eyes. "Why, how should that be?" Suddenly the frown disappeared, to be replaced with an impish twinkle. "Why, it is because of that silly hat you are wearing. It is indeed a hat for an ancient, not for a man of such strong and youthful mien!"

She jumped suddenly on the tips of her toes and snatched the flat velvet cap from his head. "There now! That is better." Tossing the hat in the air, she then caught it deftly, laughing at him.

"Give it back, Magdalen." He held out his hand, unable to respond to her mood.

"No, I shall not!" Still laughing, she danced away from him. "If you wish for it, my lord, you must catch me first."

"Magdalen, I have neither the time nor the inclination for this," he said, irritated now.

Magdalen did not hear the irritation. She was too enwrapped in her own exuberance. She danced behind an apple tree, shaking his cap in taunting invitation, grinning at him from around the trunk.

"I am not in the mood for games," he warned, snapping his fingers imperatively. "Would you give me my hat, please."

"Oh, you are just pretending to be a gray-beard," she declared, still convinced she could draw him into her game. She tossed his cap into

the branches of the apple tree. "Now see what
you have made me do, Master Graybeard."

With a muttered exclamation, Guy turned on
his heel and strode out of the orchard, leaving
Magdalen still standing beneath the tree, the
laughter dying from her eyes, a sudden tremor
on her soft mouth.

She felt embarrassed, as if she had committed
some childish solecism and been dismissed by a
weary, exasperated guardian. She had miscalculated, she realized, nibbling miserably on her
thumbnail, remembering how tired he had
looked. Perhaps the strain of d'Auriac's visit had
told on him also, but in different ways. Perhaps
he *was* too old to feel the simple exuberance of
relief, and she still an annoying babe who had
not acquired the gravity and wisdom of experience. Unfortunately, Magdalen didn't think she
wished to acquire those things if such acquisi-
tion would mean an absence of the high spirts
that she had been feeling. But they had simply
led her into trouble, they always had. It was a
melancholy reflection.

She looked up into the branches of the apple
tree where perched Guy's burgundy velvet cap,
its jeweled pin gleaming against the bare gray
bark. An experimental jump confirmed it was
too high to be reached from the ground. She
was not dressed for tree climbing and had

enough wisdom at least not to attempt that. Disconsolately, she wandered through the orchard in search of a long stick with which to poke it down.

That achieved, she returned to the castle, her pleasure in the day sadly diminished as she wondered how Guy would greet her at dinner. She wasn't sure which would be worse: that weary disapproval of the orchard, or the overt displeasure that had driven him from her. Maybe she should discover in advance. She turned the velvet cap over in her hands. Returning it would give her a pretext for disturbing him, and maybe he would see it as an apology and put aside his annoyance.

She was about to go in search of him when she saw him crossing the court, deep in conversation with the master of pages. With a resurgence of her embarrassment in the orchard, she put the cap behind her, suddenly shy of being seen publicly holding the evidence of her foolishness. She stood uncertainly in the shadow of the donjon, watching his approach and debating her own.

Guy saw her as his discussion with Master Edward drew to a close. "Some further hours at the quintain should improve the lad's marksmanship," he said absently, his eyes on Magdalen. "Use the swinging target. A few thumps from that after an ill-placed lance have been known to improve skills with some rapidity."

The master of pages chuckled. "You speak truth, my lord. But young Paul's a timid lad."

"Then he must learn to overcome his timidity," Guy said briskly. "It will stand him in bad stead, and he is ill served with too much gentleness."

Master Edward bowed to the undeniable truth. Ten-year-old boys destined for knighthood had a hard row to hoe, and little would be gained by pandering to their youth and diffidence. Young Paul must learn to handle the great lance on horseback, and if a few unseating thumps from a heavy flour sack were needed to teach him the consequences of failure, then so be it.

Guy nodded in farewell and strode across the court to where Magdalen was standing. His annoyance had vanished almost as swiftly as it had arisen, and he found himself now curious as to why she should be standing there so still, with her hands behind her back and an air of penitent anxiety that somehow amused him.

"Magdalen? Did you wish to speak to me?" He came up to her, greeting her, one eyebrow raised interrogatively.

"I wished to give you back your hat," she said, bringing the cap out from behind her back, brushing a dried leaf from the border. "You left it in the orchard."

"How careless of me," he said solemnly. "I thank you, my lady, for your attention." He took it from her, and his eyes laughed at her. "How did you contrive to get it down? It was much too high for you to reach."

"I poked it down with a stick," she said, the anxiety gone from her expression. "I ask your pardon if—"

"There is no need for that," he interrupted. "Let us go to my study. There are one or two matters I would discuss with you." He laid a hand gently on her shoulder and turned her toward the donjon.

Magdalen accompanied him readily, her step once more light. Outside the study, however, they found Olivier waiting with the watchful patience of one accustomed to waiting and accustomed to making the most of the activity.

"You said to come for your instructions, my lord," he said, acknowledging Magdalen with a bobbing motion of his head. "And the means of travel," he added.

Guy frowned. He had forgotten his summons to Olivier when he had invited Magdalen to accompany him. It was an unfortunate lapse since he could hardly conduct this business with the servant in front of the lady. Neither could he postpone his discussion with Olivier, since the sooner the spy left on the heels of Charles d'Auriac the better.

"Come within," he said, opening the door. "Magdalen, I must ask you to wait here. I will not be many minutes."

Magdalen regarded the firmly closed door with a raised eyebrow, aware that she did not care to be left standing outside in the passage like a summoned servant or a suppliant. What private business did Guy have to conduct so urgently with the olive-skinned, agile, bright-eyed man of Provence? A mysterious man, Magdalen had always thought. He came and went, and as far as she could tell, had no clear-cut, official function in the Lord de Gervais's household. But it had always been clear to her that he was on unusual terms with his lord.

She had first noticed him, clinging like a shadow to Lord de Gervais, his eyes everywhere, when they had come to Bellair to fetch her after their return from France. Since then, she had been aware of him only occasionally. He was the kind of man one forgot about unless he did something to attract attention. And she could not remember his ever doing that, except now.

Behind the heavy oak door, Guy handed Olivier a fat purse. "You will be able to insinuate yourself into his household, I trust."

"No doubt, my lord," Olivier said with calm confidence, taking the purse. "I have been to some pains to gain the confidence of the laundress in their company. She believes me to be dissatisfied with my present employment, and . . ." He shrugged his bony shoulders, stating the fact without emphasis or particular interest, "I think she will be happy to see me again. She will enable me to find kitchen work with them while they travel and in Paris."

"You are certain you have not come to the notice of d'Auriac? I'll not have you running unnecessary risks," Guy said, frowning.

Olivier shook his head. "He's not a man for poking around the kitchens, my lord. One servant looks much like another, and it's the chamberlain who does the hiring. I doubt the *sieur* has ever knowingly laid eyes on me."

Guy nodded. Migrant workers, picking up domestic or laboring work where and when they could, were not unusual and were certainly not the concern of the head of the household. He was sure there were many such coming and going at Bresse and he would know nothing of them unless they committed some offense that required his adjudication. Charles d'Auriac would not recognize Olivier. "Be watchful, then."

"How long should I remain with the *sieur's* household?"

"Until you have discovered something worth telling," Guy said, going to the window, looking out over the plain. "I would know most importantly what he intends regarding the Lady Magdalen, Olivier. But I trust you to judge what else I need to know."

"I will send messages in the usual way?"

Guy nodded. "There are always minstrels, pilgrims, troubadours who can carry news. It has worked well enough in the past."

He saw Olivier to the door and smiled invitingly at Magdalen, who had a rather martial light in her eyes. "I do beg your pardon for keeping you without," he said. "But my business with Olivier was of a private nature."

"I assumed it to be so, my lord," she responded a little stiffly, coming into the room. "What was it you wished to discuss with me?"

"Oh, come now, pippin!" He took her in his arms, pushing up her chin with his thumb. "Cannot you guess?"

"I did not mean to be foolish in the orchard," she said, as usual all sense of grievance leaving her under his smiling regard, the caressing tone.

"I was unpardonably ill humored," he said,

moving his thumb to her mouth. "And you were merely exuberant."

"Oh." She moistened his stroking thumb with the darting tip of her tongue. "And I thought I was being willful and childish and sadly vexing."

He laughed warmly. "I thought you were, too, but I have since changed my mind. I missed you this morning when I awoke."

"I did not wish to disturb your sleep. You sat late in the night."

He nodded. "There was much to be done . . . What is it, love?" A strange expression had crossed her face, a look of puzzlement, of astonishment.

"I do not know," she said slowly, looking down at herself, her hand moving to her belly. The strange little flutter came again from deep within her, a flutter like a bird's wings. She raised her head, her eyes strangely bright. "It is the child," she said in hushed wonder. "The child is quickening, Guy."

Gently, with the same wonder, he placed his hand on her belly beside her own. "You cannot feel it yet," she said. He shook his head, smiling.

"Soon you will," she asserted. "Our child grows apace, my love."

Ten

"BROTHER FELIX SHOULD be returning soon, Father Abbot."

"And with news to put our poor son's soul at ease, I trust." The abbot resumed his measured pacing along the paved terrace above the abbey vegetable garden. "His strength returns, it seems, by the minute." He gestured to the figure in the plain wool robe of a lay brother, laboring in the vegetable garden below, swinging his hoe with easy, rhythmic movements.

"He is a man of the sword, young and strong," the monk responded. "Such bodies heal well even from such fearsome wounds as our brother suffered."

"If God so wills, Brother Armand, if God so wills," the abbot gently reminded. "I doubt youth and strength would have prevailed without the timely assistance of the charcoal burner and your healing skills."

Brother Armand put aside the compliment, as was expected of him. "What skills I have, Father, are God-given."

"Of course . . . of course," placidly agreed the abbot. "But whatever their genesis, our son has cause to be grateful to them." He turned toward the great gray stone building of the abbey behind them. The last wintry rays of the afternoon sun caught the delicate flat arcading on the square, unbuttressed towers standing at its four corners.

It was a sight that never failed to uplift the Father Abbot, and he let his eyes rest upon it for a minute before gathering his cloak about him. "I must talk with Brother Gareth about the pilgrims arrived from Canterbury. Our almoner had some doubts as to whether the guest hall would accommodate them all in seemly fashion." He smiled, a knowing smile for one who lived apart from the world. "Brother Gareth is always perturbed by the presence of women pilgrims. I believe he fears some improper journeyings between the dorters if he is not very vigilant. I must reassure him that the power of prayer is sufficient to safeguard the spiritual health of our cloisters."

The abbot moved away with deliberate steps, his robes fluttering in the February wind, rising sharply now with the setting of the feeble sun.

Brother Armand remained where he was, watching the gardener at work, his eye assessing the movement of the body, noting where there was residual stiffness, noting that the young man still stopped frequently to draw breath, resting on his hoe. It had been seven months since the charcoal burner had dragged the hurdle with its unconscious burden to the postern gate of the abbey, seeking the monks' skills for a man so close to death it seemed impossible that he would remain in this world.

There had been nothing to identify the man. His body had been stripped by whoever had attacked him, and he wore only a shirt and hose, not even his boots left to him. Brother Armand had noticed immediately the hard muscle and sinew beneath the body's broken surface, the calluses on his hands and the stronger muscular swell in his right arm, all signs of a man who lived by the sword. His shirt, torn and bloody though it was, was of the finest linen, cuffs and neck embroidered with delicate stitching. It seemed reasonable to conclude that the wounded man was of knightly birth and had been set upon by outlaws.

They had not believed he could live, but he had clung to life with an astonishing tenacity, barely conscious most of the time, yet submitting with the trust of an infant to the nursing, the feeding, and the cleansing, and with the stoical courage of a man of war to the agonies of his broken body.

It was growing dark, and soon the bell for vespers would summon the abbey's inhabitants, monks, pilgrims, and chance travelers alike, to the chapel. The evening chill would not benefit a man newly arisen from his sickbed. Brother Armand called to the man in the garden.

Edmund de Bresse looked up at the shout and waved a hand in acknowledgment. He was reluctant to go inside, however, relishing the physical labor, for all that hoeing between rows of cabbages was neither dignified nor particularly strenuous labor. But his body, so long deprived of movement and exertion, seemed to stretch with pleasure, to come alive again, bringing him awareness of his whole body, of muscle and sinew and the blood flowing strong in his veins. For one who had almost crossed the frontier into death, who had hovered for many weeks in the gray, twilight land of near death, this recognition of his body, even in its complaints and the stiffness of disuse, brought the sweetest joy.

He had little memory of the attack, remembered vaguely the agonized crawl through the undergrowth when his assailants had left him for dead. He had wanted to lie still and die; death had beckoned most strongly, offering surcease from his pain, but some stubborn will to live had driven him to crawl on his hands and knees away from the blood-drenched ground on which he lay. He remembered the clearing, the pile of faggots beside the tumbledown hut, the strange fog through which he saw the bearded face peering down at him. And then he remembered nothing else; only pain was coherent and then the terror that he would live but would not be whole.

He had not known why the fear should be so all-pervasive, so consuming of his conscious moments, until the time when he opened his eyes and the fog was not there. The pain was still present, but it was no longer everything, it was an addition to himself, not intrinsic to himself. His first thought was of his wife, a wife who could not have a husband who was not whole. He had flexed fingers and toes, run his hands over his shape beneath the blankets, and had sought confirmation from the calm-eyed monk watching at his bedside.

He had spent many days drifting in healing lethargy, thinking of Magdalen, seeing those clear gray eyes, the rich mass of hair, her mouth so redolent with promise. He had been content to lie in the infirmary, thinking of her when he was not asleep, and dreaming of her when he was not awake. But in truth the two states had been very similar, as much as anything because of the potent draughts fed him by Brother Armand, draughts that kept him still as his body knitted. And then, as his strength returned and

the strength of the potions was diminished con-
sonantly, had come the knowledge that the
world to which he belonged was continuing
without him and he must do something about
reentering it. And with that knowledge had
come the anxiety that now tormented him. If he
was believed dead, what had become of Magdalen? Had Lancaster given her to some other
knight in the interests of power or alliance,
while he had been lying here dreamily recuper-
ating?

The Father Abbot had been sympathetic but
insistent that the patient was in no fit state to
leave the care of Brother Armand. One of the
monks would be leaving in three days' time on
a journey to their sister abbey at Swindon. He
would make a detour to Westminster on the
way back and carry a message to the duke.

Edmund glanced up into the darkening sky
where rooks cawed, circling the bare winter
treetops, the flock gathering for the night.
Brother Felix had been gone three weeks. If he
did not return by tomorrow, Edmund would
leave here anyway. He was strong enough now
to accomplish what could not be more than two
days' walk to Westminster at the easy pace ne-
cessitated by a man not yet robust. The abbey
was isolated, tucked away from the well-

traveled roads, its brotherhood given to prayer and meditation and the pursuit of learning rather than involvement in the temporal world. They received hospitably enough those guests and pilgrims willing to penetrate the forest this far in search of a night's lodging, but their work was more in the scholarly realms of books and texts, in the meticulous, exquisite illustration of those books and texts than in feeding and correcting the souls of ordinary folk. Edmund's urgency had failed to impress them. It belonged too much to the world of men. But it was time now for him to take his own life in his own hands again.

The bell for vespers sounded from the chapel, and reluctantly he left his cabbage patch, returning the hoe to the little shed and making his way to the chapel, feeling the good earth beneath his fingernails, the roughness of his wool habit against his skin, the plain, elemental sense of being alive. And he went to give thanks for the gift of life.

Brother Felix hurried into the chapel just as the last peal of the bell died. Edmund, taking his place in the pew reserved for the lay brothers of the abbey, saw him, and his heart jumped joyfully. He found it hard to concentrate on the office, but it was one he had heard from earliest childhood, and concentration was not necessary for its correct performance. As he left the chapel, Father Abbot beckoned to him.

"Brother Felix has returned, my son. He brings you a letter from the Duke of Lancaster." The abbot smiled at the young man's eagerness as he turned to the messenger. They had all heard the ravings of the patient during the dark days of his delirium, and they all knew of one Magdalen who occupied the nooks and crannies of the fevered brain, and they now knew that he had raved of his wife, his pregnant wife, whom he seemed to love with a very great love. There were those in the abbey who felt such a great love would be better directed heavenward, but the abbot had come late to monastic life and knew the joys and perils of the flesh. He smiled upon the young man's love.

Edmund took the rolled parchment, heavily embossed with the Lancastrian seal. His fingers trembled slightly as he broke the seal and unrolled the sheet. Lancaster's message was concise. He expressed satisfaction that his son-in-law still lived and commanded his presence at the Savoy as soon as he was fit to travel. His lady had journeyed into Picardy soon after her husband's disappearance, to make good the de Bresse and Lancastrian claims to her husband's fief in his absence, and it would be well for her husband to join her with all speed to lay to rest troublesome rumors of his death. The message ended simply enough, recommending the recipient to God's continued grace.

"The news pleases you, my son?" The abbot had been watching Edmund's face.

"Yes, indeed, Father Abbot." Edmund re-rolled the parchment. "But I must leave here and journey to Westminster without delay. The duke commands my presence."

"Then you must negotiate your release with Brother Armand," the abbot said with a laugh. "He will not want his good work undermined by your overtaxing your strength. I ask that you heed his wishes."

"I would not be so wanting in gratitude, Father, to do otherwise," Edmund said, gracefully but with perfect truth. "But I believe myself strong enough to essay the journey."

"Let us go in to supper, and you may talk with our apothecary later." The abbot walked toward the refectory, Edmund in a fever of impatience at his side. But he controlled his impatience and performed the serving tasks that came to his hand as a lay brother before taking his place at the long table. He had asked permission to serve the abbey and its brothers during his convalescence, giving thanks with the most humble of tasks for their care and God's mercy. In the service he had discovered a peace and contentment unknown to the knight working at war, but he was now ready to take up sword and spurs again, to pursue glory and honor in the name of England and St. George, and to pursue his wife in the name of love and lust.

The next morning, clad still in the robe of the lay brother, a monk's sandals on his feet, a simple cloak his only protection against the February cold, a heavy staff his only defense, Edmund set out to walk to Westminster. His way lay through the woods, but they presented no danger to a traveler dressed as he was, and if he felt the eyes of the wood's outlawed inhabitants upon him, from undergrowth and treetop, there was no threat in the surveillance.

He arrived at the Savoy when the household was at supper and was received by the duke's chamberlain with flattering attention and the information that his grace would receive him as soon he had refreshed himself. He would find his apartments undisturbed, and his squire and pages would be summoned from supper in the great hall to attend him. Edmund was unaware that these arrangements had been designed to preserve for public consumption the duke's tale that the Sieur de Bresse was taking an extended absence from court, but he was too weary to question such comforting details. A barber was summoned to close-crop his black hair and trim the beard, grown during his illness and to which he found himself now so accustomed he could not imagine being without it. He dressed in tunic and hose beneath a burgundy velvet surcote, a silver belt girding his loins, his two-pronged dagger sheathed at his hip, and he felt the wonderful resurgence of his old self as energy flooded back to muscle and limb.

In the inner chamber behind the presence chamber, John of Gaunt received a man, thinner and paler than the eager, intense young knight of the lists at Westminster on that hot August afternoon. There was a look in his eyes that Lancaster recognized. It was the look men wore after deep suffering, a look that banished a man's youth once and for all.

Edmund knelt to make submission to his overlord and father-in-law, aware of a tension in the duke, an assessing watchfulness as he sat in his great carved chair beside the table, playing with the massive ruby on his middle finger.

"Tell me what you can remember of your assailants," Lancaster said without preamble, indicating that Edmund should rise. He gestured to a page to pour wine and then dismissed him.

Edmund told the tale as best he could, wondering why his father-in-law should be interested in details of an outlaw attack. They were common enough occurrences. The duke's vivid blue gaze never left his face and he stroked his little forked beard, making no attempt to interrupt. When Edmund had concluded with his description of the monks' care and skill at the Abbey of St. Jude, his listener said nothing immediately. It was hot in the womblike room, and Edmund felt suddenly dizzy, aware that he had eaten little after his exhausting walk and that the wine was making him light-headed.

"Sit down, man!" the duke exclaimed as Edmund swayed and grabbed the edge of the carved oak table. "God's nails, you're but barely recovered."

Edmund dropped abruptly into an armless chair, too faint and sick for a minute to protest sitting in the duke's presence. Lancaster himself refilled the jeweled goblets and pushed one across to Edmund. "Drink, your blood's thin." He waited until Edmund had obeyed and some color had returned to his gaunt cheeks. Then he said, "It's time you understood the danger in which you and my daughter stand. Lord de Gervais and I thought to circumvent it without involving either of you, but it seems it cannot be done."

Edmund listened as John of Gaunt told him of the de Beauregards' mission as agents of the French king, of their intention to wrest the de

Bresse fiefdom from the influence of the English and return it to France. Not a word was said of a foiled and bloody assassination attempt in the fortress of Carcassonne, or of the circumstances of the birth of the girlchild on whose life depended the de Bresse fealty to the English king. He was told only of a family, fiercely loyal to France, enraged that one of their own, Magdalen of Lancaster, should be used against France, and of their determination that Lancaster's plans should come to ruin by whatever means, foul rather than fair, came to hand.

"So you must be on your guard," Lancaster concluded, rising from his chair. "When you journey into France, you must take with you a force sufficient for protection against attack, covert or open. Lord de Gervais is with Magdalen at the moment, holding your fiefdom for you. When you reach there, he will be free to return to my side." The duke pulled at his beard again. "I have need of him and of his counsel. The peasants grow unruly, and the damned Lollards seize any opportunity for fomenting unrest. It comes to something when the king and his ministers sit uneasy at government because of the whines of villeins."

"I will gather together a force without delay, my lord duke." Edmund had risen with his overlord, but his legs still trembled, and there was a mist before his eyes. "I will summon all who owe me allegiance."

"Requisition in my name what vessels you need," Lancaster directed, with princely carelessness dismissing in advance the prior claims of merchant-owners. "I will expect you to leave within three weeks."

But Edmund woke in the morning with a return of the fever that had ravaged him in the early days of his recovery. For a month he lay upon his sickbed, and when he was sufficiently recovered, he faced the frustration of a series of spring gales and high tides that kept all ships in harbor. It was the end of April before he had gathered his force and they were ready and able to take ship for France.

MAGDALEN WAS STANDING half dressed in her chamber on a warm April morning, absently stroking the hard mound of her belly, reflecting that the child within had been less active than usual for the last day or so, when water gushed from her body in a startling torrent.

She stared in disbelief at the puddle at her feet, then her voice lifted in alarm. "Erin! Erin!"

"What is it, my lady?" The woman came in from the privy chamber, where she had been sorting through piles of linen newly returned from the laundress.

"Look!" Magdalen pointed to the floor, her face ashen. "It is coming from me."

"Nothing to alarm you, lady," Erin said, customarily placid. "The child is coming."

"But it is too early. And why is there all this water?"

"An eight-month babe," Erin said. "They survive as well as most. Are there pains yet?"

Magdalen shook her head, still bemused, but reassured by Erin's calm manner. "Just the water."

"That has to happen sooner or later," Erin told her, "or the babe cannot be born."

"Why not?"

Erin shrugged. She had no idea why these things happened, only that they did. She had assisted at enough births to know what needed to be done if matters proceeded ordinarily, and there were other women in the castle who were more experienced.

"I'll send for the midwife, my lady," she said. "You had better lie down, and I'll bring towels to make you more comfortable."

Gingerly, Magdalen lay down on the bed, submitting to Erin's attentions because she had no choice but to trust those who knew what was happening to her better than she did. She knew little beyond the absolute basics of the process of birth, having been brought up by the spinster

Lady Elinor, whose own knowledge had been scantily theoretical, and there had been no other woman to enlighten the girl.

It occurred to her now that she should have asked more questions of Erin and Margery, who did know about these things, instead of drifting merrily oblivious in her love-lost world for the last eight months.

"Tell me what happens," she demanded, sitting up against the pillows, since lying down seemed unnecessary.

Erin scratched her nose. "Well, there'll be some pain, my lady, and then the child comes."

"Much pain?"

Erin didn't want to frighten the girl, but neither could she see much virtue in lying to her. "Some women have more than others," she said.

"Much?" Magdalen insisted.

"I believe so, my lady."

"I wish my lord were here," Magdalen said.

"Birthing's women's work, lady." Erin went to the door. "I'll fetch the midwife now."

The door closed behind her, and Magdalen sat gazing at a dancing sunbeam on the quilt. She touched her belly again, wondering what was happening inside her. Maybe birthing was women's work, but she would be comforted at the thought of Guy's presence in the castle. But he was gone with his knights to attend a tournament at Compiegne, under the auspices of the Duke of Burgundy. Ordinarily, she would have accompanied him for the three days of feasting and revelry, but her condition had prevented it. It had not occurred to either of them that she was close enough to her time to make his own absence unwise.

The midwife came in with both Erin and Margery. She was an old woman with gnarled hands and graying hair beneath a grimy coif. Her voice had a curious high-pitched whine, and Magdalen took an instant dislike to her.

"I would have Erin and Margery attend me," she said, drawing back from the woman. "I have no need of your care, *beldame*."

"No need for fear, lady," the woman whined, drawing back the coverlet. "I've seen many a child into this world . . . and out of it. And mothers, too," she added, prodding Magdalen's belly before proceeding with a more elaborate examination.

Magdalen lay rigid beneath the probing, rigid with distaste and fear, convinced that no good would come to her from this woman. The first pain came so suddenly, was so sharp, that she cried out with a species of indignant surprise.

"Start wailing now, my lady, and there's no knowing what you'll be doing later," the *beldame* declared, laying a hand on the tight abdomen.

Magdalen pushed the hand away with all her force. "I will not have this woman in here," she stated. "Get you gone, *beldame!*"

Erin and Margery, alarmed at this vehemence, encouraged the muttering crone to leave the chamber. "She knows much, my lady," Margery said, coming back to the bed.

"She has the evil eye," Magdalen said. "She will have my child born squinting or crooked of limb. I will not have her near."

The two women shrugged. Women in labor were known for their strange fancies. Soon enough, the Lady Magdalen would be too absorbed in her own struggle to heed who attended her.

By midafternoon, Magdalen lay in an exhausted stupor, her body momentarily resting from its toil. When she could think at all, she was aware only of bewildered indignation that anyone should have to endure this atrocious thing. Why had she not been forewarned? Why was this happening to her? What had she done to deserve it? Was it the wages of sin? Of the mortal sin that brought this other life in combat with her, it seemed, grappling with her, and yet they should surely be fighting together? Did this happen to everyone, or was it special because of her sin? Through her disordered, fevered brain the thoughts ran. Tears glistened at the corners of her eyes, and despair ran deep as the pain built again, inexorable, eternal, unendurable—yet it must be endured.

Erin held a water-soaked cloth to her lips, and Magdalen sucked greedily, too weak to drink from a cup. Afternoon became evening, and the two women attending her were white and tense as the pains seemed to die down, the exhausted body on the bed to sink into a state resembling a trance rather than sleep.

"We must summon the midwife," Erin said. "She must pull the child from her body."

Margery shuddered. They both knew what happened then, a child in pieces, the mother torn, bleeding to death more often than not; and if not, then the death-dealing fever always came in such cases.

"Perhaps she needs to rest, then she will able to help the child," Margery said uneasily. "My lord will be greatly angered if aught were to happen that could be prevented."

They both knew this to be true, both remembering the night on the ship and his joy when he knew that the Lady Magdalen would live.

Erin soaked the cloth again and gently bathed Magdalen's face. Her eyelids opened, and for a moment her eyes were unclouded with the mesmerizing pain.

"Lady, we must summon the midwife," Erin said in low-voiced urgency. "The child will not be born."

Magdalen shook her head weakly on the pillow. "I will not have her ... not yet." She seemed to the watching women to gather herself together, as if for one final effort. The pain scudded over her face again, her breath coming in shallow gasps as she struggled to contain the agony.

The moon rose in the dark sky, hanging, a perfect crescent, in the chamber window. The two women counted their rosary beads in passionate whispers.

GUY DE GERVAIS WAS removing his armor in his tent outside the lists on the plain beyond the castle of Compiegne. It was early evening.

"Wine, my lord," Geoffrey proffered the cup. "It was a well-fought joust, my lord, at the last."

"Mmm." Guy acknowledged the compliment absently. He went to the door of the tent, sipping wine. The air was fresh and pleasant on his face after the stifling heat of visor and helmet, and his body moved fluidly, released from the confining plates of armor. He was weary, but pleasantly so, and the prospect of the banquet that would end the revels, followed by his bed, filled him with contentment. Or should do.

He frowned, watching the evening star prick the darkening sky. He could be back at Castle de Bresse in two hours. The thought appeared unbidden in his head. But why should he ride at night? His companions would not appreciate either the effort or the danger, and if he rode out they must accompany him. Ridiculous, when there was a banquet, good company, a comfortable bed, and an easy ride home in the morning light on the morrow. He turned abruptly from the tent entrance.

"We return to Bresse, Geoffrey. Inform the knights-at-arms and the rest of the household. We set out immediately."

The party made good speed as the evening became full dark. No one questioned the Lord de Gervais's peculiar, whimsical decision, but they rode with haste and vigilance, supperless, tired after the day's combats, anxious to be off the roads and behind castle walls. They kept their complaints among themselves, not a whisper reaching their overlord as he rode at their head, a frown etching his brow, his mouth taut.

He did not know why he was doing this, only that the decision had made itself and could not be gainsaid.

It was ten o'clock when they arrived at the

Castle de Bresse. Magdalen did not hear the imperative note of the herald demanding that the drawbridge be lowered to admit the lord of the castle. Her women heard it, however, the sound coming resonant through the casement, opened to let some cool air into the room where the heat of suffering hung heavy.

"It is my lord," Erin said, bending to Magdalen, wiping her brow. "My lord is come, lady." She did not know whether the suffering woman heard the words or could understand them, but she repeated them, hoping that they might offer comfort.

"She's all but gone," muttered the *beldame*, approaching the bed cautiously. Magdalen had still not permitted her to touch her, although she no longer had the strength to forbid her the chamber. "She and the child will be dead within the hour unless I can pull the child from her."

"No!" Somehow the words penetrated the laboring woman's absorption. "You will not touch me."

Shaking her head, the crone withdrew into the shadows. She'd offered her skills. If they were rejected, then the consequences were nothing to her.

"But my lady—" Erin began, but her words died as the door of the chamber flew open.

Guy de Gervais strode in, pulling off his

gloves, his face pale beneath the weathered tan. He had been told at the gate that the Lady de Bresse had been laboring long to bring forth her child, and the atmosphere in the castle had told him all he needed to know. Everywhere he saw the grim faces of those who expected the worst at any moment.

"How is she?"

"Bad, my lord," Erin said bluntly. "The child will not be born, and my lady is at the end of her strength."

He approached the bed and stared down in despairing disbelief at the changed countenance on the pillows. Her eyes were sunken in deep purple hollows in her face where the skin was drawn tight over the bones, revealing the skull beneath, as if the flesh were already gone from her. Her mouth, that wonderful, full, passionate mouth, was set in a fine line of suffering.

"She will not let me near her, my lord," whined the *beldame*. "I would pull the child from her. It is the only way to save her, but she will not let me touch her."

"Guy?" It was a whispered exhalation, and he bent low.

"I am here."

"Send her away. Do not let her touch me."

He stood in dread and irresolution, knowing that if he ordered the midwife to do what she could, then it would be done. But if Magdalen, even in this extremity, could express such a wish, then surely he must comply.

"The priest, my lord." Erin spoke softly. "We should send for Father Vivian to hear my lady's confession."

"I am not dying." The whisper came again from the bed. "I will not die."

"Send for Father Vivian. He may wait outside, in case there is need. And you, *beldame,* get you gone." Guy made these decisions, unsure what had led him to them but sensing their rightness. But now he found himself at a loss. Magdalen had retreated again into the twilight world of endurance. His hands shook with the need to help her, and his soul was cold with dread as he stared down at the ravaged face from which all life seemed to have gone.

"I go to the chapel," he said suddenly. On his knees at the altar rail, he would wait out this dreadful time. "Send for me immediately if she is . . ." He did not finish because he could not say what he believed in his ice-bound heart was now inevitable. That loving, laughing, passionate, willful soul was going to leave this world and leave him to face the wasteland of loss as he had done once before.

He reached the door. There was a sudden rustle of movement behind him. He turned back to the room, his hand on the latch. Erin and Margery were bending over the foot of the bed.

"What is it?" His voice sounded thin and scratched in the room where a hushed and urgent expectancy had replaced the dull hopelessness of inaction.

"The child . . . It comes, my lord," Erin told him. "But my lady cannot help it. She is gone from us."

"No!" He ran back to the bed, dropping to his knees at the head, touching the cold, still face on the pillow. "No, it cannot be!" His fingers brushed her mouth, then stilled, lightly covering her lips. He was not mistaken. The faintest stirring of breath touched his skin. "She is not dead," he said quietly as a feeble, attenuated cry sounded in the room.

Magdalen's eyes opened, and to his joy he saw lucidity in their pain-haunted depths. "Over." The one word was all she could manage.

"It's a girl, my lord." Erin came up to the head of the bed, holding something in her hands. "She is small but appears sound, even after such a struggle."

Guy stood up and looked at his daughter, lying exposed for his inspection on a blanket. Such a pathetic, bloodstained, wrinkled mite to cause so much suffering, he thought, gently covering the child before taking the bundle from Erin.

"Magdalen, here is your daughter." Kneeling again beside the bed, he laid the bundle against her cheek.

"Healthy?" Her eyes opened again. Her hand moved feebly to touch the child. "She is but an eight-month babe."

"So were you," he told her, smiling, moving the child to her breast, closing her hands over the living package. "I remember your father saying."

He saw a light flicker in her eyes, as if the seemingly irrelevant scrap of information made a comforting sense, as if it connected her with the child she now held. Then the delicate, blue-veined lids closed over the light, her hands slackened and fell from her breast. But the faintest tinge of color had crept into her cheeks. It was not color so much as a patina overlaying the grayish hue of before, a patina that indicated the true sleep of recuperation.

"God is merciful," Erin whispered. "If there is no fever, my lord, I believe she will live . . . and the child, too."

"We will tend her now, my lord." Margery took the baby from her mother's breast.

Guy looked at the two women who both

bore the signs of acute exhaustion. They had been watching at this bedside for eighteen hours. "I will dower you both for this day's work," he promised. "For your loving care of my lady . . . and for your loyalty," he added quietly, but with an emphasis they could not mistake.

"Our loyalty does not need to be bought, my lord," Erin said.

"But it may be rewarded." He went to the door. "Send for me when your lady is strong enough."

Magdalen slept for many hours. She slept as they cleansed her of the residue of birthing, as they changed the linens on the bed and the sun came up on a balmy spring day, filling the chamber with healthful scents and breezes. She slept through the thin wailing of her daughter and was but barely conscious as they put the child to her breast and the warm life-giving fluid began to flow beneath the desperate, hungry suckling of the infant mouth.

She awoke as the sun went down. The chamber was quiet, infused with a great sense of peace. Languidly, she turned her head on the pillow. Erin and Margery lay on pallets beside the bed, both dead to the world. A wooden cradle stood at Erin's hand, a hand which lay slackly on the rocker, evidence of the work it had been doing before sleep had overwhelmed the woman. Magdalen could not see within the cradle and effortfully she turned on her side, propping herself on an elbow to lift her head from the pillow. She could see little more than a minute mound beneath a white coverlet, but when she leaned over the edge of the bed, she could see the crown of the tiniest head, tipped with a faint fair down.

Exhausted afresh, she fell back again, smiling to herself. If she kept very still, she could hear the infant's breathing. There were tiny disturbances to the even tenor, little catches and snuffles that for a moment alarmed her until she recognized a curious rhythm to them. She wished she could reach out to her child but knew it to be impossible. Curiously, the horror of the child's birthing had receded. Oh, she could remember the despair of relentless pain, the terror of helplessness, but it was a mind memory, not a bodily one.

The noise from the cradle changed, the snuffles became quick sucking noises, then a thin wail pierced the chamber. A rush of anxiety, unlike anything she had experienced before, flooded Magdalen as the pathetically intense wail rose. She struggled up, aware only of the compulsion to reach the child, to satisfy whatever need was causing her such distress. But Erin was already staggering up from her pallet.

"Hush now, lovely," the woman murmured, rocking the cradle.

"Give her to me, Erin."

"Ah, you're awake, my lady. It's the breast she wants." Erin lifted the child from the cradle. "She's wet. Let me change the breachclout first."

"It doesn't matter," Magdalen said, holding out her arms. "I cannot bear to hear her cry so piteously."

Erin wrapped the damp baby in an extra layer of toweling and gave her to her mother. Magdalen moved her nipple into the tiny opened mouth, looking down in wonder at the life she had nurtured. A clenched fist pushed into the swell of her breast as the babe pulled, suckled, lost the prize, wailed instantly, found it again and settled down, her cheeks growing round with contentment.

"Where is my lord?" Magdalen tore her eyes from the entrancing sight at her bosom. She knew he had been there in the last hideous hour of her labor, but the memory was smudged, a vague memory of determination, some infusion of strength that had driven the acceptance of death from her soul. "He has seen his child?"

"Yes, my lady. Shall I send to him? He said we

were to summon him when you were strong enough."

"Do so, but not until the child and I are fresh and fragrant again." Magdalen chuckled, a weak chuckle but nonetheless her own. "I am rank with sleep, Erin, and my hair is tumbled. And this little one is needing. She cannot be presented to her sire in this state."

Erin touched the sleeping Margery with her toe, and the woman rolled over with a groan. "Wake up, sluggard. My lady needs hot water and spiced gruel, and the child must be bathed before my lord comes."

Margery rubbed the sleep from her eyes and looked at mother and child. She nodded her satisfaction, despite her weariness. "I'll go to the kitchen. My lord would not have the bells rung to announce the child's safe delivery lest they disturb my lady's rest, but they can be rung now."

She hastened from the room, and within half an hour the bells from the four towers began to peal the joyous news of the birth of an heir to the de Bresse fiefdom. A male heir would have been preferable, but this little girl would provide the currency to maintain the stability of de Bresse dependents under the ultimate suzerainty of the Duke of Lancaster.

Guy listened to the jubilant pealing as he

crossed the court from the garrison. He had tried to spend the hours since he had left Magdalen in ordinary activities, tried to behave as if the life of mother and child were important to him only in terms of the discharge of a vassal's duties and responsibilities to his overlord. He held within himself the bittersweet joy, the piercing poignancy of a fatherhood that he could not openly acknowledge, and the unfathomable gratitude for the gift of Magdalen's life, so nearly lost to him.

On impulse, he turned aside into the orchard, where beneath the trees daffodils and bluebells massed in heady springtime profusion. He picked an armful, his fingers sticky with their juices as the thick stems broke for him. Abruptly, powerfully, he was reminded of the juices of love, spilled with so much delight, and he inhaled deeply of the fragrance in his arms, a fresh, youthful fragrance so redolent of Magdalen.

Carrying the bouquet, he left the orchard, climbed the outside stairs, and made his way to Magdalen's apartments. The door stood ajar. He pushed it open. Erin and Margery were not there, only Magdalen sitting up in the big bed, still pale but smiling at him. She held out her hands in welcome.

He closed the door softly behind him and trod to the bed. "You are feeling stronger, love?"

"Immeasurably," she replied. "What beautiful flowers." She lifted the sleeping baby from her nest within the crook of her arm. "Your daughter, my lord."

Guy let the flowers tumble to the bed, scattering in scented yellow, blue, and white across the coverlet. He took the child as Magdalen scooped up the flowers and buried her nose in the blooms, smiling with her eyes as she saw the soft melting of the strong features, the delicate exploration of a fingertip accustomed to sword and steel.

"Zoe," she said. "I would christen her Zoe, my lord. The gift of life."

"Zoe." Again he touched the tiny snub nose with the tip of his little finger. "But it's hardly a Plantagenet name, sweetheart."

Magdalen's face hardened. "She does not have to bear a Plantagenet name. She is our child, Guy, and will bear the name we bestow upon her. A name of love, not of dynasty."

He raised the child and lightly kissed the wrinkled forehead in benediction. "Zoe, then," he said softly. "In affirmation of life and of love."

Eleven

EDMUND DE BRESSE STOOD on the forecastle
of the *St. Anne* in the fresh dawn, watching as
the ramparts of Calais became defined in the
early mist lying over the smooth water. Running before the brisk dawn wind, they passed
within the harbor walls, the pennons of Lancaster and de Bresse flying at the masthead to
match the standard of England, lilies and leopard, flying from the welcoming ramparts.

Edmund felt his spirits lift, the energy so long
depleted in his body surge anew as they approached the familiar quay, gateway to the roy-
ally disputed territory of France and to his own
fief. Within that fief lay his wife and his child.
The child must have been born in the last few
weeks. Had he sired a male heir? Did the child
live? The latter question always served to make
the former unimportant. Whatever the child's
sex, it was still his heir. And the child's mother?
Had she survived the birth? There were so
many hazards he'd heard tell of, even if she survived delivery: the fever, the milk leg, the flux,
and the wasting.

Please God to have kept her safe, he whis-

pered in an agony of anticipation. They had
been parted, it seemed to him, as soon as he had
discovered a world wherein his love for Magdalen of Lancaster was the defining characteristic. Her image filled his waking moments; the
soft, supple lines of her body filled his arms during the long reaches of the night. He had recognized that his passion was unshared. His wife
did not feel such a one for her husband. He
knew she liked him, accepted her marriage and
everything that went with it. But she gave him
no more than friendship and acceptance. It was
a recognition that disappointed him, but with
the optimism of youth, the confidence of a man
who had done and seen and succeeded as he
had, he believed that she would come to love
him as he loved her. He would teach her the
ways of loving, and in his arms she would at last
respond with the ardor and delight he took
in her.

Gulls wheeled and called, swooping low over
the deck looking for littering scraps. Sailors
were running to their stations now, preparing to
drop the square-rigged sail as the vessel drew
closer to the quay. On the quay stood the har-
bormen, ready to receive and make fast the massive ropes once the ship dropped anchor.

Edmund stayed on deck, enjoying the bustle.

His squire and pages would see to the ordering of his possessions and their unloading. Making landfall this early in the day meant they could set out for Picardy as soon as the three ships were docked and horses, men, arms, and provisions were assembled. If they met no delays, they should not have to spend more than five nights on the road. He would send a herald on ahead with an escort of lancers to alert his wife and household to his arrival. A small party, traveling on swift horses, could expect to reach the Castle de Bresse a day earlier than the main body, and his wife would be ready to welcome him with full honors on the morrow.

The sun came up on a May morning, a delicate cobweb of a morning, and he was reminded of another May Day, when he had gone out before dawn to pick marigolds by the river before the first touch of sun had dried the dew. It was a posy for his betrothed, a lively, dancing sprite of a girl with a long plait and sparkling gray eyes and an impatience with his obedience to courtly etiquette. He could see her now on that long-ago morning, distributing his carefully picked flowers among her companions, thanking him gaily for his gift as if it had not been specially offered. And he could feel again his own chagrin. He had kissed her later as they played around the Maypole and the girls—children and maidens—ran squealing from the pursuit of swains, both serious and playful.

He had kissed her out of chagrin and a fierce determination to stake his claim to her attention. Had things changed between them that much in the intervening years? Wasn't he still trying to stake his claim to her attention? Oh, she accorded him all the public respect a wife must accord her husband, but when they were alone, he knew he craved so much more than her easy smile, relaxed companionship, willing participation in their bed. He wanted her to match him. He wanted to feel that perhaps he had the edge, that she could possibly want more from him than he was prepared to give . . . He wanted to feel that she could feel as he did.

He lifted his face to the sun. In this land, he would begin anew . . . *They* would begin anew. His memory of hovering in death's antechamber was still a vivid spur to the enjoyment of life and gratitude for God's mercy. He was in many ways newborn, and his life stretched ahead, a blank parchment on which he would write what he chose. He would inscribe his love, and he would create the rhyming couplet.

An hour later, the herald, charged with the news of the imminent arrival of the Sieur

Edmund de Bresse, galloped out of the town and down the white, winding track toward the plains of Picardy.

GUY WALKED INTO the pleasaunce under the brilliant blue of the May sky. The scent of lilac hung heavy. He heard the soft strumming of a lute coming from the center of the garden where a fountain plashed into a stone bowl and doves cooed from the dovecote set among thyme and rosemary, sage and marjoram in the herb garden.

He trod softly, hoping to catch the little party unaware, to watch unespied for a moment. He was remembering another May Day when the woman now sitting with her baby was herself a child. An eager, impetuous, laughing, loving child, who had begged him for a silver penny and pouted because they had traveled too fast to enjoy the jongleurs and other sights of the journey to London.

He stood behind a laburnum, concealed by the mass of golden flowers drooping on leafy stalks, a smile on his lips as he watched. Theo was playing his lute, singing softly. The lad had nimble fingers on the strings and a sweet, well-pitched voice. Erin and Margery sat stitching tiny garments with lace edging, a basket frothing with cambric and lace between them as they sewed for the baby. The baby slept in her mother's arms.

Magdalen was sitting in a cushioned chair in the shade of a willow tree, playing idly with the fat yellow catkins drifting in her lap. She was dressed in a simple cotehardie of ivory linen, a white silk snood confining her hair, and her face in repose showed him a deep contentment, the eyelids lowered languidly over eyes that he knew would be quiet, her mouth soft . . . but as sensual as ever. She was still a little pale, but it was not the pallor of ill health, more of the necessary peaceful lethargy of recuperation.

"I know you are there, my lord." She spoke softly, turning her head toward the laburnum, a smile on her lips. "Do you come to spy upon us, sir?"

"No, I came but to see how you did." Laughing, he stepped out of concealment. "That is a pretty song, Theo. If you paid as much attention to your Latin as you do to your singing and playing, you would be more at ease in body and soul, I believe."

"Oh, for shame, my lord," Magdalen protested. "To offer a compliment as excuse for castigation is of all things the most ungenerous."

Theo was blushing fiercely at this reminder of his recent troubles at the hand of the master of pages. Guy took pity on him. "You are right, my lady. I withdraw the castigation and leave the compliment. Would you find Geoffrey, Theo, and tell him that I will ride out within the hour."

The relieved page made good his escape, and Guy, still laughing, sat down at a stone bench beside the dovecote. A bowl of corn sat on the paving stone, and he scooped up a handful, holding out his palm, flat and still, as he watched Magdalen and his daughter. A dove alighted on his palm with a whirr of wings, delicately took a morsel of corn and flew off.

"Where do you ride, my lord?" Magdalen moved the sleeping infant to her other arm.

"To Seriac. There is some trouble over the raising of taxes," he said easily. "The farmers need reminding that the Sieur de Bresse must have his revenues if he is to provide adequate protection for his vassals." Another dove came to feed from his palm.

"It is tame work for a knight," Magdalen said. "Do you not find it so? You would prefer to be campaigning, would you not?"

"I do my overlord's bidding," Guy replied with a smile. "For the nonce, I am content." He tossed the corn to the ground, where it was swooped upon by a bevy of doves, and held out his arms. "I would hold the child, if you think I will not wake her."

"She will be hungry soon, anyway." Magdalen reached over to lay Zoe in her father's arms. "She has grown, do you not think? Do you find her heavier?"

Guy considered the question. In truth, the child was so light he could barely feel her in any substantive way, but then he was accustomed to hefting the great weight of sword and lance, so perhaps it was not surprising he should feel this diminutive creature as no more than the weight of a butterfly. He gave Magdalen the answer she desired and expected, however. "A little, I believe." He touched the baby's nose, the cleft of her chin, and she snuffled, the little mouth pursing, her nose wrinkling. He laughed in sheer delight at the tiny perfection of her.

Zoe's mouth opened abruptly on a thinly demanding cry, her eyes scrunching. Reluctantly, Guy returned the baby to her mother. "She has need of you, I believe."

"I will go in and feed her." Magdalen handed the child to the waiting Erin and accepted Guy's arm to stand up. She leaned heavily on him for a minute. "I am becoming stronger, but it is so tedious. I shall be glad to go riding and hawking again."

"All in good time," he said. "I will take you within." He held her arm as they left the pleasaunce and returned to Magdalen's apartments.

She sighed with relief as he eased her down onto the bed.

"I will permit myself to feel feeble for one more week. Then I am determined to be quite well and strong again."

"Remember that you are feeding the child, lady," Erin said. "If you would put her to a wet nurse, you would regain your strength all the quicker."

"That I will not do," Magdalen declared with the firmness of one who has reiterated the statement many times.

"Then you must not complain," Guy counseled. "I must leave you now, but I will return by vespers." He kissed the top of her head. "Rest now."

Half an hour later, with his knight companions, their squires, and a small troop of men-at-arms, he left the castle on a mission of intimidation. It was, as Magdalen had said, poor work for a knight, but it had to be done. He did not like doing it, however. The French peasantry were already over-burdened with the taxes that had been raised to pay for the long years of a war whose outcome affected them only in terms of how much depredation they had had to suffer, and many of the more substantial peasantry were still struggling to pay off the ransoms of their menfolk.

He could enjoy the ride, however. Spring had come late this year after a more than ordinarily wet winter, and the deeply rutted roads had been impassable for many weeks. Now, however, they were crowded with the usual medley of travelers. A merchant and his pack train moved cumbersomely to one side as the de Gervais herald blew imperatively for passage, but around the next corner the de Gervais party gave right of way to a courier wearing the tabard of the papal court of Avignon, galloping with his escort as if escaping the devils of hell. A pardoner, with his bag of papal indulgences, sat in the budding hedgerow, enjoying the sunshine and touting for traveling custom among peripatetic sinners. They passed a peddler whose sack hung open on his back, and Guy drew rein, attracted by a wooden doll with painted eyes and a tiny doll carriage designed to be drawn by mice. It was absurd to buy such a toy for a little girl as yet but two weeks old, but he did so, half embarrassed and half delighted, thinking how Magdalen would laugh at him.

But as he continued on his way, his reflections, prompted by the thought of Zoe, turned to more disturbing matters. The bad weather had meant that they had lived without much news of the outside world, since travelers and pilgrims stayed beside their hearths when snow drifted thick or the rain churned the roads and lanes into a mire. As soon as conditions had made it feasible, he had sent a messenger to London, to John of Gaunt, with news of his granddaughter's birth, but he could not expect a response for another month. The response would contain further commands for the prince's vassal, he was certain.

The isolation made him restless, and with the budding trees and the busily building birds had come the need to venture into the outside world again, to discover what was going on in the circles of power he had inhabited in the past. His overlord would not leave him forever as proxy suzerain of the de Bresse fiefdom. In fact, it could be said his present task was accomplished. The castle was securely held, its chatelaine well established, a healthy heir in the nursery. Charles of France could stake no legitimate claim now. And all messages from Olivier indicated that the de Beauregards had other fish to fry; their interest in their cousin died beside a series of intrigues involving a bridegroom for Philippe de Beauregard's daughter.

The Duke of Lancaster must surely now have another use for Guy de Gervais. He would also have a husband in mind for the Lady de Bresse, who could not be left husbandless for much longer.

With the news of the birth of Zoe, Guy de Gervais had included a request to wed the child's widowed mother. He had decided he had nothing to lose by making the request, although he was well aware that Magdalen of Lancaster was too valuable a prize to be given away for nothing, and as he had thought before, he had nothing left to give Lancaster that his overlord did not already possess.

He said none of this to Magdalen, who seemed not to recognize the inevitability of an end to their idyll. She ignored his hints that she would soon have another husband, behaving as if such a thing were inconceivable, and he did not know how to break through such self-deception. But if he were honest, he had not chosen to break through it. He had told himself she should be left to enjoy a serene pregnancy and, now, that she should have peace and quiet in which to convalesce. But he was going to have to face up to the task sooner rather than later.

They were dispiriting thoughts to take on a May Day ride through the spring countryside, and it was a severe countenance he showed to the recalcitrant villagers of Seriac. Their spokesman, the village elder, faltered beneath the lord's impassive, blue-eyed stare as he sat his horse outside the tavern, listening apparently unmoved, to the tale of crops lost through brigandage and the destruction of the copse that hitherto had supplied the village with sufficient wood for all its needs.

Lord de Gervais looked around the circle of anxious men and women, small children clinging to skirts, peeping out at the magnificent, terrifying party of armored knights wearing over their mailshirts the blue and silver jupons emblazoned with the golden dragon of Gervais, carrying their great swords and lances at rest atop their majestic horses. The village elder had fallen silent, pulling unhappily on his straggly white beard, shuffling his clogs in the dust.

Nothing would be gained by wringing from these already wrung withers the last drops of sweat and blood and tears, Guy realized. They must be given time to sow new crops, to find an alternative wood supply. But they must also pay some tribute to their overlord. He would take the tribute in labor, Guy decided. Two days a month from every able-bodied man over the age of sixteen.

The villagers received the judgment initially in a stunned silence. They had expected no mercy; it was not a quality of life in this war-ravaged land. But slowly the realization that they had been granted a respite seeped through. Smiles, blackened or toothless but all genuine, appeared on the weary faces. Hands reached up to touch the dragon of Gervais embroidered on the lord's blue and silver saddlecloth, the braided mane of his palfrey, the gleaming silver of his harness.

Guy was not unused to the wondering worship of peasants. It had been accorded him when sieges had been lifted, villages rescued from brigands, isolated farms and cottages offered protection. Such grateful reverence was a knight's due in return for his obligation to offer such services to the defenseless. But he quickly grew impatient, and after a final word to the village elder, he signaled to the herald to blow the note of departure. The party wheeled and left the village of Seriac.

They arrived at the Castle de Bresse just as the bell for vespers was ringing. Guy paused only to divest himself of the sword and dagger at his belt, both of which he gave to Geoffrey, before hurrying into the chapel, followed by the rest of the party. Magdalen was sitting at the front, before the altar rail, and he could sense an extraordinary strain in her body as he slid into the pew beside her.

She gave him a taut smile and handed him a parchment. It bore the seal of Lancaster. Frowning, he put it unopened beside him on the bench, as if reproving her for bringing such temporal matters into this holy place in the middle of the evening office. But the white parchment seemed to take on a glowing illumination, to become a menacing presence as it sat between them. Once or twice, he was aware that she touched it, tracing the seal with a fingertip.

It was the first communication from England since the winter storms had put an end to sea travel, and Magdalen knew that it boded ill. She had wanted to open it, but the messenger had said it was for the eyes of the Lord de Gervais. He said he had been overlong upon the road, that his ship had gone aground off the coast of Brittany, that he had barely escaped with his life. He had been desperately anxious that the Lady Magdalen should understand the difficulties and dangers attendant upon his journey and should acknowledge that he had now discharged his duty by the safe delivery of the duke's message to the suzerain of de Bresse, even though it was delivered four weeks later than it should have been. Knowing her father, Magdalen could only sympathize with the messenger's anxiety.

She had wanted to open it but had not had the courage, too inhibited by the scruples of conscience that forbade prying into the affairs of others, for all that she knew the message must concern her. It was for this reason that she had brought it into the chapel, hoping that Guy would waste no time in opening it. Instead, he had simply laid it down and frowned at her, so she sat discomfited and overweaningly anxious as the rolled parchment seemed to burn against her thigh through the fine material of her gown.

Father Vivian droned through the office. Magdalen knelt, stood, prayed as her neighbor did, without thought or concentration, anxious only for the end of the tiresome ritual. It came at last. Father Vivian pronounced the benediction, and Guy tucked the parchment into his belt and moved out of the pew, offering Magdalen his arm when he reached the aisle. She tried to hurry, but she was prevented by the measured pace he set as they preceded the rest of the household into the beginning dusk.

"I wanted to open it, but I thought it might have vexed you," she said breathlessly, as soon as they reached the court.

"I am glad you restrained yourself," he replied. "Such an act would undoubtedly have displeased me. And you can have had no reason for doing such a thing."

"But what does it say?"

"How can I know that when I haven't yet opened it?" He paused to say a few words to the seneschal who had followed them from the chapel, while Magdalen stood in a fever of impatience at his side, wondering how he could be so calm and apparently untroubled by that burning, malevolent paper bearing her father's seal, pushed so casually into his belt.

"I will go to my study," he announced finally. "Geoffrey, attend me. I would remove this chainmail and my sword belt before supper."

"May I not come too?" Magdalen could not believe he would exclude her.

But Guy wanted to read it alone. It must have been sent some time before he had dispatched his own messenger to Lancaster, and he needed to know in private whether its contents obviated his own request to wed the widow. He did not think he could handle Magdalen's response to whatever was contained in the message until he had handled his own.

"You may come to me in my study in twenty minutes," he said. "I wish to refresh myself first." He strode off on the words, Geoffrey following him, leaving Magdalen standing openmouthed in the court.

With a muttered exclamation that was not in the least seemly, she went up to her own apartments. She had been feeling much stronger after an afternoon's rest, but now tears prickled ridiculously behind her eyelids. They were tears of weakness, she knew well, having found them most inconveniently frequent since Zoe's birth. It took little to trigger them, and her present apprehension and hurt were sufficient spur.

In the seclusion of his study, Guy forced himself to wait until Geoffrey had taken his mailshirt and sword belt, poured him wine, and left the room before opening the duke's letter.

Its message was short and clear: Edmund de Bresse had survived the assault last summer, had recovered from his wounds in a nearby abbey, and had returned to the Savoy in February. He had then been taken ill again but was now well on the way to full health and strength. It had not been possible to convey these glad tidings to Edmund's wife earlier because of winter travel restrictions, but Edmund de Bresse was shortly taking ship for France to resume his duties as grand seigneur of Bresse. On his arrival, Lancaster ordered the immediate return of his dearly beloved vassal, Guy de Gervais.

Guy stood immobile for many minutes, holding the document, staring sightlessly at the stone wall of the chamber. If Lancaster had presented another prospective husband, he might have been able to press his own suit, counting on the duke's longstanding friendship. But the reappearance of Magdalen's husband left him in the falsest of false positions. He had been Edmund's guardian and mentor since the lad was ten years old, and Edmund was entitled to expect only honest dealings and true faith from his uncle.

Instead, that uncle had cuckolded him, albeit unwittingly, and bred a bastard child on the body of his wife.

A shudder of self-loathing went through him, leaving him cold and sick, as he had not been since the first time he had killed. He had been a young page at Poitiers, but had grown to manhood in the few short hours of that battle.

He knew now only that he must leave this place without delay, must leave the woman who had entranced him with her passion and her beauty and her willful determination to follow the path of her choice: must leave his child, leave her to the man who by rights should have sired her. He must leave this place of sin and the woman who had led him into sin, must seek absolution, and, shriven once again, he must start life afresh.

And the prospect of that life filled him with the deepest desolation, stretching ahead into an infinite wasteland. A fitting punishment for his sin. He would do penance every day of the rest of his life.

The door opened without ceremony, startling him. He swung round to face it.

"What is it?" Magdalen went deathly white as she saw his face . . . so unlike his face, a mask obliterating all the life, the love, the humor she knew so well. Her hand went to her throat, plucked at the strand of pearls she wore. "Guy, what has happened?"

He saw the woman who had brought him to this, who had brought them both to it, with her intemperate passion, her blind and selfish pursuit of her own desires. And he recoiled.

Magdalen felt the recoil like a blow. Uncomprehending, terrified of what she did not understand, she stood staring at him. "Please . . . I beg you, my lord . . . tell me what has happened." The whispered plea seemed to stick in her throat, and she massaged the slim column with long, restless fingers.

Guy forced himself to focus on her, to see her distress, to remember her present physical frailty, and as he did so, his love rose strong and invincible again. "Come here," he said gently, opening his arms to her.

She seemed to collapse in his embrace, shaking with a terror she could not define, a terror brought about by the look she had seen in his eyes.

He held her securely as he told her of her father's missive. "You may expect your husband here at any time," he finished, his voice as expressionless as it had been throughout.

Magdalen drew back, tilting her head to look up at him. Now that she understood, she was filled with a great calm. "I knew Edmund was not dead. Indeed, I have tried to tell you so many times."

"How could you have known it?"

She shrugged. "I did. But when I brought up the subject, you became so wretched it seemed easier to leave it alone."

A sudden stab of apprehension, of premonition, lodged cold in his soul. "You understand what this means, Magdalen?"

"It is difficult," she said, "but I have thought long about what I must tell Edmund—"

"You will tell him nothing!" he interrupted in horror, unable to grasp truly what she was saying. "I will leave here as soon as your husband arrives. He will know nothing . . . *nothing*. Is it understood?"

She shook her head with that stubbornness he knew so well, her eyes clear and amazingly untroubled. "No, you do not understand. I cannot live without you, Guy, and we will manage this as others manage it. My father lives openly with Katherine Swynford. She has borne his bastards. There are others, so many others—"

"You do not know what you are saying!" His voice was harsh with shock and revulsion. "You are dishonored, your husband is dishonored, I am dishonored by what has happened between us. Your husband has the right to take your life and mine for the shame visited upon him, and I would not deny him that right. But there is no reason that he should be made to suffer. No one apart from ourselves and your women knows of this. It will die now . . . as if it had never been." But he knew as he said it that it could never be as if it had never been.

"No." She shook her head in blank incomprehension. "You cannot speak like that. I know you do not mean it. What of your child? You cannot just cast her aside. There is a way to manage this—" She broke off on a sob of pain and fright, her hand pressed to her cheek where the scarlet imprint of his hand burned like the desperate fury that had fueled the swift and sudden blow. She stared at him, her eyes distraught, dumb with shocked betrayal.

Through the foggy rage of despair, Guy de Gervais saw not Magdalen but the image of her mother, the woman who had spun her web of mortal sin and treachery around so many men and brought them all to destruction. Isolde de Beauregard had used the power of her body and her deep sensuality to entrap, and her daughter, empowered in the same way, was following the same course. Charles d'Auriac had fallen beneath that spell. Guy had watched it happen, had seen the lust, the hungry need in the man's eyes, a need that transcended whatever family purpose he had for the cultivation of his cousin.

Edmund de Bresse was bound in her toils, lost in love and desire from the first time he had taken her to his bed. And Guy himself had fallen victim to the devil's power of her, a power that now sought to entrap him because she wanted him and for no other reason. She cared nothing for the hurt and shame her husband would suffer, a man who loved her as deeply as Guy did himself. Edmund de Bresse must be sacrificed to her passion, as she would eventually and inevitably sacrifice her lover.

Yet, even as he thought this in his blind despair, he knew that there was an innocence to her sorcery, an innocence her mother had not evinced. Magdalen's webs were spun without the desire to cause hurt or to achieve some nefarious purpose; they had no motive but that of love and passion. The power she wielded was no fault of hers. She was innocent of treachery and she bore on her face the mark of his hand raised in anger against her.

"Ah, sweetheart," he said, his voice a low throb of remorse. "Forgive me." He took her again in his arms, and again trustfully she yielded to his embrace as if he had done and said nothing to breach that trust.

"Why?" she whispered through her tears. "I do not understand what I did that you should strike me."

"Forgive me," he said again, moving backward to the deep stone windowsill, sitting down, drawing her tightly against him, his palm smoothing over the hurt, a finger tenderly smudging the tears as they rolled down the damask skin. "You were saying such things, such impossible things, I could not help myself."

She shuddered against him in the aftermath of shock and distress but said nothing further, now too unsure of her ground to know what could safely be said, or how to express her conviction in such a way that it would not bring a resurgence of that frightful anger. Later, when she had thought things through and could speak in a considered fashion, she would try again.

"Do you forgive me?" he whispered into her hair, stroking her back.

"Yes . . . yes, of course . . . always," she murmured brokenly. "I do not mean to cry so, but I do so easily at the moment . . ."

"Hush," he said helplessly, stabbed afresh with the most dreadful sorrow at what he had done. "Dry your tears, now, for they are the worst punishment you could inflict upon me, love."

Magdalen sniffed and wiped her eyes with the long pointed sleeve of her gown. "I cannot find my handkerchief."

Guy went to the table where stood a pitcher of water. He dipped his own handkerchief into it and gently bathed her face. "There, that is better. In a little while, you will look yourself again, and no one will know at supper that anything untoward has occurred."

"My thanks." She tried to smile. "But I do not want any supper tonight."

"You must," he insisted, but still gently. "The news from England must be announced in the great hall, and no one must think that the news is a matter for anything less than rejoicing. The Sieur de Bresse returns to his wife, his child, his household, and his vassals. We must celebrate and put all in motion to receive him with due honor. And I must prepare to depart this place. My task is done."

Words of protest bubbled up despite her resolution to think before she spoke again on the subject. But as if he would forestall her, Guy's blue eyes darkened abruptly in warning and the words were stillborn. "I do not know if I can bear to sit through supper in the hall tonight," she said, instead. "Could I not be excused because I am still not fully recovered?"

"No." His voice was flat, admitting no possibility of argument. "Your absence on such an evening for whatever reason would be inexplicable. Go to your apartments now and compose yourself. The summons will sound soon."

Magdalen left him immediately. In the privacy

of her own chamber, she examined her pale face where the gray eyes seemed washed out and overlarge, and a faint shadow colored her right cheek. But it was nothing that cool water would not repair. She still did not fully understand what Guy had said to her. He could not possibly contemplate leaving her and his daughter, so she must have misinterpreted him. Or perhaps, in the shock of the news he had not been expecting, he had reacted without due thought, had failed to see the matter clearly.

Since she had never believed her husband to be dead, the news was no shock to her. She had hoped in her secret heart that the news would never come, but she had not allowed it to trouble her love. Her love had never been troubled by external events. It was simply the life-defining fact on which her existence depended. Nothing had been changed by Lancaster's news . . . except Guy.

A niggling voice spoke the thought in her heart. There had been a dreadful moment when the man in the study had not been the Guy she knew, the man she loved, and he had looked at the woman he loved as if he loathed her.

Ice enclosed her heart, and the blood in her veins seemed to run cold and sluggish. Nothing on earth could change what was between them.

Only witchcraft, only the satanic powers of witch and warlock, could turn such golden goodness into something evil and harmful. The power of love could only bring sweetness and balm; it could do no harm. But he had talked of shame and dishonor, of death as just punishment for what they had done, as if their love were indeed a powerful force for injury. He had talked of their love as if it were sullied, had come from the stews of mankind not the celestial planes of divine commitment.

But he had been speaking from the distemper of shock. Tonight, in the big bed, she would talk with him, would ease his troubled soul with the truth of an innocent love, and they would decide how best to manage the tangle.

Magdalen entered the great hall at his side, a little pale but perfectly composed. She had met his anxious scrutiny with a small gallant smile that had wrenched his heart even as it assured him that she would not fail to perform the part expected of her.

They took their places on the high table, then Guy signaled to the herald to blow the call for attention. The noise in the hall died down, the minstrels laid aside their instruments. Lord de Gervais rose slowly to his feet. His voice was steady, his smile seemingly indicative of genuine pleasure in the news as he informed the people of Bresse that their liege lord would be returning to them.

The news was received with polite enthusiasm. The young Edmund de Bresse was little known in his castle, and they had become accustomed to the just and predictable rule of the Lord de Gervais, whose touch was always sure, whose prowess on the field brought honor to all who rode with him, whose care and tutelage of the young Lady de Bresse had drawn only admiration. Change was always disturbing and rarely for the better.

The enthusiasm became more marked, however, when Lord de Gervais declared that he and the Castle de Bresse would host a tourney in honor of the returning lord. There would be three days of feasting, jousting, and all manner of revelry in which the household would take part. They all knew that material benefits would most certainly accrue from the influx of visiting knights and their ladies, in addition to the license such entertainment would grant them, and a cheer of approval rose to the smoke-blackened rafters of the great hall.

Magdalen accepted the congratulations of those around her with a calm smile and ate and drank sparingly. Somehow, Guy's announcement made Edmund's imminent return tangible;

the image of feasting and jousts, of entertaining such a host of guests—the Lady Magdalen de Bresse at her husband's side in their own domain for the first time ever—stunned her with its reality. But it would have to be done. Whatever arrangements they could make to manage the tangle of love, the appearance must be maintained. She was her husband's wife.

Suddenly, she remembered what that would mean in all its facets. She remembered Edmund's ardor, the love in his eyes that she had treated with light friendliness, assuming that it would die when he found himself a paramour, as he would, as all young knights did. She remembered the conjugal bed they had shared from January to August. What took place in it had not troubled her unduly, but neither had it particularly pleasured her. She had lent herself to her husband dutifully, passionlessly. Passion she had reserved for Guy de Gervais to whom she had given herself; to whom she had given herself, it seemed, in spirit since he had ridden into the life of an eleven-year-old child, waiting with increasing impatience for her destiny to come for her.

She must resume all aspects of her wedded life with Edmund, even if it was done in the full knowledge of her other life with Guy de Gervais. Edmund would—must—understand where her heart lay, but he was still her husband, and as such was entitled to her body. And Magdalen did not know how she would be able to submit now that she knew what the true marriage of body and soul entailed.

It grew hot in the hall, and she was glad when Guy, alert as always to her fatigue, rose from his seat. They left the hall and the household to continue their supper as they pleased, going out into the cool night air.

Magdalen drew a relieved breath. "May we walk a little, my lord? I have need of the air."

"If you wish it. But not for long, as I have much to accomplish before your husband arrives." It was said in a flat, matter-of-fact tone, and Magdalen could only guess what an effort it cost him to speak in such fashion.

Disconcerted, she looked up at him in the dim light of the flambeaux held by sentries at the far corners of the inner court. He seemed to have withdrawn from her. "We need not walk, if you do not wish it," she said. "I will come to you later, when all are gone to their beds."

"No, Magdalen," he said, in the same flat tone. "You may not come to me in that way again. Did I not explain that to you?"

"But . . . but . . . ?"

"No!" He turned on his heel and went toward the outside stairs.

Desolation and confusion swamped her. How could he forbid her company at such a time? How could he deny that there were things they should talk about? Things to be arranged? Comfort they could take in and of each other? But he was denying *her*. He was denying the woman he had loved, the woman who had borne him a child, the woman who loved him more than life itself. And he must not be permitted to do so.

She had always known that this tangle would be for her to manage. She had always suspected that Guy's inner, honorborn doubts lying beneath the force of his love would raise their heads and bring heartbreak if she permitted them to do so. So she must take matters into her own hands.

In her own apartments, she found Erin and Margery agog with the news, but they were too sensitive to press their lady, whose apparent pallor and listlessness seemed at odds with a certain energy they could detect flowing though her.

She fed the baby with her usual loving patience and then allowed her women to prepare her for bed. Zoe slept with the women in the antechamber. If she woke hungry in the night, they soothed her with honeyed water so that her mother's rest would not be disturbed. It was a satisfactory arrangement from many aspects, not

least in that the Lady de Bresse generally slept
the night peacefully in the arms of the Lord de
Gervais.

Once Magdalen was alone, she sat beside the
open window, where the dark blue velvet of the
night sky was pierced with myriad diamond-
studded configurations, and the air was scented
with lilac and lavender, and she prepared herself
for the meeting—the confrontation—that she
must have with Guy de Gervais once the lights
were extinguished. The bell for compline rang,
and she determined to wait until matins
sounded. At that time even Guy would be in his
bed. In a household where the first gray streaks
of dawn signaled the beginning of a busy day,
few eyes remained open after compline. Her
own eyes drooped, however, as she sat, her elbow propped on the stone sill, and she dozed
fitfully as the castle put itself to bed.

At midnight, the matins bell rang, and she
awoke hastily, blinked the sleep from her eyes,
and set off on her mission of persuasion.

She had but recently resumed her nighttime
journeying within the walls between her own
apartments and the lord's chamber. These journeyings had led to the warmth and comfort of
his arms, the skillful, tender caresses of a man
who knew that loving sharing could take many
forms and did not always have to involve the

transcendent heights of passion that could only truly be reached by the robust in body.

Tonight, though, she hesitated outside the door to his chamber, apprehensive. He had forbidden her to come to him, and she was so ill accustomed to defying him that it took all her resolution, all her conviction that she was right to do what she was doing, to enable her to lift the latch.

The chamber was in darkness, the curtains drawn around the bed, and she stood for a moment uncertain what to do, how to announce her presence to the sleeper within the enclosure.

"Guy?" She whispered his name, treading softly to the bed, her hand raised to draw back the curtains.

"God's blood!" At the barely suppressed fury in the oath, she shrank back, her hand still on the curtain. "I told you you were never to come to me in this fashion again." He sat up, reaching sideways for flint and tinder. Candlelight flickered, darkness became gloom. His eyes glared, as hard as the flint in his hand. "Go back to your own apartments now, Magdalen."

"No, please, you must understand." She realized she was still gripping the curtain, her knuckles whitening as she seemed to be holding on to the heavy velvet as if it could provide concrete support.

"No, it is you who must understand," he said, with a resurgence of his earlier harshness. He swung out of bed, his naked body a dark shadow in the deeper shadows of the bed-curtains. He reached for his long robe and drew it around him. "It is finished, Magdalen. What must I do to enable you to understand that fact?"

She shook her head, biting her lip fiercely. "It cannot be over. My love for you is my life. We have a child together."

"And you have a husband!" He prised her fingers loose from the curtain and took her shoulders. "You have a husband deserving of your loyalty even if you cannot give him love. And now that I know your husband lives, I will not break faith with him. God knows, I have a lifetime's sin upon my soul as it is, without compounding it."

"But do you not love me?" The simplicity of the question left him momentarily speechless. It should not have surprised him, since he knew so well that it was the only fact of any significance for Magdalen.

"You must hold me," she said now. "Please, I feel so lost, so alone, so afraid. Please hold me. No more than that."

He could not deny her. Every fiber struggled to resist what he knew would bring only further heartache as it simply postponed the final wrenching agony of their parting. But he could not deny her as she stood there in all her warm, living flesh, the gray eyes glowing with promise and appeal, the vibrant dusky hair tumbling down her back, her mouth, full-lipped and rosy, parted in the urgency of her plea.

Even as he took her in his arms and held her tightly against him before slipping into bed with her, still holding her, he wondered if he would ever be free of her spell.

She fell asleep almost immediately, exhausted by the searing emotional anguish of the evening, trusting in the safety of his arms; somehow, even in sleep, managing to convey to him her conviction that she would never lose the security of his arms, would never be without his love to uphold her, whatever he might say to the contrary.

And Guy de Gervais did not know what to do to bring her to an understanding of the realities. When a man did not know himself how such a separation was to be endured, how could he possibly help such a one as Magdalen of Lancaster, who was so blindly determined in her beliefs, to come to an acceptance of their parting and of where her loyalties must now lie?

Twelve

HERALDS WENT OUT from the Castle de Bresse into the neighboring towns and fiefs, announcing the upcoming tournament to honor the return of Sieur Edmund de Bresse. The announcement reached as far afield as the rue de Berri in Paris. Charles d'Auriac set about his own preparations.

Within the castle, preparations were under way from the kitchen to the garrison, and the Lady Magdalen had little time to speculate on the future. Guy was absent for long periods of time, and when he was within the castle he was always closeted with the sergeant-at-arms, the seneschal, or the chamberlain. He gave up all attempts to discuss the future with her, trusting that Edmund's arrival would finally impress the facts upon her in a way that mere contemplation so signally failed to.

Each night, she continued to slip into his bed but made no demands upon him other than that he should hold her while she slept, and in truth he was more than content to do so, although he lay wakeful most of the night, arming himself for the long nights ahead when he would sleep alone without the warm, fragrant, sweetly breathing shape of her molded to his side.

When he would sleep alone, aware that the warm, fragrant, sweetly breathing shape of her would be molded to her husband's side.

In Paris and in Roussillon, the scattered members of the de Beauregard clan received the information that Edmund de Bresse had not died in that murderous assault in the forest at Westminster.

Bertrand de Beauregard initially poured his fury on his son Gerard, who had been dispatched incognito to England the previous summer with the responsibility for removing Magdalen's husband, by whatever method came to hand or particularly appealed to him.

"The men were paid well," the patriarch said. "You paid them for a job that they failed to perform."

"It is impossible, my lord, to believe that he could have survived such wounds," Gerard said, white around the mouth, all too well aware of the danger of failing his father's commands. "The men swore he was dead when they left him."

"And you believed them?" his father questioned scornfully. "Did they bring you the body in proof?"

"No, my lord," his son miserably confessed.

"But I had no reason to doubt them. They had served us well in the past in similar tasks, and in truth it would have been difficult for them to transport the body to the hostelry in the city where I was staying."

"Fool!" declared Bertrand. "I am surrounded by idiots and incompetents. The woman has given birth to an heir, albeit a girl child; Lord de Gervais has secured the fief, militarily and legally, against any form of attack or annexation; and now the husband is coming to take his place and presumably sire yet more children in the name of Lancaster on your base-born cousin!"

He drew his dagger from his belt. The ruby eye of the sea serpent glinted in the sun as he drove the dagger point hard into the oak table, where it shivered beneath the nose of Gerard de Beauregard, who, with the exercise of supreme self-control, did not flinch.

"Charles is the only man among you with either wit or courage," Bertrand said. "And where is he, in the name of St. Christopher? Amusing himself in the court in Paris." He pulled the dagger free of the oak and threw it instead at the wall behind Gerard's head. Again his son did not flinch. This was a favorite game of his father's when angered, one he had played when his sons were tiny and throughout their growing. The dagger did not always miss, nor was it always intended to, and all his sons bore scars on hand and thigh earned when the game had become overtly punitive.

"My cousin said he would wait out the winter in Paris," Philippe now said, hesitant lest he draw the fire toward himself. "He will waste less time if he is lodged within eighty miles of Bresse when he makes plans for the abduction."

"And what good will the abduction of the woman do us now, you fool?" snapped his father. "When her husband, liege lord of Bresse, vassal of John, Duke of Lancaster, holds undisputed sway?"

"We will arrange his murder, my lord," Gerard said, reaching behind him to pull the dagger free of the paneling. He handed it, hilt first, to his father. "Poison . . . a hunting accident . . . It can be done. It has been done many times."

"But your bungling has wasted nearly a year!" The dagger inscribed a delicate arc through the air, to land shivering in the wood at the far end of the table. It appeared this time to have been launched without threat, more in the interests of marksmanship, and his sons relaxed infinitesimally. "If it weren't for that, we could expect to see Magdalen of Lancaster and her child in the fortress at Carcassonne before the summer solstice."

"It will still be done," Gerard said, pledging himself heedlessly, knowing it to be the only means by which he would return to his father's good graces. "I will go myself to Paris and join my cousin. I will undertake to remove Edmund de Bresse, and my cousin will do with the woman what he has always intended to do."

But before Gerard could leave Roussillon, a courier arrived from Charles d'Auriac in Paris. The courier was an olive-skinned, agile man with shrewd black eyes, eyes that were everywhere at once; but his demeanor was so retiring, his position as courier between Charles d'Auriac and the de Beauregard strongholds in Roussillon so well established in recent months, that no one noticed his eyes or the fact that he seemed to like the shadows. The message he carried was simple. D'Auriac believed he had at hand the means of removing Edmund de Bresse without a hint of suspicion falling upon any member of the de Beauregard clan, and his plans were well in motion for the abduction of Magdalen of Lancaster, which would also be accomplished without any indication of who lay behind it. He expected to have the woman and her child delivered to the fortress at Carcassonne within a few weeks.

Some time during the next few days, the household at Toulouse became aware of the absence of the olive-skinned courier. It did not concern anyone; such fee-paid servants came and went frequently enough. They were not bound to a master as his serfs were. The only person for whom his disappearance was a cause for regret was a little laundress in the household of Charles d'Auriac on the rue de Berri in Paris.

MAGDALEN WAS SITTING on the broad stone windowsill of the small round turret chamber that so long ago it seemed she had discovered and designated as a trysting place for the snatched moments of daytime loving that she and Guy had found so entrancing. There had been none of that for many weeks now, and slowly it was beginning to dawn on her that Guy intended there should never again be such wonderful moments of illicit joy.

She was at a loss. There was a distanced look in his eyes now, and even when he held her, she felt a spiritual withdrawal. But she clung to the belief that for as long as he was with her, for as long as he continued to hold her, something would happen to make things right again. He would recognize that they were bound to each other, bound indissolubly by the ties of love that transcended any man-made ties, the ties imposed by John of Gaunt for his own ends.

It was midafternoon. An early bee buzzed at

the window of the bastion room. She drew her knees up, leaning her back against the hard stone wall of the window embrasure. She heard the imperative blast of an arriving herald at the drawbridge and listened idly to the identifying exchange, listened but did not fully understand. Her eyelids drooped as she looked down on the outer court from her turret window. There were so many comings and goings these days that she was but vaguely curious to see the new arrival's standard.

The herald and his escort rode from the *place d'armes* into the court. The falcon of Bresse flew at his horn.

Slowly, she turned sideways on the sill to see directly down into the court. Guy de Gervais appeared from the garrison court. He walked over to the herald. Magdalen could not hear what was said, but after a few minutes Guy turned aside and moved toward the bastion, disappearing from Magdalen's sight as he stepped through the arched door below her. The herald and his escort dismounted as attendants came out to welcome them, took their horses, and escorted them to the quarters allotted them.

Guy did not know how he knew where to find Magdalen, but his steps took him along the empty corridor of their own volition. The door to the turret room was ajar, and he saw her sitting on the windowsill, her head resting on her drawn up knees, her eyes on the court below.

"Your husband will arrive on the morrow," he said, stepping into the room.

Her head turned slowly on her knees. The gray eyes held his gaze, calm and direct. "Yes," she said. "I assumed that was the message."

"You will leave the women's wing now and remove to the lord's apartments," he said. "It is right that you should be established there when your husband arrives."

"What of you?"

"I will take up residence in the guest hall until after the tourney, when I will return to England."

"You cannot go. You cannot go and leave me here."

"Come with me." He waited until she had slipped from the windowsill, then turned to the door. "Come with me."

Chilled by the masklike impassivity of his face, the sense that he was about to do something irrevocable that she could not forestall because she did not know what it was, she followed him down the passage and out into the sunny court. There, ordinary life was continuing amid an air of excitement: servitors scurried, voices called, dogs barked, a hammer rang on wood from the lists being erected on the hill behind the castle, smoke rose thick from kitchen chimneys, and the aroma of roasting meat filled the air, mingling with the fomenting yeast from the brewery and the acrid tang of manure from the stables. It was an ordinary afternoon in May, infused with the pleasurable excitement of a great tourney to be hosted, and the prospect of fifty knights and their ladies and attendants to be housed and fed and entertained in a style appropriate to the wealth and power of de Bresse.

Guy de Gervais strode to the chapel, Magdalen following. It was dim and cool within, the heady smell of incense from the midday office lingering with that of the candles burning at the tomb of St. Francis, the patron saint of the chapel of Bresse.

The tomb lay in a pillared alcove to the right of the altar and it was here that Guy went, still saying nothing to his equally silent follower.

At the tomb, he lit another candle and held it high. Magdalen felt a weight of solemnity descend upon them both, and a weight of apprehension on her soul. "What are we doing here?" she whispered, her tongue moving for the first time in an eternity, it seemed, forming the words hesitantly, as if she had been rendered mute and was only now given back the power of speech after long silence.

"You are going to swear on the bones of St.

Francis that you will never, by word or deed, give your husband, Edmund de Bresse, the least reason to doubt your fidelity or the parentage of your child."

She shook her head. "You are telling me I must deny you . . . must deny our love, everything that has been between us."

"Yes, I am telling you that you must deny those things," he said. "Swear on the bones of St. Francis that you will never give your husband the least reason to suspect what has happened between us."

"And if I do not?" She clutched at her throat, recognizing the futility of her question. If he would deny her, then what purpose was there in her own steadfastness?

"Swear." Taking her hand, he laid it upon the cold marble effigy. The candle he held aloft flickered in this dim, cool, holy place, and a bead of wax fell hotly upon her hand, contrasting acutely with the deathly cold beneath her flattened palm.

Magdalen swallowed, feeling the movement of her throat beneath her other hand. "Why would you deny us?"

"Swear. And then you will make your confession and you will be shriven." His voice was quiet and gentle, but the imperative and the determination could not be ignored.

"On the bones of St. Francis, I deny our love." Her voice choked, shook, her hand on the cold stone trembled, and her soul screamed its denial of the words he had forced her to say.

"You swear that you will never lead your husband to doubt the paternity of your child or to suspect what has happened between you and me."

Her head drooped. "I swear." It was a bare exhalation in the cold gloom, but Guy released her hand that he still held on the tomb.

"You will make your peace with God when you choose," he said in the same quiet and gentle voice. "As shall I."

They left the chapel, going out into the heedless sun.

The following morning, the Sieur Edmund de Bresse rode up to his castle to claim his domain and his wife, who rode out with the Lord de Gervais and a welcoming party of knights and their attendants to meet her returning lord on the plain before the town.

Edmund heard the alerting bells ringing from the four towers of Bresse when he was two miles away, the sound carrying across the plain in the clear morning air, and he knew he had been seen and identified. His heart leaped against his breastbone. Excitement surged into his toes. How was she? How would she greet him? What of their child? Questions he had asked himself over and over in the last weeks, and within the hour they would be answered.

Magdalen sat her roan palfrey. It was the first time she had ridden since Zoe's birth, but she was too numbed, mesmerized by shock and spiritual pain, to find the exercise in the least enjoyable. She was dressed in a gown of silver cloth, a pearl-encrusted silver fillet confining her hair. The silver and pearl against the milk-white pallor of her skin gave her an ethereal quality, it seemed to Guy. Even her mouth, usually so warm and red and vibrant, was today the palest pink, and her eyes held none of their customary sparkling vitality; they were large gray pools of limitless depth and a haunting, mysterious sadness.

Guy did not think he had ever seen her looking more beautiful or more desirable, and he had never been more aware of the deep sensual currents running beneath that pale surface. The contrast between that vibrancy that could not be diminished even by sorrow and the still, calm sadness was more powerfully arousing than he could have believed possible. It was unnatural, bewitching, a serpentine power that could be harnessed so easily for evil if once her innocence were breached.

For himself, he could only function by taking

each minute of the day, one at a time, proceeding in orderly fashion to the moment when he could abandon the anguish of her presence and lose his grief once more in the violent pursuits of the sword. In the clash of steel, the smoking reek of blood, the agonized clamor of battle, he would find himself again, be freed of his guilt, lose the softness of the lover and remantle himself in the grim visage of the warrior.

Edmund saw the woman riding beside the Lord de Gervais, coming toward him across the plain. He could not make out the details of face or form, but he knew his wife. With an exultant cry, he put spur to his horse and galloped toward them, drawing ahead of his company. His horse reared to a halt before the first line of the welcoming party, lips drawn back over the bit as his rider hauled on the reins to arrest his stride in mid-gallop.

"My lady," Edmund said. "I rejoice to see you well."

"You are well come, my lord," Magdalen said. "I thank God in his mercy for your deliverance."

"The child?"

"A daughter, sound in limb and healthy."

Edmund smiled, and all his love and joy was in the smile. He gazed around the sunny plain, embracing every blade of grass, every peeping daisy with his contentment. Then he turned to Guy de Gervais.

"I owe you much, my lord."

The words stabbed into his very vitals, but Guy managed to smile. "God is indeed merciful, Edmund." He raised a hand in signal and the party turned their horses, Edmund falling in between his wife and Lord de Gervais.

"How is my daughter christened, madame?" He turned eagerly to Magdalen.

"Zoe," Magdalen said. "For the gift of life. Her birth was long and difficult." She saw from his nonplussed expression that he did not know how to respond to such a piece of information. Her pale lips smiled as she reassured him, but the sadness remained in her eyes. "It is not unusual, my lord, with first babies, and it is in the past now."

"Yes." He returned the smile. "But Zoe is an un-Christian name, my lady."

"Pagan?" Her eyebrows rose slightly. "It disturbs you, my lord?"

Edmund frowned. There was a note in her voice that made him uncomfortable, and he *was* disturbed by the name she had given their child. Philippa, Elinor, Katharine, Gertrude—these were proper names for girl-children of royal and noble blood.

"The child bears also the name Louise," Guy said quietly, "as I am certain your wife was about to tell you."

"Yes, my lord," Magdalen concurred, despising herself for that urge to taunt her husband, yet knowing that it had come from an instinctive anger that he should have attempted to criticize a decision made by herself and Guy for *their* child.

But Edmund was guiltless. She must never lose sight of that.

"Castle de Bresse is to host a grand tourney in honor of your return, my lord," she now said. "My Lord de Gervais thought it would be a fitting occasion for such ceremony."

"Ah, I can think of no greater pleasure." Edmund was enthusiastic. "But I have had little opportunity in recent months to practice my skill at combat, and I fear I am sadly weakened in my arm."

"Then you will have a se'enight in which to practice," Guy said. "I will gladly offer my services as partner in the garrison court and the tilting ground. Your strength will return soon enough with your skill." Easily, he led the conversation to matters of combat, talking to Edmund as he had done in the past with the familiarity of the mentor, questioning him about

Lancaster's affairs and the court at the Savoy Palace. Magdalen, for the moment ignored and glad to be so, rode in silence between them.

Heralds blew the note of welcome as they rode beneath the arch into the *place d'armes*. The knights of the garrison were drawn up to greet the returning seigneur, and Magdalen slipped from her palfrey and took the stirrup cup of welcome from a page, offering it herself.

Edmund drained its contents in one gulp, then sprang from his horse. "Let us go within, my lady. I would see our child, and there is much that we have to say to one another after such an absence." He gave her his arm, and she laid her silver sleeve upon the turquoise brocade of his tunic, thinking numbly how pretty the two colors were together. Unable to help herself, she looked over her shoulder to where Guy stood immobile beside his horse. Her eyes held a desperate plea, but he turned from it so she could not see his own piercing pain.

Abruptly, she was reminded of the day when Edmund had come to Bellair to claim his wife, and in his haste and his youthful impetuosity, he had hustled her inappropriately from the great hall and, with the same haste and impetuosity, had taken her virginity and consummated their marriage in an urgent, hurtful scramble.

She seemed to be living the experience again, except that Edmund had more finesse now, was surer of himself, and clearly felt no need to assert his claim and his right to his wife with the precipitate insensitivity of the past. But then he didn't know . . . And he was not to know, was he? She had sworn on the bones of St. Francis to deny her love and the last ten months of a loving idyll.

"The child is with my women," she said, moving toward the outside staircase. "You will remember the way to the lord's chamber, I daresay. Lord de Gervais has made many improvements to the castle and fortifications in your absence. You will wish to discuss such things with him without delay." She heard her voice rattling on in an attempt to distance him from her, to pretend this wasn't happening, that she was not going to the great conjugal chamber with her husband, was not about to present a child to him as his own—a child whose father meant more to her than life itself, but who had decreed that she must do these things and live this lie.

She led him to the antechamber of the lord's apartments. Erin and Margery jumped to their feet, making reverence to their lord, offering thanks for his deliverance. He heard them out impatiently before saying, "Dismiss your women, my lady. I would wish you to show me my child."

Magdalen waved the women from the room and went to the cradle. Zoe slept, flowerlike. At the foot of the cradle sat the doll that her father had bought her from the peddler. The tiny doll carriage stood on the windowsill above the cradle. Zoe was never to know they had been a father's gift.

"Do you wish me to waken her, my lord?"

He shook his head, gazing down at the tiny mound with its soft red-gold down on the crown of her head. He looked at his hands, turning them over in curious wonder. They seemed so enormous beside the delicate frailty of his daughter.

Magdalen bent to the cradle and gently lifted the sleeping baby. "Hold her, Edmund," she said, touched by the wonder in his face.

"I am afraid to," he whispered. "I might break her."

"No, you will not." Her smile this time reached her eyes, and she laid the child in his arms. He held her awkwardly with none of the sure, confident ease of Guy de Gervais. But Edmund had had no experience as yet.

"Zoe," he murmured. "I mislike the name, Magdalen. Let her be named Louise."

"No," Magdalen said, and her mouth hardened.

"I bore the child, Edmund, and I gave birth to her. I claim a mother's right to name her."

Edmund had rarely seen the sterner side of his wife, but he had long bowed to her assurance, to the barely acknowledged fact that he could not gainsay her if she chose not to be gainsaid, be he her lord or no.

"If you wish it, then so be it." He handed the child back to her. "Let us go into our own chamber now."

Magdalen laid the baby in the cradle and went ahead of her husband into the adjoining room where she had spent so many glorious hours, had shared a lifetime of bliss and passion—bliss and passion that must last a lifetime, she amended.

"I will pour you wine, my lord." She filled the jeweled cup from the pitcher on the table with the rich ruby wine of Aquitaine and brought him the cup.

"Drink with me." He held the cup to her lips, and she drank. "I have been tormented with my need for you," he said, trying to find the words to describe his agony of mind during the fever delirium, his terror of her loss, or of finding himself in some way not whole and therefore not worthy of her.

She listened to him without speaking, without moving, her great sad eyes never leaving his face. Then she took the cup and gently kissed his mouth. "Edmund, I am not worthy of such love."

He groaned and wrenched her against him, crushing her slender fragility against his chest so that she could feel the sharp metallic prick of his mailshirt through her gown. "I need you, Magdalen. Please, *now*."

But she pulled back, her face grave although her eyes were compassionate and understanding. "Not yet," she said. "It is still too soon after the birth. I cannot yet."

His whole body shook as he fought to bring his ardor under control, to stop himself from possessing her in a violent ravishing violation that would injure them both. His face was gray with the effort as he felt the sensual promise of her body, enticing him, drawing him toward some dark and swirling pool of desires as yet unspoken and unfelt.

"How soon?" he rasped finally, taking up the cup again, raising it jerkily to his lips. "How long must I wait? It's been ten months, Magdalen, since I have had a woman."

It had been a month since Zoe's birth, and Magdalen knew she would not be able to procrastinate for much longer. But she could not face such a thing yet . . . not yet, while Guy de Gervais remained within the same walls . . . not yet, when the memories of passion in that great bed were so agonizingly vivid . . . not yet, not until the keen edge of her love had been blunted just a little.

"A week or two," she said. "I am suckling the child, and it takes my strength."

"Then put her to the wet nurse." A harshness bred of frustration had entered his voice.

Magdalen shook her head. "No, Edmund, I will not expose her to another breast. The milk could be weak and thin, not as healthful as her mother's. I will not risk my baby's health."

He sighed, but the painful urgency of a minute ago had died, and he heard the sense in her words. "I will try to wait in patience."

"I thank you for your forbearance, my lord." She kissed him again, and there was no mockery in her words. "I will help you prepare for the feast. Your household will all be assembled to do you honor at dinner. Shall I have your squire summoned with your belongings?"

When Edmund de Bresse and his lady took their places on the high table at dinner, Guy de Gervais watched them. It seemed to him that they were both pale and strained, but Magdalen was fulfilling the duties of her position without fault, and the role of lord sat easily upon her husband now. Edmund de Bresse was no longer the eager, fiery youth of last year. Like John of

Gaunt, Guy had read in the young man's eyes the history of his suffering, and like John of Gaunt, he knew that Edmund had left his youth behind that afternoon in the forest of Westminster.

That night, Edmund lay beside his wife, conscious that she also was wakeful, yet he had no words to broach the silence. He did not know how to talk to her. If he could show her with his body how he felt, reveal his love in deed rather than word, he was certain this painful tension between them would dissipate. But she had said he must not touch her, so he lay stiffly away from her, terrified lest his leg should brush hers and the contact destroy his hard-won and hard-held control.

Suddenly, Magdalen pushed aside the quilt and slipped to the floor. "I will sleep on the truckle bed," she said, bending to pull the pallet from beneath the high-standing bed. "I feel your torment, and I will not exacerbate it in this way."

Edmund said nothing, simply turned on his side and closed his eyes tightly. Magdalen crept beneath the blanket on the pallet and lay staring up into the gloom. She was wracked with fatigue, but had gone long beyond sleep. Her legs twitched with a restless ache; her mind was horribly clear, thoughts, memories, futile plans tumbling ceaselessly. But she had to sleep. If she did not, then her milk would dry up and Zoe would suffer. And the more she told herself she must sleep, the further from sleep she became.

Across the inner court, in the guest hall, Guy de Gervais was also sleepless. But unlike the two in the lord's chamber, he was making no attempt to sleep.

"How serious a threat do you believe this to be?" He poured mead into two pewter tankards and handed one to the man sitting opposite him.

Olivier took it with a nod of thanks. He had arrived that evening, slipping through the postern gate just before the curfew had been rung. "Hard to say, my lord. The Sieur d'Auriac believes he can bring off the Lady Magdalen and remove her husband without help from Toulouse. From what I've seen of him, he doesn't make idle promises . . . or threats," he added with a grimace. In his sojourn in the d'Auriac household, he had seen plenty of evidence of the latter. Charles d'Auriac was not a pleasant man.

Guy frowned. He was now under orders to leave his erstwhile charges to manage their own protection and return to London. Edmund had told him that afternoon of Lancaster's warning to him of a potential threat from the de Beauregard clan. From what little Edmund said, it was clear how much Lancaster had omitted. It was not for the prince's vassal to repair that omission. He could do no more than alert Edmund to Charles d'Auriac.

He stood up and strode to the window. It was too dark to see anything but stars and a fitful moon, but he could see in his mind's eye every sentry position, every watchman in every bell-tower. He knew the subterranean passages that ran beneath the castle to ensure that supplies could be brought within in case of a siege. There was a permanent garrison of fifty knights, vassals of the Sieur de Bresse, and two hundred men-at-arms. What could Charles d'Auriac possibly achieve against such defenses? It would take an army to breach the walls of the Castle de Bresse, and such an armed attack by a French knight against an English knight in a time of truce was inconceivable. It would hold no just cause as motive, and without such motive to bring papal blessing on the assault, no man would attempt it for fear of damnation.

"God's bones, Olivier, but I cannot for the life of me see how he could be so confident." He turned back to the room. "I must travel to England as soon as the tourney is over. I will leave you here, but ensure that if Charles d'Auriac pays another visit he does not see you. He will undoubtedly recognize you now. Watch over the Lady Magdalen and get word to me if you sense aught amiss. It is understood?"

Olivier was not happy at the assignment, and his position was sufficiently privileged for him to make that clear. But his lord was adamant. Olivier would remain in his lord's stead. He knew everything there was to know, and if the Lady Magdalen was in need of protection, he was to provide it regardless of cost.

Guy sent the man to his bed then, and contemplated his own. It was cheerless, offering only loneliness, but Lord de Gervais was a man of war, and he knew how to banish the inconvenient thoughts and the body's recalcitrance in order to catch sleep whenever the opportunity arose. He had done what he could to ensure Magdalen's continued safety. He had done what he could to ensure her marriage would be unsullied by their sin. He had done what he could to ensure Edmund would not suffer from his uncle's breach of faith. There was no more he could do, and his grief was his own, his healing in his own hands . . . if they were capable of such work.

In the next days, he spent most of his time with Edmund in practice combat in the garrison court, riding out to hounds, watching him tilting at the quintain as if he were again a page or squire in training.

Edmund presented a cheerful, eager face to his uncle, listening attentively to matters of business relating to the household or garrison, accepting all suggestions for entertainment, but Guy de Gervais knew something was awry.

There was something false and strained in his apparent contentment. Guy had known the young man too long to miss it, and anxiously he speculated on the cause. Magdalen would not have broken her oath. Indeed he knew she had not done so. The consequences of such a confession would far transcend Edmund's present restlessness and unhappiness. But something was wrong between them. Guy suspected the root lay with Magdalen. He could command her silence, but he could not command that she treat her husband with the affection and respect he deserved. He could not command her to banish unhappiness, to put the past behind her and look to the future. He could command himself to do that, and if he failed, that was between himself and his conscience. But Magdalen's behaviour had direct repercussions on Edmund, and her husband was suffering evident disquietude. His eyes never left her, watching her every movement, hungrily resting upon her when she was still. And if she was aware of this, she gave no sign, simply continued with what she was doing, offering her husband a word, a smile, a gesture

now and again in such a casual manner, border-
ing almost on carelessness, that Guy could feel
Edmund's hurt. Why could Magdalen not
feel it?

But Guy thought he understood what was
happening. It was Magdalen's unwitting sorcery
again. From the depths of her innocence, innocent of her power, she could not help but
wound those whom she bewitched. Edmund
needed her love, and she was withholding it. On
the third night, in his own restlessness, he discovered that Edmund's distress had a more concrete dimension.

Guy was walking on the battlements, sleepless
and unwilling to put himself to sleep in the ways
that he knew. In the donjon slept his child and
the woman he loved. He had not seen his
daughter alone since Edmund had arrived, had
forced himself to sit on the sidelines when
Magdalen had brought the child into the hall or
the family parlor, longing to hold Zoe, yet
knowing he dare not because of what he might
reveal. Instead, he had had to watch Edmund's
evident delight in the child and his maladroit yet
eager attempts to hold her and play with her, secure in the belief that the child was his. The denial of his fatherhood was a wound that cut so
deep into Guy's soul, he did not think it would
ever heal, but he must live with it, though it

gape for the rest of his life. But he must see the child again before he left. He could not leave without one last kiss upon that tiny brow, one last look at the petallike face, one last deep-drawn inhalation of the sweet milky smell of her.

He became aware of Edmund, standing against the parapet, outlined against the midnight blue-black of the sky. Edmund believed himself alone, and for once his unhappiness was undisguised, easily read in the strain in the broad shoulders, hunched beneath the short cloak, in the set of his head as he gazed outward as if what was inward was too painful for contemplation.

"Edmund?"

The young man turned, painted a smile upon his face. "My lord. You are up late."

"It's a lovely night. But what of you? You practiced long and hard today. Surely you are tired?"

Edmund shrugged. "Awearied enough, I daresay. But tormented."

"By what?" Guy drew closer, his voice gently inviting.

Edmund trusted the man under whose care he had grown to manhood, and he found himself blurting out his pain without thought. "I have such need of her," he cried in low-voiced anguish. "I cannot describe such need. But she says it is too soon after the birth, and I may not take her. But I am consumed with need." His knuckles whitened against the parapet as he clenched his fists.

Guy understood the need. It was one he had endured himself all too often during the long watches of recent nights. He could tell this young man that there were ways of assuaging that need that would not injure the woman's newly healed body . . . They were ways he had practiced himself with the woman in the last weeks, bringing them both gentle release in verdant fields of satisfaction. But he found that he could not pass on such knowledge, not now . . . Not to this man, about this woman.

So he said, "Come, there are simple enough avenues for release, Edmund. We will go into the town."

Edmund looked as if he would argue, but Guy de Gervais was already striding to the steps. He, too, would take his need and assuage it in the stews of the town. There were times when the boil must be lanced.

They rode out by the postern gate, both silent. It was not the first time they had ridden together on such an errand. During the years of their earlier campaigning, Guy had often steered the hot blood of youth toward the relatively safe havens of conventional release. He knew that suppressed ardor ill served a man during a campaign when the opportunities abounded for violent possession among the defenseless. In Guy's experience, such excesses rarely afforded the taker much satisfaction and usually generated further excess as a means of assuaging angry frustration. More importantly, it took a man's mind off the task at hand. Lack of concentration was as deadly in the field as lack of armor.

He knew that Edmund had once yielded to the seductive power of the victor, tumbling with a reluctant widow in a barn while her husband lay dead in the yard outside. And he knew that Edmund's remorse had been as violent as the emotion that had fueled the assault. He was not a man for whom rape was the natural reward of victory, and it seemed he was not a man to force himself upon his wife.

How long would Magdalen continue to withhold her body as well as her love? Guy wondered bleakly. The prospect of her submission to her husband filled him with limitless revulsion, yet he knew it must happen according to the course he had imposed upon them both. He could command it of her before he left this place . . . but he knew he would not. Edmund must find his own way to his wife's heart, and find the key to unlock the sensual secrets of her body. They were both young and fresh to the world. He knew Magdalen did not hold Edmund in dislike. If it had not been for him, they would have dealt together in great harmony, and he must live with that knowledge.

Such reflections made him ill disposed to break his companion's silence as they rode down the hill and into the town. The curfew had sounded at sundown, instructing craftsmen and laborers to cover their fires and cease working once the light became too dim for good work to be done. Some parts of the town were not sleeping, however. There was some work that was best done when the light was dim, and it was toward those streets that Edmund and Guy directed their horses.

Lantern light fell upon them from the unshuttered windows of taverns, and sounds of laughter and raised voices came from doors opened onto the rutted lanes. Muted giggles reached them from dark corners and shadowed doorways, squeaks and muffled protests as the lowliest women of the town plied their trade wherever the ground was dry or the wall straight.

Edmund drew rein outside the sign of the Black Ram. "I would drink first." He spoke almost curtly.

Guy took no offense. "Where we are going, you may do both." He pointed down the lane. "The house at the end, Edmund."

Edmund nudged his horse into motion again, reflecting that Lord de Gervais had spent part of his boyhood and youth in this place, with his elder half brother. It was hardly surprising he should know its secrets better than Edmund, who had left at the age of ten and returned five years later only to fight for his inheritance. He had as yet spent no time in the enjoyment of his demesne.

The house at the corner was shuttered and quiet, but Guy seemed unperturbed. He swung from his horse, and immediately a grimy lad appeared from the shadows to take the reins. The door opened before they could step up to it and a tall woman stood there, holding a lantern high. Her dress was plain and neat, her hair tucked into a starched cap.

"My lord. You are well come." Her voice was soft as she moved aside, still holding the lantern aloft, inviting them within.

"I bid you good even, Jacqueline." Guy moved past her. "The Sieur Edmund de Bresse." He indicated Edmund behind him.

"My lord." The woman bowed. "My hearth is honored."

This was no whorehouse of the kind to which Edmund was accustomed. They were in a central room, swept clean, candles trimmed on the table.

"Griselde?" The woman called softly yet imperatively. A door opened and a girl entered, small, round, rose-cheeked, wiping her hands on her apron.

"Yes, madame."

"My daughter," Jacqueline said to Edmund. "Bring wine, *petite*." She smiled at Edmund, inviting him to sit on a settle against the hearth wall. "You will take wine, my lord?"

"With pleasure." Edmund looked questioningly at Guy, who simply smiled and sat down on the opposite settle, stretching his legs appreciatively.

Griselde brought wine and pewter tankards and poured. Then she sat beside Edmund, engaging him in a low-voiced conversation.

Guy turned to the older woman. "You have settled the matter of the blacksmith's goat, Jacqueline?"

She laughed and sipped her wine. "The old rogue was forced to acknowledge that his wretched animal had eaten my cabbages when I put some bitter aloes on the turnips. They caught that goat nicely when he slipped through the fence for a further forage. Old Girard was spitting, I can tell you. But the town tribunal found that the goat had been ill tethered and ordered Girard to make restitution."

"You have a new row of cabbages?"

Jacqueline laughed richly. "Better yet. Cabbages *and* a new fence. I managed to persuade the tribunal that the goat had destroyed my fence in its enthusiasm for my vegetables."

"And had it?"

Jacqueline was well aware that Lord de Gervais could overset any ruling of the town tribunal, but she had no hesitation in admitting that the fence had been broken before the goat's depredations. Tonight was not an occasion when the Lord de Gervais would be in evidence.

They both laughed, and Guy became aware that the two on the settle had disappeared. It was as it should be.

"Will you come, my lord?" Jacqueline asked directly, gesturing to a door on the far side of the hall.

Guy had intended to take his pleasure with Jacqueline, to seek easement of the aching flesh with the woman who he knew would offer it in a spirit of companionable friendship that made nonsense of her profession. But he hesitated.

"You are sorely troubled, my lord?" Jacqueline refilled his tankard, her tone matter-of-fact, accepting his hesitation and moving on from it.

"Aye." He sighed but did not expand.

"It's a trouble of the soul," she said.

"Of the soul," he agreed.

"It cannot be eased in the flesh?"

"I had thought it could, but now I doubt it." He closed his eyes, leaning his head against the back of the settle. "It goes deeper than the body, Jacqueline."

"But it is also of the flesh?"

He nodded. "In part. But it is the part that is of the soul that cannot be eased." He drained his wine cup and glanced toward the opposite door. "The lad is sore in need of comfort. Griselde will do her work well?"

"You know that she will, my lord." Jacqueline spoke with quiet dignity, and he made a small deprecating gesture as if apologizing for casting aspersions on her daughter's skill.

"It is a powerful woman who can reach a man's soul," Jacqueline said.

"A woman of a powerful innocence," he responded. "A woman whose birth was accursed, who comes from tainted seed, yet she has an innocence and a sweetness that a man would die for."

"Men do not die for innocence and sweetness," Jacqueline observed.

Guy laughed without humor but in resigned acknowledgment of the woman's truth. "No, they die for the temptress. They die for one more journey into the dark toils of passion."

"The woman who can combine innocence with the dark toils of passion," mused Jacqueline, sipping her wine, "now that is a woman with power." She laid down her tankard and her hands rested in her lap, lightly cupped. "It is such a woman who troubles you, my lord?"

"Me and the lad," Guy said.

"Ah." Jacqueline nodded. "But the young lord will find respite with Griselde. You, my lord, will never find respite with another woman."

It was a statement, one which Guy made no attempt to dispute because he knew it to be true.

Slowly, he rose to his feet. "I'll take my leave, Jacqueline. Make sure the lad returns to the castle before prime." He laid a heavy purse upon the table. "You have given me ease."

A smile touched her mouth. She left the purse on the table and went with him to the door. She saw him onto his horse.

"Have a care for Edmund," Guy said as he made to depart.

"The young lord will come to no harm in my house, my lord."

"I know it." He raised a hand in farewell and then rode out of the town, back to the castle and his bed in the guest hall, eased in some fashion by his sojourn with the woman who had taken his virginity when, like her daughter now, she was but a girl in her mother's house some sixteen years ago.

Thirteen

THE FIRST GUESTS began to arrive three days later. Knights and their ladies, they came with their squires; their pages; their men-at-arms, falconers, minstrels, grooms, and horses, both palfreys and the great destriers that would be ridden in the lists.

There was no time for the castle's three troubled inhabitants to indulge in grievous thoughts. The heralds' horns blew from dawn till dusk, announcing arrivals. The Sieur de Bresse and his chatelaine were there to welcome each new party to their court. The feasting went on all day since travelers could not be sure to arrive in time for dinner or supper. There were mummers and jongleurs, acrobats and dancers in the courts and the pleasaunce.

Magdalen had no domestic duties to attend to since these were all assumed by the seneschal, the butler, and the grand chamberlain. Her only responsibility was as hostess, a duty she found onerous, but she was grateful for the need to be always smiling, always talking, always watchful of her guests' comfort. It ensured she went to bed tired enough to sleep.

Edmund seemed to throw himself into the revelry, apparently relishing his position as host. He never came to the bed in the lord's chamber until the night was far advanced and his wife asleep. Instead, he sat up with his knight companions, drinking, playing dice, singing, and telling stories, as the musicians grew wearier and the stars began to fade.

Guy de Gervais left the management of the revels to the Lord and Lady de Bresse, although out of habit his eye was ever watchful, ready to step in should the need arise. His contact with Magdalen was of the most commonplace, and he did nothing to encourage anything more, treating her with a distant courtesy and confining their conversations as much as possible to times when they were in company. He felt her torment as keenly as he felt his own, and he knew it would not lessen until he left her finally. Only then, away from the dust and ashes of an unfulfillable love, could they find some way of piecing together their lives. But to leave before the tourney would cause remark and would certainly disconcert Edmund, so he moved in the fog of anguish, smiled, talked, laughed, and only Magdalen, from her own anguish, guessed at his.

The day before the tourney was to commence, the Sieur Charles d'Auriac declared himself a contender in the lists. His herald blew the challenge from beyond the drawbridge, and the rules of chivalry decreed that the contender be welcomed.

Magdalen had somehow persuaded herself that she would never again come face to face with her cousin, and she was ill prepared for the effect he had upon her when he entered the great hall at dinner, striding up to the dais, gauntlets in hand, silver spurs jingling, a gold embossed tunic over his mailshirt. He was all smiles, bowing low as she rose from the table, her hands clammy, her nerves jumping.

"Cousin," he said. "I understand you are safely delivered of a daughter. Pray accept my felicitations."

"I thank you, *mon sieur.*" She managed to return the courtesies, although all the fear and revulsion she had felt for him in the past returned in full measure. "You are not acquainted with my husband, I believe."

Edmund stepped forward. Guy had warned him of d'Auriac's connection with the de Beauregards, but he knew, as did Guy, that there was nothing to be done in these circumstances except welcome the man as warmly as they had the other guests.

"I bid you welcome to our tourney, *sieur*," he said. "And offer you the hospitality of my hearth and my board." He gestured to a seat at the high table, and Charles took it with a smile of thanks, his squire and page moving smoothly into place behind him.

"Lord de Gervais, I am glad to see you again." Charles nodded pleasantly to Guy, sitting opposite him.

"Indeed," Guy said calmly. "It is a noble company we have drawn for this tourney. Do you have in mind to issue a private challenge, or will you confine your participation to the melee?" His eyes were lowered to his goblet that he was turning reflectively between his hands, and no one but Edmund could guess the importance of the question. Would another attempt be made to turn knightly sport into death dealing?

Charles d'Auriac shrugged easily. "The melee will please me well enough, Lord de Gervais. Although I'll not refuse a private challenge from any that may issue it." His eyes ran around the table, where all were listening to the exchange. "It is indeed a noble company you have drawn, my lords."

Magdalen rose abruptly. "Pray excuse me. I must go to my child." She left the hall with an impatient stride, her surcote of emerald velvet swirling around the apple-green cotehardie beneath. Edmund frowned and glanced instinctively at Guy de Gervais, a question in his eyes.

It was unlike Magdalen to behave so precipitately in company. But Guy seemed not to see the question. He drank deeply of his wine and cut into the haunch of venison on the platter before him, continuing to engage the new arrival in conversation.

There was dancing in the hall after dinner and a play performed in the inner court by a traveling guild of actors. Magdalen did not reappear, and Edmund, disturbed, went in search of her. She was not to be found in her apartments, and her women said they had not seen her, had assumed she was still at table.

Guy saw him emerge from the donjon, his face creased with anxiety and a certain annoyance. "Something troubles you, Edmund?"

"I cannot find Magdalen," Edmund said. "She left the table so abruptly, discourteously almost, and now she is nowhere to be found."

Guy glanced toward the tower and upward to the small window of the bastion room. "You will find her up there, I expect," he said, disclosing their secret place with a lacerating sorrow. But it was no longer a special place, it could not be, and must be divested of all past magic. "I have noticed Magdalen goes there to be private when she is disturbed."

"But why is she disturbed?" Edmund absently

watched the wheeled platform on which the play was being enacted. An actor inside a donkey's skin was portraying Balaam's ass with great gusto and much vulgarity, his antics causing considerable hilarity to the assembled audience, both noble and ignoble, the latter gathering on the outskirts of the court, abandoning their tasks until such time as they should be chased back to them.

"She does not care for her cousin," Guy told him in a low voice. "But you must not permit her to show it. It is a most powerful revulsion she has, but she must control it in d'Auriac's company, for it will do her little good and maybe some considerable disservice."

"I will fetch her," Edmund said. "I will tell her she has nothing to fear from his presence."

Guy nodded. "I do not believe she does at the moment. There is nothing he can attempt here and now. But you must be watchful, for I believe he has some plan."

Edmund's mouth tightened. "I will permit no harm to come to my wife."

Charles d'Auriac, standing a little to one side of the laughing, applauding circle of playgoers in the center of the inner court, watched the two men covertly, wondering what had led to their low-voiced colloquy, heads together in a privy corner of the court. Maybe he was the subject under discussion. A smile touched his mouth. They could guard themselves as they pleased. His weapon would slip beneath the strongest guard. There was no defense against the weapon Charles d'Auriac believed he held in the palm of his hand.

Magdalen looked startled when her husband pushed open the door of the bastion room. She was sitting on her favorite perch on the broad stone sill. "Why, my lord, how did you know to find me here?"

"Lord de Gervais told me."

A needle of betrayal drew a bead of heart-blood, and she turned her head back to the window without a word.

"You must return to our guests," Edmund said, stepping into the room. "Indeed, Magdalen, it is most discourteous of you to absent yourself in this manner."

"I know it." She turned back to him. "But I cannot endure my cousin's company. It has always been so."

"Lord de Gervais told me. But you must not let that lead you into discourtesy." He spoke gravely, finding the task of upbraiding his wife a strange and uncomfortable one, yet at the same time feeling a prickle of pleasure. He had the right, and exercising it implied an intimacy that could only afford him gratification and reassurance.

"I loathe him!" she said, softly fierce. "He means me harm, Edmund."

"I will not permit him to harm you." He took her hand tentatively, afraid she might withdraw it. But she let it lie in his.

Guy de Gervais had said those same words to her, and she had believed him implicitly. She did not believe her husband had the same power to protect her from harm, but it would benefit neither of them to show her doubt. She smiled and slipped from the windowsill. "Yes," she said. "I know you will, Edmund. Let us return to our guests; it must seem strange that we are both absent."

CHARLES D'AURIAC SETTLED down to observe. He had no other plan for this visit. The next step must wait until Guy de Gervais had left de Bresse on his return to England. But he would put the opportunity for observation to good use. Before vespers that evening, he made the acquaintance of the baby, the daughter of Edmund de Bresse.

The Lady de Bresse was walking in the pleasaunce with a party of guests, minstrels playing softly from the rose garden as the afternoon dipped into evening. She carried the child in her arms as she strolled, occasionally breaking off her conversation to smile down at the baby, who was wide awake, gray eyes examining her surroundings with a placid intelligence.

"Your daughter, my lady?"

At d'Auriac's quiet observation, Magdalen jumped, and her arms tightened, instinctively protective, around the child, whose mouth opened on an equally startled wail.

"Hush, pigeon," Magdalen whispered, rocking the child gently. Zoe's cries ceased and she stared unblinking at the Sieur d'Auriac, bending over her.

"A beautiful child," he commented. "Her hair is a most unusual color." He smiled, looking across to where Guy de Gervais stood to one side of the garden party, as watchful in his own way as d'Auriac. The dying sun set his bare head aflame.

Cold, an icicle of steel, twisted in Magdalen's belly as she followed the direction of d'Auriac's eyes. Edmund was standing beside Guy, his hair as dark as night.

Abruptly, Magdalen moved toward the two men, not thinking but suddenly desperate for the protection the two would offer the child who in some sort belonged to them both. "My lords, do you not think Zoe has grown apace in the last days?" She held out the child to them.

Guy had not missed her panic. He had felt it although he could not hear what had been said.

Now he took the child from her and immediately felt her relaxation. It was as if, with the child in his arms, Magdalen felt safe. "She is twice as heavy as when last I held her," he said calmly, his eyes locked with Magdalen's as he imparted his reassurance. Reluctantly depriving himself of the joy of holding his daughter once again, he handed the baby to Edmund. "What think you, Edmund?"

Edmund took Zoe, still a little awkwardly, but his proud smile as he gazed upon the child brought the anguish of remorse rising, gall and wormwood, in Guy's soul, and it brought a deep satisfaction to the observant Charles d'Auriac.

"I will take her within," Magdalen said hurriedly. "It is near time for vespers, and she should be in her cradle." She took the child and moved to the gate of the pleasaunce, where Erin stood waiting to take the child as soon as her mother should decide she had had sufficient of the evening air.

Charles d'Auriac noticed other things than the red-gold down thickening to a curly thatch on the child's head. He was aware of the currents of unhappiness running between Edmund de Bresse, the Lady Magdalen, and the Lord de Gervais. He was aware of them because he had the nose for distressful secrets, could smell them out as a predator can smell on the wind the blood of an injured prey.

He saw the way Edmund de Bresse looked at his wife, followed her with his eyes, in moments of repose gazed at her with a hunger that d'Auriac understood well. The man lusted after the woman, that Charles could understand, but there was something else as well. Something else that he wanted from her that she was not giving him. That, Charles did not understand, but he did not trouble himself over it. All that was important was that the husband was as bound in the serpentine coils of her sensuality, in the hot, whirring promise of her body, as were de Gervais and d'Auriac. Such a husband would be fertile soil for the seeds Charles would sow. His observation of Guy de Gervais offered him little information except that the man held himself aloof from the woman, and Charles d'Auriac knew from his past visit that that was unnatural for Magdalen de Bresse and Lord de Gervais. So what could explain such a withdrawal? It was a rhetorical question Charles asked himself.

THE THREE DAYS of jousting seemed interminable to Magdalen. But this time, it was not simply boredom that made it interminable. She had reached a point of desperation that matched Guy's. Now, it had to be over quickly. She had come to accept that it was over, that she had to face her life with the last ten months fading into a memory that only the reality of her child would underpin. The present knife edge of have and have not was all but unendurable. And that knife edge was compounded by her cousin's presence. The close of these three days would see the departure of Charles d'Auriac as well as Guy de Gervais.

So she sat in the loge and smiled, waiting for the final melee that would bring present torment to an end and begin the misery of the future. In her lap she held a handkerchief of Bretonne lace, delicate as filigree. When the rival contestants in the melee entered the lists, riding up to the loges to acknowledge their interested ladies, she stood up and leaned over the rail.

"My Lord de Gervais. I beg you will carry my gage with my prayers for your safety and success." She held out the handkerchief.

"With honor, lady, if I have your husband's permission to do so," Guy said, not a flicker of his surprise evident in voice or look.

Edmund wore Magdalen's scarf of gold tissue tied around the golden falcon on his helmet. A tinge of honest pleasure showed on his cheekbones. "My lady shall have two champions this day."

Guy bowed his acknowledgment and reached

to take the flimsy piece of lace. "I have a pin, my lord." Magdalen leaned further over the rail and fastened the favor herself to the sleeve of his jupon. "God and my heart go with you," she whispered, and it was as if she had given him her final farewell.

He let his visor drop and turned his horse, riding to the far side of the lists, his own team of combatants falling in beside him.

Steel clashed, mighty blows fell upon helmets, horses charged, wheeled, pounded the earth, sending great clods flying up to scatter the spectators with dust and mud. Unhorsed men reeled, dazed and battered, to be helped from the stockade by their attendants, supported to the apothecaries in the tent set aside for their ministrations, or, if their wounds were not too severe, to their own tents.

At the end, there were three knights of Guy de Gervais's side left mounted and but one of the opposing side. Magdalen's two champions and Charles d'Auriac were the three victors.

"A well-fought joust, my lords," Magdalen said, even as she thought of the violent struggle, the hideous battering blows that had been given in the name of friendly rivalry and knightly sport.

"I would beg a favor also, cousin." Charles d'Auriac put up his visor, his face etched with the physical strain of the last violent hour. "It may be after the event, but I would claim a reward for championing my Lady de Bresse."

Magdalen plucked a flower from the vase standing at her elbow. "My lord." She tossed it to him, although she knew it would have been more gracious to have handed it to him. D'Auriac caught the bloom neatly, but something flared in his eyes, and Magdalen felt again that graveyard fear.

She did not know how she endured the feasting that night. The great banquet that drew the tourney to a close also, it seemed to her, was putting an end to all possibility of happiness in the lifetime to come. She ate almost nothing, toying with a little fish aspic, pushing a lark pasty to one side of her platter, spurning the swan and peacock.

"Why do you not eat?" Edmund lowered his head to ask the question against her ear. "It looks most strange in you. As if you do not find your own hospitality good."

"I have no appetite," she said, her voice as low as his. But she allowed her page to serve her a portion of stuffed roasted suckling pig with mushrooms, and she nibbled on a fruit wafer when dessert was passed, sipping the accompanying spiced wine, normally her favorite drink, although tonight it was tasteless on her tongue.

She tried to respond to Edmund's efforts to cheer her, but her smile was brittle, her attention abstracted, and after a while he gave up. He had become accustomed to her strange abstractions although they puzzled and saddened him. He did not know what else to do except leave her in them, hoping that the reason for them would be revealed in time, or that maybe they would just go away and the Magdalen he remembered would be restored to him. She may not have loved him, but she had never been less than friendly and companionable.

The days of revelry were to end with a magnificent display of fireworks in the *place d'armes*. The townspeople crowded onto rooftops and scattered over the hillside, the better to view the spectacle, and the castle servants packed the battlements. In the *place d'armes*, tiers had been set up to accommodate the guests. Magdalen deliberately moved away from Edmund and took a place beside Guy de Gervais. In the noise of the display and the excitement of the spectators, much could be said that might otherwise draw remark.

Guy smiled courteously as she sat down beside him, but his eyes were wary. "Do you enjoy the *feux d'artifices*, my lady?"

"I have but once before seen a display, my lord," she responded in the same easy tone. "But

I remember finding it hard to believe. There were castles and fountains in the air . . . and so many amazing colors."

"I trust you will find this as impressive."

A great gasp went up from the spectators as the entertainment opened with a flashing sparking facsimile of the de Bresse standard, the great golden falcon seeming to soar in the sky. It was followed almost immediately by the hissing dragon of Gervais, the rose of Lancaster, and finally the lilies of France, the last pretty compliment drawing appreciative applause from the French knights and their ladies.

Under cover of the applause, Magdalen said softly, "I will bring your child to the chapel after matins if you wish to bid her farewell."

Guy turned his head to look down at her, his expression unreadable in the fizzing, exploding, color-shot darkness. "After matins." Then he returned his attention to the fireworks.

Edmund had still not come to bed when Magdalen crept into the antechamber where Erin and Margery were snoring beside Zoe's cradle. Gently, she lifted the sleeping child, wrapped the blanket securely around her against the night chills, and returned with her to the big bedchamber. She slipped from the room by the internal passageway and down a winding staircase that led by a hidden door into the inner court. She could hear voices from the hall, slightly slurred now but amiable enough, and knew Edmund was still up with his guests and knight companions. He would not come to bed until certain she was asleep.

Keeping to the shadows, she crossed the court and entered the chapel. Her eyes were unaccustomed to such complete darkness after the torch-lit court outside, and she stood against the heavy door, her heart pounding uncomfortably, her eyes straining into the blackness. Then she caught a flicker of a candle behind the altar.

"Guy?" Her whisper sounded like a shout in the dark silence. She stepped forward, her slippered feet rustling across the cold flagstones. "Is that you, Guy?"

The candlelight flared yellow suddenly, emerging from the darkness, and she saw his bulk shadowed against the pillar. "I am here." His voice was soft and steady.

Clutching the baby, she ran toward him. "I could not bear to part without—"

"Hush," he said gently, taking her in his arms, drawing her behind the altar. "Hush, now."

"Must it be?" she said, her head against his chest, the babe still pressed to her bosom.

"It must be." Taking her chin, he lifted her face. "One last kiss, sweetheart. I will feed upon the memory to my death."

It was a kiss of searing sweetness. Magdalen's tears mingled salt with the sweetly familiar taste of their joined mouths, and her wet cheeks pressed against the weathered face above her as if she would grow into his flesh and be never parted.

The child in her arms whimpered and snuffled, and slowly, each breath a lancination of loss, they drew apart. Guy took his daughter from Magdalen, lifting her against his face, inhaling her baby smell, burying his lips in the damask roundness of her cheeks. Her tiny hands curled against his face, the rosebud mouth pursed, suckling as if the child knew only one reason to be awake. He gave her his finger, and she gripped it in her minutely perfect, dimpled fist.

Guy de Gervais had not wept since he had left his own babyhood behind. He had lost friends and comrades in hideous circumstances both on and off the battlefield. He had lost his dearly beloved wife after months of agonizing sickness. He had faced the fact that he must lose his second and greater love. But he had not wept. Now his eyes were brightly sheened with grief at the knowledge that this little daughter would never know her father. He would never see her smile or take her first steps, hear her lisp her first word. He would never hear her call him Father, and he would never be able to guide her into womanhood with all the loving care he had within him. So much love he had within him, and those on whom he ached to bestow it, he must put from him.

"Take her and go," he said, laying the child in Magdalen's arms again and turning away from them, turning toward the concealment of the darkness behind the altar.

She hesitated for a minute, then turned and slipped wraith-like into the body of the chapel. Her own grief was too deep for tears, like the deepest wounds that do not bleed for a long time.

She stepped through the oak door and into the semidarkness of the court. Zoe whimpered again, and she hushed her gently, moving swiftly toward the outside staircase, now no longer concerned with concealment.

Charles d'Auriac, standing in the doorway of the great hall, saw her emerge from the chapel. His eyebrows lifted in surprise. He remained where he was, the noise of the revelers behind him growing muted now as the day's combat and liberal doses of malmsey took their toll. One by one, the late revelers went past him on their way to their beds. Servants extinguished candles and torches in the hall. And, finally, Guy de Gervais emerged from the chapel. He went directly to the guest hall. Only then did Charles leave his post and seek his own bed.

Magdalen entered the antechamber, closing the door quietly behind her. Her women did not seem to have stirred in her absence. She was laying the baby in her cradle when the door to the main chamber opened.

"Where have you been?" Edmund's whisper was a trifle thick, and he leaned unsteadily against the doorjamb.

"Zoe was wakeful," she replied calmly. "I thought a little walk might soothe her. See, she is quite sleepy again now."

"It is strange behavior, to walk a baby in the middle of the night," Edmund grumbled, stepping aside to let her pass into the bedchamber. "Where would you go? I have been waiting and worrying this half hour past when I found you gone."

"I walked around the inner court . . . and went into the chapel." She began to unpin her hair as she talked, turning away from him toward the cedar chest where her brushes and combs stood.

"Into the chapel! In the middle of the night, Magdalen!" Edmund swayed slightly and sat down on the edge of the bed. He was undressed and in his long robe.

"One may say one's prayers at any time, may one not?" she replied, reaching for her brush, beginning to draw it through the rich sable tresses falling to her knees.

Edmund felt rebuked. He knew he was a little drunk, and her assurance in the face of his vague befuddlement put him at a disadvantage that was becoming an all-too-familiar condition of their relationship. He stood up and crossed the woven carpet toward her.

"I would do that," he stated, taking the brush from her suddenly nerveless hand.

Magdalen made no protest, lowering her head beneath the firm brushstrokes. She knew what was going to happen and felt now only the deep resignation she had felt when he had first bedded her. She had procrastinated long enough, and she knew she did not have the right to continue to refuse him. What did it matter anyway?

She turned to face him when his hand on her shoulder bade her do so. His eyes were filled again with that desperate need he had shown the first day he had arrived and had since hidden from her and controlled with his nighttime absences.

"I can wait no longer for my wife," he declared, and she could feel the current surging beneath the rigidly held body. It was not a current that could be resisted. She would not be able to prevent him tonight even if she had intended to do so.

She said only, "My lord."

He took a deep shuddering breath at her submission, his hands moving to her gown, fingers fumbling awkwardly with the hooks. She had changed her ceremonial dress of the evening before taking Zoe to her father in the chapel, and now wore only a simple linen tunic over a white shift. She made no attempt to help him, however, as he loosened the gown, pushed it with rough haste from her shoulders, and removed the shift similarly.

She remembered that first time, when he had not taken the time to remove her clothes in his urgency. Now she felt his trembling hands moving over her nakedness in loving wonder, and while she could summon no physical response to his caresses, she could be touched by his tenderness, stirred by the almost awed joy in his gaze. She stroked his face fleetingly and saw his delight in the skimming gesture of affection. And she felt remorse and compassion and the depths of her unworthiness to be the object of this great and guiltless love.

"Ah, my love . . . love . . . love . . ." he whispered, bearing her backward to the bed. Husky endearments broke from his lips as he came down with her, but his need was so keen, so long kept at bay, so long an agonizing hunger that it could be curbed no longer. For a moment, he held himself above her, desperately trying to bridle the rampant forces of his passion, knowing she was unready and terrified of hurting her in her unreadiness this first time after she had given birth. But with a soul-deep groan he yielded to the wild, plunging forces of lust that drove him to her center, drowned him in the enchanted well of her body, lost him in the bewitched forest of her body, brought him swirling and gasping out of a maelstrom that left him inert upon her soft and tender flesh.

Magdalen lay still beneath him, feeling his weight crushing her breasts, squeezing the breath from her, feeling his sweat-slick skin clammy against the cool dryness of her own. She wondered how it was possible to be so distanced from another's passion when that passion was being poured into one's own body. She wondered how the same act could be so dissimilar between different people as to have no points of contact, to be deserving of a different name.

Edmund slowly came to himself. He lifted his head where the black hair stuck wetly to his forehead and the residue of passion lurked in his unfocused blue eyes. He looked down at her still face, the quietness in her eyes.

"Can you feel nothing for me?"

There was such a desperate sorrow in the question, a grief that she understood, that spoke to her own. Lifting her arms, she took his head and drew it down to her bosom. "I feel much for you, Edmund. But you must give me just a little time."

There was a tenderness in her voice that brought him immeasurable comfort. She stroked his back, smoothed his hair, eased him gently to lie beside her, feeling him slip into the sleep of satiation.

It was a sleep that eluded Magdalen, who kept vigil for her lost love, dry-eyed and steadfast throughout the night as if she were on her knees on the cold stone before the altar rail. At dawn, she heard Zoe's morning plaint, and she rose and went next door to feed her.

Erin was already tending to the child, changing her breech-clout, whistling softly at her from between her teeth.

"Ah, good morrow, pigeon." Magdalen bent to kiss the wailing child. "Never mind such niceties, Erin. She is hungry." Scooping up the baby, she sat down on the stool beneath the window and gave the child her breast.

From the court below came sounds of the beginning day. Voices, scurrying feet, commands, and the herald's horn followed on the heels of the bell for prime. The guests would all be leaving before midmorning, and the urgency of departure filled the air. Magdalen sat enclosed in the absolute privacy that came when she was feeding her child. Only the two of them existed in this solitude and she was only vaguely conscious of Erin and Margery setting the chamber to rights, bringing her a cup of honeyed mead, preparing the baby's bath.

Edmund's sudden appearance in the doorway was a momentary violation of this privacy, something he had never done before, but she looked up and smiled at him.

"I give you good morrow, my lord."

"And I you, lady." He ran a hand through his disordered hair and came over to look down at the child still nuzzling at the breast. He shook his head in a gesture of bemused wonder and smiled at his wife. "So pretty," he said.

"You had best get dressed, my lord." Magdalen laughed slightly. "Your guests will be leaving, and you must bid them farewell."

"We must both do so."

She shook her head. "No, I beg you will excuse me, Edmund. I slept ill and am feeling fatigued. I will keep to my apartments this day. You will explain that I am unwell."

"But are you truly so?" He looked anxious. "It was not—"

"No," she reassured him quietly. "But I am truly fatigued."

"Then I will make your excuses," he said. "It will be such a turmoil anyway that you are well out of it." He bent to kiss her, still with some of the hesitancy of the last two weeks, but with more assurance. She did not return the salute, but neither did she turn her head away.

She sat beside the window throughout the morning, listening to the bustle of departure. She did not see Guy de Gervais and his knights ride out, but she felt his departure as if some part of herself had been wrenched from her, and the tears spilled heedlessly onto her joined hands in her lap. Erin and Margery hovered helplessly, and when she gestured that they should leave her, they did so with some relief.

Magdalen was not in the *place d'armes* to hear Charles d'Auriac say to her husband in jocular tones that he wished to claim a kinsman's right to hospitality for another week while he awaited a summons from his uncle at Toulouse.

She was not in the *place d'armes* to hear her husband reply as he must: that his lady's cousin should consider the Castle de Bresse as his own.

Fourteen

CHARLES D'AURIAC BEGAN his campaign of whispers before Guy de Gervais was out of sight upon the plain on his way to Calais.

"Your lady will doubtless be melancholy now that Lord de Gervais has left."

Edmund looked surprised at this casual observation. "She has always held Lord de Gervais in high regard, ever since she was a child in his household during our betrothal." He walked toward the garrison court. "I have some business with the sergeant-at-arms, d'Auriac. If you would care to ride to hounds after dinner, I will have order sent to the stables."

"Perhaps my cousin would accompany us," Charles said, falling in step with his companion. "On my last visit, she was with child, and the Lord de Gervais would not permit her to indulge in such exercise."

Edmund made no response, and Charles continued, "Such care as he had for your wife can only be commended."

Edmund felt the first prickles of unease at the soft-spoken words, but he didn't know why he should, unless it was something in the tone; it was too sweet and soft, reminding him of decaying fruit. Or was it in the gray eyes, so like Magdalen's yet so unlike in their narrowed coldness? "I believe it to be so," he responded neutrally. "Lord de Gervais has stood in place of her father, Lancaster, these last months."

"And in place of her husband, surely?" The gray eyes flicked sideways, swift and thin as a snake's tongue. Again Edmund didn't respond because he didn't know how to.

"My cousin carried her child well," Charles went on. "In late December, when I was here, she bore no signs of her pregnancy. Indeed, if it were not for the care Lord de Gervais took of her, one would not have guessed at her condition." They had reached the garrison court, and d'Auriac stopped just inside the arched entrance. "I will leave you to your business with the sergeant-at-arms, but will gladly join you with the hounds after dinner." He turned and left, his short cloak fluttering in the breeze.

Edmund stood watching his departure, a puzzled and uneasy frown creasing his forehead. Something had been said yet not said, but for the life of him he could not pinpoint what it was.

Before dinner, he found Magdalen in the antechamber of the lord's apartments, sewing with her women. He noticed immediately her drawn countenance, her pallor, the sadness in her eyes. He had been aware of those things before, but for some reason they seemed more pronounced now. Was it perhaps because he had been given a reason for her melancholy? A reason that had not occurred to him before.

"The guests have departed?" she asked, laying down her needle.

"All but your cousin," he replied. "He is to stay a further week."

Her hand flew to her throat, her eyes filled with a species of terror. "The Sieur d'Auriac remains?"

"As I have said." Edmund sounded impatient. "He awaits a summons from Toulouse."

"You must tell him to leave." Her voice was low but contained a fierce determination informed by fear. "He intends me harm."

"I will not permit him to harm you," he said as he had done before, but this time he read the disbelief in her eyes.

"Lord de Gervais has gone from here," she said in flat, dull truth.

"Do you believe only he can protect you? I have said I will do so." Edmund's voice rose with his hurt and an anger that seemed to have come from nowhere. "Leave us!" He spoke sharply to Erin and Margery, who hustled from the chamber without a word. "Well, answer me. Do you believe only Lord de Gervais can protect you?"

Magdalen was silent as she mastered her fear and marshaled her defenses. "I had come to rely upon him," she said finally. "He has been at my side for many months. You must understand that, Edmund."

"I suppose I do." He went to the cradle where the baby lay cooing. "You have never said when our child was born."

"You have never asked," she replied calmly, picking up her needle again, only the slight tremor of her fingers betraying her agitation. "She was born in April."

Edmund's frown deepened. "But should she not have been born in March?"

"First babies are often a week or so late, I am told," she replied, keeping her eyes on her sewing. "It is hard to be exact about such matters."

It sounded reasonable enough to Edmund. The child's dimpled fists were waving randomly, plucking at the air in front of her face as if she would capture some golden dream, and her soft contented cooing mingled with the lazy droning hum of a bumblebee at the open window. It was too serene a scene for ugliness, yet ugliness had entered his mind, and he could not put it from him.

"We go out with the hounds after dinner," he said, turning back to Magdalen.

"I will keep to my apartments until my cousin has taken his leave." She looked up from her sewing, her face closed and determined.

"No, I insist that you take your place as his hostess." Her refusal to see her cousin seemed to underscore her lack of trust in her husband's ability to protect her, and the hurt and anger rose anew. "It is not right that you should hide from a guest, whatever your dislike of him."

"It lies much deeper than dislike, Edmund." Her head lifted with that unconscious yet unmistakable Plantagenet arrogance and determination that Guy would have recognized. Edmund did not recognize it. Guy de Gervais would have prevailed over that arrogance and determination. Edmund de Bresse could not.

They argued for many minutes, Edmund becoming angrier as Magdalen became colder and more resolute. She refused to have anything to do with her cousin and would remain in her apartments, indisposed, until he took his leave.

Baffled and frustrated, he left her finally, the door shivering on its hinges with the force of the slam. Zoe jumped at the bang and wailed. Magdalen picked her up and rocked her, hum-

ming soothingly. But it was as if the child felt her
mother's agitation and fear, and she would not
be soothed.

Magdalen stood at the window, looking down
on the inner court. In Guy's absence and
d'Auriac's presence, she felt more vulnerable
than she had ever felt in her life. She understood
Edmund's hurt, but she could not help it.
Edmund de Bresse was as a film of parchment
against the power of Charles d'Auriac to hurt.
She knew it in the deepest recesses of her soul;
the knowledge flowed through her body with
her blood. And her terror grew with the recognition that she did not know why he would
wish to harm her, or how he intended doing so.
She knew he lusted after her, knew that it
was this hunger that crawled like the sticky slime
of a slug's trail across her skin, that filled her
head with the terrifying images of the oubliette.
But she also knew it was not just her cousin's
concupiscence that threatened her.

There was some secret here that Guy had
known and had chosen not to share with her.
And he had ridden away, leaving her in ignorance and fear, to face her cousin's malevolence
without his protection. Tears of anger mingled
now with the tears of loss she had been shedding
all morning, mingled and were indistinguishable
as the emotions became indistinguishable.

Magdalen did not know it, but her refusal to see her cousin played perfectly into his hands. Had she been beside her husband, the hints and innuendo would have found less fertile soil. But in estrangement, Edmund had no counterbalance for d'Auriac's clever malice.

Edmund's pride was hurt that he had failed to compel his wife's obedience, and more so that he had failed because she did not trust in his strength. He knew d'Auriac possibly posed a threat, either to Magdalen or to himself, but like Guy de Gervais, he could not imagine how he could put such a threat into practice from within the walls of the Castle de Bresse. There was always poison, of course, but Edmund ate only from the dishes d'Auriac ate from first, and he knew Magdalen's women prepared her food themselves. Knives in the night were too hard to cover up afterward, and d'Auriac could not stand openly accused of the murder of John of Gaunt's daughter or son-in-law. So for the moment, there was nothing to fear.

But Edmund was a man of action and of limited imagination. He saw threats only in terms of the physical. An honest man, a guileless man, he could not plumb the devious depths of an evil mind and was no proof against d'Auriac's whispers.

It was a word here, a word there, but it was

relentless. D'Auriac talked of little else but Guy de Gervais and Magdalen de Bresse, and whenever Edmund was in his wife's company the whispers were reinforced by her patent unhappiness and by his earlier recognition that something had changed her from the friendly companion of the past into this remote and rather forbidding woman. She no longer refused him her body, but he knew she was absent in spirit. Even her gentle kindness in their bed, he began to feel as a form of tolerant pity rather than the promise of a future love, and the cold steel of wounded pride twisted in his gut.

"It is interesting your daughter should have such unusual coloring," d'Auriac remarked on the third morning as they rode through the outskirts of the forest of Compiegne, a pack of lean deer hounds in full cry ahead of them. "But of course she has the de Gervais blood in some measure, does she not? That red-gold hair is so distinctive."

Why had he not remarked on Zoe's hair coloring? His own was black as night, Magdalen's as dark and richly brown as sable. A wild fury surged in the young man's breast at the soft, insidious words of his companion, but no insult had been given, no statement made that could be challenged. He was related to Guy de Gervais and so, therefore, was his daughter, although the shared blood would be running thin in his children. But the poison seeped, and his arrows flew awry throughout the day.

Before supper that day, he stood above his daughter's cradle, examining the sleeping child with the poison corroding his soul. Her hair promised to be thick and wavy, glinting red and gold in the evening sunlight. Her eyebrows were faint lines, but they were straight and fair. He glanced at his wife, sitting in contemplative silence by the window. Her eyebrows were the same rich sable as her hair, and they were delicately arched. His own he knew were black and unruly, almost meeting over the bridge of his nose.

"You will come down to supper," he said to Magdalen.

She shook her head. "Not until my cousin takes his leave of us."

"You are neglecting your household duties as well as those of hospitality."

"The seneschal and the chamberlain can manage quite well without me for a few days. If any has a question, I am here to answer it."

"I bid you, as your lord, to come down to supper." He didn't expect the command to have any effect, anticipating it would slide off that smooth, resolute composure like water off an oiled skin.

But Magdalen said simply, "Very well, my lord. If you so command."

His surprise was evident in his slackened jaw, the widening of his eyes. He tried to find satisfaction in her submission but could not and heard himself bluster that it was time she learned obedience. And then he felt foolish and stood in awkward silence before saying, "We will go to vespers together."

"As you wish, my lord," she replied in the same flat tone.

Even more baffled and frustrated by this abrupt capitulation, he strode from the chamber completely ungratified. In truth, Magdalen had yielded because suddenly it seemed not to matter. Her grief and loneliness had become so all-pervasive in the days since Guy's departure that she had ceased to fear her cousin; or, rather, her fear had ceased to be important.

Erin and Margery were so relieved that their mistress had decided to bring an end to her enforced seclusion that they chattered like magpies as they helped her dress for the evening. If it hadn't been for their encouragement, she would not have troubled unduly over her dress, but they were so shocked at her inclination to attend in the great hall in the simple tunic she had been wearing all day that she let them have their way and stood compliantly while they clothed her in cream damask and a scarlet surcote trimmed with silver fox. They brushed and braided her hair before fastening her headdress of cylindrical gold cauls attached to a gold head-band over her brow. A filmy white veil stood out at the back, brushing her shoulders bared by the wide, low neckline of her gown.

All the care of her women, however, could not disguise the shadowed hollows beneath her eyes or add color to her pale cheeks. Charles d'Auriac, seeing her for the first time since Guy de Gervais had left, was jolted by the ethereal quality sorrow lent to the previously vibrant, glowing countenance. It lessened his lust not a whit, because in no wise was the distinctive nature of her sensuality diminished by her stillness and her pallor.

He watched her during the evening office, and he saw the restless anxiety of her husband, the covert looks he sent in her direction, the questioning, uneasy glances of a man no longer certain. Charles d'Auriac was satisfied. It would not be long before the man would challenge the woman, and he did not believe the woman in her present distress would be able to dissemble adequately to persuade the man of her innocence.

At supper, he was at some pains to be pleasant to his cousin. She responded with the habitual level courtesy she had shown him ever since she had recovered her manners after their first meeting. But as always he could feel her revulsion, the shrinking of her skin when his arm brushed hers as he passed a platter or reached for the great dipper in the tureen of broth. His own anger rose with a powerful purity that she should treat him in such fashion, but it added zest to his desire. It would not matter in the end how she felt, how deeply she was repelled by him.

Magdalen heard the voices in the hall as a dim buzz, the plucking and twanging of the minstrels in the gallery as a barely noticeable resonance. Between the anxious, speculative glances of Edmund on her left and the ill-concealed, predatory hunger of her cousin on her right, she felt as if she were being pressed to death between heavy stones, as she had heard tell they did to the felons in Newgate. Her eyes were fixed on her cousin's white hands, the long white fingers encrusted with jewels. There was something almost effete about his hands, yet she had seen him wield a great sword and place a lance with a strength to match any knight's.

As soon as the platters of peeled nuts, medlars, fruit wafers, and marchpane pastries had been passed with the jugs of hypocras, she rose from the table.

"I beg you will excuse me, my lords. I am a

little fatigued, and the child will soon need feeding."

Charles d'Auriac paused as his dagger slowly peeled away the brown decayed skin of a medlar. His gray eyes flicked sideways and upward to where she stood beside him. "Do you pay another midnight visit to the chapel, cousin?"

"I do not understand you." Her lips were bloodless.

"Oh, I thought you were in the habit of taking your child to the chapel after matins." He smiled, aware of Edmund's close gaze. "I saw you leave there with the child the other night as I was leaving the hall on my way to the guest hall." He turned his dagger in his hands, smiling still. "Lord de Gervais had the same need for late-night prayers, it seemed. I daresay he was keeping vigil before taking his leave the next morning. It is, after all, the custom of many knights before setting out upon a journey."

"I know nothing of my Lord de Gervais's customs," she said steadily, although her stomach was quivering and she was aware suddenly that this was the threat, that she was looking into the abyss of his malice. But it made no sense that he should betray her to Edmund. "I do not know if he kept vigil or not. I bid you good night, *mon sieur*." With the exercise of immense self-restraint, she managed not to look at Edmund, to see how he was reacting to d'Auriac's strange statement, because she knew if she looked at him he would read her dismay, a dismay that could only be explained by guilt.

She left the hall, her step measured, acknowledging the salutes of the household still supping in the body of the hall. Outside, she drew breath desperately, trying to rid herself of the suffocating feeling. The air was still warm, and she longed for the cold, purifying blasts of winter, for ice crackling beneath her feet and the purity of snow. This air was too hot, too clammy, too clinging, and it would not fill her lungs properly. Smells of cooking hung heavy, and a wave of nausea rose with shocking suddenness. She blundered into a dark corner of the ward and vomited.

Afterward, she stumbled up the outside stairs and along the passage to her own apartments. Erin and Margery exclaimed as she staggered in, holding the long pointed tippet of her sleeve to her mouth, her face deathly white beneath the gold headdress.

"My lady." Erin leaped to her feet. "Whatever has happened? Are you ill?"

"Something I ate at supper," she said, sinking onto a stool. "Bring me clean water to drink and some mint leaves to chew."

She drank greedily of the water they brought

her while they undressed her, murmuring sympathetically even as they shook their heads over the splashes on her gown and slippers. But finally she was in her robe, her hair brushed, her face and hands clean, her mouth freshened with spearmint.

"Leave me now. I would sit up alone awhile." They left her seated beside the window, gently rocking Zoe's cradle. Something dreadful was going to happen . . . something more dreadful than the great pit of loss in which she had been struggling to keep afloat for the last weeks. She tried to gather strength, to prepare herself, and when Edmund came in, his face livid, his eyes blank, as if the person who normally inhabited them was somehow absent, replaced with only a spirit of despairing rage, she greeted him calmly, as if she did not see his desperate hope that he was in error and his equally desperate certainty that there was no error.

"Why would you go to the chapel . . . take the child to the chapel after midnight?" His voice rasped painfully.

"I explained that Zoe was restless," she said. "I thought a walk would soothe her."

"Why would you walk her in the chapel?"

"I felt the need for some solace."

"Solace with Lord de Gervais?"

There had been no solace with Guy de

Gervais that night. She shook her head and spoke the truth. "No, I did not seek solace with Lord de Gervais."

"But he was there?" He stepped toward her, his hands open, but whether to reach for her in threat or need she could not tell.

She tried to lie. "I do not know if he was or not." But she knew the truth was in her eyes. She had sworn on the bones of St. Francis to do or say nothing to lead Edmund to suspect the truth, but *she* had not brought him to this point. And how could she help it if her eyes would not lie?

His hands caught her upper arms, pulled her to her feet. *"He was there!"*

"Edmund . . . Edmund, please, do not do this," she heard herself whisper as they drew closer to the edge of the abyss.

"Why would you take my child to the chapel at midnight for a tryst with Lord de Gervais?" His fingers gripped so tightly the blood throbbed against the vise they formed.

The child in the cradle stirred, whimpered softly in her sleep.

Abruptly, Edmund released Magdalen. He swung toward the cradle, staring down at the sleeping child. "Whose child is she?" There was so much pain in his voice that Magdalen, even in her own pain, wanted to reach for him, to offer him what comfort she could. But as she struggled for words, he swung round again, his eyes great burning holes in his ghastly countenance. "Eternal damnation on your black soul! *Whose child is she?*"

Her hands opened in a gesture of defeat, of acceptance, of despair.

"Tell me she is not mine, damn you, tell me!" His voice had dropped to barely a whisper, but the force was undiminished.

But she could not tell him because she had sworn not to. So she just stood there, helplessly silent, unable either to deny or to confirm.

Edmund waited for the words he knew he must hear, and her continuing silence seemed to add to his agony. Blind in his despairing rage, in his hurt that cut more deeply than any asssailants' knives, he still remembered the sleeping child. He shoved Magdalen through the door into their own chamber.

"Tell me she is not mine!"

"I can tell you nothing," she whispered.

He hit her, but she knew this was not the worst. And when he bore her backward to the bed, raging in broken incoherence that what she had withheld from him she had given to another, she knew that this was not the worst, either. And when the violence of his despairing rage had worn itself out upon her body and he rolled away from her, his sobs muffled against the pillow, she lay very still beside him, feeling only sorrow and pity, yet knowing that to express either at this moment would exacerbate his suffering.

After a few minutes, he flung himself from the bed, laced his hose again, and went to the chest where he lit a candle. The yellow light flared in the dark chamber. He came back to the bed, holding the candle high and looked down at her as she lay, her eyes unblinking, meeting his gaze.

"You betrayed me," he said, his voice now without expression. "But greater by far is the betrayal of Guy de Gervais. He has broken faith with me, has bred a bastard on the body of my wife, and I will kill him for that."

"Ah, Edmund, no," she said softly. "He did not break faith with you. He believed you dead. Be revenged upon me if you must, but not—"

"I will kill him," he interrupted. "He will meet me in combat, and one of us will die." He turned away from her. "I care not if it is I. I cannot live dishonored." With a sudden movement, he pulled the curtains around the bed, leaving her in merciful dark seclusion, and flung open the door, bellowing for his squire and pages.

Magdalen lay and listened, her heart dead within her, as he gave orders to ride out within the hour, he and his knight companions, his squire and pages. They would ride day and night until they caught up with Lord de Gervais.

What had mad Jennet said to a bored eleven-year-old girl on a long-ago February day: *The day will come when you'll pray for all to stay the same. Bad though 'tis, you'll wish it to stay for fear of the worse that is coming.*

And she knew that she would give anything at this moment for the bad that had been: for Guy to be going on his way, leaving her to make what life she could with the guiltless Edmund, who had not deserved the knowledge of unwitting betrayal.

Now, one of them was going to die at the hands of the other. She knew that in fair combat Guy de Gervais could not lose. Edmund might have youth on his side, but the other man had strength and experience and a skill exceeding that of most men. But she also knew that Guy would not kill Edmund, not even as a matter of honor in a challenge, not over this issue. He would bow his neck beneath the sword rather than strike the fatal blow against the man he believed he had dishonored.

There was love and blood in her hand. That also mad Jennet had said. The love of men. And out of the love of men, blood would be shed.

She rose in the now empty chamber and went

to the window. The inner court was ablaze with torchlight, men scurrying, horns blowing as if it were full day. She wondered what they must all be thinking of this astonishing start of the Lord de Bresse, to set out in such haste in the middle of the night. But no one would question his bidding except maybe his closest knight companions . . . and what would he tell them?

They left as the chapel bell rang for lauds and the night was at its lowest ebb. Magdalen remained at the window. The silent emptiness of the court after the preceding bustle was echoed in the chambers of her heart as she contemplated the meeting between the two men who loved her, one of whom she loved too deeply for words, the other whom she loved in friendship and could never wish ill.

As the sky lightened in the east, another departure took place. Charles d'Auriac emerged from the guest hall with his own companions and attendants. Their horses were brought, and they rode from the castle without a word of farewell. Magdalen should have felt relief, but nothing could pierce her present grief and dread.

Charles d'Auriac rode off, greatly satisfied. Such a neat and pleasing plan he had concocted to rid the world of Edmund de Bresse. He had seen both men in combat, and he knew that

Edmund was no match for Guy de Gervais. The latter could not fail to kill that ardent and impulsive young man, and no one could implicate the de Beauregards in his death. Meanwhile, Lady Magdalen remained in the castle unprotected by either of her lovers, who would be too busy spilling blood over her to concern themselves with her safety. He couldn't help but smile at the neatness of it all as he prepared to move the operation into its second stage.

Fifteen

EDMUND MAINTAINED A merciless pace under the stars that night. He said nothing to anyone, and his expression was so closed and forbidding no one dared ask what calamity had precipitated this mad ride along the dark and dangerous roads. They were a small party, only four of his closest companions, their squires and pages, the squires leading spare horses.

Edmund did not know whether he would come upon his quarry before de Gervais reached Calais, but it mattered little. If de Gervais had taken ship to England, then Edmund would follow him there. He would meet up with him eventually. But he knew Guy was in no great hurry and assumed he would be taking the journey in relatively easy stages, stopping early for the night with hospitable barons or religious orders. If Edmund rode night and day, they should be able to make up the three-day start on the second day.

At dawn, they broke their fast at a mean hostelry in Roye where they learned that the party in the blue and silver de Gervais livery had passed through without stopping two days earlier. They changed to their spare horses and rode on through the long midsummer day. Only Edmund was unflagging. He seemed like a man possessed, possessed of abnormal strength and endurance, certainly. In normal circumstances, they could expect to accomplish thirty miles a day; those they pursued would do no more. At the pace Edmund was setting, they were accomplishing twice that, changing their exhausted horses at staging posts along the way.

That evening, he realized that he could not continue to push his companions as he was pushing himself, and they halted at a roadside tavern. His companions slept in their cloaks on the earthen floor of the one room while he himself, red-eyed with lack of sleep, the dust of the road coating his hair and clothes, paced the yard outside waiting for the stars to fade so that they could begin again. He slept for twenty minutes, sitting on the ale bench against the tavern wall, and woke with a guilty start, as if the sleep had in some way detracted from his sacred, honor-bound mission. Until he was avenged, he was a knight dishonored and should not be able to find bodily ease in any fashion.

At noon, they learned that the de Gervais party had stopped the preceding night at Arras as guests of a local baron. Edmund could smell his quarry now, and as they dropped onto the flat meadowland outside Bethune that evening, he saw them encamped by a river, a cluster of tents, the dragon pennon of Gervais fluttering in the breeze.

For the two days and nights of their journey, he had thought of nothing except this moment when he would confront the man who had broken faith with him, the faith of a lifetime, who had cuckolded him, who had bred a bastard on his wife. Now he paused at the crest of the rise looking down on the meadows and the encampment. None of his companions knew why he was pursuing Guy de Gervais with this madly obsessive speed, but a challenge could not be issued in private. Could it be issued without giving all and sundry the shaming truth, a truth he would keep to himself if he could?

Lord de Gervais, walking in melancholy mood beside the river as the rich aromas of roasting meat from the cooks' braziers rose in the balmy evening air, brushed at a cloud of midges. He saw the party of horsemen on the ridge, outlined against the pink sky, but the setting sun was in his eyes and he could not distinguish any identifying marks. They were a small party, he reflected, unless it was an advance guard for a larger force. If they were simply passing travelers, he could not fail to offer them the shelter of his own camp and the protection of his own watchmen and fires throughout the night.

It was a displeasing reflection, since he preferred his own company these days, eschewing even that of his knight companions. In truth, he had not hurried on this journey to Calais, knowing that he lingered in France because he could not endure the finality of leaving the shores where Magdalen and his child would remain until—unless—John of Gaunt summoned them to England.

But even that prospect brought only heartache. He did not think he could suffer again as he had these last weeks since Edmund's return, holding himself away from her, pretending less intimacy than he had had with her even before they had become lovers. That intimacy, of course, had been that of child and guardian and was no longer convincing between a virile man in his prime and a vibrant young woman; so what was left but the distance and formality of acquaintances? It was unendurable; better to have no contact at all than that.

He turned back toward the encampment as the party of horsemen came down the ridge. He would ask the Duchess Constanza for the hand of the Lady Maude Wyseford if it had not already been bestowed elsewhere in his absence. On that dull, stolid, dutiful body he would father children and lose as far as he could the memory of a quicksilver nature and sweet sensuality, red lips parted in mischief, gray eyes darkening with passion, rich sable hair glowing in a rippling tide to her knees. And he would lose as far as he could the memory of a gray-eyed babe with fat dimpled fists whom he'd held at the moment of her birth.

Casually, he looked toward the party of approaching horsemen. The falcon of Bresse flew at the herald's trumpet, now clearly visible despite the fading light. Edmund, riding at the head, was in armor beneath his black and gold jupon, his hand at his sword, and there was something about his posture that the older man recognized immediately as belonging exclusively to the very young and ingenuous—the urgent, rashly idealistic resolution of one about to right a wrong, scorning all consequences as immaterial to the vital, honorable importance of his self-appointed mission.

Guy knew why he had come, looking as he did. There could be but one explanation. He did not know how Edmund had come by the knowledge that had driven him to cover so many miles at such reckless pace, but he did know that he must forestall him before his consuming need for vengeance brought further calamity.

The approaching herald blew his alerting

note, and the party rode into the encampment. They were immediately recognized, and grooms and attendants ran forward to take their horses and offer the stirrup cups of welcome.

Guy moved at a more leisurely pace toward them. Edmund had flung himself from his lathered mount and stood looking around him, his eyes wildly seeking Guy de Gervais. Guy took in the condition of the horses, the dust-coated, red-eyed, disheveled appearance of Edmund and his companions. The cool space that always settled around him before he went into battle came to him then. This was a battle greater than any he had fought, and he must win it. He must win it for Edmund and for Magdalen and for little Zoe. He could feel his heart beating slow and steady, the relaxation in his muscles that came before he would require of them the ultimate exertion.

"I give you good even, Edmund." He stepped into the circle.

Edmund spun round to face him. His eyes were feral in his livid face, his lips a thin drawn line, the exhaustion of a man who has pushed himself physically and spiritually beyond endurable limits etched upon his countenance. He said nothing but began to fumble with his mail-plated gauntlet while the group around them stared, for the moment uncomprehending.

"*No!*" Guy's voice rang out in the sudden silence. The one word was invested with so much authority that Edmund's fumbling fingers were for a moment stilled. Then he shook his head, like someone momentarily blinded, and began again to wrench at his gauntlet.

"I said *no!*" Again the commanding voice rang out. Edmund's eyes began to focus as old habits pushed aside the fog of his rage-born, single-minded purpose: habits of obedience to that voice, habits of trust in that voice.

"Don't be a fool, man!" Guy spoke again with the same force. "Come with me." Without waiting to see that he was obeyed, he turned on his heel and strode out of the fascinated circle and down to the river.

Edmund stood irresolute for a minute. He could hardly throw down his gauntlet to the man's back. His eyes ran around the circle, and he read their knowledge of what he had been about to do. Once the gauntlet lay publicly upon the ground, the path was immutable. But he had intended it to be so.

He wrenched off his glove and almost ran after Guy de Gervais, whose broad back, the set of his red-gold head, the long, easy stride from the hip were all so familiar, had so often provided the ultimate reassurance in danger and uncertainty.

Once out of earshot of the audience in the camp, Guy stopped and turned, waiting for Edmund to reach him. Edmund was breathless; his silver-laced gauntlet was in his hand. With a sweeping gesture, he flung the gauntlet at Guy's feet.

Guy said quietly, "You have dropped your glove, Edmund." He turned and walked away a few paces as if the thrown gauntlet were of no importance.

Edmund stood where he was. "You have wronged me!" he declared, his voice carrying on the still evening air.

Guy paused. Without turning round, he said, "Pick up the glove, Edmund."

"You refuse my challenge?" It was inconceivable that a knight should do so within the laws of chivalry.

Guy remained with his back to Edmund, but he spoke clearly. "When you have heard what I have to say, you may issue your challenge if you so wish. Then I will take it up. But for now, *you* will retrieve your dropped gauntlet."

Deflated, robbed suddenly of the driving purpose, the absolute knowledge of the wrong done him and the only redress he could take, Edmund bent to pick up his glove.

Only then did Guy turn around, and there was deep sorrow and a wealth of compassion in his eyes as he looked at the young man in his bewilderment, his hurt, his unutterable exhaustion. But he allowed none of that to sound in his voice. "You are too weary to hear me sensibly or to discuss anything without resorting to foolishness. You and your companions will sup and take your rest. In the morning, we will talk of this."

"I will not break bread at your table." Edmund spoke with revulsion. "You have made a whore of my wife."

Guy shook his head wearily. "Nothing will be gained by this intemperance, Edmund. You will eat and you will sleep. Tomorrow, you may call your wife whore, and you may call me what you will, but *not now!* It is understood?"

Edmund yielded again from the same force of habit. He turned with de Gervais, and they walked together back to the encampment. His own traveling companions were already taking their ease at the long table set beneath the trees, tankards of wine at their elbows, relaxation flowing through their travel-weary bodies. They had been vouchsafed no reason for their journey, but now understood its purpose although not what lay behind that purpose. But they also understood that there were to be no dramas that evening. Their lord had lost the febrile intensity that had kept him in the saddle these last two days, although without that intensity, his soul-deep unhappiness was more in evidence.

Guy courteously invited Edmund to take his place at the table. He talked of this and that, casual but ever watchful, engaging his knightly guests in conversation. Edmund was silent throughout, and it was from one of his companions that Guy learned that the Sieur d'Auriac had not left Bresse with the other contenders at the tourney. He made no comment, although he was in no doubt as to the significance of the information.

When they had supped, he gestured to a group of tents clustered to the right of the encampment. "Sirs, I beg you will take your rest. You have need of it, I believe, and those tents are at your disposal if you so wish."

He remained at the table after they had left, sipping his wine, brushing idly at moths diving into the candle flame. Mosquitoes whined from the marshy sedge beside the river, but he barely noticed them. Had Magdalen broken her oath? Or did Charles d'Auriac, and therefore the de Beauregard clan, lie behind this diabolical situation?

If he could not persuade Edmund to withdraw the challenge he was so determined to make, then he must in honor accept it. And in honor, he could not kill the man he had wronged. So he must allow himself to fall beneath the other's sword and lance. But how was it possible to do that? He had all the reflexes of a man accustomed to fighting for his life; they were intrinsic to the way he thought, the way he moved. How could he lose them at will? Or control them? And it would be the equivalent of taking his own life—a mortal sin from which, logistically, there was no hope of absolution. Only confession and absolution would bring him to a state of grace.

He felt the terror of hell's torments as he looked into the candle flame. They were very real terrors, an eternity of damnation in indescribable torment. At least the pains of this world had their limits. The tortured body on this earth finally found peace. While he lived, he could endow a convent, have masses said for his soul, buy some redemption for past sins. But there was nothing he could do to avoid damnation if in effect he took his own life.

But with Edmund's blood upon his hands for such a cause, he could not endure his own life.

He took no rest that night.

Dawn broke, clear and cloudless. A heron skimmed over the river. Edmund de Bresse emerged from his tent. He yawned, stretched, and for a moment looked like a young man with not a care in the world. He saw Guy de Gervais, still sitting on the plank bench beneath the trees, just as he had left him the previous evening. He turned and went down to the river, splashed water on his face, untrussed in the seclusion of the bullrushes, then walked back to the bench beneath the willow trees.

Guy's page brought a pitcher of ale and a round of wheaten bread to the table. The lad looked uneasy, aware of the strange, threatening atmosphere hanging over people who seemed to be behaving in perfectly ordinary fashion—except that his lord had not sought his bed all night and was looking gray and haggard in the unforgiving light of morning.

"Leave us, Stefan," Guy said. "Bring water to my tent in half an hour." He poured ale and handed the tankard to Edmund. "Drink, and then we will walk away from here and talk of what must be talked of away from the ears of others."

Edmund followed the instruction, accepting now that Guy de Gervais would direct the situation. He was refreshed, calmer, but nonetheless resolute after his night's rest.

They walked away from the encampment, far along the riverbank until there was no possibility of ears, accidental or otherwise, to overhear them. Then Edmund spoke with the fierceness of the previous night, but without the hysteria.

"You have wronged me. You have made a whore of my wife and bred a bastard upon her body. Will you deny this?"

Guy shook his head. "I can deny the terms but not the facts." He heard Edmund's whistling breath at this admission and spoke again swiftly. "In a minute we will talk of both. Did Magdalen tell you of this?"

"What difference—"

"*Did she?*"

"Yes, I suppose she—" Edmund stopped, remembering that dreadful scene. Magdalen had not told him. He could see her now, standing so still and quiet, her hands opened in defeated admission when he had hurled his accusations at her. But she had not told him.

Slowly, he shook his head. "She did not tell me, but she did not deny it."

"Who told you?"

But no one had told him. Just whispers . . . innuendo . . . odd little remarks that had somehow formed a picture. "No one told me. But what difference does it make?" His anger resurfaced. "You do not deny that you—"

"Edmund, this is important." Guy interrupted him again. "What part did Charles d'Auriac play in this?"

Edmund was silent.

"He did play a part, didn't he?"

Edmund nodded. "He seemed to know that you . . . that the child . . . He said things that made me suspect. But what difference does it make?" he cried again.

"Not much, perhaps," Guy said quietly. "But one must give him credit for his cleverness. It is a brilliant strategy, designed, you understand, to remove you from this earth, as they once failed to do."

Edmund stared. "To remove me? How?"

"I think the de Beauregards rather assume that in fair combat I would prevail," Guy said, his voice as dry as the desert wind. "You would die at my hands. They would not be implicated. They have but to remove Magdalen, and the de Bresse fealty would lie open for the taking. Charles of France would be grateful, and the de Beauregards would be once and for all revenged upon Lancaster and most fittingly through his daughter."

"Revenged upon Lancaster?"

"I think it's time you knew the truth. It is John of Gaunt's secret, but he has kept it from you long enough. Let us walk a little way."

Edmund listened to the dark tale of that night in the fortress at Carcassonne, of his wife's birth amid blood and treachery. He heard of Isolde and the power she had to entrap, to bring men to their deaths when it suited her clan, and he heard, beneath the measured tones, and the temperate language, the unspoken parallels.

"Magdalen has that power," he said.

Guy nodded. "But she is innocent, Edmund. Her mother's family will use her and the power she has been given to destroy us both, but Magdalen herself is not responsible."

"She betrayed me."

Guy said nothing. There was nothing to say.

"And you . . . you took from me what was mine. I loved . . . love . . . her." Edmund's anguish now stood alone, his desperate rage somehow exhausted, only his sense of betrayal left.

"You were dead," Guy said. "I believed you to be dead. And I too loved . . . love . . . her, Edmund. But I swear to you that had I not believed you dead, I would have cut off my hand rather than break faith with you. I will go from here. Neither you nor Magdalen will ever see me again. You are both young, and you have a life and a love to share. Do not throw it away at the manipulation of the de Beauregards!"

The last sentence was spoken with a fierce desperation. Edmund looked around him, at the blue morning sky, the dawn mist on the river. A flock of curlews rose calling over the bullrushes, and there were marsh marigolds and rich yellow buttercups beneath his feet. There was a sweet taste to life, and he remembered the long months of agony as he had fought to hold on to that. Would he throw it away now?

"What happened to my child? The child she was carrying when I was attacked."

"There was a fearful storm on the voyage over. Magdalen lost the child then."

"And then she bore yours." Bitterness laced his voice. "She bore your child and pretended it was mine."

"It seemed the best course," Guy said with difficulty. "But I will not expect you to acknowledge my child as your own. I will take her, if you so wish it, and you and Magdalen will begin anew."

Edmund said painfully, "Magdalen would never give up her child."

"I believe she would, if you asked it of her," Guy said. "She will understand that you cannot love another man's child, cannot be expected to nurture another man's child as your own."

Edmund thought of Magdalen and her baby. He saw her sitting beside the window, her head bent over the child at her breast, the soft curve of her mouth, the lovelight in her eyes. "I could not ask it of her."

Guy felt a great peace enter his soul. He knew he could not himself have asked it of her. "Go back to your wife," he said softly.

"She does not love me," Edmund said, in pain and bitterness. "It is you she loves."

"She has always loved me," Guy said, as softly. "Since she was a child. She told me so first after my wife died, the day before you and she were to be wed. I took no notice, thinking it but the infatuation of a child. But she is a Plantagenet, Edmund, and they are a passionate breed. When they love, they love hard. It is for you to teach her to respond to your love."

"She will never forget you."

"I will become a memory in time. She will bear your children and as she loves them, she will love you. You will grow together in love." How it hurt to say such things, to say them with the sincerity that must convince Edmund. Did he truly believe that he would become a faded memory for Magdalen? Did he wish it?

No, he didn't wish it, and he didn't believe it. But he knew he must try to do both.

"Go back to your wife," he said again. "You have left her alone, and she has need of your protection."

"She believes that only you have the power to protect her." The bitterness was still there.

"Then you had better convince her that she is

in error!" Guy spoke sharply, as if impatient with a show of petulance. Edmund flushed.

"You have proved yourself on many a field, Edmund," Guy said, gently now. "In knightly sport and in battle. No one will impugn your courage or your ability to defend those who look to your for defense. And if your wife does so, then it is for you to correct her."

"It seems I have much to accomplish," Edmund said with a wry smile. But it was a smile that warmed and eased Guy de Gervais. Both the smile and the words told him that he had won this, the hardest fight he had yet fought.

"Then go to it," he said. "As soon as your horses are sufficiently rested, for I dare swear you will ride them as hard on the return as you did on the coming."

"The spur will be different," Edmund said.

Guy de Gervais knelt slowly on the grass, among the marigolds and the buttercups. "I ask your forgiveness for the wrong I have done you, Edmund. And I ask you to believe that it was not meant."

"Ah, no!" Edmund put his hands out to the kneeling man, knowing absolutely at this moment that Guy de Gervais would never deliberately have injured him. In fact, in the deepest recesses of his soul, he now acknowledged that he had always known it. "I do believe it, and if there is aught to forgive, then I do so freely and with all my heart."

"And you must forgive Magdalen," Guy said.

"I love her; how can I do else?" Edmund seized Guy's hands, pulling him to his feet. "I will make her love me."

Guy nodded. "Go back to the camp. I would be alone for a while."

Edmund left him immediately. Guy watched him go, saw the renewed spring in his stride, felt as if Edmund's anguish had simply been passed on to him, to augment his own burden. And he felt it to be a just penance.

He walked for an hour along the riverbank, recognizing within his grief the relief that he no longer bore the weight of deceit. It was over, and there was every hope that Edmund and Magdalen would now be able to begin their life together anew, unsullied with betrayal. Edmund had too generous a soul to visit vengeance upon the child that was not his. And Magdalen . . . Magdalen had affection for Edmund and a deep well of sensitivity and compassion. She would not withhold herself in her husband's need, and in time that affection would deepen. They would have babes of their own and . . .

But he could not follow the thought any further, however much he believed he deserved the self-flagellation. He must return to the camp, send

Edmund off to his wife, and put on his own life. There would be work for him to do in England, and in that work he would find surcease.

He gave order when he reached the camp that they would remain until after dinner and resume their travels at noon. The horses of the de Bresse party would be sufficiently refreshed by then, and for himself it mattered little if they only made a half-day journey.

If any speculated as to what had caused the precipitate pursuit of Edmund de Bresse, they kept their speculation to themselves. It was clear enough at dinner that the two men were in accord, that there were now no gauntlets about to be thrown, no challenges issued and taken up. The food was good, the wine flowed freely, the shade of the willows kept the midsummer sun from roasting the diners, and if there was a haunting sadness in the blue eyes of Lord de Gervais, then it was no concern of his guests.

The lone horseman careening down the ridge to the encampment was seen first by one of the men-at arms standing watch on the perimeter of the camp. He called out the alert that was then taken up by the herald.

Guy stood up, shading his eyes against the sun. He had little difficulty recognizing the figure crouched low over a long-tailed gray stallion. Olivier rode abysmally, slouching and jouncing like a flour sack. Apprehension took solid form. Only news of Magdalen could have brought Olivier, riding so recklessly, upon them.

"Who is it?" Edmund stood up, too, his hand still around his wine cup.

"My servant, Olivier," Guy said shortly. "I left him to . . ." He swallowed the rest of the explanation. Edmund would not want to hear that Guy de Gervais had left his own man to keep watch over Magdalen with instructions to bring him immediate word should any ill befall her.

"He is in some sort a spy," he said. "He had instructions to watch the doings of d'Auriac and the de Beauregards as and when he could."

"Then he brings ill news?"

"It is to be assumed so." Guy was already moving away from the table, his voice clipped with worry. Edmund followed him across the flattened grass of the meadow to where Olivier had ridden into the encampment. He had met no challenge from Lord de Gervais's watchmen, being well known, and now tumbled in an ungainly heap from his horse as a groom took the bridle.

He stood rubbing his back, a frown of discomfort on his swarthy brow. " 'Tis a scurvy means of travel, my lord. I've ridden nigh on a hundred miles in a day and a night."

"For a man who detests riding, that is indeed

some feat," Guy said as easily as if he did not know that Olivier could only bring disastrous news. "The Lady Magdalen . . . ?"

"Taken, my lord." Olivier bent double, his face screwed with pain.

"Taken? God's nails, man! What does that mean?" Edmund, agitated beyond containment, stepped forward.

"Give him time." Guy waved him down. "He has not ridden this far and this fast to keep it from us." He gestured to a hovering page. "Bring wine and set a platter of food upon the table. Come, Olivier, you have need of food and drink and rest while you tell your tale."

"I'll not sit, my lord," Olivier said frankly, moving to the table, where he leaned heavily upon it for a minute before he took the cup of wine the page held for him and drank its contents in one swift gulp, his throat working. Then he sighed with relief and put the empty cup on the table.

"Two nights ago, the tocsin sounded from the town. The garrison went out in answer. In their absence, an army laid siege to the castle."

"An army? Frenchmen in a time of truce?" Guy refilled the wine cup, his voice incredulous.

"Brigands," Olivier said, taking the cup again. "That bastard knight, Courtney Durand."

"Durand?" Courtney Durand was an English

knight turned mercenary. His company of brig-
and knights were at the fee of any who could pay
them, and they were notorious for their ferocity,
their success, and their lack of scruple. They ter-
rorized wherever their fee took them, from the
Swiss Alps to Naples, from Paris to Rome.

"Courtney Durand has taken my wife?"
Edmund was whiter than milk. "How could he
breach the walls of Bresse?"

"The garrison were lured away, my lord,"
Olivier explained, passing a hand wearily over
his face where sweat and dirt caked hard. "Then
engaged in battle beyond the town. There were
some three hundred lancers, pikers, and archers
who laid siege to the castle. They breached the
walls with bombards, sent fire arrows over the
battlements. Lady Magdalen directed our own
archers and we did some damage, but nothing to
the point. The savages were in the town, too."
A shudder of distaste rippled across his face.
"They sacked the town . . . You could hear the
screams, smell the burning . . ." He paused to
refresh himself from the cup again, and Edmund
swore violently. He should have been there to
defend his castle, his vassals, his wife.

"Go on, Olivier." Guy's face was strangely
still, and he ignored his companion's intemperate and guilt-ridden outburst.

"Well, as I said, the Lady Magdalen did what

she could, but in the end it was surrender or be sacked. She knew the rules. If the castle yielded, there would be mercy. If she held out . . ." Olivier shrugged. Those were the rules of war. Everyone understood them. "They demanded only herself and the child. She parleyed for the safety of the rest and immediate withdrawal from the town."

"And did they agree?"

"Yes, my lord. Very courteous it was, after that, almost as if they weren't after plunder at all." Olivier rinsed his mouth with wine and spat a red stream upon the ground, as if to indicate his opinion of such a ridiculous idea. "If you'd seen the town when they'd left you'd take their courtesy at its proper value." He wiped his mouth with the back of his hand, adding, "My lady showed much courage."

Guy nodded, unsurprised. "She is a Plantagenet."

"They have taken her for ransom," Edmund said in tones of one struggling to understand.

"The hand of the de Beauregards is behind this," Guy said impatiently. "And employing such a force, there is no doubt but they intended to succeed this time. There is no question of ransom, although that is what you and the rest of the world are to believe. How did you escape, Olivier?"

"Through the underground passage." The spy shrugged as if such means of egress were quite ordinary, as indeed they were to those who knew of them. "But you are correct, my lord. They have taken the lady and the child to Carcassonne."

"You heard this said?"

"Of course, my lord. I would not leave until I knew where they were taking them."

"No, of course you would not." Guy, even in his preoccupation, managed the flicker of a smile. "I did not mean to doubt you, my friend."

"We must go after them!" Edmund spoke in stifled tones. "Immediately."

"Yes," Guy said. "We must and will. But let us make plans first. Nothing will be gained without due thought and attention. We must match their care with our own. She is in the hands of the de Beauregards, and that is no light matter, Edmund."

He kept to himself what he feared might be planned for her at the hands of Charles d'Auriac, whom he knew to be the force behind the abduction, because it would do Edmund no good to share in those fears.

Sixteen

THE BOLT FROM a crossbow found its mark with an ugly dull thud. A scream rose, unearthly in its extremity of anguish. Such dreadful damage they did, those great bolts, much worse than the clean piercing of the arrows of the longbowmen; but not as bad as the spiked head of a mace, or the dreadful double blade of the battle-ax that was now rising up before her, wielded by a figure encased in plates of armor, his visored face a metal blank. She opened her mouth to scream, but no sound came forth.

Magdalen woke in an icy sweat, shaking with the terror images of her dream. Tonight they had been dream images, but two days ago they had been reality. She lay on the thin pallet, straw crackling beneath her when she moved to pull the blanket up to her chin, staring upward in the darkness at the canvas roof of the tiny tent. Roistering, drunken shouts came from outside her flimsy shelter, voices raised in song and frequently in altercation. She heard a woman cry out, and she shuddered. Two days ago, women from the town of Bresse had cried for mercy from sunup to sundown.

Beside her, Zoe slept peacefully, oblivious of the noise and the intrinsic threat it held. Magdalen assumed that if she and the baby were being held for ransom, no harm beyond their captivity would befall them. But while her head told her this, her heart heard the riotous sounds from the camp outside, the violent edge to the merriment, and her head would not rule her heart.

Pushing aside the blanket, she got to her knees and crawled to the tent flap. The night outside was lit with braziers and pitch torches of this brigand army. A rustle of cloth, a shuffle of booted feet on the grass sounded to the right of the tent, and she ducked back inside instinctively, then cautiously peered out again. An armed piker stood in the shadows of the tent, his back to her. There was something about his stance that told her he was not idling there. He had a purpose.

As if aware of the watcher, he turned around. His eyes were incurious as they rested on Magdalen's face framed palely in the tent opening. Then he turned frontward again, standing with his legs apart, one hand closed over the pike at his side.

A watchman, Magdalen decided, retreating again. Whether he was there to keep her in or others out, it mattered little. Someone had a care for her safety, and that in itself was comforting.

She sat cross-legged on the pallet, all desire to sleep long gone, wondering for the hundredth time since that terrible debacle whether she could have done anything to avert her present captivity or to save the lives that had been lost. The alarm had come in the dark hour before dawn and the garrison had ridden out, exactly as they had done that time when Guy had led them to repel a brigand attack. Remembering that incident, she had thought little of this expedition, had simply directed the preparations for receiving the returning warriors and tried to keep under control the memories of that last occasion, memories that brought stinging tears to her eyes. But once the garrison had left, a second, massive force had appeared from the woods at the rear of the castle. They had gone through the town like a knife through butter, and the screams and the fires had begun.

She had known what was expected of her. As lone chatelaine of the Castle de Bresse, it was for her to direct the defense. She had stood on the battlements, and men had died beside her with the bolts from the crossbows ripping through flesh and bone, unhindered by the links of chainmail. Fires had started all around from the fire-tipped arrows pouring in from across the moat, and the pounding mortars from the bombard had set the walls shaking. It was the noise she remembered most vividly . . . that and the moment when the walls were first breached. Armed men had poured into the *place d'armes,* giant figures embodying violent death with their maces and their cleavers, and, unable to bear further slaughter, she had instructed the herald to blow the note for parley . . .

Footsteps sounded outside the tent, and her heart jumped into her throat. The tent flap was pushed aside.

"The watchman seemed to think you had need of something." It was the brigand chieftain, the Englishman who had set the terms for the surrender; a big man with a gray-flecked beard and shoulder-length hair, and the eyes and mouth of one who followed no code of morality or of honor. Yet his voice was soft, and his manner had been courteous from the moment she had surrendered herself, the child, and the castle.

He ducked into the small space and sat down, unbidden, on the end of her pallet. "You'll be ill advised to show your face beyond that opening again this night." He folded his arms and regarded her with a certain avidity. "My hold's tenuous at best, and nonexistent when the drink's in them."

"And the bloodlust," she said coldly. "But

you'd think they'd had their fill of rape and murder at Bresse."

He laughed. "An appetite that once whetted only grows, lady."

Magdalen recognized the look in his eye. She had seen it in the eyes of men before, men who loved her and men who simply lusted. She pulled her cloak more tightly around her.

Leaning over, he moved a finger beneath her chin. She drew back, but there was nowhere to go. So she sat rigid, trying to stare him down. He laughed again and ran his finger over her lips. She jerked her head to one side. "Will you emulate your men, then?"

"Why should I not?" he asked softly. "There's something powerfully arousing about you, sweeting. Offer me a little softness, and there's no knowing what I may be able to offer you in return."

"My freedom?" she shot at him.

"No, not that, I fear. That is not in my gift." Before she could question this statement, he had caught her chin between finger and thumb, and his mouth was coming down on hers.

She brought her knee up into his stomach, not hard enough to do any damage because of the smallness of the space and the awkwardness of her position on the pallet, but he drew breath sharply nevertheless and abruptly released her.

"I do not think you dare to violate the daughter of John of Gaunt," she declared, finding herself no longer frightened in the face of this tangible threat.

He sat back and laughed. "What care I for Lancaster . . . or his daughter? I owe no fealty to anyone, and I abide by no man's laws but my own." He sat looking at her for a minute that seemed very long to Magdalen. Then he shook his head. "I do, however, give loyalty to the man who fees me, for as long as I am in his pay. And I do not think the Sieur d'Auriac considers you to be a part of my fee. A man thinks twice before dipping his toes in waters rightly belonging to any de Beauregard."

"The Sieur d'Auriac?" Horror stood out in her eyes. "I am not held for ransom?"

"Not by me, lady." He shrugged his wide shoulders, and the intricate design of woven leaves on his tunic seemed to ripple as if touched by a breeze. "I have been paid to bring you out of the Castle de Bresse and deliver you and the child to the fortress at Carcassonne . . . in good health," he added, shaking his head again with a regretful chuckle. "So, if you will not play willingly, then I must leave you to your chaste bed, since any effort to take what you refuse to give can only lead to some diminution in your good health." He ducked toward the tent opening. "I

give you good night, lady. Since I value my fee
at least as much as you value your honor, I will
double the watch outside. They will have orders
to restrain you, should you attempt to leave the
tent without permission."

But Magdalen was not listening. She was staring into the abyss, knowing now the ultimate
terror. Every time she believed matters could
not be any worse, they became so. She was in
the hands of her cousin with no hope of protection or rescue, since no one knew the truth.
And somewhere on the road to Calais, her lover
and her husband would by now have met in
bloody combat.

She looked upon an expanse of malevolence,
felt herself wandering in a void of menace. She
could not lay hands upon it, take the threat, examine it, disarm it with understanding. It simply
cast its great black shadow over her, and instinctively she lay down on the pallet, curled tightly
on her side beneath the blanket, and drew the
sleeping baby against her breast.

Her cousin's hand was now clearly revealed in
all of this. It was he who had betrayed her to
Edmund, his intention to achieve Edmund's departure from Bresse in the short term, his death
in the long term. There was now no representative of the Duke of Lancaster holding Bresse
for England. She and the child were vanished

and would never be seen again. The fealty of Bresse would revert to France as soon as Charles of France sent someone to take it. And she would be in her cousin's hands.

She saw those white hands, beringed, manicured, somehow soft as if decayed. Yet she knew they were not soft. She saw his eyes, narrowed with that hunger that sent the slug's trails across her skin, brought the stench of the oubliette to her nostrils. She felt the aura of his evil enveloping her as it had done on that very first meeting outside the tavern in Calais. Her future seemed very certain.

Panic fluttered, grew bright and strong, and she fought it with muscle and sinew of body and mind until she had subdued it and it lay below the surface once more. She must face what was to come alone, and, for Zoe's sake, she must face it with a mind cleared of the obscuring trappings of fear.

The days grew hotter as they journeyed south. They kept away from towns and camped in the countryside at nightfall. There were little breakaway excursions into solitary farms and small villages by small troops of Durand's army. The men would return with a glazed, surfeited look in their eyes that sent shudders down Magdalen's spine, and a drunken ribaldry that was somehow shamefaced. Their chieftain did nothing to prevent these diversions, but when two men failed to return to the main body of the army with their companions, he tracked them down, discovered them in a drunken stupor in a barnyard, and summarily hanged them as deserters before they were sober.

Magdalen rode her own horse, the babe cradled before her. Two pack mules bore her possessions. She had been instructed to bring all her clothes and jewels, which had not surprised her; she had expected to be robbed of them. Now it seemed she must put a different construction on the provision. Her women had not been permitted to accompany her, and Durand had offered her the services of a slatternly girl traveling with the baggage and at the service of any who chose to take what she had to offer. Magdalen had at first refused the girl's services, but had realized rapidly that caring single-handedly for a baby on a march of this kind was not easy. She hadn't realized how much washing had to be done, when all such things were seen to by Erin and Margery. So she accepted the woman's help for the menial tasks and struggled daily with the lack of privacy that made feeding the child and caring for her own personal needs a continual ordeal.

There was not a waking moment when she was not striving for a means of escape. Plans rose to be as quickly discarded. She looked longingly at the towns they passed. Surely in those crowded streets an opportunity would present itself, a sympathetic person would be found. But their road lay on the byways rather than the highways and she was kept so well guarded, surrounded by armed men at all times, that her chances of catching anyone's eye were so remote as to be not worth considering.

The terrain changed as they left the lush, green, river-threaded lands of the Dordogne. The vineyards of Roussillon lined the dusty hillsides, and the Pyrenees threw their southerly shadow. There was a sense of limitless space that came with the presence of the sea, for all that it was too far to be more than a hint on the horizon.

They reached the great fortress of Carcassonne at the end of the fifth week of their journey. By that time, Magdalen was so wearied of travel that her fear of journey's end had taken second place to the acute discomforts of every day. The only blessing was that Zoe appeared completely unconcerned by this change in her routine. She slept as easily to the gait of the horse as she had done in her cradle beneath the window at Bresse. She was awake a lot more of the time these days and would gaze around her with placid yet bright-eyed curiosity, sometimes sucking her fist, sometimes waving her arms in the air with gurgles of enjoyment.

Magdalen would not permit the slatternly servant to touch the child, so the two grew together in mutual dependence, the baby accepting only her mother's care and the mother finding in the child the only reassurance, the only reminder that there was a world outside this burning summer travel. Fear was lodged deep in her soul, and the dust caked her skin and hair, caught so deep beneath her fingernails it was impossible to imagine them clean again. Her throat was always dry and scratchy so that there was never enough water to lubricate it and never enough air to clear her nose of the hot trapped dust that made her sneeze constantly.

But in Zoe she saw what had once been and in Zoe she saw what must be . . . the future she must enable her daughter to have, whatever the future might hold for herself.

Her first sight of the fortress monastery dominating the mountainous countryside from its commanding hilltop position brought the terror alive and vivid again. The lilies of France and the hounds and hawk of Beauregard flew side by side from the donjon. It was a dark, menacing, massive pile of stone. The approach through the town sprawled across the hillside was a sunless ride through narrow, fetid cobbled streets overshadowed by the great walls of the fortress.

It was midday when Durand left the main body

of his army encamped outside the town and rode with his prisoner and a small escort of pikers and archers up to the fortress. Magdalen's arms tightened around the baby as they reached the drawbridge across a moat, wider and deeper than any she had seen. Durand's herald blew his note. It was answered from within, and the portcullis rose slowly as the drawbridge was lowered.

A dark, dank stench of old never-dried stone floated from the entrails of the fortress as Magdalen and her child rode to face the horror it contained. She was trembling, and Zoe wailed in sudden sympathy, her little face screwed up with unidentifiable unease.

The cry strengthened Magdalen. "Hush, pigeon," she soothed, lifting the child to kiss the plump cheek.

They rode beneath the arch, into the *place d'armes,* thronged with men-at-arms. Cowled monks in the brown corded habits of the Franciscans mingled with the warriors, hurrying on their own business, God and war inextricably bound here as they were in the minds of all men.

They rode through the *place d'armes* and into the inner ward, where attendants hurried from the donjon to greet them. A woman in nun's habit, a harsh-featured face beneath the stiff starched wimple, came over to Magdalen as she was helped from her horse.

"I am Sister Therese, lady. You will come with me."

Magdalen followed the nun into the donjon. The air inside was chill despite the midsummer heat, and there were no floor coverings on the stone passages or wall hangings to block the draughts. The nun led her through a circuitous maze of passages, up twisting staircases, and stopped outside an iron-bound oak door.

"For the moment, you are to be lodged in this apartment." She raised the heavy latch and opened the door onto a small, well-swept chamber. The only light came from a narrow slitted window high up in the stone wall and from tallow candles that burned on a long pine table beneath the window. There was no fire in the hearth, but the hangings to the bed looked clean, and there was a wooden cradle on rockers beside the bed.

"There is a latrine beyond the garderobe." The nun gestured to the door in the outside wall. "You will be brought hot water for you and the child, and meat and drink. If you have need of anything further, there is a bell beside the door." She indicated the hand bell on a table. "When they are ready to see you, I will come for you."

Her face had remained set in its original, forbidding lines throughout this brief communication, her speech delivered with a degree of indifference, as if she were simply reciting by rote. She offered Magdalen no sign of fellow feeling, no hint of sympathy, and Magdalen's questions died in the face of an impassivity that seemed to indicate little or no interest in the captive woman's fate.

The door closed on the nun, and the heavy wooden bar fell into place with a dull finality. Magdalen examined her surroundings. The chamber was furnished with the bare necessities, offering no clues to the intentions of her captors. In a few minutes, the latch was lifted and a serving wench appeared with a steaming pitcher which she took into the garderobe. Beneath her arm, she carried a pile of toweling which she set beside the pitcher.

"My thanks," Magdalen said. "I'll be glad to wash away the dust of the road." She smiled at the girl. "How are you called?"

But the girl merely stared at her with frightened eyes and scuttled from the chamber.

It was not reassuring, but Magdalen turned to the soothing tasks of caring for the baby. She was washing her when the door again opened, admitting this time two burly varlets, who deposited her own trunks in the middle of the floor.

There was something both comforting and

discomforting about having her own possessions again. For the first time in weeks, she could change her clothes in the privacy of four walls, but the presence of her trunks, of the familiar possessions in this dim chamber, seemed to impart a finality to her present residence, as if she must learn to call this place home.

She had fed Zoe and changed her own clothes before the serving wench reappeared, this time with a tray bearing bread, meat, and wine. It was simple fare, but Magdalen found she could not eat. The meat would not be swallowed however much she chewed, and the bread settled in a solid lump in her throat. Apprehension was now filling the gap left by the accomplishment of her physical tasks. She drank a little wine, hoping it would give her some courage, and paced the small chamber, waiting.

It was late afternoon when the nun returned for her. The sun was still hot and bright, but the day might as well have been dull and overcast for all the sunlight penetrating the little slitted window. Magdalen was chilled and rubbed her hands together as if it were midwinter. When she heard the latch being lifted, she turned to the door, and the cold was in her soul.

Sister Therese came in. Her eyes were a muddy brown, without depth or warmth. "You are to come now. They are ready for you."

Magdalen bent to pick up Zoe, who sat propped against pillows on the bed, shaking a wooden rattle with an air of great concentration.

"The child is to remain here."

"No!" Magdalen forgot her own fear in the face of this new threat. They would not separate her from her baby, not in this place. "The child goes where I go."

"She stays here, lady." The nun looked significantly over her shoulder to where two brawny men-at-arms stood. They stepped into the doorway.

"You will have to kill me first." Magdalen issued the dramatic threat with composure now. She knew instinctively that for the moment she herself was to be unharmed, and if she stood her ground they would have no choice but to accede to her demand. Her arms were wrapped tightly around Zoe, and her gray eyes glared their implacable message.

There was a short silence when the coiled tension in the room seemed almost palpable. Magdalen did not move in her Plantagenet determination, and her eyes did not so much as flicker. Sister Therese touched her wimple; it was a gesture of uncertainty.

"The child will not be harmed," she said slowly.

Magdalen's eyes went to the two men standing in the doorway, and she said nothing.

"I swear to you that she will not be harmed," Sister Therese said, and there was a placatory note in her voice.

Magdalen thought rapidly. She knew she would want no distractions when facing whatever she was about to face. The child was her weakness, as well as her strength, and she could not afford to reveal that weakness to those she was about to confront. "You will swear on the cross you wear that my child will come to no harm in my absence." Her voice was low and steady.

The nun touched her crucifix. "I swear it. She will come to no harm while you are gone from this chamber. If you wish it, I will remain with her. You are to go with the men."

Gently, Magdalen laid the baby in the cradle, tucking her up securely. Zoe blinked sleepily and seemed not ill content with the arrangement. Magdalen kissed her brow and then straightened.

"Very well," she said. "I leave her in your charge." Strangely, their roles seemed to have been reversed and she was in control, making the decisions instead of having them made for her. It gave her courage.

She walked out of the chamber, and the nun closed the door gently behind her. The gentleness reassured Magdalen since it seemed to indicate some consideration for the child, a desire not to startle her with a sudden noise. The two men-at-arms silently fell in on either side of Magdalen, forming an escort.

They progressed in silence down endless passages, past hurrying pages and anxious servitors. Couriers and men-at-arms moved with a stolid purpose, cowled monks with measured pace. None offered the woman and her escort more than a passing glance, and Magdalen wondered if such sights were common enough in this vast fortress dedicated to so many purposes, both religious and secular.

At a door set into a bastion wall, her escort stopped. One of them rapped with his staff. The door was opened, and the man who stood there smiled his thin smile at Magdalen.

"Such a pleasure, cousin," Charles d'Auriac said, bowing. "I bid you welcome." He gestured sweepingly that she should enter the tower room.

Magdalen felt his evil, but she was accustomed to it and had prepared herself well for this first encounter. She was not, however, prepared for the massed wall of malignancy that seemed to shimmer before her eyes as she walked past her cousin and faced the four other men in the round chamber.

They were sitting at a rectangular table in the center of the room. Fingers of light came from the slitted windows set at eye level around the wall. A branched candlestick in the middle of the table augmented the light and threw golden shadows. Four pairs of gray eyes regarded her as she stood uncertainly just inside the doorway.

"I bid you welcome to your mother's family, Magdalen, daughter of Isolde." A heavy-set man, older than the others, spoke from his place at the head of the table. None of the men rose at her entrance. "I am Bertrand de Beauregard, your mother's brother and the head of this family. You will accord me the reverence due your uncle and the head of your family."

He was her uncle. She could read it in his face, in the resemblance they shared. He did not look in the least like her, yet something told unmistakably that they were of the same blood, as she had known it with Charles d'Auriac. And courtesy decreed that she make her reverence.

She ignored courtesy. "I have been brought here under duress."

"You were removed from your mother's family without consent and have been brought back to them." His voice was harsh, but she sensed that the grating note was habitual and that he was not at the moment angered by her refusal to obey his demand.

"I have never known my mother's family. I do not understand how I was removed from them." She held herself very still, aware of Charles behind her, so close she could almost feel his breath on her neck. Her skin crawled at his proximity, but he was a known danger and for the moment she put him aside, concentrating instead on the unknown embodied in this burly man, whose gray eyes pierced the world from beneath massive shaggy brows above a large, pointed nose.

"That will be explained to you. For now, you will acknowledge your place in this family."

"I am the Duke of Lancaster's daughter," she said, lifting her head. "It is to him I owe filial reverence." She had moved to the end of the table and now stood facing him, her hands flattened on the cool oak surface.

There was a flash of blood-red as something caught the pointer of sun from one of the window slits. The next instant she was staring in disbelief at her hands on the table. Between the middle and index fingers of her right hand a dagger shivered, the ruby-eyed sea serpent glinting. It was impossible to believe that the dagger was not pinning her finger to the table, yet she felt no pain and could see no blood. Her eyes lifted slowly, appalled, to the man at the end of the table.

"Pay attention," said Bertrand. "You talk too much and listen too little."

She swallowed, moistened her dry lips, gingerly moved her fingers apart. A tiny bead of blood showed where the dagger had nicked the skin of her middle finger. The silence in the chamber was profound.

"My lord uncle," she acknowledged finally, bowing her head.

Charles d'Auriac reached over her shoulder, pulled out the dagger, and sent it skidding across the table to his uncle. Magdalen noticed distantly that the entire surface of the table was scarred with incisions like the one just made. Her sense of unreality increased. What had happened was clearly accepted as a usual method of discipline in this group.

Bertrand laid the dagger on the table at his right hand. "Niece," he responded. "You are most welcome. My sons, your cousins . . ." His hand moved in leisurely fashion, indicating the three men at the table. "Gerard, Marc, and Philippe. Your cousin Charles, you already know. His mother was sister to myself and to your mother."

"What do you want of me?" She managed to frame the question, to keep her head raised, despite the deep chill of terror in her belly.

"Why, your allegiance to the de Beauregards,

niece," Bertrand responded gently, leaning back in his chair. "You are one of us. You belong to us, as your mother belonged to us. We would embrace you."

The embrace of the serpent. Her eye fixed on the serpentine head of the dagger, and the malevolence of her mother's family swirled around her in choking possession. "I am a Plantagenet," she said, summoning the last drop of defiance, her eyes never leaving the dagger. Next time, she knew, it could draw real blood.

But Bertrand made no move toward the weapon. He leaned back in his chair, looking up at her with narrowed eyes. His voice was suddenly quite soft. "You were born in this very chamber, daughter of Isolde."

"Here?" She had always known she'd been born in France, but beyond that had neither asked for nor been offered further information. "In this room?"

She looked around the bastion room, its thick stone walls, flagstone floor, and great hearth, empty now, but on the winter night of her birth a fire would have been kindled. A shiver lifted the fine hairs on her spine. She was standing in the room of her birth, among her mother's family. And she had known only the cool green lands of England, the drear wilderness of a border fortress, the lush arrogance of the Plantagenet court. Only these had informed her sense of herself, of who and what she was, of her place in the world. And now she was standing where some woman had gone through the agonies of birth to bring her into the world . . . agonies she had gone through herself . . . agonies that she knew welded a mother to her child. The sense of the room seemed to seep into her blood, through her pores, like the presence of the mother she had never known. Had Isolde de Beauregard died in this room? Had she died here in the moment of birth, or afterward, in some other chamber?

"Did she die here?" She uttered the question on the thought.

Something in Bertrand's gray eyes flickered, a serpent's darting venom. His voice was still and cold, almost disembodied, as if it emerged from the mouth of a corpse. "Your father poisoned her in this room . . . and here she suffered her death agony at the moment of your birth. Lancaster took you from her dying body."

The horror swirled around her. She grabbed the edge of the table, her knuckles whitening as she hung on to the hard solidity in an effort to keep upright as she absorbed what had been said. "My father killed my mother?"

Softly, his words falling into the cool light of early evening, Bertrand told her. He told her of her mother's gifts, her power to bewitch men, the way they had harnessed those gifts, that power, to work for the good of the family. He told her how Isolde had set out to entrap Lancaster and how her plan had been foiled by the prince. He told her her mother cared nothing for Lancaster, had seduced him simply to achieve his death for the greater good of France and the aggrandizement of the de Beauregards. The words were soft, but their meaning was as marble, ice cold and indelible. She had been conceived in hatred and born of a murderous revenge.

So this was the secret Guy de Gervais had kept from her. She understood then so much . . . understood that dreadful moment when John of Gaunt had rejected his eleven-year-old daughter . . . understood his continuing aversion . . . understood the strange, oblique remarks Guy de Gervais had made about her resemblance to her mother, how he would never expand, would stop as if he had already said too much . . . understood his recoil when she had blindly stated her belief in following the dictates of passion. She understood then that the effect she had on men, the hungry gazes of the men at her father's court, the lusting of her cousin, of the brigand chieftain, the passionate loving and lusting of Edmund and Guy, was the effect her mother had

had on men. She was the daughter of Isolde de Beauregard, and these men, Isolde's family . . . *her* family . . . intended to put her to the same use to which they had put her mother, employing the same innate powers.

And all the love she had felt from anyone was suddenly tarnished like old brass, green and spoiled. It was aroused from tainted roots, despoiled and despoiling. She felt as she had done all those years ago, when Guy de Gervais had told her that John of Gaunt was her father. The same desperation, confusion, excoriating hurt of the soul swamped her. And this time there was no loving, understanding figure in whom she reposed absolute trust to lead her to understanding.

But she was no longer a child. The same experience could not engulf her as it had once done, and she had no need of an omnipotent guardian to make sense of the world for her. She had a core, her own core, and she clung to it, facing these men with their uncanny resemblance to herself, these men who were telling her she was of them and belonged to them, telling her that she would work for them because she owed them family fealty as her mother had done. She would reject their taint.

"No!" she said.

She recoiled with a gasp as the dagger drove

into the very edge of the table a fraction of an inch from her belly.

"Pull it out and give it back to me," Bertrand said, his voice as cold and calm as ever. She obeyed because she could not imagine doing otherwise, drawing forth the blade, seeing its keenness shimmer in the candlelight as she pushed it along the table so that he would have it to use again.

"There comes a time, niece, when I grow awearied of make-believe," Bertrand said almost casually, polishing the ruby eye with the end of his dagged sleeve. "Have a care."

"I have a husband—" Magdalen began shakily.

"Edmund de Bresse is dead." It was Charles d'Auriac who spoke. He had been standing behind her, but now he moved round the table so he could see her face. "You know he is dead. He has challenged your lover, the man who betrayed his marriage bed. There could be but one conclusion to such a combat."

"Guy de Gervais would never deliberately have Edmund's blood upon his hands." She spoke with the clarity of absolute confidence and felt the sudden attention from the men in the room. This was not something they had ever considered. The recognition brought her renewed courage, and an imprudent touch of scorn laced her voice. "Having wronged

Edmund as he believed he had done, he would never take his life in fair combat."

"What nonsense is this!" Charles exclaimed, but they could all hear the hint of uncertainty in his voice. "What possible choice could he have? He is far and away the stronger combatant."

Magdalen's eyes met his. "I do not know what choice he would have," she said quietly. "But I do know he would be more likely to choose his own death than Edmund's." It was the truth and it tore at her to say it, but because it did, her conviction was unassailable. The quality of the silence in the room changed, sharpened, and she could feel Charles's unease.

"The courier has not yet returned with confirmation?" Bertrand raised an eyebrow.

"Not yet," Charles said. "Something must have delayed him upon the road. But there is no doubt as to the outcome. No man would choose his own death over another's." He managed to sound dismissive.

"You couldn't imagine it, could you?" Magdalen looked at him with contempt, then her gaze ran around the table. She forgot her fear under a surge of contemptuous loathing and the belief that while blood ties might connect her with these men, those ties were as nothing compared to the ones that connected her with the Lord Bellair, Guy de Gervais, Edmund de

Bresse, and John of Gaunt. Those ties had their roots in shared codes of honor and morality, in the knowledge of what was right and wrong, in the knowledge that people would in general prefer to behave well rather than ill, even if their own goals were not served thereby.

"None of you could understand it," she said. "Because it comes under the name of honor— something you do not understand, something you cannot—"

The dagger buried itself in the door behind her. It had sped past her ear, so close she could feel the air vibrating with its passing, so close the skin of her cheekbone burned in response and her right eyelid fluttered uncontrollably at the thought of what nearly had been.

Nausea rose in her gorge, her shock so powerful she was afraid she would be sick where she stood. She fought it, closing her eyes tightly against the image of the right side of her face sliced cleanly with the dagger, losing herself in this private struggle to bring her shattered nerves into alignment again, to quell her heaving belly, to still the violent tremors of her knees and hands, the wild pounding of her heart.

Her face had a gray cast, blue tinged her set lips, and the five men watched her struggle with interest. They all knew the fear of that dagger, even for those accustomed to it, even for those who were no strangers to the battlefield horrors of mutilation, the pain of wounds.

When she finally opened her eyes, her battle won, there was the faintest look of respect in the eyes regarding her. But when Bertrand spoke, there was no acknowledgment of that respect.

"Daughter of Isolde, you belong now to your mother's family. You will work with us as your mother did, and you will put aside all previous allegiances. Your cousin Charles has expressed the wish to manage your obedience to this family. When the courier brings us confirmation of your husband's death, you will wed your cousin. In the meantime . . ." He glanced significantly at d'Auriac, then shrugged. "In the meantime, we leave matters in Charles's hands, to be managed as he sees fit."

Magdalen shook her head in mute dread. In the tension of the last half hour, her very personal fear of Charles d'Auriac had been subsumed under her need to stand up to these men, to stand true to her core, to reject the taint they would put upon her. But now the full horror of her situation rose vivid and implacable. She was without rights or protection, in her cousin's power, and he had been given leave to wield that power as he chose.

She looked at him, and he read the panic in her eyes. His own eyes contained the hunger she knew well and the calm satisfaction of one about to achieve a long-awaited goal.

"I will never swear allegiance to this family," she said, her voice a mere thread. But she had managed to speak through her fear.

"It will be for your cousin to persuade you otherwise," Bertrand said, sounding suddenly bored with the discussion. He got to his feet and went to a table against the wall where a pitcher of wine and tankards stood. He poured and drank. "Take her away. Bring her back when you have done your work."

Charles d'Auriac bowed to his uncle in acknowledgment. "Cousin," he said with gentle mockery. "Shall we go?" He moved to open the door, where the dagger was still implanted in violent reminder of the phantasmic savagery of the last half hour.

What choice did she have but to go with this man into whatever species of hell he had planned for her? She walked past him, drawing her surcote aside as if she could not bear to touch him. His smile grew thinner.

When they reached her chamber, he opened the door and curtly dismissed Sister Therese, sitting beside the cradle. He stood looking down at the sleeping child. "You continue to nurse her?"

There was something sinister in the question, something that set her skin crawling with alarm, yet it was reasonable enough on the surface. Just the sight of him standing so close to Zoe brought sick quivers to her belly.

"Yes," she said. "Do not wake her."

He turned away from the cradle. His eyes rested on her, speculative and rapacious. "So, I am to make a good and loyal de Beauregard of you, cousin."

"Never!"

"That is a long time," he observed. "I do not believe it will take so long." He moved toward her, and she forced herself to stand her ground, knowing that if she showed her fear it would only render her more powerless.

"If you but knew how long I have waited for this time," he said softly, standing over her, his body seeming to become massive in its closeness. Her eyes were fixed on a sparrow hawk embroidered on his tunic. The bird seemed to dip and curve with each breath he drew. "I know you do not hold the marriage bed sacred, cousin, but you will stray from ours only with those to whom I send you."

"You would make a whore of me!" Her voice was a whisper of outrage.

"You were born of a whore," he said. "A whore who knew how to do her work well." His finger brushed her cheek, and when she recoiled, he put a hand on her shoulder, holding her still. "You also know how to do that work well. You have proved that you can satisfy a husband and a lover at the same time. You have the power of the temptress in you, too, Magdalen of Lancaster. You are your mother's daughter, and we will harness that power for the good of the family and the good of France. And through you we will be revenged upon Lancaster for the murder of Isolde."

He brought his mouth down on hers, hard and bruising as he forced her lips open. For one dreadful instant, his tongue lay upon hers. Her hand went up and raked his cheek, her nails leaving livid lines. He pulled back with a vile oath just as the child awoke and a hungry wail filled the chamber.

Magdalen moved instinctively toward the cradle, but the hand on her shoulder closed painfully. He looked down at her for a moment that seemed to stretch into eternity.

"See to her!" He released his grip on the curt instruction.

Magdalen hurried to the cradle. She lifted the child, trying to calm herself so that Zoe would not sense her agitation. Under the cold gray gaze of Charles d'Auriac, she changed the baby and then fed her, turning sideways to the watcher, drawing the sleeve of her surcote over her exposed breast as if she could thus preserve some modesty. But his voracious eyes did not once leave her.

Her appetite satisfied, Zoe was inclined for play. She sat on her mother's knee as Magdalen refastened her gown, and stared around the chamber, her eyes wide as she included Charles d'Auriac in her examination.

"Put her down," he instructed in the same curt tone.

"But she is not ready to sleep yet," she protested. "She has only just wakened."

The marks of her nails had reddened against his cheek, and there was a deep, cold fury in his eyes. "Leave her." He strode to the door, flinging it open. Outside stood the two men-at-arms who had escorted her earlier.

He gestured with his head toward Magdalen. "Take her down."

"What . . . ? Where . . . ? I do not—" Stammering, she stood up, retreating as they advanced on her, the child still in her arms.

"Give the child to Sister Therese. You will not wish her to go where you are going."

The nun had entered the chamber after the soldiers, her features as harshly unmoving as before. Magdalen's terror surpassed anything she had ever felt. "Where . . . ?" But the one-word question was a mere whimper. The nun took the child from her nerveless arms.

"To a place where you may reflect at leisure, cousin," Charles said. "Take her!"

The two men grabbed her arms. She struggled for a minute before realizing the absolute futility at the same moment that she realized d'Auriac was watching her pathetic efforts to free herself with a sardonic smile, the scarlet marks of her nails standing out even more vividly now. She yielded abruptly. Whatever they were going to do with her, she could do nothing to avert it.

She walked between them, although they still held her arms, and they went down . . . down and down until she could smell the cold earth and knew they were below ground level. The darkness of the passages was lit infrequently by pitch-pine torches in sconces, and the walls oozed a greenish slime. They saw no one, and she began to shake with cold and terror.

At last they stopped. A trapdoor was set into the floor at their feet. Magdalen knew immediately what was below it. The oubliette of her nightmares.

It took both of them to grasp the massive ring bolted to the slab and haul the door open. She cowered on the edge of the black hole yawning at her feet. Then she felt the hand in the small of her back and knew they would push her. God alone knew what she would fall into. She dropped to her knees at the edge and slowly lowered herself into a darkness so black it was beyond imagination. The stone slab crashed closed above her, and a scream ripped through her. It came back at her, and then there was silence . . . the most absolute silence, as absolute as the darkness. She thought her heart was going to stop with her terror. What was in front of her? Was she standing on the edge of some deep shaft, some pit that would swallow her if she took a step? She shrank back, felt something cold and wet against her back, but at least it was solid. She was breathing in little petrified sobs. Blindly she moved her hands to either side of her. They encountered cold, slimy, oozing stone, then her fumbling fingers closed over a steel ring. She leaned backward and tears of relief filled her eyes at finding something solid to hold on to. Her heart was pounding so violently in her ears that the noise filled her head. Her feet were wet. She was standing in water. How much water? Now she heard a steady trickle from somewhere, but the darkness was so complete it was disorienting, and she could not decide whether the sound came from right or left or ahead.

She was entombed, the great weight of the earth pressing upon her head. There was no air; it was as if a thick velvet cloth were being held over her mouth, and her chest began to close, her lungs heaving, hurting as she grabbed for the air that was not there. Her body was bathed in an icy sweat, and she knew she was going to die.

But she hadn't been put here to die.

Slowly, the thought took hold. She began to see the words, shaped in her head. *She hadn't been put here to die.* She heard them, spoke them, rolled them around her tongue.

Zoe was safe, and they would let her out of this place. But when? What else was down here, invisible? Rats, snakes in the walls, in the water, beetles, spiders . . . Before she could stop it, another scream escaped her. Again it was returned to her, and the silence, broken now by the incessant dripping, took over.

Courtney Durand was dozing the doze of the justly satiated in his tent below the walls of the fortress of Carcassonne. He had been paid for a job well done and now took his ease, one hand lazily stroking the curving hip of the woman who had led him to that ease during the long, somnolent hours of the summer afternoon. The taste of wine and garlic and the rich sausage of Toulouse was upon his tongue, and the woman was full-breasted and eager, lifting to his touch, her mouth stained with wine, her rich earthy scent of sweat and fulfillment and the beginnings of arousal stirring him anew. She moved over him, taking him within the capacious welcome of her body, and for a moment he saw a pair of wide, candid gray eyes, a full, passionate mouth, a sloping white shoulder above the wide-necked cotehardie hinting at the subtle curves beneath.

His turgid flesh shrank. The woman looked down at him, startled, a little aggrieved. He pushed her off him and stood up. The tastes on his tongue were now sour and he grimaced, pouring wine from the pitcher on a low table, drinking it down in one deep gulp. He reached for his purse, shook out a handful of coins, and tossed them toward the woman. They fell in a bright, jangling shower upon the ground.

She scooped them up, pulled on her shift and coarse linen gown, thrust her feet into her sabots, and disappeared without a word through the tent flap.

"My lord?"

"What is it?" It was a snarl, and the page flinched as if expecting a blow.

"A man to see you, my lord. He says he has an urgent message."

"From whom?"

"He will not say, my lord. He says it is for you alone."

Durand pushed past the lad and stepped out into the late afternoon. His hose was untrussed, his tunic unbuttoned, but there was no one to whom he would make apology for such dishevelment.

A lean, agile, swarthy-skinned man was sitting on a pack roll beneath a tree. He was eating olives and spitting the pits with a careless indifference to where they fell. As Durand emerged from his tent, he stood up.

"I've a message for you, Sir Courtney."

"From whom?" Durand scratched his chest.

"My lord." The man seemed to think that sufficient. He turned to rummage in the pack roll.

"Haven't I seen you somewhere before?" Durand examined the figure with a frown.

The man shrugged. "Could be. I'm to be found here and there." He drew forth a parchment and handed it over, then resumed his seat and began again on the olives.

Courtney Durand read the missive. He read it twice, and a slow smile spread over his face. He glanced over his shoulder at the fortress, looming in its malevolent mass at his back. His smile broadened.

"An interesting challenge," he murmured. "You may tell the Lord de Gervais that I find his proposition appealing. The figure named seems sufficient, and our combined forces might pre-

vail with cunning. I await his arrival most
eagerly."

Olivier nodded, got to his feet, slung his pack
over the sturdy roan tethered to the tree, untied
the horse, swung awkwardly onto his back, and
trotted off.

Courtney Durand laced up his hose and but-
toned his tunic, feeling the evening sun on the
back of his neck. It was indeed an interesting
and appealing proposition: having taken the fee
of the de Beauregards to deliver the lady and her
child into captivity, he would take the fee of the
opposition to effect their release. He laughed
aloud, the sour, jaded aftermath of surfeit
vanished.

THE BLACK TIME was interminable. She was
engulfed, only the death grip of her fingers on
the steel ring keeping her hold on reality. Her
legs ached from standing, but she could not sit
while holding the ring, and besides, there was
the water at her feet and she did not know what
else. So she stood, her back welded to the oozing slime of the wall. When the stone door
above her crashed open, the sound was so terrifying in the absolute silence, she let go the ring
and slipped forward onto her knees. Her hands
sank into a viscous mud, and she cried out. But
she didn't fall any further, and there was light

behind her now. Her eyes hurt for a minute, stinging from the acrid smoke of pitch and tallow. She struggled back to her feet, but before she could orient herself to her dungeon, hands seized her arms and she was hauled up, out of the oubliette. The slab crashed down on her prison and she was in the passage, trying to control her sobs.

The same two men-at-arms stood impassive, waiting for her to get to her feet. She saw the slime coating her slippers, drenching the hem of her gown and surcote. Her hands were black with it. She could not see the wildness in her eyes, the ghastly hue of limitless terror on her face. Her escort saw it, but it was usual for those released from the oubliette, and their flat peasant eyes, accustomed to cruelty, did not remark the signs of suffering.

They took her back, up and up to where the air smelled fresh and the cold of the stone was that of an aired stone, stone that saw the light of day. But it was full night. She could see only blackness filling the slitted windows, occasionally a silver star glimmer. They opened the door of her chamber, and she stepped in.

Sister Therese was there, holding a wailing, desperately hungry Zoe. Charles d'Auriac lounged against the far wall. His eyes read and understood every terror-filled moment she had spent, and the cold gray gaze was touched with satisfaction.

"The child is hungry," the nun said, holding out the baby.

Magdalen looked at her hands. She could not touch her child with the indescribable filth of the oubliette upon them. Without a word, she went into the garderobe. The water in the pitcher was cold, but she scrubbed her hands with a vigor that belied her absolute exhaustion . . . the exhaustion of a spirit that has clung to sanity by a merest thread. Satisfied, she took Zoe and sat down, heedless of her wet and filthy hem and slippers. As the child suckled, some element of peace entered her. She would not look at her cousin, who remained by the wall watching, but as her body responded to the baby's elemental needs, she began to feel her own hold on reality reassert itself.

But when the child was fed and comfortable once more, Charles d'Auriac went again to the door. "Take her down."

The two men-at-arms entered the room.

"No . . . please . . . I cannot . . ." She heard her plea, would have given anything not to have made it, but could not help herself.

Her cousin touched his cheek, touched the raw striations made by her nails, and said nothing.

They took her back, down and down, and they locked her again in the impenetrable timeless darkness.

TEN MILES OUTSIDE ORLEANS lay the decomposing body of the courier who'd been sent to discover and bring report to Carcassonne upon the outcome of the combat between Edmund de Bresse and Guy de Gervais. The body lay tumbled in the ditch where the band of thieves had left it, its news locked forever in the whitening skull.

GUY DE GERVAIS, EDMUND de Bresse, and Courtney Durand met in the shadow of the fortress, their forces melding without ceremony or insignia, offering no apparent threat to the watchmen of Carcassonne, who saw only the brigand army so recently in the fee of the de Beauregards.

Seventeen

THE ACHE IN her legs mercifully passed, a deep numbness taking its place. Long before then, she had lost all sensation in her feet, finally deadened by the icy water in which she stood. No longer able to feel anything, she could only imagine what was crawling around her ankles, clinging to her skirts. But this time even terror had its limits, and finally she drifted into an almost trancelike state, retreating from hell by removing herself from her body, physically aware only of her fingers curled around the steel ring, holding her upright. When they lifted the trap door, she could not move, and they had to reach down and prise her cramped fingers loose before hauling her up into the light.

Her legs would not hold her, and she crumpled in the passage, uncaring. One of the men-at-arms picked her up without comment and she lay limply in his hold, her mind and spirit still somehow floating above her inert bodily shape.

It was full daylight, and she closed her eyes tightly against a brightness that yesterday she had found dim and gloomy. She heard Zoe's cries before they reached the chamber, and abruptly mind and body became one again. With the fusion came the resurgence of fear and the dread knowledge that she could not preserve her reason through another such period of incarceration. Following instinct, she gave no indication of her return to full awareness and stayed limp and unresponsive in her bearer's arms. When he carried her into the chamber, she remained inert.

Sister Therese was holding Zoe, rocking her back and forth in a futile effort to still the frantic screams, so piercing they seemed to go straight through one's head. No one else was in the room.

The trooper set Magdalen on her feet, and deliberately she crumpled to the ground again.

"Put her on the bed," the nun said. "She has to feed the child."

They picked her up and put her on the bed, where she lay unmoving. Sister Therese put the screaming Zoe into her lap and hastily pulled up the pillows behind her. "Sit up, now," the nun said with anxious impatience. "Your child is hungry."

With a supreme effort of will, Magdalen made no attempt to soothe Zoe, but lay as if she still

inhabited the trancelike world of her imprisonment, her eyes closed.

The troopers left the chamber, and the nun
stood looking down at the immobile woman
and the screeching baby. Then with an almost
imperceptible shrug, as if to say she had done all
she could, she turned and left the chamber.

Magdalen heard the heavy wooden bar fall
into place with a dull thud. She lay still for a further minute, then caught the child to her breast.
Zoe was not impressed with her mother's desperate kisses and nuzzled frantically. Magdalen
unfastened her bodice, the screams died on a
gulping sob, and a deep quiet entered the dim
chamber.

Magdalen found that her mind had a bell-like
clarity. As the blood returned to her feet, the
pain was excruciating. The muscles in her legs
cramped violently with the renewal of sensation,
but the pain served to concentrate her mind. If,
apart from feeding Zoe, she preserved the appearance of one physically and spiritually broken
by the oubliette, then surely nothing would be
gained by returning her there. The last two periods had been punitive as well as coercive, she
was in no doubt, but if her cousin saw her in this
broken state, he would surely feel adequately
avenged for the raking marks of her nails. And

for as long as she remained apparently physically incapable of anything but feeding the child, the matter of her compliance would have to be postponed.

She would not be able to convince them for long, but it would buy her some time, and at the moment, she could only think ahead an hour or two at a time. She was abruptly overtaken by an invincible weariness, like a great black blanket dropping over her. Her eyes closed while she still held the child at her breast.

Sister Therese, coming in an hour later, found the woman still asleep and the baby lying placidly at her side. She had brought a tray of food and bent to wake the sleeping woman, who she knew had not eaten since the previous midmorning.

Magdalen woke but turned her head from the food. She refused to speak, but staggered off the bed to wash and change Zoe, put the child in her cradle, and drag herself to the latrine behind the garderobe. She exaggerated the pain and effort of her movements, and finally tumbled back on the bed, closing her eyes. Uneasy, but uncertain what else she should do, the nun left her.

Alone again, Magdalen ate a little of the venison pasty on the tray and drank some of the wine. She was feeling much stronger, although she dared not let her mind return to the timeless terror of her imprisonment. She knew only that she could not endure more of it. Curiously, she did not entertain the obvious means of avoiding further coercion. She would not yield.

She slept fitfully throughout the day, closing her eyes tightly whenever she heard the door open as it did several times. The visitor did not come into the room, however, merely checked on its occupant and left again. She looked after Zoe but deliberately left herself unwashed and uncombed.

Charles d'Auriac came in at the end of the afternoon. He had planned to leave her alone all day, alone to recover her strength and to allow herself to feel that her ordeal was finished. The shock of being taken down again, to spend the hours of the night in the oubliette, would be so much the greater after the day's respite that he had every expectation of achieving her submission by first light on the morrow.

He was not prepared for what he found, however. She lay on the bed exactly as she had been brought up that morning, the filth of the dungeon on her clothes, her hair matted, her face streaked. Her eyes looked blankly at him, almost through him.

"Sweet Jesus! Why have you not cleaned yourself?"

She made no response, not even a flicker of an

eyelid. He crossed to the bed and took her chin between thumb and forefinger, staring down into her face. The blankness of her eyes did not alter. Had he miscalculated? Believed her stronger than she was? There came a point, he knew, when physical coercion ceased to be fruitful, a point when the victim withdrew from the pain into a private world of illusion and thus from the power of the interrogator. But it could not have happened so soon. He went to the door and bellowed for Sister Therese.

"How long has she been like this?"

"Since they brought her back this morning. She has fed the child, but little else."

"Has she spoken?"

"No, my lord."

He turned back to the bed. It was as if she did not know they were talking about her . . . as if she did not know they were in the room. "Get her cleaned up," he said. "I will return later."

Magdalen offered neither resistance nor assistance as the nun and a serving wench took off her filth-encrusted clothes. She let them wash her, comb out the matted tangles of her hair, dress her in a linen shift and a loose robe. She gave no indication of her relief at being thus rid of the reek and mire of the dungeon. They encouraged her into a chair beside the empty hearth, brought her the baby, offered her broth and wine. Passively, silently, she submitted.

It was dark when her cousin returned. She was still sitting in the chair, her hands clasped loosely in her lap, the candles unlit upon the table. It was as if she were unaware of the darkness.

He struck flint, and light flared from the candles. She did not look toward the light or acknowledge his presence in the slightest way.

"So, cousin," he said, approaching her, holding the candle high so that its light fell upon her face, as desirable in its pale stillness as ever it was in the glowing vibrancy of health and happiness. "I wonder how you will respond to my kiss tonight." He held her face with one hand and brought his lips to hers. She endured, still and cold as a marble effigy. Abruptly, he released her and went to the door.

"Take her down!"

Scalding terror filled her. She had failed. But she somehow remained immobile, her eyes fixed on a dip in the flagstones at her feet. Her neck ached unbearably with the strain.

He looked at her closely for some sign that his instruction to the two troopers had pierced her absorption. He could detect no change in posture or expression. As the two men moved toward her, he gestured to them to stop. If it was genuine, her present state of mind bordered on madness, and if he had her confined again so soon, she might well slip over the edge. She would be no good to them then, and he could not afford to risk all by being overzealous.

"Get out."

The men left, and he put the candle on the table again. "In the morning I will have your submission, cousin, and you will give your allegiance to Bertrand. If I do not have it, you will rot in the oubliette, and your child with you." She gave no indication that she had heard him, and with a wash of frustration he caught her under the arms and pulled her to her feet. "Do you hear me, cousin? You *and* the child."

She must not respond. She would not respond. Over and over in her head she said the words until the internal chant obscured all else. She fell back in the chair as he pushed her away from him, and she let herself fall and lie as limp as any doll.

The door banged on his departure and she began to shake, but she had won herself a night's respite.

GUY DE GERVAIS LOOKED up at the sky. It was heavy and overcast, the air sultry, as if a summer storm were brewing over the Pyrenees. But the lack of moon or starshine couldn't be better for their purpose.

"Do you think she is asleep?" Edmund's voice came softly through the darkness. "Do you think they have harmed her?"

Guy turned, making out the dark bulk of the other man. Like himself, Edmund wore chain-mail and carried his great sword and shield. Their suits of full plate armor would not be needed until the fighting began. First they would parley. "Do not think about Magdalen," he counseled, as he had counseled himself countless times during the weeks of their pursuit. "You cannot serve her by worrying over her."

"But she has such fear of her cousin."

"Fear will not kill her," Guy said shortly. "She has courage and nimble wits." But the thought of her alone and afraid at times tormented him beyond endurance.

"All is ready." Courtney Durand loomed out of the shadows. "The town watchtower has been taken, and there'll be none to sound the tocsin." There was no intensity in his voice or expression. He had no interest beyond amuse-ment and coin in the present enterprise. Any in-terest he might have had in the Lady Magdalen was surpassed by too many men, he realized, for it to be worth pursuing. "We will leave the fires and torches burning in the camp so all looks undisturbed, and we will be in position by first light."

Through the dark, shadowed, sleeping town, forty lancers moved almost soundlessly, horses' hooves muffled with sacking on the cobbles, only an occasional jingle of a bridle to betray them. Behind them came pikers and archers, troopers bearing great bundles of faggots and the long siege ladders. Those townsmen who heard them cowered behind their shuttered windows. In the absence of the tocsin, the only sensible course was to mind one's own business and be thankful that the armed men showed no interest in the town or its inhabitants.

The town streets lapped the fortress walls, and the men had moved from the shadows of the former and under the overhang of the latter without venturing into the open. The watchmen at the fortress towers looked outward to the distant horizon for threat. They saw the dark huddle of the brigand encampment, the usual nighttime flares glowing in the dark, just as they had done for the last several days, since the brigand chieftain had delivered his captive to the fortress. They did not look immediately beneath them because they had no reason to do so. If the town had been threatened, the tocsin would have sounded. So they did not see the stealthy, creeping menace moving into position, preparing to bridge the moat and assail the fortress walls with their bombards, obscuring fires, and siege ladders.

But as the first faint lightening appeared over the mountains, the air was rent with the insolence of a dozen bugles, like so many barnyard cockerels throwing their challenge to the day. The pennons of the knights banneret were raised at the moment that the standards of Bresse, Gervais, and Lancaster lifted to a gust of dawn wind from the mountains. The heralds blew their note again.

Within the fortress, there was utter confusion. Men ran to the battlements, staring down at the armed force massed at the walls. Bertrand de Beauregard was hauled from sleep by a white-faced squire—white-faced because of how his lord would react to what must have been someone's incompetence.

The knight commander of the garrison followed hard on the heels of the squire and, as Bertrand was strapped into his armor, told him whose standards flew in challenge at their gates.

"God's nails. You say the standard of Bresse flies?" Bertrand cursed his squire as he struggled with the steel greaves of his armor. "Fetch d'Auriac!"

Charles was already there, pale but resolute, as yet unarmored. "My lord."

"You guaranteed his death!" his uncle spat.

"I still guarantee it," Charles said steadily. "This time by my own hand."

Bertrand looked at him, then shook his head impatiently. "The man has more lives than a cat!" He strode past his nephew into the outer ward of the fortress, and up to the battlements. "Call for identification and for the purpose of this challenge." As if he didn't know it!

The herald blew his note, and they watched as a herald from the opposing side rode up to the lifted drawbridge. His voice rose clear in the dawn: "The Lord de Bresse is come for his wife, the Lady Magdalen. The Lord de Gervais is come, as representative of John, Duke of Lancaster, for Lancaster's daughter, the Lady Magdalen."

Bertrand took the jeweled cup of wine proffered by his page and drained the contents before replying. "Tell them we will have an answer for them in an hour."

The herald relayed the message, and Bertrand left the battlements. His sons and his nephew were gathered in the outer ward. "Come," he instructed curtly. "We must take counsel." They followed him to the bastion room, where the early sun showed fingers of dust on the scarred table. Pages scurried with jugs of wine but were curtly dismissed.

"Well?" Bertrand said. "I await an explanation."

All eyes turned to Charles d'Auriac. He was still a little pale but otherwise seemed unmoved. "It seems I was in error," he said slowly.

"The woman was right, you mean," Bertrand said. "If you had had the sense to do the job yourself . . . if your cousin had had the sense to do the job himself . . ." Here he glared at Gerard, who had been feeling a certain satisfaction that his cousin had also failed in his set task.

"This time I will," Charles said again.

"Of course, you want the woman for yourself," Marc said with a sly smile. "That is a powerful incentive, cousin."

"So is pride," Charles snapped back. "I do not fail."

"So what do you suggest?" Bertrand sounded suddenly genial, as if this squabbling pleased him. He poured wine. "We have an army laying siege at our gates over a woman and a baby."

"Durand is with them," Philippe remarked. "The mind of the mercenary is most curious."

"Hardly curious," Bertrand said. "He has a nose to sniff out coin and cares not who pays or for what."

"But can we withstand such a siege?" asked

Gerard. "It is the devil's own luck that we should all be gathered here together. There is none outside to bring reinforcements."

"They are well equipped for assault," Bertrand said. "And Durand has no difficulty in raising fresh troops whenever he needs them. We will be outnumbered soon enough, however heavy the losses we may inflict upon them."

"There is no need to withstand a siege." It was Charles who spoke. Absently, he poured himself wine and spoke directly to his uncle. "We will use the woman. It will be her first task for her family." He smiled. "She will bring her husband and her lover to their deaths."

"You have broken her?" Bertrand frowned. "You believe she will obey you in this so soon? You believe you can compel her to betray de Gervais and de Bresse?" He shook his head. "You are overly optimistic, my friend. It is a fault of yours."

But Charles continued to smile. "You forget the child. If the child's life is in danger, she will betray anyone." He stroked his chin. "I do not know why I did not think of it before."

"But we want the child, too," Marc said. "She will grow to be a de Beauregard more completely than the mother ever will be."

"True enough, which is why I didn't consider it before," Charles agreed. "But in this instance,

I believe the sacrifice will be worthwhile . . .
not that I think for one minute we shall be
obliged to make the sacrifice."

Bertrand nodded. "Continue."

"She will go out to them, and she must bring
them within the fortress to parley. How she does
so will be up to her, but she must be convinced
that the child dies if she fails . . . She will not
fail," he concluded with quiet conviction. "I
have seen her with the child."

"Then I suggest we present our kinswoman
with the alternatives without delay."

Magdalen had heard the bugles' challenge but
could see nothing of the outside from the high
slitted window. But the sound sent the blood
coursing through her veins, embodying hope although she did not know why. It was always
possible that if something beyond the walls was
occupying her family, they would leave her
alone for a while longer. She had not forgotten
her cousin's threat of the previous evening, and
the long hours of the night had failed to bring a
new plan to mind.

Sister Therese came in, and for once her face
showed some expression. "Come, you must
hurry and dress," she said. "You and the child
are to go to the battlements."

Magdalen made no response. Her performance of the previous day had worked well

enough then and it was still all she had at the
moment. She remained listless and silent, but offered no resistance to putting on the clothes
thrust at her. Defiance must be saved for great
matters. Taking up the wakeful Zoe, she followed Sister Therese from the chamber. The
thought of fresh air and sunshine encouraged a
spring to her step, and she had difficulty maintaining a dragging pace and lowered head as
they emerged from the bleak gloom of the donjon into the inner ward. She looked up to where
the standard of Beauregard fluttered with the
lilies of France from the topmost rampart of
the keep. Who was challenging that standard?

Her uncle and cousins were gathered on the
outer battlements. Archers ranged along the
ramparts, longbowmen with arrows already to
their bows, crossbowmen laboriously cranking
the unwieldy bolts. Men were bringing pails of
water to line the walls, ready to be poured upon
the fires that the besiegers would light to provide smoke cover for the scaling ladders.

Magdalen recognized all these signs of a
fortress preparing to withstand an assault. She
had ordered the same herself a few weeks ago.
But who would be attacking the de Beauregard
stronghold of Carcassonne? Again a tiny spark of
hope flickered crazily.

She climbed the steps, preserving a lethargic

passivity of face and step, and walked toward the group waiting on the battlement. Zoe was waving her arms around and gurgling with pleasure in the balmy morning, the swooping rooks, the fluttering flags.

At the edge of the ramparts, Magdalen looked down. Her legs almost gave way beneath her. She could see Guy, astride his massive war horse, his red-gold head bare, his standard snapping. Joyous love, overwhelming relief that he was alive, safe, that he had come for her, flowed sweetly in her veins. All appearance of passivity vanished. She wanted to call out to him; she wanted to shout her love to the bright blue skies. She saw Edmund just behind him, and her relief at his safety was no less piercing. That they were both here, had both come for her, could only mean that some agreement had been reached between them. She would not be responsible for the death of one or both. Their blood would not be in her hand. In that moment, she knew that in gratitude for God's mercy, she would put Guy de Gervais from her as all but a memory to lighten the soul's darkness, and she would embrace her husband with what love she had left to give.

"Yes, cousin. It would seem your champions are come." Charles spoke, dryly sardonic, shattering the intensity of her thoughts. "I see you have recovered your senses. That is fortunate because we have work for you to do."

All her joy seeped away from her with the certainty that she was about to face a further ordeal. Her mother's family was not going to yield her up without a fight.

"Stand up here and show yourself. Let them see what they have come for." Bertrand indicated a step in the parapet. "No, do not take the child up there. It is dangerous."

Somehow, she found she had relinquished Zoe to her cousin Philippe, whose hands took the child before she had time to think beyond her eagerness to see more clearly over the parapet. A hand went under her elbow, and she was standing on the step, exposed well above the rampart.

Guy saw her and, despite the distance between them, some spirit flew between them, joined them in a moment of intense communion. Her hair was unbound, held back from her face by a simple wooden fillet at her brow, and the wind sent the rich sable mass swirling around her shoulders as it flattened her gown against the lissom lines of her body.

"Magdalen!" Edmund, less restrained than Guy, couldn't resist calling to her, but the wind snatched at his voice. "Is she unharmed?" he said in desperate anxiety to his companion.

"I believe so," Guy returned quietly. In that moment of communion he had felt that she was whole, but he had also felt something else, and he could not control his unease as she stood so exposed upon the parapet. He had felt her fear.

"You may stand down now." Bertrand spoke behind her, and she stepped backward to the flat broad solidity of the battlement. She turned to take Zoe, but Philippe held the child away from her.

"Give her to me," she said, trying to still the panic rushing dizzily to her head.

"No. You have a task to complete first," Bertrand said. "When it is done to our satisfaction, the child will be returned to you."

"What do you mean?" She now knew terror greater than that of the oubliette and a moan escaped her, her hands reached pathetically for her child.

"Charles will explain."

She turned to d'Auriac, who was smiling his thin smile. "You will go to your husband and your lover, and you will invite them into the fortress to parley. When they pass through the gate, the child will be returned to you. If you fail. . . ." He reached over and touched the baby's cheek with a negligent forefinger. "If you fail, she will die . . . A pike thrust, and you may fish her body out of the moat."

"No! You could not—" But she knew they could. Her hand plucked at her throat. "Please . . ."

"Bring them within the fortress," Charles said.

"And you will kill them?"

"Them or the child. The choice is yours."

This was the abyss. She had been drawing ever closer to it, but each time she had thought she had reached it, she had been wrong. Now, she was there.

"How?" She could barely form the word. Her throat was as dry as leather, and there seemed to be no breath in her lungs.

Charles shrugged. "My dear cousin, that is for you to decide. You will know what arguments will serve best. You know those men, after all." He was softly insulting. "Let us go down."

They all left the battlement. In the court below, Sister Therese still stood. She accepted the child without surprise. "Take her away and keep her with you at all times," Bertrand said. "Her mother has work to do."

Magdalen watched, enwrapped in blackest despair, as the nun carried the child back to the donjon. If she could save them all with her own death, she knew at that minute that she would do so. But she had not been given that choice. She must entice Edmund and Guy to their deaths.

She must go to them with loving eyes and open arms, words of promise and appeal on her lips. She must call to the love they both bore her, and they would do what she asked. She would bring them to their deaths with the vow of love, just as her mother had condemned so many enemies of the de Beauregards. She was her mother's daughter; she had her mother's power.

Without a word, she began to walk toward the outer ward and the arched gate of the fortress.

"You have one hour, cousin," Charles called softly, and she felt his words on her back like a knife in the night.

They let her out through the postern gate and lowered the drawbridge. She walked slowly across it, aware of the eyes of archers and pikers on the battlements, aware of the eyes of her mother's family, watching her every step. Guy and Edmund had dismounted and stood at the edge of the drawbridge as she came forward. They made no attempt to step upon it, governed as they were by the rules of chivalry ensuring that during parley no advantage must be taken of an enemy's dropped defenses.

She stepped off the drawbridge onto the cool green grass of the bank along the moat. The two men stood very still. Oh, how she needed Guy's arms around her at this moment! How she yearned for his body against hers, enfolding her with his love and his passion and his strength. And oh, how she felt Edmund's burning need for her to turn to him, to take those things from him.

So she went to neither of them.

She held out her hands in a gesture of mute supplication, her face deathly white under the sun, her eyes haunted with her terror.

"What is it?" Guy said softly. "What have they done to you?"

"I am to bring you both within the castle, or they will murder our child," she said, knowing now that she could never have told him anything but the truth.

He looked up toward the watchers lining the battlements, then he turned away. "Come with me." The instruction was curt, masking the depths of fury threatening to chase all reason from his brain. "You too, Edmund."

They followed him out of the sunshine, into the first shadowed street of the town. There he stopped and turned to them. His eyes ran over them, assessing, and he knew Edmund could do nothing for Magdalen at the moment. It wasn't a lover she needed with a lover's needs to obscure her own. So he opened his arms to her. "Come here, pippin."

She fell against him with an incoherent sob and he stroked her hair, gently soothing, as if she were again the little girl he had comforted and reassured. And she gave way to the terror, dropping her defenses for the first time since they had parted in the chapel at Bresse and he had ridden away from her.

Edmund, from his own horror at what she had told them, watched without jealousy. He knew he could not give her what she was receiving from the other man, and the knowledge brought him sorrow but now no sense of betrayal.

"Enough," Guy said finally, when her dreadful, wracking grief had yielded to gulping sobs. "Plantagenets do not give in or give up. Remember who you are, Magdalen of Lancaster."

She raised her tear-streaked face from his chest. The faintest indentation of his mailshirt beneath the tunic showed on her cheek, so tightly had she been pressed against him. "I am the daughter of a whore, sent to do a whore's work."

Edmund exclaimed and Guy's face darkened, but he said no words of denial. There were none. "How long have they given you to do this work?"

She was not hurt by the lack of denial. She had simply stated the truth, and the pain was her own. "One hour," she said. Her tears had dried, and her body seemed to be emptied of all emotion, even fear. Only a cool, dark void remained within her.

"It's not long enough," Guy said, turning to Courtney Durand, who had been standing in the shadows, drawing his own conclusions from the scene. "What do you think, Durand?"

The brigand chieftain said nothing for a minute, wondering why, now they'd got the woman, they didn't simply leave the place. Children were expendable, and that one was so young anything could happen to it in the next few years. But he hadn't been paid to advance what he sensed would be an unpopular viewpoint, so he said finally, "The lady must parley for more time."

"I do not know if I can," she said.

"You must."

"Magdalen?" Edmund spoke her name hesitantly.

She remembered that moment on the battlement when she had sworn to give her husband all she had to give, and she realized that in her desperate need for Guy's strength she had not yet acknowledged Edmund. She went quickly toward him, her hands outstretched. "Forgive me."

He gripped her hands, remembering painfully

the violence of their last time together. "Forgive me for what I did to you," he said in a low voice. "I have regretted it every minute—"

She shook her head in vigorous denial. "I have not thought of it . . . will never think of it."

He longed to take her in his arms, but he could not, not here, so he just held her hands and devoured her face with his eyes. "I have been so afraid for you."

"Edmund . . . Magdalen." Guy's voice called them to him softly. He and Durand had been talking to Olivier, who in customary fashion had appeared silently and usefully. "Magdalen, you must return and negotiate a further two hours before we will enter the fortress."

"They will kill—"

"Be quiet and listen."

Abashed, she fell silent, aware of the strangest resurgence of strength and optimism under the brusque, commanding tone.

"Olivier knows where the underground corridor is located," Guy said. All well-constructed castles had them, narrow passages running from the dungeons of the donjon, beneath the walls and the moat to the outside. Only thus could supplies be brought in during a siege and couriers escape unseen. Such corridors could not provide egress for large numbers; they were narrow, low-roofed dirt tunnels, and their location was in general known only to the castle commander. But on one of his spying visits to Carcassonne, Olivier had contrived to discover the whereabouts of this one.

"Comes up in the saddler's in the town," Olivier said, picking his teeth. "Starts below the armory in the garrison court."

"We are going to send a small force through the corridor," Guy said. "They must have time to get in place within the walls before Edmund and I enter. You will tell the de Beauregards that Edmund and I are prepared to discuss a ransom for you and the child and will come in peace to parley. We will bring our squires and pages and two knights banneret apiece as escort, and we will come in two hours."

"And if they will not accept that?"

"You must ensure that they do."

Magdalen absorbed the flat statement.

"Could we not send a herald with the message?" Edmund said tentatively. "Magdalen could stay safely here—"

"They will kill Zoe," Magdalen interrupted, her voice shaking. "I thought you understood that. If I do not return within the hour, they will kill her. And if you do not enter the fortress, they will kill her."

"I would not ask it of you," Guy said gently, "but I can think of no alternative. You must trust that we will come for you both."

"What else must I do?"

"If it is possible, you must get yourself and the child into the outer ward. We will raise the portcullis from within as soon as we are able, to admit reinforcements. When it is raised, you must leave immediately. You are not to concern yourself about anything that is happening within the courts. You are simply to save yourself and Zoe."

"I will tell them that you have made it a condition of parley that you see both the child and myself on the parapet, unharmed, in an hour," she said, a slight tremor still in her voice but her mind now clear and resolute. "That way, they must give Zoe back to me, and I will ensure they do not take her from me again."

Guy nodded. "Return now, pippin. You must be strong for just a little longer."

She paused, shaking her head infinitesimally. Her voice very low, she said, "No, Guy, you are mistaken. I must be strong for a lifetime."

He knew what she meant, the final, absolute relinquishment of love. "And I also," he said as quietly. "Go now."

They escorted her back to the drawbridge.

She crossed without a backward glance and slipped through the postern gate. The drawbridge was pulled up behind her. Her uncle and cousins awaited her in the *place d'armes*.

"Well?" Bertrand demanded.

"I will tell you in a minute." Magdalen put up her chin. "I have not broken my fast this day, my lord, and I am faint for lack of food."

"By the Holy Rood, you are your mother's daughter," Bertrand said into the stunned silence. He gave a sharp crack of laughter. "Many times I have seen Isolde put up her chin in just that manner."

"I am also a Plantagenet," Magdalen said, thinking of all the minutes she was using up in this exchange. But she must not go too far. "May I eat?" She put the request in a conciliatory tone.

"They will come?" It was Charles who spoke the harsh question, and she turned to look at him, reading to her surprise a hint of anxiety in his voice, as if there was something personal riding on the success of this betrayal. She hid her satisfaction and dropped her eyes. Her voice was low, with a note of defeated submission.

"They will come. But there are conditions."

"Come, there is no reason to discuss this in the open court." Bertrand swung on his heel and strode to the donjon. "Bring meat and drink to the bastion room," he instructed a page trotting at his heels.

Magdalen tried to eat as if she had not had a decent meal in weeks, thinking all the time of the men crawling beneath the earth to shoot up where they were least expected, like the unruly suckers of a giant oak. But she could not procrastinate for long and finally told them of the conditions, making the telling long-winded and disjointed, as if the evidence of her success in this evil had to be dragged from her.

"You told them we wished to discuss ransom?" Bertrand cut a thick slice from the sirloin on the table. "A good enough invention, I daresay."

"But they will not come if they do not see me and the child on the parapet first," she said, trying to keep her desperate anxiety from her voice. She had to have Zoe again in her arms; without the child none of this was worth anything.

"What has the child to do with it?" Charles demanded.

Bertrand waved him down as he chewed solidly for a few minutes, and Magdalen waited, her eyes on the table lest they read her dreadful apprehension. "I see no reason why not," her uncle pronounced finally. "A reasonable man would see that what he wished to ransom was ransomable. It simply indicates that he comes in good faith. Let her have the bratling. We can take it from her any time we choose, if it's necessary to punish her failure or again compel her obedience."

Cold dread at this calm statement was followed immediately by sweet relief. The two emotions turned her joints to butter, her gut to water, and she had to hold unobtrusively to the edge of the table until the weakness left her legs and belly.

"Why would they wait two hours?" Marc asked. "They are positioned outside the gates. They could ride in without such delay."

"I think they wished the priests to celebrate a mass," Magdalen improvised. "Lord de Gervais does little without prayer beforehand."

Bertrand grunted. It was common enough. "Very well. You and the child will show yourselves upon the ramparts."

"And when they ride in," Charles said softly, "you will be in the *place d'armes* to welcome them, cousin. So that you may see the welcome we accord them."

She shuddered. They would force her to watch as the two men she had betrayed were cut to pieces under the flag of parley. They all saw her shudder, and the horror in her eyes was genuine enough to encourage the belief that she did not doubt such an outcome.

DURAND, WITH THIRTY men, followed the agile, speedy Olivier through the earth corridor. They carried no light. The fire of a torch would have been impossible to carry, bent double as they were, and would have reduced what little air they had. They were armed only with knives and wore only leather gambesons as protection against whatever weapons they might face when the fighting began. But there was no choice for a man who must make his approach on his hands and knees.

Outside the walls, Durand's brigands in flat-brimmed siege hats, hide shields strapped to their backs as protection against missiles and arrows from the ramparts above, milled around in apparent idleness, yet they were prepared to run to the walls and light their faggot fires once the call to arms was blown from within. The men on the ramparts watched impassively. In the present state of parley, neither side would make overtly aggressive moves, but each was ready for the moment when, or if, they were called for.

Guy and Edmund sat their war horses, waiting to ride to the drawbridge. They were now in full ceremonial armor, lances fixed in the sockets to the right of their breastplates, visors up for the moment. Their escort, also armed, squires carrying the standards, gathered around, horses shifting on the moat's narrow bank, scenting the possibility of battle. They all knew the trap into which they were about to ride. Guy watched the sun, waiting for the second hour to be up. The great ball of midmorning heat lifted above the far rampart. He signaled, and the herald raised his trumpet and blew the note of parley.

They dropped their visors and rode forward as the portcullis was lifted, the drawbridge lowered. Within the *place d'armes,* Charles d'Auriac let his hand rest on his great sword. His uncle and cousins, also fully armed and mounted, did the same. A troop of pikers circled the court. Magdalen, holding the baby, began to step by inches into the sheltering darkness beneath the walls. So intently were they all watching and waiting, the small steps passed unnoticed.

A deep hush enveloped the court, as deep as the shadows cast by the fortress walls. Beyond the walls, sun shone and ordinary things were happening. Within, there was only the expectant hush before treachery. The clanging drop of the portcullis behind the entering men signaled the end both of silence and of waiting. Charles d'Auriac drew his sword with a great cry of challenge, but Guy de Gervais had his lance poised in the same moment and rode at him with his own war cry, savage and exultant, bursting from his lips. The lance hit true, toppling d'Auriac from his horse. His squires were hauling him to his feet as confusion erupted. Thirty men leaped from the shadows of the garrison court, knives in hand, their challenging cries mingling now with the clash of steel as the armed men in the center of the court engaged in combat. Guy was off his horse now, intending to pursue d'Auriac with sword and on foot, but before he could do so, Philippe was riding down upon him.

Magdalen screamed and Charles turned. He had pushed up his visor, and there was murder in his eyes as he saw her with the baby, clinging to the shadows. He came toward her, a hulking armored figure, sword gripped in his two hands, raised to cleave her in two.

"Treacherous whore!" The accusation rang out above the battle noise, a mad, wild fury behind it. For precious seconds Magdalen was paralyzed by the sight of that great cleaving blade. Zoe was screaming against her ear. Then she turned and ran. Tripping over the cobbles, stumbling against the wall, clutching the child, she ran frantically as the massive figure lumbered behind her. She ran for the battlement steps, not thinking beyond the need to escape the clamorous murky confines of the court, up into air and space and sunlight.

She could hear him behind her, could see the huge shadow of the raised sword on the steps above her. Her breath came in gasping sobs, and the child in her arms continued her dreadful, terrified screaming. She stumbled on the top step, lost her footing for one petrifying moment, could almost hear his breath behind her, recovered, staggering upright, leaping away from the steps as he rose, massive in his steel plating behind her. There was smoke everywhere. The men at the foot of the walls outside had lit their fires at the first sound of steel. The archers were firing down upon them, hurling rocks and pails of water to put out the fires. Black smoke rose, choking, obscuring. Magdalen found herself backed against a low break in the ramparts. She could feel the wall against her thighs, and the sense of the drop behind her left her back icily exposed as she stared at death in the shape of her cousin bearing down upon her, his gray eyes as cold and murderous as the steel upraised in his two hands. He ran at her, and she ducked sideways. The sword came down in an almighty sweep, meeting only air. Unbalanced, he tottered at the edge of the parapet, fighting the great cumbersome weight of his armor. Then, as she watched, numbed, he toppled very, very slowly over the edge, his sword pulling him down it seemed, down into the choking smoke, his cry lost in the deafening clamor around her.

"Holy mother, sweet Jesus." She was murmuring the incantations over and over, standing immobile, holding the screaming child, then she was running back to the steps, her only thought to get down to the court, to discover Guy and Edmund alive in all that death-dealing clamor. At first, she could make out nothing, identify no one. They were all on foot now, the huge war horses pulled aside by squires, where they blew through their great nostrils and pawed the earth, tossing their caparisoned heads.

There was fierce fighting at the gatehouse as Durand's men fought for control of the portcullis. She knew she should somehow make her way around the fighting to the gates. Possibly the postern gate would be untended, and she and Zoe could slip out of this murderous havoc. But she did not do it. She stood, straining her eyes, desperately seeking the blue and silver standard of Gervais.

She saw him finally, hand to hand now with Bertrand, the dreadful clash of sword on sword resounding, so heavy it seemed impossible they could remain upright whether giving or receiving the blows. She felt sick and cursed her weakness, fighting the wash of nausea, standing rooted in dreadful apprehension as the two men, both massive-framed, both skilled and experienced at this horrendous art of murderous combat, battered each other with deadly ferocity. There was a moment when Guy seemed to stagger, unbalanced. Bertrand raised his mace with a cry of exultant savagery. The wickedly spiked ball came hurtling down. Magdalen could hear her own voice screaming incoherent incantations with a lunatic fervency, resounding in her ears, filling her head. Then miraculously Guy seemed to recover, to sidestep the brutal death embodied in the mace, and it was Bertrand who went down to the cobbles, his head at an odd angle, crimson blood pumping from his neck. Guy ignored his fallen enemy and simply turned back to the fray, and Magdalen realized on the periphery of her intelligence that his apparent stumble had been a feint, intended to catch Bertrand off guard, his shield lowered.

The urge to vomit threatened to overwhelm her in the weakness of relief, and only the need to hold tight to the still screaming Zoe kept her on her feet. She was shaking, her hair damp with the sweat of fear, when a triumphant shout came from the gates as the portcullis was raised and into the *place d'armes* poured the rest of Durand's men. Her heart lifted with a sudden surge of exaltation as powerful as the terror that had gone before, matching the crowing of the invading herald's trumpet. Arrows flew, and the archers on the ramparts turned from the besiegers outside to the intruders in the *place d'armes,* pouring down a hailstorm of feathered death . . .

Indiscriminate feathered death . . . One of those arrows found its way between the links of Edmund de Bresse's gorget as he raised his head. Magdalen watched, disbelieving in this moment of triumph, as the black and gold jupon crumpled to the ground. Then she was running through the death and the arrows and the swords and the sweating, bleeding, screaming men to where he lay. She fell on her knees beside him, still holding the child. His page and squires were there, and somehow they managed to pull him to the side of the court, out of the melee.

"We have to get the arrow out, my lady," the squire said, pushing up the wounded man's visor. "Raymond must pull it while I hold his shoulders."

Edmund's eyes flickered, rolled up in his head, but he was still breathing. Magdalen began feverishly to unbuckle his armor, but she was still holding Zoe, and it was almost impossible to perform such a task with one hand. The squire had grasped his shoulders now, and Raymond, twelve years old and come to manhood that day in the blood-drenched courts of Carcassonne, seized the feathered arrow and pulled. It came out with a spurt of blood, and Edmund's breath became a choked scream.

"Ah, no . . . not Edmund!" Guy was there beside them, his voice a low moan of sorrow. "Quickly, we have to unbuckle him, then I can carry him out of here." With the help of the other two, he went swiftly to work, and Magdalen knelt at Edmund's head, her finger over the hole in his throat as if she could close the wound. But the blood pulsed against her finger, welled over the dike.

"He still lives," she said, over and over, as if the constant repetition would ensure the continued state.

Around them the fighting continued, but Durand's men were in the ascendancy, and the five of them seemed to occupy a space that had nothing to do with what was going on around them. At last they had Edmund out of the iron cocoon, and Guy was able to lift him. Magdalen had to take her finger from the wound, and she watched in despair as his lifeblood spurted forth.

Guy carried him out of the fortress and down through the silent, deserted streets of the town. The townspeople had fled their homes at the first fighting and were streaming across the plain, well aware of the carnage and plunder that would ensue if the brigands won the day.

In the encampment only the apothecaries, the priests, and the lads caring for the pack animals remained. Guy laid his burden gently upon the ground, and Magdalen set the baby down and again put her finger over the wound. The page ran for the apothecary, but Guy called swiftly, "Bring a priest, first, Raymond."

"He still lives," Magdalen said again.

Edmund's eyes opened, and for a minute there was recognition in them. He tried to speak, but his voice was so faint she had to bend her ear to his mouth.

"I loved you," he said.

"I know." She clutched his hand. "And I loved you as I was able. Forgive me that it was not enough."

Edmund's eyes frantically sought Guy, who bent his head to catch the thread of breath that formed the words. "It is right . . . right . . ." Magdalen wiped a trickle of blood from his mouth and tried to hush him, but he continued with a desperate effort. "Right that you . . . you have each other now." Then his head fell back as the final effort took the last breath of his strength.

The priest was there, murmuring the words

of absolution over the dying man. Magdalen held his hand as her tears poured heedlessly, uselessly. Then she felt the moment when Edmund's spirit left him. She looked up at Guy and saw his own eyes filled with tears. Gently, she laid Edmund's hands upon his breast and bent to kiss his cold face.

"Requiescat in pace." There was such finality in the priest's benediction.

She picked up Zoe, who had fallen asleep on the grass, still sobbing in her confused fear, and she walked away, leaving Guy to his own vigil.

Eighteen

THEY BURIED EDMUND in a grove of poplars. The clash of steel, screams of pain, cries of challenge or triumph continued to come from the fortress, and the air was blackened with smoke. Against the violent backdrop of his death, they wrapped Edmund in his standard and buried him with decency and honor and reverence, and when a mass had been said for his soul, there was no more the living could do for him.

In midafternoon, the standard of Beauregard came down from the donjon of Carcassonne and the men of Bresse and Gervais began streaming back to the brigand camp, leaving the mercenaries behind within the town and castle, at their reward of plunder and looting. There must be no implication that a vassal of the Duke of Lancaster had wantonly attacked a castle held in stewardship for the king of France during a truce between their two countries. The fortress of Carcassonne had been attacked by Durand's brigand army in search of plunder and ransom. A daring attack, certainly, but no one would consider it extraordinary. Men like Durand scorned the need for righteous cause to underpin aggression, as if they were immune from the threat of hell's torments, clearly choosing immediate gratification over the body's eternal peace; and there was none to tell the tale of an abducted woman and child and a rescue that had brought full circle a bloody train of events begun at the woman's birth.

So the men of Bresse and Gervais, their clandestine and uneasy partnership with Durand's brigands now over, gathered quietly around the dragon of Gervais and moved out on the north road as the sun dipped over the mountains.

By nightfall, they had put ten miles between themselves and Durand's encampment. They made camp on the bank of a tributary of the Garonne, outside a small village. The villagers cowered fearfully as the armed troop of weary men rode through, faces blackened with the smoke of siege fires, blood spattering their tunics, their wounded on litters with the pack animals. But they left the village unmolested and lit their fires on land that was not good pasture and did not bear as yet unharvested crops.

Magdalen rode beside Guy, but neither of them had spoken beyond the merest commonplace. Edmund's death lay heavy between them, unabsorbed, its significance unprobed. Her possessions had been retrieved from the fortress so she was able to care for Zoe when they made camp. The child seemed to have forgotten the terrors of the day, secure now in her mother's arms and lulled by the horse's gait as she had been during the long weeks of the journey from Bresse to Carcassonne.

Magdalen's small tent had been pitched beside the much larger one flying the dragon of Gervais, and when she had fed and washed the baby, she carried her out into the soft, torch-lit dusk to where Guy sat at a small table, a wine cup in his hands, staring into some inner world. He was quite alone, his attendants at a discreet distance, and he did not appear to notice her immediately. She found she needed an invitation to sit beside him, so she hovered uncertainly at his elbow until Zoe gave a sudden squeal of delight as a firefly glowed abruptly in front of her face.

He looked up and smiled tiredly at the child. "Give her to me." He took Zoe and sat her on his knee. She chuckled, and her fat fingers grabbed at the embossed dragon on his tunic. "How you've grown, little pigeon," he said, bending to kiss her, and she seized his hair, still chuckling.

Magdalen sat down on a low stool. "May I drink?"

He pushed his wine cup toward her and began to tickle the child's stomach. She flung herself back against his supporting hand, laughing in unrestrained glee. Magdalen drank some wine and said, "What do we do now?"

"Return to Bresse," he told her. "I must ensure that the fief remains secured for Lancaster after Durand's attack. The garrison will have returned eventually, but I must see for myself. An empty nest makes fat pickings for predators."

Magdalen made no immediate response. She had not been asking quite that question.

"Olivier has gone to England carrying the news of this day's work to Lancaster," Guy continued, absently stroking the baby's cheek. "Riding alone, he can make perhaps a hundred miles a day. Allowing for inevitable delays and a few days' wait in Calais for a ship, if the wind is fair, he should reach Southampton within three weeks."

"Yes," said Magdalen. She was at a loss, not knowing how to penetrate Guy's mood, which, while not hostile, was certainly withdrawn from her.

Theo came quietly across the grass toward them. "Will you sup, my lord? All is prepared."

"I will sup apart," Guy said. "You may serve me here."

Magdalen bit her lip, suddenly swamped with a desolate uncertainty at the conspicuous lack of invitation to share his meal.

"I'll put Zoe to bed so that you may eat in

peace," she said, her voice sounding small. "Would you bring my supper to my tent, Theo?"

Guy made no demur, seemed not to notice what she had said. He simply relinquished the child and resumed his contemplative silence as she left him.

Magdalen tossed on her thin pallet throughout the hot summer night. She could not understand why they could not draw together in their shared sorrow over Edmund's death. He had been a friend to both of them, and they could surely comfort each other. At dawn, she got up and went outside. Guy was still sitting at the table, and she could not tell whether he had been there all night or, like herself, had awakened early after a disturbed night.

"Good morrow, my lord." The dew-wet grass soaked her slippers and dampened her ankles as she went toward him.

He looked up, frowning slightly. "You are awake betimes, Magdalen."

"As are you, sir." She stood at the table, her knuckles resting lightly on the edge. "We are both unhappy. Can we not help each other?" Her voice was very soft.

The frown in his blue eyes deepened. "How? Edmund died because of us. How can we assuage each other's guilt in that?"

She touched the back of her hand to her lips, hearing his anguished misery, struggling to contain the hurt of his words and to find the right ones of her own. "There is sorrow, deep and abiding sorrow. But must we bear the guilt for his death?"

The bleakness in his eyes was suddenly replaced with a rapier thrust of anger, and she recoiled instinctively.

"If you had not broken your oath, Magdalen, Edmund would still live."

She shook her head in bewilderment and pain. "No . . . I did not break my oath. I said nothing—"

"He discovered the truth from you."

"But . . . but it was my cousin who told him . . . who led him to believe—"

"And you did not deny it, did you?" There was now just harsh anger in his voice. His hands lay flat upon the table, and his bright blue gaze went through and through her. She shook her head numbly. "Had you denied it, he would have believed you because he bore you such love he would have accepted your word in anything. He *wanted* your denial, and you would not give it to him. None of this would have happened if you had stood fast to your oath."

"You are saying that it is I who am responsible for Edmund's death." Her voice was a bare whisper as she read that dreadful revulsion in his eyes, and her own defiled blood moved sluggishly in her veins.

Guy did not reply.

"It is because I am my mother's daughter," she went on in a faint, distant voice. "Edmund loved me, and that love led to his death. All those men who died up there yesterday died because of the love Edmund bore me . . . That is what you are saying."

Again there was no reply. "I did not mean him to die," she said in the same threadlike whisper. "I cannot help the taint of my blood that makes these things happen." She brushed her hair from her face as the sun came up. "I may be born of a whore, in a moment accursed, but I would prefer my own death than to cause that of others in the manner of my mother, even if I cannot help it."

She walked away from him as he still sat, unmoving and silent. She walked down to the river. The sun began to dry the grass beneath her feet, fell warm on the back of her neck, and she sought the cool green gloom of a copse of elder and poplar, as if its shadowy depths suited her soul better than the heedless sun rising in promise on another day.

Guy had barely heard her words. They had fallen soft and deadly as poisoned rain, and only

in the silence of her departure did their residue
sound a note of foreboding. He had spoken out
of anger and grief at such a cruelly abrupt ending to a young man's life, but such endings were
a part of life. He had witnessed many such and
grieved for many young men; ordinarily he
would have absorbed the fact, and the anger and
grief would have settled, finally to be forgotten.
But guilt and remorse added an extra dimension
to this death. He had made peace with Edmund,
had received his forgiveness, yet his death re-
vived the wretchedness of betrayal. When
Magdalen had denied the guilt—hers, his,
theirs—he had lashed out in a furious need to
implicate her in his own thicket of remorse. He
had intended to wound her as he was wounded,
and it was only as he heard her words again that
he realized she still bled from her own wounds,
those inflicted by the de Beauregards during the
long days of her ordeal at Carcassonne. He had
laid his own stripes across those she already bore
at a moment when she had needed his love and
his comfort, as she had offered him her own.

Whatever the future might hold for either of
them, their love was still as vital a force as it had
ever been. He rose abruptly to his feet.
Magdalen's distress had been of no ordinary
quality, and he was suddenly afraid of what had
been said and done between them. There was

nothing further he could do for Edmund, but the living had need of him as he had need of her.

Her footprints were fading in the grass as the sun dried the dew, but he followed them to the copse. It was quiet, the night's cool still lingering. A woodpecker rat-tatted. Something rustled in a bramble bush. He called her and heard only the empty echo of his voice imprinted in the air. Fear twisted around his heart. He saw those gray eyes, candid as always, filled with a self-disgust that he had done nothing to eradicate. He heard her voice, so soft yet pulsing with revulsion. Twice, she had called herself the daughter of a whore, and on neither occasion had he denied it. He hadn't denied it because it was true. But Magdalen had not been talking of the fact; she had been talking of the spirit that lay behind the fact. That, he could and should have denied immediately. In his own absorption, in what he now recognized as the need to punish her for his own pain and guilt, he had left her unrelieved in the morass of self-contempt and what she believed had been his contempt.

"Magdalen!" He called her again, his voice rising with anxiety, but still there was no response.

Sunlight glimmered at the end of the bramble-strewn path he trod, and the trees gave way to a

broad meadow. He stepped into the light. The
river ran between wide banks, dark brown water over flat stones, the silver glint of trout, the
flat sharp-fanged head of an eel in the mud, a
dragonfly swooping low, the feathered silver of
a weeping willow drooping over the gently
moving water. A peaceful scene, one untouch-
able by malevolence, by vengeance, by a poisoned love of the past.

A little bridge of logs lay across the river a few
hundred feet away. A fragile handrail of sagging
rope had been slung alongside. Magdalen stood
on the logs, facing the water, her hands gripping
the rope. Her head was bent, and her hair fell
richly brown across her breast.

He came swiftly toward her, but she didn't
look up, not even when he reached the bridge
and placed one foot on the logs. They shifted
with his weight, then settled.

"You must not wander so far from the camp,"
he said, stepping carefully beside her.

"They are evil," she said, still not looking up.
"And I belong to them . . . I am of them. It is
not possible to love one of them, only, it seems,
to be drawn to them . . . to be drawn into their
evil. I have drawn you. I drew Edmund . . . as
my mother drew my father. Mad Jennet said
there was love and blood in my hand. I did not
then understand how much."

"I love you," he affirmed quietly, looking along the river, allowing the peace of the scene to inform his words, to heal his soul. "You are the daughter of Isolde de Beauregard and John of Gaunt. And I love you. You have borne me a child. And I love you."

"My mother was a whore."

"But you are not."

"Am I not?" She turned vigorously, and the logs trembled beneath her. "I betrayed my husband doubly and led him to his death. You could as easily have died at Carcassonne. How many men died there because of who I am and what I have done?"

"You are not responsible for your birth or for the evil of your mother's family, the evil that led to Edmund's death. I spoke heedlessly out of my own pain, and you must take nothing I said into yourself, except this: I love you."

"You cannot. I bewitched you. How often have you said so? But you do not love *me*."

"Once upon a time," Guy said thoughtfully, "there was a little girl who became very tiresome when she was told something she didn't want to believe . . . so tiresome, in fact, that those who loved her lost all patience." He caught her chin, forcing her to look at him. "The years don't seem to have eradicated that tendency. You grow tiresome again, Magdalen of Lancaster." He was smiling at her, his finger lightly running over her mouth. "I love *you*. And it does not matter whose daughter you are."

She looked into his eyes and read their truth. She saw the grief still there, the haunting remorse that would take a long time to fade, but she saw the truth of his love, a bright strong flame through the shadows, a flame that could only purify the past. And she saw that he would now allow it to do so. Secure in that love, she could lay down her own defiling heritage, trust once again in the simple fact of her own love, the love she bore the man and their child, a love that could only be a driving force for good. "Hold me," she said, as she had so often done.

"When there is solid ground beneath my feet," he replied. "I have no wish to swim."

A tremulous laugh hovered on her lips, then she turned and leaped lightly along the logs to the far bank. Guy followed her as speedily, but he had barely touched ground before she was in his arms and he was engulfed with his own need. It had been so long since he had last held her this way, so long since he had felt the sinuous, lissom curves beneath his hands, smelled the warm, womanly fragrance of her hair and skin. She reached against him, her hands palming his scalp, her body pressed urgently to his, and a hot, hungry passion swept through them in an all-consuming tide. Her tongue was on his, his on hers, her teeth nipping his bottom lip, his hands pushing aside her skirts, probing, delving, opening in the warm, humid furrows of her body, and she moaned against him, desperate for his skin upon hers.

They came together still clothed, hands scrabbling to push aside confining material, their bodies twisting to fit into each other with the familiarity of much shared intimacy and the piquancy of long deprivation, so that it felt familiar yet at the same time new and fresh.

She felt she must hold him within herself forever, the throbbing, pulsing presence inside her that was intrinsic to her self. She felt she could forever bear the weight of his body upon hers, pressing her into the earth so that she was one with the earth and one with his body, the goodness from each flowing inside her, through her.

He felt he was encompassing her with his body as she was consuming him with hers. They were one under the sun and upon the earth. They were one in life and in death, and their blood mingled hot with the juices of love in a transcendent, healing tide of joyous affirmation.

Epilogue

JOHN OF GAUNT'S long fingers pinched the wax falling from the candle on the table in the womb-like privy chamber at the Savoy. The ruby on his ring glowed deeply crimson as his finger moved into shadow, sparking purple-red fire when it caught the candlelight. He rolled the wax ball between finger and thumb, enjoying its malleability, its warm softness.

The messenger, dust-streaked, exhaustion etched on his swarthy face, dimming the natural brightness of his black eyes, stood against the door, head bowed, shoulders drooping.

Lancaster tapped the parchment lying open on the table before him. The paper crackled in the overheated silence of the room. "Seek your rest, man," he said abruptly. "You must have ridden day and night to arrive here so speedily."

"True enough, my lord duke," Olivier said. "But my lord instructed me to bring you the news with all speed."

"You are a faithful and obedient servant," the duke said. "But go to your rest now."

"When may I take an answer to my lord?" Despite his bone-deep fatigue and the man to whom he spoke, Olivier's voice still had a certain obduracy.

John of Gaunt frowned. "I see no call for an answer. Your master has simply informed me of certain facts, to whit: the death of Edmund de Bresse, the fall of the de Beauregards at Carcassonne, and the vulnerability of the fiefdom of Bresse. Do you see the necessity for an answer therein, Master Courier?"

Olivier raised his head. "I believe my master expects an answer, my lord duke."

A sharp crack of laughter escaped the duke. He jerked his head toward the door. "Go to your rest, loyal courier. If I discover aught to respond, then I will apprise you of it as soon as you are rested."

Olivier bowed low and slipped soundlessly from the privy chamber.

John of Gaunt again perused the document in Guy de Gervais's sharp black script. Then he rose and went to a small jeweled chest set upon a shelf in a niche in the wall. He lifted the lid and took out another parchment. It bore the same black script.

He sat down again, smoothing out both documents on the table. He was remembering that moment beside Magdalen's bed when he and Lord de Gervais had told her of her husband's disappearance, and he had felt the powerful surge of passion between his daughter and de Gervais and had recognized it because he had felt its like with the girl's mother.

When he had assumed Edmund de Bresse to be dead, Guy de Gervais had asked his overlord for the widowed hand of Magdalen of Lancaster.

But Edmund de Bresse had not then been dead, and John of Gaunt had put the letter aside, deciding in kindness that it was best to pretend it had never been written. Now Edmund was dead in truth, and Guy de Gervais had informed him of this, and of Magdalen's rescue, and of the destruction of the de Beauregard threat. This document, however, contained no plea for the widow's hand.

But it was there, nevertheless. The courier, Olivier, knew it to be there.

He sat back, mentally reviewing potential suitors for his daughter's hand. Another French connection could yield powerful allegiances. Then there were the Italian Viscontis. Rich and powerful, bandits in essence, but all too eager for a royal alliance. There were several young English lords whose absolute loyalty could be bought with the gift of such a bride. The girl had a proven ability to bear children. Where would it be most useful to plant his Plantagenet seed?

Without volition, his hand moved to the deep

pocket in his furred gown. He drew out the enameled miniature and gazed for long minutes on the face of the woman he loved and could not marry. Katharine Swynford was not of the blood that made royal brides, even were he free of his wife, Constanza of Castile. But he loved Katharine and he knew he would snap his fingers at the conventions of breeding if he were free.

There were no such conventions preventing the marriage of Guy de Gervais and Magdalen of Lancaster, only a father's desire to dispose of his daughter as advantageously as possible.

John, Duke of Lancaster, took a sheet of parchment from the press, mended his pen, and began to write to his vassal, Guy de Gervais, Earl of Redeforde. He wrote fluently for many minutes, and at the end sanded the script, and without rereading it, folded the parchment, dropped wax from the candle upon the fold, and sealed it with his great ring.

The following day, Olivier set out on his return journey, the duke's parchment sewn into the lining of his doublet.

He arrived at the Castle de Bresse a week after his lord's return from Carcassonne. It was a tawny gold day of early autumn, and the castle wore the orderly air of a place under the command of its master, as if assaults, breached walls, and abduction had never disturbed the smooth pattern of daily life.

He found Lord de Gervais and the Lady Magdalen in the pleasaunce, playing with the child whose red-gold hair and gray eyes offered the promise of an unusual future beauty.

"You have made good speed, Olivier," Lord de Gervais said. He was counting sunflower seeds into Zoe's rosy palm as she sat on his knee, showing her how to hold her hand out to the softly murmuring doves. It was not an entirely successful exercise, but one that seemed to amuse the baby mightily.

Guy shifted his hold to encircle his daughter with one arm and took the duke's parchment with his free hand. "Go to your rest, Olivier. We will talk further when you are refreshed." He waited until the courier had slipped with his usual discretion from the pleasaunce before breaking the Lancastrian seal. Zoe gleefully snatched at the parchment, and he captured her grasping fingers in his encircling hand, holding them firmly as he read. Finally he looked up.

Magdalen was sitting back, her lap brimming with the embroidery silks she had been sorting. The warm glowing vibrancy was back in her face, her lips softly parted, the candid gray gaze containing love and the knowledge of its fulfillment. Her contentment was as one with the soft golden surfeit of the autumn garden, and he knew that for her it mattered nothing what John of Gaunt said. She knew that their love could not be touched by her father's manipulations. John of Gaunt would decree, but she and Guy de Gervais would find their own way.

But he had not been able to share her resignation or her calm certainty. Therein lay the difference between them, a difference that had always been there and always would be. The thought pleased him with its encompassing of the future, a future that he could now allow to enter his soul.

He smiled. "We go to England, pippin."

"Why so?"

"To be wed. His grace of Lancaster sees fit to bestow the hand of his dearly beloved daughter Magdalen upon his loyal vassal, Guy de Gervais, Earl of Redeforde."

" 'Dearly beloved'?" said Magdalen. "I believe my father lies."

"Do not be tiresome."

Her eyes closed for a minute under the soft autumnal sun, and a tiny, secretive smile played over her lips as she remembered all that had been and contemplated all that was to come. She opened her eyes. Guy was watching her, his own smile, comprehending and amused, illuminating his face.

"I love you," he said.

"Yes, I know," she returned. "I even believe you love me as much as I love you."

"You are learning, it seems." He set Zoe on the ground and stood up, reaching down a hand to pull Magdalen to her feet. "I think it's time this little one went for a sleep, don't you?"

Magdalen stood up, heedlessly scattering embroidery silks in gay profusion on the grass at her feet. Zoe seized the bright swatches with a gleeful chuckle as her parents moved out of the sunlight under the golden canopy of a beech tree.

"She'll be happy enough for a little longer," Magdalen whispered, lifting her face imperatively. "We can have a little interlude under the trees."

"Or we could simply let matters take their course," he replied, grazing the curve of her cheek with his lips.

"Or we could do that," Magdalen agreed, tracing his ear with a delicate fingertip before standing on tiptoe to nip the lobe. "Yes, I think we should certainly do that. It's always the best plan, I've found." He laughed against her mouth.

Zoe yawned, settling down amid the bright

colors of her carpet to sleep. It was quiet in the warm, late afternoon garden, only the soft rustles of an affirming love mingling with the indolent drone of a wasp and the sharp chatter of a starling.

JANE FEATHER is the *New York Times* best-selling, award-winning author of *The Accidental Bride, The Hostage Bride, A Valentine Wedding, The Emerald Swan,* and many other historical romances. She was born in Cairo, Egypt, and grew up in the New Forest, in the south of England. She began her writing career after she and her family moved to Washington, D.C., in 1981. She now has over four million copies of her books in print.